Torpedoed!
The *R.M.S. Leinster* Disaster

"At such a tale, who could forbear to weep?"

Virgil *'Aenid'*

Dedicated to my mother
Eileen Lecane (née O'Brien) 1932 – 1994,
my father Philip Lecane,
and my wife Kate Lecane (née Grant)

Torpedoed!
The R.M.S. *Leinster* Disaster

By Philip Lecane

Published in 2005 by
Periscope Publishing Ltd.
33 Barwis Terrace
Penzance
Cornwall TR18 2AW

A CIP record for this book is available from the British Library

ISBN No 1-904381-29-4

Printed in England by Anthony Rowe Ltd
Eastbourne

CONTENTS

FOREWORD

It has been a very real privilege to have been asked to write a foreword for this remarkable book. I was taught to read very young and for eight-five years I have been reading books whenever I could find a free half hour. Among the regular mountain of books that have come my way in all these years I have read very few as good as this. Philip Lecane's book is a masterful and strictly accurate presentation of the historic drama that led to more lives being lost in the Irish Sea on an October morning in 1918 than any other marine disaster in all of Ireland's history.

A potential reader finds it hard to get deep into a book where every incident recorded until the very last pages occurs on the sea, with which they may not be well acquainted. That reader can cheer up at once. Philip Lecane writes with an accuracy and vividness that inevitably draws the reader into the story. The author has the ability to give life to individual details and dramatic actions by the patient and disciplined thoroughness of his research. Time and time again as I read his description of events such as the saving from drowning of a ship's passenger evidently bound to perish, he brings those persons, the saver and the saved, to life again after more than eighty years. In doing so he brightens with reality this story of the sinking of an Irish owned passenger ship by a German submarine whose young crew, convinced that they were helping save their country from imminent invasion, were never again to see their homes and loved ones, as their vessel struck a mine off Scotland on their way back to Germany.

Philip Lecane has no need to pour out words on the awfulness of war. Just to tell the story as it happened, often in the words survivors of the sinking used to their rescuers or to newspapermen when they got ashore, is enough to make any reader hope that no such event can ever occur again. I am sure that the first thought of many readers of this magnificent book will resemble my own -- how appalling that political leaders can allow the affairs they are supposed to be promoting to get into such a mess that decent men have to inflict horrors on other humans, as here dramatically told, and then die horribly themselves.

John de Courcy Ireland

ACKNOWLEDGEMENTS

I owe an incredible debt to my wife Kate, my father Philip and my late mother Eileen for all their love and support. Apart from my family, my chief supporters during the research and writing of this book were Dr David Murphy, Liam Dodd, Tom Burke M.B.E., Frank Coffey and Jimmy Taylor, all from the Royal Dublin Fusiliers Association, Dún Laoghaire Historian Brian Smith, American Historian Dwight R. Messimer, German Researcher Dr Stefan Graf, Ronald Clifton, Historical Information Officer of The Western Front Association, Australian Historian Jeff Kildea and Author Roy Stokes. Special thanks to the crew of uboat.net, especially Jörn Jensen, Michael Lowrey and Brian Vigliette. My grateful thanks to Dwight R. Messimer who kindly allowed me to use a map he drew for one of his own books. My thanks also go to the following who helped in various ways. John Cave, Richard Burnell and Stephen Hunt of the Holyhead Maritime Museum, Christine Bradshaw, the late Robbie Brennan, Noel Brien, Nick Broughal, Tamsin Bunnay, William Byrne, Seán Connolly, Ian Coulter, Adrian Crotty, Marcus de Burca, Sally Copeland Keogh, Joe Devereaux, Conor Dodd, John D. Clarke, Jeff Evans, Hal Giblin, Seamus Green, Pat Hogarty, John Hughes, Trevor James, John L. Liffiton, Ron Mahoney, Michael McGovern, Billy McGrath, Patrick McNamara, Michael Merrigan, John Moore, Bernard Murnaghan, Brian Moroney, Seamus O'Connor, Niamh O'Doherty, Cathal O'Shannon, Jim Scannell, the late F. E. Smith, Dr Philip Smyly, Jim Strawbridge, Christine O'Sullivan and Declan Whelan. Thanks to the staff of the following libraries: the Gilbert Library, Deansgrange, Dún Laoghaire, Pembroke and Tallaght public libraries, the National Library and the Irish Labour History Museum. To Frieda Carroll, Archivist of the Genealogical Society of Ireland, Catherine Malone of the Dún Laoghaire-Rathdown Heritage Society, Allison Wareham of the Royal Naval Museum, Lesley Thomas of the *Wrens* Museum, Lieutenant-Colonel (Retd.) Angus Fairrie, Regimental Headquarters The Highlanders, the staff of the R.A.F. Museum, Hendon, the staff of the Commonwealth War Graves Commission, Captain Henshall, Assistant Regimental Secretary, The Royal Dragoon Guards, Royal Army Medical Corps, Historian R.L. Barrett-Cross, the staffs of the Royal Norfolk Regimental Museum and The Keep Military Museum, (The Military Museum of Devon and Dorset). For permission to reproduce various accounts and photographs I am grateful to John Cave, Holyhead Maritime Museum, Joe Maher, Deputy General Secretary of the Communications Workers Union, Ireland, Dr Philip Smyly, Dún Laoghaire Maritime Museum Jane Smythson, Publications Manager of *The Life Boat* and the staff of the U-boat Archives, Cuxhaven. I am grateful to the following people for information on postal staff on the *Leinster*. (Postal workers names are given in brackets.) Kathleen, Ann and Jean Attwooll (Jennins Attwooll.), Brendan Bradley (Joseph Bradley), Bill McMahon (William Maxwell), Fr. Fergus O'Donoghue S.J. (Thomas O'Donoghue), Peggy Glendon, Tom Kelly and Frances O'Hanlon (Joseph Robinson), Annette McDonnell and Pauline Farrell, (Adam Smyth), Charlie Wakefield (William Wakefield), Gladys Warbrook (James Warbrook). My thanks to the following people for information on members of the *Leinster's* crew. Eric Anthony (Robert Anthony), Frank Coffey (Chief Stewardess Mary Coffey and Quartermaster Henry Tyrrel), Mairín Cullen (Chief Stewardess Mary Coffey), Dinah Jordan and Ollie Gray (Philip and Tom Connolly), Gerard Crangle (First Officer Patrick Crangle), William Byrne (Chief Fireman John Donohoe), Ninian Faulkiner and John Lush (Second Steward John Flood), Seán M. Redmond (Seaman Frank Kehoe), Margaret Rogerson, Andrew Mooney, Dolores Loughlin and John Loughlin (Seaman John Loughlin), Liam and Lena Donovan (Fireman William Maher Leslie Owen (Seaman Hugh Owen), Haulwen McClean and Robert H. Williams (Second Stewardess Louisa Parry), Peter Scott Roberts (Fireman Richard Roberts), Brian Ellis (Chief Purser Hugh Rowlands) and Mairwen Carr (Fireman John Williams). I am grateful to the following people who gave me information on *Leinster* passengers. Declan Byrne (Robert Alexander), Marilynn Hearne (Lieutenant Robert Bassett), Jim Strawbridge (*Wren* Josephine Carr and Nurse J. M. Fannin), Jim Herlihy (Lance-Sergeant Michael Cooke), Joy O'Gorman (Elizabeth Ellam), Declan Jones (Anthony Jones), Maureen O'Brien, Anne O'Brion and Des Guerins (Michael Joyce M.P.), Chris Knuckey (Lance-Corporal Frederick Knuckey), Brian White (Lady Phyllis Hamilton), Kate Healy Coburn (Lizzie Healy), Nora Hedworth (Second Lieutenant Thomas Hedworth), Chris Murphy and Liam Dodd (Private James Hickman), Will Lockhart (Francis Higgerty), Mary Jacques (Private Joseph Hill), Peter Power-Hynes (James and Clare Hynes), Peter Wood (Robert Kerr), Margaret Cross and Kathyrn Rundle (Lieutenant Francis Laracy), Michael Lee (Captain Ernest Lee), Jane Smythson (Arthur Lewis), Peter Trigueiro (Private Andrew McCartney), Donal Hall (Regimental Quartermaster Sergeant Samuel McKenna and Robert Wilde, Works Manager Great Northern Railways, Dundalk), Doris Hodgins (Robert Wilde), Marion McNally (Clare McNally), Ann O'Carroll and Jim Strawbridge (Nursing Sister Henrietta Mellett), Violet Milne McIntyre (Captain Edward Milne), Thomas Gallagher (Private Philip O'Brien), Christine O'Sullivan (Leading Seaman William O'Sullivan), William Lennon and Francis Loughrey (Gerald Palmer), Dr Arnold Burrows, Liz Jones and John Phillpott (Sergeant George and Minnie Phillpott), Aideen Byrne and Annette Proffitt (Lucy and Sheelah Plunkett), Des McCloskey and Marie Lawlor (Private James Rathcliffe), Rupert Jeffares,

General Manager of Howth Yacht Club (Club Secretary John Ross), Darren Blackmore (Fanny Saunders), Irene Jones, Irene Watson, Dave Roberts and Anne Roberts (Private Ezekiel Thomas), Dr Margaret Elmes (Maud Elizabeth Ward), Mary Horgan (Able Seaman David White), Roger Imes (Corporal John Williams) and Patrick Woodgate (Private Thomas Woodgate).

My thanks to Dr John de Courcy Ireland for taking time from his very busy schedule to read my book and for writing such a generous foreword. My special thanks to Innes McCartney of Periscope Publishing who had the vision and courage to publish the book.

I am grateful to all those who gave me pictures of their *Leinster* relatives. Unfortunately, for reasons of space, it has not been possible to publish them all. Finally, I spoke with many people over the course of my six years of research. I would like to thank anyone I may have inadvertently forgotten to mention. Please believe that no slight was intended.

In the third century before Christ an Irish prince named Maen returned from exile with an army of Gauls and reclaimed the kingship usurped by his grand uncle. Maen's soldiers had an unusual broad pointed spear called a *"Laighen"* (pronounced Layen). The province where they settled was afterwards called *"Laighen." "Ster,"* derived from the Scandinavian word *"Stadr,"* a place, was later added. The English name of the province became *Leinster.*

Source: *"The Origin and History of Irish names of places."*
by P.W. Joyce.

The crew of the *R.M.S. Leinster* came from the towns of Kingstown (now Dún Laoghaire*)* and Holyhead. There is a peninsula on the coast of Wales south of Holyhead. During the Roman occupation of Britain a band of lance-men from Ireland occupied the peninsula. The area is today known as the Lleyn peninsula. The names 'Lleyn' in Wales and 'Leinster' in Ireland have a common origin in the Celtic word for lance.

Source: *"Holyhead: The Story of a Port."*
by D. Lloyd Hughes and Dorothy M. Williams.

11

INTRODUCTION

The Forgotten Tragedy

"Forgetfulness transforms every occurrence into a non-occurrence."
Plutarch

On the morning of 10 October 1918 the Royal Mail Steamer *Leinster* left Kingstown (now Dún Laoghaire), Co. Dublin for Holyhead in Wales. On board were 771 passengers and crew. It was a month before the end of the First World War and Ireland, as part of the United Kingdom of Great Britain and Ireland, was at war with Germany. Thousands of Irish men and women were serving in the British forces. Since late 1917 the Kingstown to Holyhead mail boats had been attacked a number of times by German submarines. They had, however, always managed to avoid being sunk or damaged. But the *Leinster's* luck was about to run out. Shortly after leaving Kingstown the ship was sunk by two torpedoes fired by submarine UB-123. Many of those on the ship died in the sinking. Others lost their lives in the sea while waiting for rescue ships to arrive. According to figures compiled by the *Leinster's* owners, 501 people died in the Irish Sea's worst maritime tragedy. In the months and years immediately following the sinking newspapers referred to *"the Leinster sinking"* in a way that implied that their readers were familiar with the tragedy and didn't require background details. Unfortunately, with the passage of time the *Leinster* sinking became almost totally forgotten. Today a mention of the *Lusitania* sinking will bring a nod of recognition from a listener, whereas mention of the *Leinster* sinking will bring a look of puzzlement. This book tells the forgotten story of the people who sailed on the *R.M.S. Leinster's* final voyage. It also tells the forgotten story of 35 young men from the submarine service of the Imperial German Navy who bravely served their country and died under appalling circumstances.

*

Walter Lord, author of two books about the sinking of the *R.M.S. Titanic,* said that it is impossible to be definite about everything that happened the night the ship sank. He said this despite the fact that he was

13

able to consult the reports of two inquiries into the sinking and was able to interview several *Titanic* survivors. There was no court of inquiry into the loss of the *R.M.S. Leinster* and no survivors were available for interview at the time this book was being researched. A further difficulty arises because some of the survivors' accounts differ from each other on particular details.[1] Given these constraints, it is even more difficult to be definite about the events surrounding the loss of the *Leinster*.

It is not even possible to definitely say how many people died as a result of the *Leinster* sinking.[2] The ship's Daily Journal contains a typed page prepared by Edward Watson, Managing Director of the City of Dublin Steam Packet Company. This gives totals for each category of people on the ship: crew, ship's gunners, postal staff, civilian passengers, military officers and military other ranks. It also gives the number of survivors in each category. From this, it is possible to calculate the number of casualties in each category. The calculations show that 501 people died out of a total of 771 who were on board. But confusion arises from the fact that Watson's figures are undated. Newspaper reports show that at least three of those rescued later died in hospital. It is not certain if Edward Watson took their deaths into account when compiling his figures.[3] Military authorities were aware that 18 soldiers boarded the *Leinster* without their names being recorded. As the military didn't want this fact to become known, it is possible that the *Leinster's* owners were not aware of these 18 when compiling the total numbers of those who were on board. Consequently, any of the 18 who died may not have been recorded among the number of dead compiled by the company.

No passenger list is available for the *Leinster's* final voyage. There are two major sources available to research those who were on the ship, contemporary newspapers and the records of the Commonwealth War Graves Commission. The former are the best source for crewmembers and civilian passengers. The latter are the best source for military casualties. Neither source, however, is totally accurate. For instance, some contemporary newspapers refer to people believed to have been on board the *Leinster*, only to report in subsequent issues that they were not on board. At least one civilian casualty, Gerald Palmer, does not appear on any casualty list. It is also accepted that the records of the Commonwealth War Graves Commission do not record all British First World War casualties. Given the constraints imposed by the available records, this book's passenger and crew list is the best that could be compiled at present. Further research may result in some changes. It would make for very tedious reading if every mention of casualties and survivors were qualified with the comment that it might not be 100% accurate. Therefore, while the reader is asked to remember that further research might result in slight changes to figures, statements about casualties and survivors are used as if they were totally accurate.

Another area of difficulty is that of establishing exactly what time the *Leinster* was torpedoed. Different sources give different times. In a final entry in the *Leinster's* Daily Journal, CDSPCo Managing Director Edward Watson said *"The Leinster left Kingstown on 10th October 1918 at 8.50 a.m. with mails and passengers. At about 9.50 a.m. she was torpedoed by an enemy submarine, her wireless message was picked up by the Ulster with down night mails which had passed the Kish at 9.42 a.m. Leinster had no escort and there were no patrols about. The boats were lowered. At about 9.55 a.m. Leinster was struck by a second torpedo and went down immediately. About an hour and a half elapsed before any boats came to the rescue. H.M.S. Lively first arrived and afterwards Patrol boats. In the interim boats had been swamped and many lives lost."* First Officer Crangle also quotes the 9.50 a.m. time in his report. But his report, as the *Leinster's* senior surviving officer, was undoubtedly Watson's source. Passenger and Consulting Engineer to the RNLI Arthur Lewis says the ship was struck at 9.32 a.m. The log of *H.M.S. Mallard* records picking up the *Leinster's* S.O.S. at 9.42 a.m. and that of *H.M.S. Seal* at 9.45 a.m. However, the log of *H.M.S. Lively* appears to agree with the CDSPCo account, by giving the time as 9.50 a.m. On another point, Watson says that *H.M.S. Lively* was the first rescue ship to arrive. Yet, while her log records that she commenced to pick up survivors at 11.12 a.m., the log of *H.M.S. Mallard* records launching a boat to pick up survivors at 10.35 a.m., while the log of *H.M.S. Seal* records picking up survivors at 10.40 a.m. As there is no way of resolving differing statements on times, I have quoted the various sources at different points of the story.

*

Declan Whelan is to be highly commended for having the foresight to interview *Leinster's* Assistant Purser Bill Sweeney on tape shortly before the latter's death in 1979. Joe Varley is to be equally commended for interviewing passenger Mary Buckley (née Hoare). Unfortunately, she proved to have very little to tell about the sinking. It is a very great pity that no one had the foresight to interview other survivors. Several of the crew lived into old age in the Dún Laoghaire area. What a wealth of information on the *Leinster* sinking they took to their graves. In the absence of readily available documented accounts, it was perhaps inevitable that some tall tales would circulate concerning the *Leinster* sinking. I mention the tall tales because some people, honestly wishing to help my research, told me stories that just did not accord with the known facts. Stories that caused me even more difficulty were those where relatives of people who were on the *Leinster* told me that their ancestors had heroically died or put their lives at risk, while saving others. At first I took these stories at face value.

Unfortunately, I was told so many that, were I were to repeat them all, it would seem as if, in an outbreak of mass heroism, half of those on the *Leinster* gave away their lifejackets to the other half. Apart from where heroism was documented, I have not been able to include such stories in the book. Again, except in one documented case, I have unable to include the numerous stories of relatives who were said to have missed sailing on the *Leinster* due to illness, over-sleeping etc.

Notes

- U-boat (Unterseeboot: literally undersea boat) was a German submarine. Submarines were referred to as boats rather than ships.

- The Royal Welsh Fusiliers were established as a regiment in 1881. In 1920 their named was changed to The Royal Welch Fusiliers, using an older spelling of the word "Welsh." However, the "Welch" spelling was, and is, a matter of great pride to the regiment. Robert Graves, among others, used it during World War One. So I have used this spelling in the book.

- As late as 1955 the rank of Sergeant was still spelled as "Serjeant" in official British documents. I have chosen to use the more familiar, though technically incorrect, spelling.

- Where a footnote merely gives a persons name (e.g. Mary Jacques), this indicates the source of information was a relative of a postal worker, crewmember or passenger.

- I have come across two or three articles that claimed, with great authority, that the aerial photograph of the camouflaged CDSPCo ship that appears in this book is not that of the *Leinster*, but one of her sisters. As the claim was made without any source references or supporting evidence, it would appear to be a case of one source making a (mistaken) claim and other sources repeating the claim. On 22 September 1973, A. C. Yeates., author of *70 Years of the Irish Mail* published in Sea Breezes July 1961, wrote to Mrs Crangle, daughter-in-law of *Leinster's* First Officer Patrick Crangle. He told her that Assistant Purser Bill Sweeney had said that the photograph is of the *Leinster*, taken from a Royal Naval Air Service (RNAS) airship a few months before she was lost. (On 1 April 1918 the RNAS was amalgamated with the Royal Flying Corps, becoming the Royal Air Force. If the airship was owned by the RNAS the photograph would have been taken prior to 1 April 1918.)

- Some details on the *Leinster* wreck, taken from the website of the Marlin Subaqua Club. Position: 053.18.810N. 005.47.510W (GPS). Twelve miles from shore, Dublin Bay. Twin-screw steamer. Steel hull. 2646 tons. Length 378 ft. Beam 75 ft. Draft 40 ft. Armament 1x12pdr plus 2 signalling guns. Depth: Top 27 m. Deck 30 m. Seabed 33 m. Lying N-S. Access with owner's permission.

I would be very interested to hear from any reader who has further information on people who were on the *Leinster*, on UB-123, or on the rescue ships.

Philip Lecane,
"Le Quesne,"
77 Windsor Drive,
Monkstown,
Co. Dublin, Ireland

I can also be contacted through the email address of the Royal Dublin Fusiliers Association: rdfa@eircom.net Please ask that your email be forwarded to me. The Royal Dublin Fusiliers Association promotes remembrance of the Irish men and women who served in the First World War. Our very informative website is at www.greatwar.ie

Notes

[1] People's accounts of the same events often differ. According to Michael Davie's *The Titanic: The full story of a tragedy* there were five conflicting accounts of the circumstances of Captain Smith's death.

[2] According to Michael Davie there isn't agreement on the number of casualties and survivors from the *Titanic*.

[3] On 29 September 1919 Watson quoted the figure of 501 deaths at the presentation of a medal to William Maher. This appears to suggest that he took deaths subsequent to the rescue of survivors into account in arriving at a death toll of 501.

PROLOGUE

"The past is the present, isn't it? It's the future too.
We all try to lie out of that but life won't let us."

Eugene O'Neill *Long Day's Journey into Night* (1956)

Ottawa, Canada, 10 October 1918.

The telegram from Dublin was completely unexpected. Its message was simple and brutal. *"Frank Higgerty torpedoed body here. Please reply. O'Kane."* Frank had not yet taken up his commission in the British Army. So how could he have been killed? But the Higgertys could not argue with the telegram. Neither could they ask it for details on the circumstances of Frank's death. They would have to wait for further information from Dublin. In the meantime they decided that Frank's body should be brought back to Canada. His would not be another lonely war grave in Europe.[1]

Like two men on mountaintops signalling to each other with semaphore flags, telegrams passed back and forth between Canada and Ireland.

Ottawa Oct 12th/18
O'Kane Post Office, Dublin Ireland

Canadian Military Authorities cabling to forward body to Canada. Arrange to have body embalmed and use effort to prevent being interred. Reply. Give particulars.
                                                                                    Higgerty

Dublin Oct 14/18
Higgerty 54 Somerset St. Ottawa

Embalming arranged cost seventy pounds. Wire draft   *O'Kane*

Seven telegrams in all passed back and forth. Eventually Frank Higgerty came home. He rests in Notre Dame Roman Catholic Cemetery on the Montreal Road, Ottawa. Higgerty's family were told that he died when the City of Dublin Steam Packet Company ship *R.M.S. Leinster* was torpedoed. But they, and the relatives of the other 500 people who died, never had the comfort of knowing the full story of what had happened. It was as if the events of that day were a string of pearls savagely wrenched asunder and scattered far and wide across the floor of history. Parts of the story were reported in newspapers of the time, other parts ended up in public records, while others still were in the personal papers of families affected by the tragedy. This book is an attempt to gather up and restring many of the pearls of information as to what happened that tragic day.

Note

[1]   Source on Frank Higgerty and the Higgerty family: Will Lockhart.

Chapter 1

The Holyhead to Kingstown mail boats[1]

"The introduction of steam has made the islands of Ireland and England one island as it were, and the voyage now, either from Liverpool to Dublin, or from Bristol to Waterford is far more comfortable and less fatiguing than a journey to York."

Hall's Ireland: Mr & Mrs Hall's Tour of 1840.

For the last half of the nineteenth century and the first quarter of the twentieth the City of Dublin Steam Packet Company played a vital part in the economic and social history of Kingstown. (now Dún Laoghaire), Co. Dublin and Holyhead, Anglesey. Twice daily the company's mail steamers carried passengers and mail between the two ports. The men and women who crewed the ships were drawn almost exclusively from Holyhead and Kingstown. Irish and Welsh accents were heard on the decks, in the passenger quarters and in the stokeholds as crew men and women laughed and joked, cursed and grumbled, sang and cried. Friendships were formed and marriages made. As is also the way with human beings, no doubt disagreements and rivalries sometimes led to longstanding hostility and enmity.

The first ever steamship seen in Dublin Port was the *Argyle*, which docked in May 1815, en route from London to the Clyde. The following year a group of Dublin businessmen formed *The Steam Packet Company*. Among them was Richard Williams of Drumcondra Castle. Using the paddle steamers *Hibernia* and *Britannia, The Steam Packet Company* ran a passenger service between Howth, Co. Dublin and Holyhead. Dissention among the directors, however, led to the closure of the company.

Within a few years of the closure of *The Steam Packet Company* the younger brother of Richard Williams entered the steam packet business. Charles Wye Williams was born in 1779, the son of Thomas Williams, Secretary of the Bank of Ireland and Mary Ann Quin/Quine. The birth probably took place at his parent's home at 2 Belvedere Place, Drumcondra, Dublin.[2] He was descended on his mother's side from Marke Quin/Quine., the second person to receive the title of Lord Mayor of Dublin (1667-1668).[3] Charles and his older brother Richard were probably privately tutored. In his early twenties Charles became managing director of a bleaching works in the Lagan Valley, near Belfast and in 1806 he built a linen mill there. In 1812 he was called to the Bar of the King's Inns, Dublin, though it is not known whether he practiced as a barrister. In the summer of 1822 he travelled to Liverpool hoping to get funding for a fleet of steamers he proposed to operate between Dublin and Liverpool. Unfortunately for him, the businessmen of Liverpool considered that the existing sail and steam services adequately met trading needs. Undeterred by this setback, Williams returned to Dublin. There he founded a steam packet company, *Charles Wye Williams & Company,* with a capital of £50,000 in 1,000 shares of £50 each. In February 1823 he returned to Liverpool and placed an order for a 200-ton wooden paddle steamer with Thomas Wilson, a Cork born shipbuilder who was based in Liverpool. Named *The City of Dublin,* the ship carried passengers, cargo and cattle between Dublin and Liverpool. By 1826 the company owned fifteen ships. Having exceeded the upper limit of the capital under which *Charles Wye Williams and Co.* was founded, new powers were sought for the company. The capital of the company was increased to £250,000 in 2,500 shares of £100 each. Charles's brother Richard was among the shareholders. Charles himself became the first managing director of the reformed company. The company name was subsequently changed to *The City of Dublin Steam Packet Company* (CDSPCo). In 1826 Charles Wye Williams was granted the Freedom of the City of Dublin for his *"efforts and talent in bringing steam vessels to perfection and rendering a passage formerly dangerous, safe and pleasurable."*[4] The CDSPCo subsequently took over *The Inland Steam Navigation Company,* a company that Williams operated on the Shannon.[5] The CDSPCo, with its headquarters at 15 Eden Quay, Dublin, now had steam vessels on Ireland's waterways and canals and on the Irish Sea.

In 1836 a Bill further increasing the capital of the CDSPCo was passed by parliament. In 1838, with Liverpool linked by rail to London, the Post Office decided that all mail to and from Ireland would be sent through the port of Liverpool. The CDSPCo secured the contract to operate the night mail packet service to Kingstown, thus beginning an association with the port and the Post Office that was to last for over eighty years. The Admiralty operated the day service from Liverpool to Kingstown.

The CDSPCo put four ships on the mail route. These were the *Duke of Cambridge, Duchess of Kent, Queen Victoria* and *Royal William.* The *Royal William* was the first ever steamer to be divided into watertight compartments. She had made maritime history before joining the mail service. On 5 July 1838, while leased by the CDSPCo to *The Transatlantic Steamship Company,*[6] she sailed from Liverpool to New York, becoming the first steamship to sail between the two ports. She completed the outward passage in nineteen days and made the return trip in just over fifteen days. After a number of Atlantic passages the *Royal William* was returned to the

CDSPCo. In 1847 Daniel O'Connell, leader of the campaign for Catholic Emancipation, died in Genoa, Italy. His body was brought back to Ireland on the CDSPCo's *Duchess of Kent*.

As the CDSPCo flourished, Charles Wye Williams moved from Dublin to Liverpool, where all the company's vessels were overhauled and repaired. In 1820 he married Mary Henry. The inscription on a loose headstone discovered by author Hazel P. Smyth in St. James's Mount Cemetery, Liverpool tells a sad story. *"Here lies the remains of Mary, wife of Charles Wye Williams, died 11th January, 1826, aged 25 years, and their infant son, died 5th March aged 9 months."* Williams lived for a time at 19 St Vincent Street, Liverpool before moving to Rodney Street. He eventually settled at *"The Nook,"* St. James's Mount. At the latter house he set up a laboratory in which he carried out many experiments in the more efficient use of fuel in steam vessels, and, in particular, the improvement of combustion and the reduction of smoke. In 1835 he was elected as an Associate in the Institution of Civil Engineers. His application was supported by Sir John McNeill, an eminent Irish civil engineer who had been one of Thomas Telford's assistants, by (Sir) William Cubitt, F.R.S. and by Robert Sibley. As detailed in footnote 5 of this chapter, Williams became a director in the P&O shipping line. The Fifth report of the shipping line, dated 30 May 1843 states: *"All of the vessels built by this company since 1840 have had introduced into them the watertight bulkheads first adapted to steam vessels by Mr Charles Wye Williams, one of the Directors of this company, which give not only additional strength but, also, unquestionably additional security in case of accident."*

Williams wrote extensively. In 1831 and 1833 he wrote pamphlets on the unemployment then rife in Ireland, and on the need to improve the navigation of the River Shannon as a means of alleviating unemployment. In 1837 he gave a paper to the British Association in Liverpool *"On Preventing the Dangers from Collision, and from Fire in Vessels,"* in which he advocated the subdivision of ships into several compartments by watertight bulkheads. What was probably the last of his numerous papers was delivered to the (now Royal) Institution of Naval Architects in 1862, when he lectured the professional engineers *"On the Construction of Marine Steam Boilers."* His first book (published 1840) was *"The Combustion of Coals and the Prevention of Smoke chemically and practically considered."* It was well received and translated into French and several other languages. His principal other published work was *"On Heat in its relations to Water and Steam."* It was initially published in 1860, when Williams was 80 years old. A second edition was published in 1861.

Williams's personal life continued to be blighted by tragedy. *Saunders News Letter* of 25 May 1840 contains the following entry. *"Died in April at Madeira aged 17 years and 11 months, Thomas Alexander, only son of Charles Wye Williams, Esq. Whatever may bring either pain or grief to the breast of so worthy a man as the regarded C. W. Williams will, while it is a cause of regret to the whole community, be shared by every person who has the benefit of his friendship and the happiness of his acquaintance, and sure we are that a sympathy, at once genuine and general, will be felt by a wide circle of his scientific associates and numerous admirers, when they shall have heard of his bereavement by the early fall of his only son who has thus fallen in the bloom of life at Madeira after a short illness and has been thus prematurely cut off from a world which he would have served and adorned by talents that gave promise of fame and may, had it pleased the Almighty to have spared him until they were matured, even have rivalled those of his respected father."*

It is not known whether Thomas was the son of Williams's first wife, Mary or his second wife, Frances. Charles Wye Williams died on 2 April 1866 at the age of 85. With an astonishing range of abilities, the Irishman with the Welsh surname and ancestry had established a shipping company that would link Ireland and Wales for most of the nineteenth and the first quarter of the twentieth centuries. He was still a director of his beloved CDSPCo at the time of his death. According to Hazel P. Smyth *"The people of Liverpool greatly respected Mr Williams and had asked him to stand for parliament, but he had declined the offer due to his many commitments."* Williams was buried in St. James's Mount Cemetery, Liverpool. J. Foster Petree (1966) said that *"Williams's grave in St. James's Mount cemetery, Liverpool, is no longer there; his remains were among the many that were re-interred elsewhere to clear the site for the (Anglican) Cathedral."* But author and maritime historian Hazel P. Smyth (1996) discovered a second gravestone in the cemetery. This read: *"Sacred to the memory of Charles Wye Williams, C.E., who died 2nd April 1866 aged 85 years; also of Frances, widow of the above, who died 2 March 1898 aged 93 years."*

As if to show that the sea can never be taken for granted, disaster struck one of the CDSPCo mail steamers five years after coming into service. Between 2 a.m. and 3 a.m. on the morning of 14 February 1853 the paddle steamer *Queen Victoria* (337 tons) was en route from Liverpool to Kingstown with 120 passengers and cargo. In a blinding snowstorm she struck the rocks near the Bailey Lighthouse, Howth, Co. Dublin. Eight passengers managed to scramble overboard on to the rocks. From there they made their way up the cliffs to the Bailey Lighthouse. The captain backed the ship off the rocks. When she was in deep water it became clear that she was more badly damaged that had first been thought. Drifting helplessly, the ship filled with water. At the mercy of the sea, she again struck the rocks below the lighthouse and sank in fifteen minutes. Fortunately, another CDSPCo ship, the *Roscommon,* was passing and picked up 45 passengers. Sixty lives were lost in the sinking, including the captain. It was the greatest loss of life on a CDSPCo mail boat until the sinking of the R.M.S. *Leinster* sixty-five years later.

As the century approached the halfway mark, Holyhead, the port that provided the shortest route to Ireland, was linked by rail to London. It was decided that the Irish mail would henceforth be shipped through Holyhead. Public tenders were invited for the Holyhead to Kingstown mail service for a period of ten years. The conditions stipulated that four vessels should be used on the route, capable of a speed of not less than 12 knots. Two tenders were submitted. These were from the Chester & Holyhead Railway Company (CHR) and the CDSPCo. The CHR were so certain they would be awarded the contract that they had purchased four paddle steamers in anticipation. Their confidence appears to have come from the fact that they already had the contract to carry the mail by rail from London to Holyhead. They also appear to have had friends in high places.

William Watson, formerly of *The Inland Steam Navigation Company* and now managing director of the CDSPCo, made an offer to the Admiralty to buy the four ships they had used on the day service between Holyhead and Kingstown. The Admiralty accepted the offer but, before the Treasury could ratify it, the CHR were made aware of the offer and intrigued against its being accepted. As a result, the offer wasn't ratified and the mail service was again put to tender. This time the figure submitted by the CDSPCo was made public, with the result that the CHR was able to tender a lesser figure. The CHR's friends in high places appear to have leaked the information about the Admiralty ships and the tender figure submitted by the CDSPCo. Perhaps this is why the CHR were so certain they would be awarded the contract and why they had purchased four paddle steamers in anticipation.

Following strong protests by the CDSPCo, the parties were allowed to tender again. William Watson, Managing Director of the CDSPCo, submitted a tender of £25,000 annually to carry the mail. As this was £5,000 less than the CHR bid, the CDSPCo were awarded the contract. The whole episode marked the start of a long and bitter rivalry between the railway company and its successors and the CDSPCo. While they didn't get the mail contract for the Irish Sea crossing, the CHR provided their own passenger service from Holyhead.

The mail service under the terms of the new contract began on 1 June 1850. The CDSPCo bought the paddle steamers *Llewellyn* and *St Columba* from the Admiralty. As the former was not immediately available, on account of a broken shaft, the company were allowed for the time being to use the paddle steamer *Banshee*. They also chartered the *Caradoc* for a few runs in the early 1850s. They put their own paddle steamers the *Eblana* (built 1849) and the *Prince Arthur* (built 1851) on the route. Between 1850 and 1860 the company's paddle steamers made the crossing between Holyhead and Kingstown in an average of 5 hours 40 minutes, at a mean speed of 12.2 knots.

At Holyhead the CDSPCo operated from the Admiralty Pier, Salt Island, near the entrance to the harbour, while the CHR ships operated from a berth inside the harbour, nearer to the railway station. Horse drawn omnibuses operated between the station and the mail boat terminus at Admiralty Pier. At the pier, passengers waited in the open air to board the boat to Kingstown. Following complaints about the poor facilities, the directors of the CHR agreed to extend the station waiting room so that refreshments could be provided. An extension line to the Admiralty Pier, with horse drawn trams, carried its first passengers on 20 May 1851. Plans for a new harbour for the mail boats at Salt Island were abandoned as being too expensive and the existing pier was extended. The CDSPCo were unhappy with the timber extension, arguing that it was inadequate to hold ships during heavy storms. As if to prove the point, their packet steamer *Llewellyn* was nearly torn from its moorings during a storm on 27 May 1860. The railway company decided to improve its own amenities at the railway station and build new inner harbour facilities for its ships. The CDSPCo set up workshops at Salt Island, where its engineers carried out repairs to the mail boats and fabricated replacement parts.

While the Government and the Post Office were satisfied with the mail packet service, there was a strong public feeling that it could be faster. With this in view the CDSPCo drew up a three-point plan. This proposed the introduction of special faster trains, larger ships capable of a speed of 17½ knots, and the sorting of mail on board the steamers. The CHR caused the negotiations to be held up. Public outcry, however, forced the companies to meet and come to an agreement. The two companies drew up a joint proposal. Among its stipulations were proposals that proper accommodation should be provided for the steamers at both Holyhead and Kingstown and that railway lines should run onto the Admiralty Pier at Holyhead and the new Carlisle Pier at Kingstown. On 3 January 1859, a contract, embodying the new proposals was completed between the Post Office and the two companies. The new contact was for a service of 11 hours between London and Kingstown, with the sea crossing to be made in a time of 3 hours and 45 minutes, with a penalty of £1-14-0 for every minute late. If a steamer were delayed reaching Kingstown the mail would be late in every town in Ireland. A delay on the Holyhead route meant that Irish letters missed the first delivery in London next day.

There were two other important developments in 1859. On 1 January the CHR was taken over by the larger London & North Western Railway. The CDSPCo now had an even more formidable rival for future mail contracts. Also in 1859, the Carlisle Pier was opened in Kingstown harbour, Co. Dublin. The pier had a rail line linked to the Dublin track. In order to meet the terms of the new contract the CDSPCo placed orders with Laird Brothers of Birkenhead[7] for the construction of three paddle steamers and Samuda Brothers of Ravenhill, on the Thames, for the construction of a further paddle steamer. The four new ships were launched in August 1860. Named after Ireland's provinces *Connaught, Leinster, Munster,* and *Ulster,* they were often referred to as the *Provinces*. They used the prefix *R.M.S.*, which stood for *Royal Mail Steamer*. The *Leinster*, which was built by Samuda Brothers, was the longest. It was 343 feet in length, as against the *Connaught* (338 feet) and the *Munster* and the *Ulster* (each 337 feet). All four ships were 35 feet in width. Passenger accommodation was good. W.S. Lindsay in *"History of Merchant Shipping"* (1876) said, *"Saloon and cabins are large, lofty and well ventilated."* The *Leinster* and the *Connaught* caused quite a sensation when they first appeared. Instead of the standard contemporary design of two-funnels, they had four. On her trials, on 27 August 1860, the *Connaught* became the first ever steamship to record a speed of 18 knots.

In the meantime the London & North Western Railway (LNWR) continued to provide a sea passenger service. In 1861 the railway transferred its Irish passenger terminal from Kingstown to the North Wall in Dublin Port. Under the terms of the mail contact, the LNWR, as the main contractors (carrying the mail from London to Holyhead), controlled not only the rates of their own rail fares, but also the rates of fares charged by the CDSPCo for the sea crossing. Early in 1880 the LNWR reduced the fares on their steamers running between Holyhead and Dublin. They refused to allow the CDSPCo to do likewise. This resulted in an increase in the numbers travelling to Dublin on the LNWR boats and a decrease in the numbers travelling to Kingstown on the mail boats. In 1881 the CDSPCo put the matter before the Railway Commissioners. Their complaint was upheld and they were allowed to reduce their fares. Shortly afterwards the Post Office told the CDSPCo that they wished to terminate the existing contract for the Holyhead to Kingstown service and invite tenders for a faster service. This sparked a prolonged wrangle between the companies, with the LNWR using their connections in the Government and the CDSPCo using their connections with the Irish Party at Westminster. The Irish lobby was very strong, as they held the balance of power at Westminster. On 1 August 1883 the tender submitted by the CDSPCo was accepted. It was ratified on 20 August.

As there was insufficient time to build vessels capable of the speed required by the new contract, the CDSPCo decided to re-boiler and modify the main engines of the existing ships. The *Provinces* were given extensive refits. The number of funnels on the *Leinster* and the *Connaught* were reduced to two. Extra passenger space and comfort was provided on all four ships, and electric light installed. The onboard mail sorting rooms were enlarged. The *Leinster* was the first to come into service with the new alterations, making her first crossing in February 1885. The company also placed an order with Laird Brothers of Birkenhead for a new paddle steamer. At the time of her launch in August 1885 the *Ireland* (2095 tons) was considered to be the fastest ship in the world. Between 1885 and 1896 the fleet average crossing time was 3 hours 37 minutes. According to Dr John De

Courcy Ireland, in size and speed, the CDSPCo ships were twenty years ahead of all other cross-channel steamers.

Between 1890 and 1892 a number of improvements were made to Irish railways and Kingstown was linked to the rest of the railway system. With railway times greatly reduced, the question of reducing sea-crossing times arose again. On 6 July 1894 the Post Office invited three different tenders. The LNWR were invited to tender for a service from London to Kingstown. Ship owners were invited to tender for a sea service that was half an hour faster, or alternatively, one hour faster. The Post Office accepted the CDSPCo's tender for a service that was half an hour faster, for a period of twenty years, subject to a year's notice thereafter. Also that year the CDSPCo placed an order with Laird Brothers for four identical twin-screw steamers. Like their predecessors, the ships were named after the four provinces of Ireland. On 27 June 1896 the *Ulster* was the first to be launched.[8] Mary Hamilton, Duchess of Abercorn christened the ship. Her husband James accompanied her. Their daughter Phyllis would be a passenger on the *Leinster's* last voyage. The *Ulster* made her maiden voyage from Holyhead on 9 February 1897.

George Henry Cadogan, Earl of Cadogan and Lord Lieutenant of Ireland, travelled to Birkenhead with his wife for the launch of the *Leinster*, the 616th ship to be built at Lairds.[9] On 12 September 1896 Beatrix, Countess of Cadogan performed the launching ceremony. It was the first time that a ship was launched by the wife of a Lord Lieutenant of Ireland. Those who believed in omens might have found two reasons for concern. The Lord Mayor and Lady Mayoress of Dublin were unable to attend due to last minute difficulties, and a thunderstorm broke as the guests sat down to lunch. On 21 October 1896 Mrs William Laird launched the *Munster*. On Saturday 27 February 1897 the *Leinster* made her trial voyage. She broke by 6 minutes the existing record of 2 hours and 30 minutes for the crossing between Holyhead and Kingstown. The launch of the *Connaught* on 21 September 1897 got very little press coverage compared to her sisters.

The normal routine on the Holyhead to Kingstown mail service was for two ships to be on the run. A further ship was on standby at Holyhead, ready to come into service if the need arose. The final ship would be undergoing overhaul or laid up. The funnels and hulls of each *Province* were painted black, their superstructures were white, and a narrow white ribband ran round the hull at gunwale level. Each of the ships had an onboard post office. Staffed by members of Dublin Post Office, it could facilitate 30 postal sorters and 250 bags of mail. With a speed of 24 knots, the 2640-ton vessels were, at the time of their launch, the fastest cross-channel steamers in the world. In their first year in service they made the crossing in an average of 2 hours 51 minutes. Their time keeping was so regular it was said that people set their clocks by them. In a sense this could be said to be literally true.

Every day an official from the observatory at Greenwich delivered a watch, set to Greenwich Mean Time, to the guard of *The Irish Mail* train at Euston. At Holyhead the watch was given to the captain of the mail packet. Upon arrival in Kingstown it was handed over to the guard on the train. When it arrived in Dublin, it was brought by an official of the Dublin Port Authority to the Ballast Office on Westmoreland Street, whose clock was always set to GMT. The same procedure was followed in reverse, with the watch being handed back to an official from Greenwich Observatory at Euston for resetting. This practice continued up to the outbreak of the Second World War.

Five years after she entered service the *R.M.S. Leinster* again made newspaper headlines. On the afternoon of 8 September 1902 there was a thick fog at the Kish Bank, off the east coast of Ireland. The *Leinster* had almost completed her journey from Holyhead to Kingstown. In the reduced visibility she rammed and sank the wooden Kish Bank light ship *Albatross*. Luckily, there was no loss of life. The crew of the *Albatross* were taken on board the *Leinster*. Having suffered no more than a few dents on her plates, the *Leinster* sailed for Holyhead the following morning.[10]

In 1908 the LNWR, who had moved their terminal to Dublin Port in 1861, said that they were moving back to Kingstown, as the dues at Dublin Port were excessive. As Kingstown was obliged to charge the same rates as Dublin, the true reason may have been a hope that they would finally capture the mail contract. Rivalry between the LNWR and the CDSPCo over berthing rights at the Carlisle Pier developed into a dispute that became known as *"The Battle of the Pier."* The pier could only accommodate two ships, one on either side of the pier. Each company had two ships in service at any one time, one on the morning run and one on the evening crossing. The dispute went to litigation, which went all the way to the House of Lords. Their lordships decided that both companies should have access to the pier, a situation that prevailed until the outbreak of the First World War, when the Admiralty requisitioned the LNWR ships.

Notes

1   Articles: J.H. Isherwood *Irish Mail "Provinces"* in Sea Breezes, M.J. Tutty *The City of Dublin Steam Packet Company* in Dublin Historical Record, and A.C. Yeates *70 Years of the Irish Mail* in Sea Breezes. Books: John De Courcy Ireland *History of Dun Laoghaire Harbour*, H.A. Gilligan *A History of the Port of Dublin*, Mike Hitches *The Irish Mail*, D. Lloyd Hughes and Dorothy M. Williams *Holyhead: The Story of a Port*, *The B & I Line* by Hazel P. Smyth (henceforth abbreviated to Hazel P. Smyth in footnotes), D.B. McNeill *Irish Passenger Steamship Services Volume 2:South of Ireland* and Roy Stokes *Death in the Irish Sea* (henceforth abbreviated to Roy Stokes).

[2] Sources for Charles Wye Williams: Articles by J. Foster Petree *Charles Wye Williams (1779-1866) A Pioneer in Steam Navigation and Fuel Efficiency* in The Transactions of The Newcomen Society, and Hazel Smyth *"Some notes on Charles Wye Williams, His Family, Their Life and Times"* in the Dublin Historical Record.

[3] Hazel Smyth says that he was descended on his father's side from Griffith Williams, 1st Baronet Penrhyn (1661). Holyhead historian Richard Burnell says that the first Baron Penrhyn (1783) was a man named Richard Pennant. I have to unable to resolve this contradiction.

[4] Hazel P. Smyth. According to the book *"The Annals of Dublin: Fair City* by E.E. O'Donnell (Dublin 1987) *"Among the muniments of Dublin Corporation in the City Hall, dating back to the twelfth century there are rolls of 'free citizens' who received a key to the city gates."* The book says that the British parliament passed an act in 1876 enabling the City Council to *"elect and admit persons to be honourary burgesses."* Presumably Charles Wye William received the earlier form of the Freedom of the City.

[5] In the late 1820s John Grantham started a small steamer service on Lough Dearg and the Upper Shannon. Charles Wye Williams. initially established *Charles Wye Williams & Co* to operate a steamer depot at Killaloe. He eventually bought out Grantham and established *The Inland Steam Navigation Company*. The latter company was taken over by the CDSPCo in 1829 (according to D.B. McNeill) or 1840 (according to J. Foster Pertree.) The CDSPCo acquired a monopoly of the Shannon trade, which they held for almost twenty years. In 1857 the Midland Great Western Railway opened a steamer service on the Shannon. This service ultimately forced the CDSPCo to cease its operations on the river. Sources: D.B. McNeill *Irish Passenger Steamship Services Volume 2: South of Ireland*. J. Foster Petree *Charles Wye Williams (1779-1866) A Pioneer in Steam Navigation and Fuel Efficiency* in The Transactions of The Newcomen Society.

[6] J. Foster Petree says that *The Transatlantic Shipping Company* was founded by Charles Wye Williams and Francis Carleton, who he says was the co-managing director of the CDSPCo. Pertree says that *The Transatlantic Steamship Company* subsequently merged with the *Peninsular Steam Navigation Company,* with Williams being given a seat on the board of the latter company. He retained the seat until 1854. (The company became the *Peninsular and Oriental Steam Navigation Company* in 1840. It continues to operate today and is more popularly known as the *P & O Line.*)

[7] The CDSPCo had a long association with Laird Brothers (later Cammell Laird). In 1829, the first boat ever built by the firm was the lighter *Wye* for Charles Wye Williams's company *The Inland Steam Navigation Company*. Lairds's second and third ships, *The Dundally* or *Lady Dundally* and an unnamed ship, both built in 1832, were also built for *The Inland Steam Navigation Company*. At that time Lairds were called the *Birkenhead Iron Works* and the ships were a new departure. They were lettered A, B and C. In 1833 Charles Wye Williams's CDSPCo ordered the *Lady Landsdowne*, an iron steamer, for the Shannon. The first iron vessel built on the Mersey, it was given the yard number of "1". According to J. Foster Petree *"This seems to have decided William Laird that he was no longer just a builder of miscellaneous iron work but was definitely in the ship building business."* Lairds's sixth vessel, the *Garryowen* or *Lady Garryowen* was also built for the CDSPCO (in 1834). John Grantham jun., a founder member of the (now Royal) Institution of Naval

Architects said that the *Garryowen* was the first ever vessel to have watertight bulkheads. Sources: J. Foster Petree and the websitewww.wirral-libraries.net/archives/ list_of_vessels_constructedbyc.htm

8 Launching of the CDSPCo ships: *The Irish Times* various dates in 1896 and 1897.

9 As the first three ships built by Laird's (for Charles Wye Williams) were not numbered, the *Leinster* was given the yard number 613. Source: The Wirral Archives website www.wirral-libraries.net/archives/list-_of_vessels_constructed_by-c.htm

10 Details of the collision with the *Albatross* from *The Irish Times* of 9 and 10 October 1902. Irish Lights, the owners of the *Albatross* put in a claim for £13,000 for the loss of the ship, but agreed to an out of court settlement of £6,000. Source: Document M3765, National Archives, Dublin.

.

Chapter 2

The Germans

"There are no roses on a sailor's grave,
No lilies on an ocean wave,
The only tributes are the seagulls' sweeps
And the teardrops that a sweetheart weeps."

German song.

26 September 1918. Heligoland Island, off the North coast of Germany. [1]

Submarine UB-123 had left its German north coast naval base a short time previously.[2] The crew had recently returned from leave. The boat's engines had been overhauled. With new torpedoes, oil and stores she was ready for her second combat mission.[3] It was standard practice for outgoing U-boats to stop at the small naval depot on the island of Heligoland. There they received up to date information on Allied anti-submarine measures, particularly on the progress of the huge minefield being laid between Scotland and Norway in an attempt to block the northern exit from the North Sea Oberleutnant zur See Robert Ramm had instructions to operate in the Irish Sea, an area in which neither he nor his boat had previously sailed. Twenty-seven year old Ramm had served on submarines since April 1916. Married, with two children, he had been given new submarine UB-123 as his first command on 6 April 1918.[4] The boat's first cruise, in July and August 1918, had been dogged by technical failures and sickness among the crew.[5] Perhaps this voyage would be more successful.

Ramm's crew comprised of two officers and thirty-three men. First Officer Helmuth Bahr was twenty-three and Second Officer Ferdinand Lohmeyer was twenty-one. Both had fought at the Battle of Jutland. Their first submarine service had been UB-123's combat mission in July and August 1918.[6] Apart from their names, rank and roles, no background details are available on the thirty-three men who formed the rest of UB-123's crew. Some general points can be made about them, however. Their average age would have been between nineteen to twenty years old. Like officers Helmuth Bahr and Ferdinand Lohmeyer, many, perhaps most, of the crew would have had their first submarine service during UB-123's previous combat voyage. The wartime expansion of the German submarine fleet, coupled with the loss in action of trained men, meant that the level of previous submarine experience in new boat crews was thinly spread.[7]

To avoid British minefields north of Heligoland., the UB-123 sailed eastwards, making her way through the Kiel Canal into the Baltic Sea. and then around the north coast of Denmark into the North Sea. While travelling on the surface the submarine's twin propeller shafts were powered by two 550 h.p. diesel engines. The boat could travel at a maximum speed of 13.6 knots and had a range of about 8,500 nautical miles. When submerged it was driven by two 380 h.p. electric engines, drawing their power from huge storage batteries and could travel for about 55 nautical miles at a speed of 8 knots.[8] The only way of recharging the batteries was to surface and run the diesel engines. These turned over electric motors, which put energy back in the batteries. Unlike modern submarines, which are designed to spend most of their time submerged, the submarines of the two world wars were really surface craft that could operate submerged for short periods of time. Because of the necessity to recharge batteries and due to their slow underwater speed they spent as much time as possible on the surface, diving only to avoid or to attack enemy ships.

Robert Ramm's submarine was 55.3 meters (181ft 5 inches) in length, 5.8 meters (19ft) in width and 3.7 meters (12 ft 2inches) in height. The boat had a double hull to withstand pressure, a diving depth of 50 meters (approximately 164 feet) and could dive from the surfaced position in 30 seconds. It had 5 cm (19.7 in) torpedo tubes, four in the bow and one in the stern. It carried 10 torpedoes and had an 8.8 cm deck gun.

To hinder German submarines sailing from the North Sea into the Atlantic the British and American navies had laid a huge minefield – known as the Northern Barrage - between the north coast of Scotland and the west coast of Norway. UB-123 successfully avoided the lethal mines and sailed into the Atlantic. Robert Ramm's submarine was on her way to bring death to the Irish Sea.

*

The major powers of the world had been at war since 1914. On one side were Germany, Austro-Hungary, Turkey and Bulgaria. Facing them was the United Kingdom of Great Britain and Ireland, Britain's colonies, France, Italy and, from April 1917, the United States of America. On land both sides became bogged down in static trench warfare. At sea the Royal Navy blockaded Germany from the start of the war, forcing the German fleet to remain in port. Putting to sea in 1916, the German navy failed at the Battle of Jutland to break the British stranglehold. Germany's fleet returned to port, where it remained for the rest of the war. Meanwhile the British naval blockade also prevented munitions and food from reaching Germany. The country was facing starvation and defeat unless something could be done to counter the blockade.

Since the early days of the war Germany's submarines were able to avoid the British blockade by sailing beneath the ocean's surface. They brought the war to their enemy by attacking merchant shipping, in an attempt to starve Britain into submission before Germany herself suffered the same fate. However, faced with protests by neutral America following the sinking of the *R.M.S. Lusitania* in 1915, Germany suspended her unrestricted attacks on merchant shipping. It was only in 1917, in a desperate all-out attempt to win the war, that she resumed unrestricted attacks. Among the counter measures adopted by the British was the sailing of their merchant ships in convoys escorted by the Royal Navy. Faced with the difficulty of attacking escorted convoys in the Atlantic, the Germans in late 1917 began to focus their attacks on the waters of Great Britain and Ireland, where convoys would disperse and where local shipping tended not to be convoyed. Late 1918 saw the German army being worn down by the relentless assaults of the Allied forces. The Germany fleet, still confined to port, was on the verge of mutiny. Meanwhile the men of the submarine service continued to attack enemy merchant shipping.

*

UB-123 was a long steel cylinder, designed to withstand enormous pressure at depth. On top of the cylinder, about midway between the bow and the stern, was a smaller structure known as the conning tower. Attached to the outside of the submarine were large tanks called ballast tanks. When the tanks were empty the submarine floated. The tanks had valves at the bottom and at the top. When both sets of valves were opened the sea came in the end of the tanks and pushed the air out the top of the tanks. The submarine then submerged due to the weight of the water in the tanks.

The required level of depth was obtained by controlling the amount of water in the tanks. Water could be expelled from the tanks by mechanically pumping it out or by admitting compressed air. The submarine's level of depth could also be altered by the angle of horizontal fins, known as hydroplanes, at the bow and stern of the boat. When approaching the required depth the diving officer attempted to balance the boat so that it neither descended further nor rose. He did this by adjusting the volume of water in auxiliary tanks at the bow and stern, and on either side at the mid-point of the boat. It required minute attention to detail, taking into account the current weight of the submarine. The weight of the boat was affected by the amount of fuel the submarine had used and the amount of torpedoes and foodstuff still on board. If a few members of the crew moved from the back of the boat to the front it would automatically decrease the weight of the rear of the submarine and increase the weight at the bow. This would cause the bow to drop and the stern to rise, pushing the submarine downwards. Crew moving from the front to the rear would have the opposite effect. Seawater is seldom homogenous. If the submarine passed into a layer of water with a different salt level or temperature it suddenly became less or more buoyant, dropping fast or refusing to drop further until the tanks had taken on more water. Particular vigilance was required at great or shallow depths. In the former instance the boat might plunge below the point at which the hull could withstand the pressure. At shallow depths the submarine might suddenly rise to the surface near enemy ships.

Every crewman on UB-123 had to be thoroughly familiar with his role in the submarine's operation. He might be responsible for working dozens of valves, switches and levers. These not only had to be operated correctly and in the proper sequence, but also in correct relation to what dozens of other men were doing at the same time. On a submarine, more than on any other sea-going vessel, each man had a very high stake in the safety of his boat. If a surface ship sank, her crew had some chance of survival. If a submarine was lost, it was highly likely that all her crew would die with her. Every crewman knew that a single mistake by one of them could be the death of all of them.

The purpose of a submarine like UB-123 was to sink enemy ships with torpedoes or gunfire. Everything else was incidental. Few concessions were made to the comfort or convenience of the crew. They were carried merely to help the submarine achieve its deadly purpose and they fitted in the spaces that were left after the machinery and weapons were installed. Space was at such a premium that a bed could not be provided for each man. As soon as one man got out of a bunk another got in, using the same sheets. This was known as "hot bunking." In such conditions privacy was non-existent. The captain was the only one to have private space. He had a desk, wash bowl, locker and bunk all jammed into a tiny space. But he had it all to himself and was the only man on board who could have some privacy when he wanted it. Of course this also meant that he was alone with his thoughts and responsibilities.

There was no bath and only one toilet for the use of the entire crew. UB-123 had to make its own fresh water by distilling seawater, using up her precious fuel supply or draining her battery. The fresh water was rationed, with each man getting a small amount per day. This was used for brushing his teeth, washing himself and his clothes. Few men shaved and no one changed their clothes from the beginning to the end of a voyage. The crew frequently could not get dry after a spell on watch. Unable to bath or shower, men were scarcely able to wash their hands and faces. The toilet could not be used below a depth of 70 feet because of external pressure. Thereafter the crew had to relieve themselves in buckets and bottles, whose smell mixed with the all-pervasive odour of diesel oil, past cooking and unwashed bodies. The officers used eau de cologne to mask body odour and the smells of the boat.

Due to the cramped confined life, everyone on board got to know each other only too well. Before a cruise was over everyone on board would know every joke that every other man on board had ever heard. A noteworthy comment or funny quip would travel through the submarine as quickly as if it was broadcast on a public address system. With everyone living in close proximity, an irritating personal quirk could soon antagonize. Occupying the toilet for more that one's fair share of time could quickly make enemies among the crew. Incidentally the toilet was the only place a submariner was ever alone, apart from the captain who could pull a curtain across the entrance to his cubbyhole cabin. Life aboard submarines was informal. While on patrol U-boat crews looked more like pirates than members of the Imperial German Navy. All who could grew beards. From the length of the crews' hair, a pretty good guess could be made as to how long a boat had been at sea. When men lived as close together as a U-boat crew did, insignia on uniforms wasn't needed to designate rank. Conventional uniforms went into lockers and didn't come out again until the submarine came alongside the dock to be received by the admiral.

There were very few choices when it came to passing off-duty time. There was no point in writing letters home. Books and magazines were read over and over until they were falling to pieces. Decks of cards continued in use long after they were worn out. Draughts and chess were popular pastimes. Whenever possible, U-boat captains would surface their boats and put up an aerial to pick up radio news. At the start of a voyage food and supplies would be crammed into every available space in the boat. The galley was little bigger than a telephone booth, with one small stove for preparing food for the entire crew. As food and supplies where consumed a little bit of extra space became available to the men. After the fresh food ran out, the crew were forced to eat tinned food and dehydrated vegetables. In the cramped conditions they could not take proper exercise. When submerged for any length of time they were subject to nausea, splitting headaches, and, if the mind were allowed to dwell on it, incipient claustrophobia.

Paradoxically, the terrible conditions, sense of vulnerability and of mutual responsibility fostered comradeship across barriers of rank. This in turn ensured that morale among German submarine crews remained high, ever in the final days of the war.

On 1 October 1918 in the Atlantic north west of Ireland, some of the crew of the British merchant ship *Karmala* (8,983 tons) saw a torpedo miss their ship.[9] While the unsuccessful attack may have been made by Robert Ramm's submarine, it is possible that it was made by U-118.[10] The latter submarine, commanded by Kapitänleutnant Herbert Stohwasser, sank the British merchant ship *Arca* (4,839 tons) north west of Tory Island, Donegal the following day.[11]

The tanker *Eupion* (3,575 tons) was owned by the British Tanker Company Ltd. of London. Built in 1914, she had a narrow escape on 12 April 1918, when a submarine fired two torpedoes at her in St. Georges Channel. Both torpedoes missed.[12] Five months later, in September 1918, she set out from Philadelphia with a cargo of oil bound for Limerick. On 3 October she was 10 miles west of Loop Head, Co. Clare when her luck ran out. She was torpedoed and sunk. Having consulted the submarine records of the Imperial Germany Navy between the two world wars, Admiral Arno Spindler concluded that the *Eupion* was sunk by UB-123.[13] Having finally sunk his first ship, Robert Ramm must have felt greatly reassured. His crew would have been doubly pleased at having sunk a British tanker. The international nature and the terrible tragedy of war is shown in the *Eupion* sinking. Of the eleven seamen who died when she was sunk, four were from neutral countries. Two were from Holland, one from Spain and one from Mexico. Of the other seven, one was from Ireland, one from Canada and five from England. The bodies of the Canadian and two of the Englishmen were recovered and buried in Kilrush Church of Ireland, Co. Clare. Another Englishman was buried in London. The bodies of the other seven rest in the Atlantic Ocean.[14]

Having sunk the *Eupion*, Ramm and his crew sailed UB-123 further down the west coast of Ireland and along the Irish south coast. They then sailed northwards into the Irish Sea with their cargo of death.

Notes

[1]   Heligoland(called Helgoland in German) is a 2.1 square kilometre (one square mile) island in the North Sea, 70 kilometres (43.5 miles) off the coast of Germany. Originally part of Denmark, the island was held by the British from 1814 until 1890, when it was handed over to Germany in exchange for the island of Zanzibar off the east African coast. Heligoland was used as a German naval depot during the two world wars. As the island wasn't big enough to have a permanent base, submarines used it as a staging post on their way from and to bases on the North coast of Germany. Sources: *Reader's Digest Guide to Places of the World* and Naval Historian Dwight R. Messimer.

2   UB-123 was part of 3 U-Halbflottille (3rd Half Flotilla), which was based at the ports of Emden and Wilhelmshaven. Unfortunately her exact port of departure in late September 1918 is not known. Source: Naval Historian Dwight R. Messimer.

3   UB-123 had her first combat mission in July and August 1918. Overhauling of engines, replacement of torpedoes, oil and stores were standard procedures before setting out on a new mission.

4   Information on Robert Ramm from research by Dr. Stefan Graf (Germany) and Jörn Jensen (Denmark).

5   Author's copy of microfilmed war diary for UB-123's first cruise, purchased from National Archives and Records Service, Washington. See *Guides to the Microfilmed Records of the German Navy 1850-1945: No. 1 U-Boats and T-Boats 1914-1918.* Index Item No. PG 61878 KTB U.B. 123, Roll 42. National Archives and Records Service, U.S. General Services Administration. Washington (1984).

6   Information on Helmuth Bahr and Ferdinand Lohmeyer from research by Jörn Jensen (Denmark).

7   Information on submarines and World War 1 U-boats from the following books: Jack Coggins *Prepare to Dive: The Story of Man Undersea*, Rear-Admiral Daniel V. Gallery *We Captured a U-Boat*, Wolfgang Hirschfeld *Hirschfeld: The Secret Diary of a U-Boat* as told to Geoffrey Brooks, Dwight R. Messimer. *Find and Destroy: Antisubmarine Warfare in World War 1*, Peter Padfield *War Beneath The Sea: Submarine Conflict 1939-1945*, Eberhard Rössler *The U-Boat: The evolution and technical history of German submarines*, Rear Admiral William Sowden Simms in collaboration with Burton J. Hendick *The Victory at Sea*, Roy Stokes *Death in the Irish Sea: The sinking of the R.M.S. Leinster,* John Terraine *Business in Great Waters,* Herbert A. Werner *Iron Coffins: A U-Boat Commander's War 1939-1945* and Gordon Williamson *U-boats of the Kaiser's Navy.*

8   Eberhard Rössler *The U-Boat: The evolution and technical history of German submarines* and Gordon Williamson, *U-boats of the Kaiser's Navy.*

9   His Majesty's Stationary Office publication *British Merchant Vessels Damaged or Molested (but not sunk) by the Enemy* (London 1919).

10   This question could be settled by examining UB-118's war diary.

11   His Majesty's Stationary Office, *British Vessels Lost at Sea 1914-1918,* (London 1919), A.J. Tennant *British Merchant Ships sunk by U-Boats in the 1914-1918 War, Guides to the Microfilmed Records of the German Navy 1850-1945: No. 1 U-Boats and T-Boats 1914-1918.* Index Item No. PG 61699 KTB U.B. 1118, Roll 30. National Archives and Records Service, U.S. General Services Administration. Washington (1984).

12   His Majesty's Stationary Office publication *British Merchant Vessels Damaged or Molested (but not sunk) by the Enemy* (London 1919).

13   Rear Admiral Spindler *Der Handelskrieg mit U-Booten,* 1914-1918, Vols 1-5 Mittler & Sohn, (1932-1966).

14   Commonwealth War Graves Commission.

Chapter 3

Departure

"Eternal Father, strong to save,
Whose arm hath bound the restless wave,
Who bidd'st the mighty ocean deep
Its own appointed limits keep:
O hear us when we cry to thee
For those in peril on the sea."

William Whiting (1860).

East coast of Ireland, *evening of 9 October 1918*

Fanny Saunders lived at 53 York Road, Kingstown. From her garden gate she could see part of the harbour and the sea.[1] On a stormy Christmas Eve in 1895 her husband Frank had left the harbour on board the Kingstown lifeboat. He never came home. The same sea, that Fanny saw every time she left her home, had made her a widow almost 23 years ago. Today a telegram had arrived. Her daughter Janet was seriously ill in Liverpool. Fanny decided that tomorrow she would leave the harbour and sail upon the cruel sea.[2]

About a mile from the Saunders home, the *R.M.S. Leinster* was docked at Carlisle Pier in Kingstown harbour. A number of passengers boarded the ship that evening. They had booked cabins for the night, to avoid having to travel to the ship the following morning. Among them was Louisa Frend, from Co. Limerick. She had left her home on 4 October on her way to visit friends in Eastbourne, England. She stayed in Rathgar, Dublin, from where she wrote to her sister telling of her intention to cross on the mail boat on 10 October.

Gerald Palmer's spine had been injured when he was an infant. As a result, he walked with some difficulty. Placed in *The Cripples Home*, Bray, Co. Wicklow, as a child, the now fifteen-year-old Gerald had recently been told that he had been accepted for training in *Barnardos* in London.[3] Tomorrow he would travel alone on the *Leinster*.

Major Charles Duggan from Hampshire and Lieutenant Robert Bassett from Cork booked into *Rosse's Hotel*, Parkgate Street, in Dublin. Both men were doctors serving in the Royal Army Medical Corps. Also staying at the hotel was Lieutenant Halse of the New Zealand Army, who had been hospitalised in Ireland for an injured left shoulder. To keep the shoulder in position he had his left arm clamped in an iron frame. Duggan, Bassett and Halse would travel on the *Leinster* the following morning.

*

Westland Row Railway Station, Dublin, early Thursday morning 10 October 1918

The mailbags arrived by road from the General Post Office and were put on board the sorting wagon.[4] When everything was ready the train set off on the six and a half mile journey to Kingstown harbour. Assistant Superintendent of Postal Sorters Richard Patterson had 20 men with him in the sorting wagon and they were already at work sorting the mail bound for Britain. A further man would join the team at Kingstown. Patterson was married and lived in Sandymount, Dublin. His family were grown up, with three sons serving in the army. In his spare time he was President and Secretary of the Dolphin Rowing Club at Ringsend. At least three of his staff were also sporting men. Tom Bolster, Peter Daly and Michael Hogan were members of the *Davis Hurling Club*. Hogan was captain of the senior team. The *Davis Club* drew its membership from employees of the post office.[5]

Most of the sorters on the train were Dublin born. Most were married, some with large families. Nearly all of them lived on the north side of Dublin city, apart from Richard Patterson (Ringsend) and John Ledwidge (Dalkey). In one of those random acts of fate, which often precede large-scale loss of life, three of the men were replacing colleagues who were ill. Charles Archer, Albert MacDonnell and William Pasker would die and three of their colleagues, who were listed for duty that day, would live.

*

Each of the CDSPCo ships on the Kingstown-Holyhead route had an on board post office, where mail was sorted. The post offices were staffed from Dublin and administered as branches of the Dublin Post Office.[6] Since mid-1861 a special date stamp had been used to frank mail sorted on the ships. Prior to August 1901 the date stamps were lodged in the post offices at Kingstown and Holyhead between voyages. From August 1901 they were permanently kept on board the ships. Each ship was issued with four steel stamps for letter post and a rubber stamp for parcel post.[7]

40

Among the sorters listed for duty that day were Jennins Attwooll, and Thomas O'Donaghue.

Jennins Attwooll was born in Dorsetshire. His father was a customs officer who was transferred to Dublin when Jennins was five years old. As he spent the rest of his life in Dublin, Jennins would doubtless have considered himself as much a *Dub* as most of his fellow sorters. Jennins was one of the older sorters on duty that day. Forty-nine years old at the time of the 1911 census, he would have been about fifty-six in October 1918. He and his wife Edith Jane (née Earls) lived in Drumcondra. They had ten children. Two of their sons were in the army. Jennins was a pipe smoker. He enjoyed picnics on Dollymount Strand, Dublin. He collected cockles there and cooked them for his family. His children were greatly entertained by his party piece, *doing the monkey* (i.e. pretending to be a monkey). To prevent getting a cold Jennins always took a raw egg before going on duty on the mail boat. He went to work for the last time on 10 October 1918.

Postal Sorter Thomas O'Donaghue was born in Dublin in 1888. He married Muriel Boyd in 1911. They settled in Kingstown, where they reared a family. Living in Kingstown was convenient for Tom's work on the mail boats. On at least two occasions he experienced the tension and horror of the war at sea. Once, he was on duty in the mailroom when a torpedo narrowly missed the ship. On another occasion he was on duty when the *Leinster* stopped to pick up survivors from a torpedoed ship. One image would stay forever etched in his memory, that of a Chinese man the mail boat crew were unable to save, who waved serenely as he slowly sank beneath the waves. Thomas O'Donoghue was listed for duty on the *R.M.S. Leinster* on 10 October 1918. One of his colleagues asked him to switch duties and Tom obliged. His colleague was lost when the ship was sunk.

Postal Sorter Adam Smyth was at home with his family at 26 Tivoli Terrace East, Kingstown on the morning of 10 October 1918, as he was not on the duty roster that day. A messenger arrived at the house to tell him that he had been assigned to replace a colleague who was ill. As he prepared to leave, his wife Elizabeth made him sandwiches. In the rush he left the house without them. One of his daughters ran after him with the sandwiches. She was the last member of the family to see him alive.[8]

*

Kingstown Harbour, early Thursday morning 10 October 1918

The *R.M.S. Leinster* lay at anchor at Carlisle Pier. The sailors who had served on the ship in her early days would have been surprised, perhaps even shocked, by the change in her appearance. When submarine attacks on British merchant shipping grew, the *Leinster* and her sisters were recalled to the shipyard for a number of modifications. The ships were painted in camouflage, giving an appearance similar to that of a warship. To add to the warlike appearance, a 12-pounder (i.e. 3 inch) gun was mounted on a platform at the stern of each vessel, just behind the boat deck. Members of the Royal Navy were assigned to each ship, as gunners for the 12-pounder.[9] A wartime photograph of the *Leinster* shows another change in her appearance from her original design. At some point the ship's boat deck, containing the lifeboats, was extended toward the stern of the ship and extra lifeboats added. It has not been possible to establish whether this change was done before or during the war.[10] The *Leinster's* interior remained unchanged. The ship had three main decks, lower, middle and upper. On top of the upper deck stood a smaller deck, with the ship's bridge and lifeboats.

On the lowest deck was accommodation for some of the crew, the post office where the mail was sorted, and first and second-class accommodation.[11]

On the middle deck was accommodation for most of the ship's crew, a storage area for mailbags, known as *"The Mail Shed"* and the first class dining room. The dining room, designed in Sheraton style in mahogany, measured forty feet by thirty-four feet. Seventy-nine people could be seated at seven tables. A large fireplace graced the head of the room. Overhead, in the centre of the room, was an elegant glass dome, which let in a subdued light. Further back on the main deck were first and second-class cabins and ladies first and second-class cabins.

The upper deck, on some ships called the promenade deck, was the only deck on which passengers could walk out of doors. On this deck, at the front of the ship, was the galley for the crew and some workshops and storage areas. This entire part of the upper deck, from the bow of the ship extending back for 70 feet, was covered over with what was called a hurricane fo'c'sle. This enabled the *Leinster* to plough through heavy seas. Water pouring over the bow of the ship landed on the covering and flowed back into the sea. Further back on the upper deck were cabins for the captain and the first officer, a meeting room for directors, a directors' state room (cabin), a galley and scullery, with a lift to bring meals down to the first class dining room, first class cabins and the first class smoking room. The first class smoking room was decorated in Jacobean style, with the doors, dados etc. being of oak and the seats upholstered in morocco leather. Behind the smoking room was the first class ladies sitting room, decorated in Louis XVI style in white and gold.

Above the upper deck stood a smaller deck with the ship's bridge and two lifeboats forward of the ship's funnels. Behind the ship's funnels – and also above the upper deck – was a boat deck with the rest of the ship's lifeboats.

*

When the mail train arrived at Kingstown harbour it took the branch line leading to Carlisle Pier, where it stopped alongside the *R.M.S. Leinster.* Hordes of porters descended on the sorting van and within a short time the mountains of mail bags had been transferred to the *Leinster.*[12] The postal sorters climbed the gangplank and boarded the ship.

A ladder of about twenty steps led from the upper deck of the ship to a storage area for mailbags, known as *"The Mail Shed."* A further ladder of about fourteen steps led to the floor of the post office. The only way of getting in and out of the post office was by way of this ladder.[13] The post office was near the bow of the ship. Forty feet long, it was approximately fifteen feet at its widest point. The floor of the post office was about three feet below sea level. Those who designed the ship obviously did not imagine a time when the sorters might need to make a quick exit from the post office.

Richard Patterson's men began to sort the mail.

*

Westland Row Railway Station, Dublin. Early Thursday morning 10 October 1918

Australian Corporal Michael Roach and New Zealander Rifleman P. J. Fahey had stayed at the Soldiers Club, Dublin. On the morning of 10 October 1918 they travelled by jaunting car to Westland Row railway station.[14] Sergeant Francis Coleman and Private Boxer Ware of the Australian Army had spent part of their leave staying in the more salubrious surroundings of the Shelbourne Hotel, St. Stephen's Green, Dublin. Having decided to spend the rest of their leave with friends in London, they also made their way to Westland Row station.[15] At 7.30 a.m., with other passengers on the way to the *R.M.S. Leinster,* the four soldiers left on the train for Kingstown. Also on the train - and travelling alone – was Australian Lieutenant Francis Laracy. His left arm was in a sling, the result of wounds sustained in France three months previously. In his right hand he carried a suitcase.

When the train reached Carlisle Pier Lieutenant Laracy boarded the *Leinster* alone. He was the only Australian officer travelling on the ship that day.[16] Australian Sergeant Thomas Coleman and Private Boxer Ware boarded the ship together, as did Lance-Corporal Roach and Rifleman Fahey. All four sat on deck.

43

Another train left Westland Row at 8.30 a.m. It arrived at Carlisle Pier later than scheduled. This resulted in a certain amount of confusion, as CDSPCo staff tried to ensure that the *Leinster* left on time.[17]

*

As Richard Patterson's men worked in the sorting office, high above them passengers boarded the ship by means of two gangways to the main deck.[18] Some had travelled by train. Others had come by different modes of transport or had spent the previous night in Kingstown. Elderly widow Eliza Jane Murphy and her middle-aged daughter Amy were from Clonmel, Co. Tipperary. They had stayed at *The Carlisle Hotel* in Kingstown. They had planned to travel on 8 October but were prevented when Amy developed a cold. They reserved berths on the *Leinster*. When they came on board, they went to their cabins and lay down. Fifteen-year old Gerald Palmer had made the short journey from *The Cripples Home* in Bray that morning. Fanny Saunders had made the even shorter journey from her home in York Road. Michael Joyce, Member of Parliament for the city of Limerick, was on his way to London. Elizabeth Ellam was returning from a visit to her daughter and son-in-law in Skibbereen, Co. Cork. Fanny Wookey's son Frederick had been lost on the Western Front in 1915. Her husband, also Frederick, owner of *Leixlip Woollen Mills* had died a few months previously. Now, with the Woollen Mills sold, Fanny was moving to England to live with her daughter. Charles Evans was on his way to take up a new post at the London offices of Guinness. He was accompanied by his wife Ella and son Charles. Fifteen-year old Alfred Curzon White King, who was travelling alone, was returning to Winchester public school from Roebuck Hall in Clonskeagh, Dublin. He was the godson of Mary Curzon, wife of the Viceroy of India. Hence his second name. But of perhaps more significance, he was the nephew of Lord Northcliff, owner of *The Times* and the *Daily Mail* and a much-hated figure in Germany. Maud Elizabeth Ward, personal secretary to Colonel Proby, had travelled from Glenart Castle, Arklow, Co. Wicklow. Lady Phyllis Hamilton had also come from Arklow, with servants Martha Bridge and Ellenor Strachan.

Robert and Virginia Frizzell had married the previous day. They arrived at the quayside with a group of relatives who had come to see them off. Possibly due to the confusion caused by the late arrival of the 8.30 a.m. train from Westland Row, they became separated in the crowd. Virginia boarded the ship. But Robert was among a group of between 30 to 50 people who were turned back at the gangplank. He would never again see the woman with whom he had planned to share his life. Yesterday he had become a husband. Today he would become a widower.

Canadian Frank Higgerty had been a barrister until March of that year, when he had joined the Canadian Army as a private. Granted a commission in the British Army, he had visited Ireland, the land of his ancestors, before setting out to take up duty. Lizzie Healy had come from Tralee, Co. Kerry, as had Chrissie Murphy and sisters Lena and Norah Galvin. Thomas Foley, brother-in-law to the tenor John McCormack, was travelling with his wife Charlotte. They were going to England to visit Charlotte's brother who had been wounded in France. The Goulds from Limerick were the largest family group on the ship. Catherine Gould was travelling with her son Michael and daughters May, Essie, Alice, Angela and Olive. They were on their way to England, where Mr Gould was employed as a munitions worker. John Ross, Secretary of the Howth Yacht Club, was going to a sea scouts conference in England. Sisters-in-law Lucy and Sheelah Plunkett were returning from a visit to Dublin.

However, most of those travelling that day were military personnel. The number of troops regularly travelling on the *Leinster* had grown to such an extent that a military adjutant, Second Lieutenant Hugh Parker, had been appointed to the ship.[19] It was his duty to supervise the embarkation of the military and to liase with *Leinster's* Captain William Birch. Among the military travelling that day were Irish men and women returning from leave, British troops going on leave from Ireland, members of the Royal Navy and Royal Air Force, New Zealanders, Australians, Canadians and Americans.

Private Joseph Hill from Leicester was travelling with 28 colleagues from the Royal Defence Corps. He was on his way home to visit his wife Nellie and their three young sons. Second Lieutenant Thomas Hedworth of the Worcestershire Regiment was going on leave to be with his wife Ada and their three children. Englishman Major Charles Duggan, Irishman Lieutenant Robert Bassett and the injured New Zealander Lieutenant Halse, who had spent the previous evening in *Rosse's Hotel* in Dublin, boarded the ship together. Military Policemen Lance-Corporal Charles Billings and Lance-Corporal Arthur Hewitt came on board escorting a prisoner. Lieutenant-Colonel Charles Blackburne was travelling with his wife Emily, daughter Beatrice and son Peter. Accompanying them was the children's governess, Rose De Pury. Major Louis Daly of the Leinster Regiment and his wife Cora were on honeymoon, having been married in Cork two days previously. Captain Hutch Cone was head of the United States Naval Aviation Forces in Europe. He was returning from an inspection of U.S. naval aviation bases in Ireland. Lieutenant Sydney Crawford of the Royal Dublin Fusiliers and his sister Letitia Hill were returning from a visit to their seriously ill sister. Their parents came to the boat to see them off.

Captain Edward Milne came on board on crutches. Born in Scotland, raised in Ireland, a member of the Canadian army, of all those on board he perhaps most embodied the international nature of the passengers. Recovering from wounds received on the Western Front, he was on his way for treatment at a London hospital. Violet Barrett was a V.A.D. (volunteer nurse) returning to duty in France. Her sister Elizabeth saw her off at Kingstown harbour. Five members of the Royal Navy were returning from leave in Cork, justifying a local saying that *"Royal Navy ships are all metal on the outside and all Cork on the inside!"* Able Seaman David White of *H.M.S. Pembroke* was travelling with Leading Seaman William O'Sullivan of *H.M.S. Carysford*. They came from Cork by train. In Dublin they met a female cousin of White's, who was returning to work in England.[20] The three of them took the train to Kingstown, where they boarded the *Leinster*. The other three Cork members of the Royal Navy were female. The Women's Royal Naval Service (nicknamed the *Wrens*) had been established less than a year previously with the purpose of *"substituting women for men on certain work on shore directly connected with the Royal Navy."*[21] *Wren* Shorthand Typist Josephine Carr was travelling with Maureen Waters and Miss Barry (first name unknown).

It seems likely that few of those travelling would have felt apprehensive about the crossing.[22] Probably fewer still would have bothered to read the emergency instructions Captain Birch had posted in various parts of the ship.[23] The newspapers were full of reports about Allied advances on the Western Front. Since 21 August 110,000 German soldiers and 1,200 guns had been captured. On 9 October the British Army had advanced to the vicinity of Le Cateau, France, a town from which they had retreated in 1914.[24] It seemed as if Germany would soon be forced to surrender. Those on board the *Leinster* would probably have felt even more secure had they known that on 6 October U.S. President Woodrow Wilson had received the following message from Germany: *"The German Government requests the President of the United States of America to take steps for the restoration of peace, to notify all belligerents of this request, and to invite them to delegate plenipotentiaries for the purpose of taking up negotiations. In order to avoid further bloodshed the German Government requests the President to bring about the immediate conclusion of an armistice on land, by sea and in the air."*[25]

The *Leinster's* crew were preparing for another voyage. Cabin staff, supervised by Chief Steward Llewellyn Lewis and Chief Stewardess Mary Coffey were helping to make passengers comfortable. On the bridge of the ship stood the bearded figure of Captain William Birch. With him were Second Officer Harry Addison, Seaman Hugh Owen and one of the ship's two Quartermasters. Owen would act as look out once the ship put to sea. The Quartermaster was at the ship's wheel.[26]

46

After boarding the *Leinster* Captain Hutch Cone of the United States Naval Aviation Forces went into the smoking room and placed his belongings on a seat. He then went out on deck and sat on a bench, watching passengers come on board. Just before the ship sailed he gave up his seat to a woman with a child. He went back into the smoking room, where he settled down to read the *Saturday Evening Post*.[27]

At 8.50 a.m. all was ready. The two gangways were removed from the portside of the ship and the ropes cast off. The *R.M.S. Leinster* moved away from Carlisle Pier. Slowly she moved through Kingstown harbour and out to the open sea.

Notes

[1] View of the harbour established by a visit to her house.
[2] Details on passengers and postal workers from their relatives and contemporary newspapers.
[3] Information on Gerald Palmer from Frank Loughery *Old Bray and its Neighbourhood* and *Sunbeam House Bray*.
[4] Dublin readers may be surprised that the mail was not loaded at Amiens Street (now Connolly) Station, which is nearer to the General Post Office. CDSPCo Managing Director Edward Watson, in *The Royal Mail to Ireland* (1917), said that after Amiens Street and Westland Row railway stations were joined by rail in 1891 *"passengers were carried through but the mails were not, and strange to say, are up to the present day carted just as they were before the connection railway was formed."* Mike Hitches in *The Irish Mail* says that *"the Dublin and Kingstown Railway carried the mails from Kingstown to Dublin (Westland Row) and they were then transferred by road to the General Post Office."* He later says *"all the mail traffic has been funnelled through Westland Row from the earliest days of the 'Irish Mail.'*
[5] Details on postal workers from newspapers, relatives, 1911 census of Dublin and Dublin street directories. Davis Club membership: Marcus de Burca, G.A.A. historian.
[6] The British and Irish Post Offices were amalgamated in 1832.
[7] O.M. Richards *Salved from S.S. Leinster*, an article from an unidentified philately journal in the archives of the Dún Laoghaire Heritage Society.
[8] Annette McDonnell *"Adam Smyth. (1875-1918) Post Office Sorter on Royal Mail Steamer Leinster,"* Journal of the Genealogical Society of Ireland.
[9] Sources on *Leinster's* camouflage Roy Stokes, Hazel P. Smyth and a wartime photograph of the *Leinster*. Sources on *Leinster's* gun crew Hazel P. Smyth and the Commonwealth War Graves Commission.
[10] The Cunard Line put extra lifeboats on its vessels after the loss of the White Star Line's *Titanic* in 1912.
[11] The lay out of the ship: *The Irish Builder* (1896), Hazel P. Smyth and the *Leinster's* ship plans. I am very grateful to author Roy Stokes for giving me a copy of the ship's plans.
[12] D.B. McNeill *Irish Passenger Steam Services Volume 2: South of Ireland*.
[13] Postal Sorter John Higgins.

14 Statement of Lance-Corporal Roach 16 October 1918 in AWM18 9953/1/1. Thanks to Australian researcher Jeff Kildea for assistance and advice in accessing the files of the Australian War Memorial (AWM), Canberra, Australia on the internet.

15 Letter 5 November 1918 from Sergeant Coleman to Corporal Russell, AWM18 9953/1/1.

16 Information on Lieutenant Francis Laracy from Australian Red Cross Society Wounded and Missing Enquiry Bureau files 1914-18 War: File 15508050, Lieutenant Francis Patrick Laracy, 1st Battalion.

17 Letter from the Commandant of the Administrative Headquarters, Australian Imperial Force, London to the Secretary of the Department of Defence, Melbourne in File AWM18 9953/1/1.

18 Contemporary newspapers.

19 I am very grateful to author Roy Stokes for a copy of Parker's report on the sinking.

20 Cross referencing of information given to me by Mary Horgan and Christine O'Sullivan.

21 Letter from Sir Eric Geddes, First Lord of the Admiralty to King George V 26 November 1917.

22 No ships had been sunk in the Irish Sea since the start of October. On 4 October 1918 the Japanese passenger ship *Hirano Maru* was sunk in the Atlantic west of the Bristol Channel and south of Ireland (at Latitude 51-12N, Longitude 7.01W). This was outside of the Irish Sea. Newspapers were still reporting on the event after the *Leinster* was sunk.

23 Contemporary newspaper reports on the inquest into the death of passenger Georgina O'Brien.

24 The "*On This Day*" section of the *First World War.org* website.

25 Gregor Dallas *1918: War and Peace* and article by Ann B. Sides "*When submarine UB-123 attacked the ferry Leinster, it torpedoed Germany's last hope for a 'soft peace' in 1918*" in Military History.

26 The men on the bridge: Seaman Hugh Owen quoted in *The Chronicle* (Holyhead) 18 October 1918.

27 Statement by Captain Cone.

Chapter 4

Torpedoed!

" Two minutes passed, the noise finally stopped and the Titanic settled back slightly at the stern. Then slowly she began sliding under, moving at a deep slant."

Walter Lord, 'A Night to Remember.'

Irish Sea, Thursday morning 10 October 1918

As the *R.M.S. Leinster* set out on her final journey, the weather was fine at Kingstown. But the sea was rough following recent storms. A wind was blowing from the south-southwest. *Leinster's* Boatswain Jim Carraher was in charge of a group of sailors who were working on deck. He later said that *"There was a fresh breeze and a heavy sea running, which increased as* (the ship) *got further out from land."*[1]

At Holyhead conditions became so bad that several Royal Naval ships had to return to port.[2] The weather at Holyhead, however, had not prevented the *R.M.S. Ulster* leaving earlier that morning. She had been taken out of service for overhaul on 7 September and had returned to duty on 5 October. Since her return her Daily Journal had recorded delays every day at Holyhead, awaiting Admiralty orders to sail. After the usual delay, she left at 7 a.m., under the command of Birkenhead born Captain Robert Newton.[3] She reached the Kish Light Vessel at 9.42 a.m. Soon afterwards she passed north of the outbound *Leinster*.

Twenty-one year old Assistant Purser Bill Sweeney was on deck after the *Leinster* left Kingstown. He spoke with passenger Arthur Adshead, Irish agent for the Midland Railway Company. Adshead pointed to a faraway ship and asked if it was the incoming mail boat. Sweeney confirmed that it was the *Ulster* coming from Holyhead, thinking to himself that the mail boat was sailing further north than he had ever seen an incoming *Province*.[4]

*

Meanwhile, like a steel shark, UB-123 was prowling the depths of the Irish Sea. Near the front of the boat was the forward torpedo room, with

49

four torpedo tubes. Six of the submarine's torpedoes were kept on racks near the torpedo tubes. Behind the torpedo room was the area where the lower ranks slept in two-tier bunk beds. Then came the compartment with the warrant officers' and the officers' bunks. Further back was the control room. This contained the main controls for UB-123's diving planes, the main controls for venting the ballast tanks, the boat's radio equipment, the navigator's table and the eyepiece for the navigating periscope. Behind the control room was the accommodation area for petty officers and behind this was the boat's engine room with a diesel engine and a motor for recharging the batteries. At the rear of the boat was a single torpedo tube and racks for the remainder of the boat's torpedoes. The submarine's batteries were located under panels in the floor of the boat. The boat could be divided into separate sealed compartments by the use of watertight doors, in order to prevent flooding in one part of the boat spreading to the rest of the submarine. On the front deck of the submarine was an 8.8 cm gun. Ammunition for the gun was kept under panels on the floor of the control room.

Above UB-123's control room was the conning tower. This area contained Robert Ramm's tiny attack position, with the eyepiece for the attack periscope. The conning tower could be sealed off from the rest of the boat by the use of a watertight door.[5]

As UB-123 did not survive its second combat mission, events on the boat before, during and after the attack on the *Leinster* are not known. However, its tactics can be deduced from similar U-boat attacks.[6] On the lookout for targets, submarines tried to stay on the surface as much as possible, so as to maximise the area of visibility. In daylight a U-boat would be ready for instant dive. A submarine could always locate a surface craft by the tell tale smoke on the horizon. On sighting smoke the submarine captain would take his boat to periscope depth. If the vessel coming over the horizon were a warship, the U-boat would usually try to avoid it. But if – as with the *Leinster* - it were a merchant ship, the submarine's captain would climb up into his attack position in the conning tower. There, using the attack periscope he would try to calculate his target's course and speed. Unless the steamer's course was going to take her fairly close to the submarine there was no hope of getting in an attack by torpedo. This was because the speed of a submerged submarine was very slow and it would need to get within 2,000 yards to fire. However, if things looked favourable the captain would manoeuvre his submarine to get within a few hundred yards of the steamer's course. In the meantime, at regular intervals, the attack periscope would be raised for a few seconds and then lowered immediately. This was to check the steamer's course and speed, as accurate knowledge of these was essential to plot a course for the torpedoes. The fact that periscopes had only to be used for a few seconds at a time made it practically impossible for lookouts like Hugh Owen on the bridge of the *Leinster* to spot them. On the other hand if a steamer was zigzagging, especially when travelling fast, it was very difficult for a submarine captain to gauge its course.

Because he was the only one with access to the attack periscope, Robert Ramm would have been the only man on UB-123 who would have seen the *Leinster* in her final moments. The rest of the crew would – literally – have blindly followed his orders in manoeuvring the submarine and firing the torpedoes.

*

On board the *Leinster* staff had just finished serving breakfast in the dining room. In the smoking room Captain Hutch Cone of the United States Naval Aviation Forces was reading the *Saturday Evening Post* and Michael Joyce, Member of Parliament for Limerick was reading a book. Many passengers were in their cabins, probably feeling tired or sea sick. On deck were the hardier souls and some of those who didn't have cabins. It was about 9.50 a.m. The *Ulster* was still visible on the horizon. On the bridge Captain Birch gave the order to begin a zigzag course, the standard anti-submarine tactic.[7]

*

Shortly before 10 a.m., from his crammed attack post in the conning tower of his submarine, Robert Ramm manoeuvred UB-123 into position on the port side of the *Leinster*. The periscope through which he observed his target was 7.5 meters (approximately 39 feet) in length. On Ramm's command the tubes containing the torpedoes were flooded and the bow caps opened. Then, when conditions looked right, Ramm gave the command to fire. A torpedo sped from one of the torpedo tubes. The front of UB-123 began to lift, lightened by the loss of the torpedo's weight. Chief Engineer Hermann Meier, at the trimming panel, immediately compensated for the loss of weight. Meanwhile the torpedo sped towards the *Leinster*.[8]

*

Sitting on the deck of the *Leinster*, New Zealand Rifleman P. J. Fahey saw what he thought was a porpoise. He pointed it out to Australian Lance-Corporal Michael Roach, who thought it was a whale.[9] The approaching torpedo had also been seen from the bridge. It missed the ship, passing across her bows.[10]

Submarines sometimes fired two torpedoes close together to try to ensure that at least one hit the target. On other occasions the captain would

51

wait to see if the first torpedo struck, before deciding whether it was necessary to fire a second one. It is not known which option Robert Ramm chose. What is known is that he fired a second torpedo.

The second G6AV torpedo shot from the submarine's tubes. Travelling 10 to 20 feet below the surface, it was in effect a miniature submarine. It sped towards the *Leinster* at a speed of 27 knots. 600 cms in length, 50 cms in diameter, it had a fuel tank containing the alcohol that powered the torpedo's motor. The motor drove contra-rotating propellers at the rear of the torpedo. A depth mechanism, set before the torpedo was fired, programmed hydroplanes to maintain a set depth. A gyro-compass linked to a rudder allowed the torpedo to maintain a set course. The torpedo speeding towards the *Leinster* was not armed at the time it left the torpedo tube. Submarines like UB-123 could not afford to carry ten armed torpedoes that might be set off by a slight jar and blow the submarine to pieces. So the detonating cap that exploded the warhead was kept a few inches away from the firing hammer. At the nose of the torpedo was a small propeller-like water vane, which turned as the torpedo drove itself through the water. The shaft of the vane had a screw thread connected to the detonating cap. As it turned it moved the detonator into line with the firing device, completing the alignment after the torpedo had travelled a safe distance from UB-123.

*

On the bridge of the *Leinster* Seaman Hugh Owen from Holyhead saw the second torpedo approaching from the port side.[11] He pointed it out to Captain Birch, who shouted *"Helm hard a-Port! Starboard full astern!"* The intention was to swing the ship to starboard, to avoid the on-coming torpedo. Before the manoeuvre could be completed the torpedo struck the ship forward on the port side in the vicinity of the mailroom, where 22 postal sorters were at work. The torpedo's firing hammer struck the detonating cap. The resulting small explosion triggered the 160 kilograms (approximately 353 pounds) of high explosive at the front of the torpedo. The exploding torpedo blew a whole in the port side of the ship, passed through the ship and blew a hole in the starboard side.

*

Captain Birch ordered *"All hands to the boat stations!"*[12] He remained on the bridge giving orders. The *Leinster* continued to turn until it was facing back the way it had come. The ship began to settle by the bow. Civilian Passenger Florence Enright was sitting on deck when she saw the second torpedo. *"I saw a thing coming along. A long grey thing with red marks, but I did not know that it was a torpedo. It crashed into the engine room and some of the stokers ran up on deck bleeding."* According to U.S. Sailor Frank Martin several people on the portside said that they saw the torpedo about forty yards off before it struck. *"It seemed to go through the ship, as I saw splinters flying out of the starboard side."* Arthur Lewis, Consultant Engineer to the Royal National Lifeboat Institution, was sitting on deck on the starboard side, a little aft of amidships. A man ran from the port side of the ship shouting *"A torpedo coming!"* The shock of the explosion was not great. The ship shivered and began to dip slightly forward. Nobody in Lewis's vicinity appeared to be hurt. Sergeants Denny and Rose of the U.S. Army were sitting in the stern of the *Leinster* when the torpedo struck. Denny hear people say that they had been torpedoed. As the shock in that part of the ship was slight, Denny went to see if in fact they had been torpedoed.

Chief Special Mechanic Mason, of the U.S. Navy was sitting aft on the starboard side when he heard a soldier shout: *"A torpedo!"* Immediately afterward a shockwave struck the *Leinster*. Mason ran to the lifeboat deck with about a dozen men. One of the men, a *Leinster* crewman, prevented further people rushing the lifeboats. Cork couple Louis and Cora Daly were on honeymoon. Shortly before 10 a.m. they decided to go on deck. As every seat was taken, Louis Daly – a major in the Leinster Regiment – decided to go to their cabin to get a suitcase for Cora to sit on. He was just returning on deck when the ship was struck. Passengers from below rushed up onto the deck. As the Dalys didn't have life jackets, Louis told Cora to remain where she was and he went below deck to search for some.

Maureen Waters, Josephine Carr and Miss Barry (first name unknown) were members of the newly formed Women's Royal Naval Service (nicknamed the *Wrens*.) Sometime after boarding the *Leinster* Waters and Barry went on deck. They were seated on the starboard side near the bow when the ship was struck on the port side. Waters later said that she didn't realize that the *Leinster* had been torpedoed, thinking that a gun had been fired on the ship. Putting on life jackets, the *Wrens* met their newly married friend Cora Daly, who was waiting for her husband Louis to return with life jackets.

Assistant Purser Bill Sweeney was on the port side of the ship, in the corridor between the saloon and the ladies cabins when Stewardess Louisa Parry called to him. She wanted to return his watch, which he had lent to her the previous evening. Sweeney said that he had something to do and would return shortly. He had only gone a few yards when the ship was struck. He rushed on deck, where Second Mate Addison shouted *"We've been torpedoed!"* First Officer Patrick Crangle was in his cabin making up the crew's pay sheets. When the torpedo struck the ship he rushed on deck. By this time the *Leinster* was settling by the head. After Captain Birch ordered the lifeboats to be launched Crangle lowered the forward starboard lifeboat level with the deck. Birch then ordered him to check on the aft lifeboats. Passengers were milling around the deck. As the *Leinster* was not sinking any further, Crangle told the passengers that the ship would remain afloat. Passenger Minnie Donnelly was in the saloon when the torpedo struck. There was a general commotion. Donnelly rushed on deck. She managed to get a lifebelt, which she put on.

Third Steward Thomas Deegan was finishing his work in the saloon when he felt a bump, as if the *Leinster* had struck a brick wall. He made his way to the lifeboat deck. Captain Hutch Cone and Michael Joyce M.P. were among those in the smoking room when someone rushed in and shouted that a torpedo was approaching. Simultaneously the ship shuddered as if it had received a terrible blow. Cone and Joyce put on their life jackets and went on deck, where both went to help with launching lifeboats. Cone decided to go to the lifeboat deck, to help with the forward lifeboats. On his way he saw a few of the engine room crew who had come on deck. Among them was a man who had facial injuries and two broken legs. At this point Cone decided to go onto the bridge, where he spoke with Captain Birch. The captain said that the ship's radio was out of action and he didn't think a message that the ship had been torpedoed would have been picked up. (In fact, CDSPCo Managing Director Edward Watson, in the final entry in *Leinster's* journal says *"her wireless message was picked up by the Ulster."* In a 1979 interview, Assistant Purser Bill Sweeney said that the *Ulster's* radio operator told him that he had picked up an S.O.S. from the *Leinster*. As will be seen later, the message was also picked up by Royal Navy destroyers.)

Birch asked Cone if he would assist with the launching of a nearby starboard lifeboat. Cone helped one of the *Leinster's* officers and a group of men with this lifeboat. At the same time he noticed that a lifeboat that was launched on the port side had few people in it. When the lifeboat he was helping with had been launched, Cone went back onto the bridge and pointed out to Birch the lifeboat that had few people in it. Birch hailed the lifeboat and Cone believed that those on board tried to return to get more passengers on board. As will be seen later, this was probably a boat that contained four or five of the *Leinster's* crew and did not pick up any passengers.

Michael Joyce M.P. had a seafaring background, was President of the United Kingdom River Pilots' Association and had survived four shipwrecks. He went to assist a number of stewards who were launching a lifeboat on the port side. Third Steward John O'Connor was flung to the deck when the torpedo struck the ship. He got up immediately and went below to the first class cabins to look for a lifebelt. After getting a lifebelt and assisting a woman passenger with hers, he returned on deck to hear Captain Birch order the lifeboats to be launched. He tried to get to the lifeboat deck, but was prevented from doing so by a crowd of passengers. He finally reached a boat near the bridge, which the captain ordered him and some of the crew to lower. They managed to get it into the water.

Chief Steward Llewellyn Lewis was at the saloon entrance, speaking with his brother William John, when the torpedo struck. The Lewis brothers began handing out life jackets. William John, who was a shore steward and was travelling on the *Leinster* as a passenger, asked his brother for a life belt. After Llewellyn helped him put one on, William John went on deck. Llewellyn Lewis continued to help passengers before heading for the bridge to tell Captain Birch that all was clear down below. On his way he met Ship's Adjutant Second Lieutenant Hugh Parker, who was looking for a life jacket. Lewis opened one of the director's cabins and got two life jackets. He gave one to Parker and another to an officer who had one leg. At this point Lewis was unable to make his way up to the bridge because a woman passenger clung onto him. He shouted up to Captain Birch that all was clear below stairs. Not receiving a reply, he shouted again. This time Second Mate Harry Addison answered *"All right!"*

The area where the torpedo had caused most devastation was in the post room. Postal Workers John Higgins, Patrick Murphy and Jennins Attwooll were sorting registered mail in a small office in a corner of the sorting room. Higgins later said that when the torpedo struck the port side of the ship the resulting explosion blew holes in both the port and starboard sides of the ship. All of the lights went out. The surviving sorters were now in the dark with the sea pouring in both sides of the ship. Higgins called to Patrick Murphy (see also the section *"Postal Sorter John Joseph Higgins"*) but the latter did not react, possibly due to shock. As the post office was rapidly filling up with seawater, Higgins decided that it was every man for himself. He partly scrambled and partly swam through a sea of floating letters, making for the ladder leading to the upper deck. When he reached the place where the ladder should have been he was horrified to find that it had been blown away. Above him he could see a pale glimmer of daylight shining through the exit hatch. He grabbed strands of, now dead, electric wire hanging from the ceiling. He held onto these until the rising water brought him up to the roof of the post office. There, after several attempts, he managed to pull himself through the opening. The postal workers' life jackets were stored on a rack in this area. Grabbing one, he noticed that the sea was already about a foot deep where he was standing. At this point he noticed his colleague John Ledwidge struggling at the exit from the postal room. Higgins helped him on deck. By this time the *Leinster* was down by the head. Major Louis Daly had returned to the cabin area to find lifejackets for his wife Cora and himself. As the *Leinster's* power had failed he had to search in the dark. Using match light to guide him, he searched several cabins before finding two lifejackets.

Boatswain Jim Carraher was on the *Leinster's* hurricane deck (the covered-over part of the upper deck from the bow of the ship extending back for about 70 feet) when the torpedo struck. The force of the explosion knocked him off his feet. He heard Captain Birch shout *"All hands to the boat stations!"* Carraher came up on the main deck. He went to boat No. 6, the middle boat, aft. There he found that a sergeant and some soldiers had climbed into the lifeboat before it could be readied for launching. Carraher tried to get them out of the boat, but they wouldn't move. With lives at risk, Carraher called a military policeman and explained the problem. The MP drew his gun and told the sergeant to get out of the boat. The sergeant appeared to be dazed and didn't move. The military policeman shot him dead. The rest of the soldiers then climbed out of the lifeboat. With the help of some of the crew, Jim Carraher prepared the boat for launch. The boat was then filled with people and lowered.[13]

Second Lieutenant Hugh Parker, the *Leinster's* military adjutant, got a life jacket from Chief Steward Llewellyn Lewis and headed for the bridge to report to Captain Birch. On the port side of the ship he found a boat being lowered by several of the crew. He saw two male passengers, one of whom he believed to be a priest, getting into the boat. He dragged one of the men from the boat and told him that it was *"women and children first."* Telling the man that he would kill him if he tried to get in again, Parker remained on the spot until the lifeboat had been launched. On reaching the bridge Parker saw Captain Birch talking with American Captain Hutch Cone. By this time the bow of the *Leinster* was down, but not completely submerged and the ship was on an even keel. Finishing with Captain Cone, Captain Birch said to Parker: *'The wires are gone, so we have not been able to send a message. I am sure the ship will float.'* Parker said that he felt that the submarine would fire another torpedo. Birch gave him a key. He asked him to go to the chart room, open the top drawer and bring him the codebooks that were there. Parker went down to the chart room.

Birch appears to have been worried about the codebooks, as he subsequently called Assistant Purser Bill Sweeney to the bridge and also asked him to get the codebooks. When Sweeney reached the chart room Parker was there. He asked Parker what he was doing. Parker said that he was getting the codes and that they were supposed to be thrown over the side if there was a danger the enemy might capture them. Sweeney told him to carry on. Parker returned to the bridge with two codebooks and Captain Birch's revolver. Birch told him to go back on deck and give orders for the life rafts to be launched. Sweeney subsequently arrived back on the bridge. Birch and he then threw the codebooks over the side. Birch ordered Sweeney to launch a small lifeboat from under the bridge on the starboard side. Sweeney called to Lamp Trimmer Robert Anthony and together they got the lifeboat into the water. Just as Sweeney was about to slide down a rope into the lifeboat, Birch called to him again. *"Go down and get that accommodation ladder out."* As it was lashed to the side of the ship, Sweeney called to Fireman Percy Lamble, asking if he had a knife. (The men who tended the boilers on Royal Navy ships were called stokers. On merchant ships they were called firemen.)

Wrens Maureen Waters and Miss Barry saw lifeboats that had been launched. They were terrified at the thought that they would have to jump down from the deck into them. In the meantime Major Louis Daly returned from his search in the darkened cabins, with two lifejackets. Cora and he then helped each other to put on the lifejackets. As one of the senior officers on the ship, Daly felt that he should stay on board to help out. He put Cora into a lifeboat that was about to be launched. Maureen Waters and Miss Barry also climbed in and the boat was lowered to the water. Michael Joyce, MP for Limerick, was helping a number of stewards who were launching a lifeboat on the port side. As the boat was being lowered the crew had difficulties in getting a woman passenger into the boat. In order to get her over the rail Joyce got into the lifeboat and pulled her into the boat. As the boat was being lowered, Joyce was lowered with it.

Stewardess Louisa Parry went into the First Class Saloon to help Chief Stewardess Mary Coffey. When the ship was struck by the torpedo Coffey got lifejackets from some of the cabins. She handed them out to passengers and to her two stewardesses. Parry then went downstairs and got some women and children to the upper deck. She then went below again. She was helping a woman and child in a cabin when the door slammed shut.

After he had seen his wife Cora safely into a lifeboat, Major Louis Daly went up to Captain Birch on the bridge. *"I found the Captain rather pessimistic. He said that the ship would only last eight minutes and he feared that the shock of the explosion had very likely disorganized the wireless apparatus, so that our S.O.S. would not have gone forth. In this, as it happened, he was mistaken."* At this point the second torpedo struck the ship.

*

After giving the order to fire one or more torpedoes, a submarine captain would lower the boat's periscope and give the order to dive. This was to prevent the submarine from being spotted. Once torpedoes were fired the captain had no control over whether they hit or missed their target. If they hit, the sound would be heard on board the submarine below the surface of the sea. If they missed, no sound would be heard on board the submarine. In either event, there was no point in increasing the risk of being seen. So the submarine would dive.

Below the surface of the sea, UB-123's crew would have heard the explosion as the torpedo struck the *Leinster*. A few minutes later Ramm would have ordered UB-123 to be taken up to periscope depth. He would again have raised the attack periscope. By the time he looked through the periscope the wounded *Leinster* had made a 180-degree turn in an attempt to get back to Kingstown. UB-123's periscope would now have shown the *Leinster's* starboard side. What did Ramm see when he looked through the periscope? Did he see the ship's deck full of military personnel, whom he felt were on their way to destroy his homeland? Did he see civilians, including women and children? Or did he see both? Why did he decide to fire another torpedo? Did he think that the *Leinster* was going to remain afloat and feel that he had to sink the ship before Royal Navy destroyers arrived and sank him? What he saw and why he decided to fire another torpedo at the *Leinster* will never be known.

Again Ramm gave the command. Again a G6AV torpedo leapt from the submarine's tubes and sped towards the *Leinster* at a speed of 27 knots, its gyro-compass keeping the deadly missile on course. As it closed on its prey the torpedo's detonator moved into line with the firing device. The torpedo stuck the *Leinster* on the starboard side. A full lifeboat that was being lowered on the starboard side was blown to pieces. Captain William Birch was blow off the bridge and into the sea.

Her mission completed, UB-123 would have left the scene as quickly as possible to avoid British warships. Behind her hundreds of human beings were struggling for their lives in the cruel sea.

*

Seaman Hugh Owen had been on the bridge with Captain Birch. He had spotted a torpedo approaching and shouted a warning to Birch. The torpedo struck as Owen ran to help with the launching of lifeboats. He later said that there had been no instructions as to which particular lifeboats passengers were to take. Owen helped get a lifeboat launched and climbed on board himself. He said that the boat was filled with about a hundred people. As the boat was pushed away from the ship, the second torpedo struck the *Leinster*. In the resulting confusion the lifeboat turned over. Out of the approximately one hundred people Owen said were in the boat, only six survived.

Boatswain Jim Carraher, who had launched No. 6 lifeboat, later testified that he saw No. 2 and No. 4 boats lowered. He said that No. 2 boat got safely to the water, but he was unable to say what happened to No. 4, as the second torpedo struck at that point. Carraher released a number of rafts. After the second torpedo exploded the *Leinster* listed to port and started to settle rapidly. Before the ship went down Carraher jumped over the side.

An American soldier helped passenger Minnie Donnelly into a lifeboat. There were about thirty in the lifeboat, of whom the majority were men. The boat had just pulled away from the *Leinster* when the second torpedo struck. *"It was as if the whole place had been rent asunder. Dense black clouds of smoke went up. Pieces of the steamer were blown into the air including the two funnels and some of the passengers were also blown up with the force of the explosion. Debris fell all around and there were agonising screams and cries for help. After the first torpedo struck, people who could not get into a boat threw themselves over the side of the vessel into the water -- men, women and children. When the second missile struck terrible panic prevailed. We could see the people jumping into the water in hundreds. Some of them -- mostly women -- appeared to have been in bed below, or to be suffering from sea sickness, for I could see them rushing about the decks very scantily clad and their hair flying loose. In about four minutes after the second torpedo struck, the Leinster split up and sank. I was a bit stunned with the shock. We could see another lifeboat full of people being capsized, and the sight of the occupants struggling in the water and their cries for help were heart rending. When the boat capsized many of them clung on to the keel and sides of the overturned craft until the nails of their fingers were absolutely torn away."*

Passenger Florence Enright had seen the approach of the first torpedo to strike the *Leinster*. She was still on deck when the second torpedo struck. *"Pieces of iron and wood flew about hitting various people, many of whom were wounded, blood flowing freely from them. The (Leinster) immediately listed and the deck went perpendicular, so that we could not stand."* Enright jumped into the water and managed to get to an upturned lifeboat. Shortly afterwards she was stuck on the head and rendered unconscious. Seaman John Lacey had been working on deck as the *Leinster* put out to sea. When he had finished his work he went to his cabin. He was there when the first torpedo struck. Scrambling unhurt from a mass of splinters, he made his way on deck. The ship was then on an ever keel, but down by the head. Lacey helped to launch lifeboat No. 4, aft on the starboard side. Another boat forward on the same side had been lowered a moment before. At this point the second torpedo struck the ship. *"The Leinster heeled over tremendously to port, I and some of my mates were flung off the top deck, a drop of 40 feet, into the water."* Shortly afterwards he managed to get into a lifeboat.

Thirty-four year old Lieutenant-Commander Colin Campbell was travelling with his wife Eileen and 4½-year-old daughter, also named Eileen. All three were lost. Sergeant Denny of the U.S. Army slid down a rope at the stern of the *Leinster*. The second torpedo struck the ship as he was on his way down. He was knocked unconscious. *"My first impression afterwards was that my lungs had burst. I was under water and must have been drawn down by the sinking of the ship. When I got to the surface and was able to get my breath back, I caught hold of a spar. I found that my right shoulder was dislocated and my arm useless. Fortunately, I had done some swimming before, so I managed to cling on to the spar. I saw at least twenty people die in the water around me. I could do nothing for them."*

Chief Stewardess Mary Coffey saw passenger Georgina O'Brien, whom she knew, standing on deck on the port side of the ship. As a crowd of people was gathered in the vicinity, Coffey suggested to O'Brien that they go to the starboard side of the ship. At that point the second torpedo struck the ship. Coffey told O'Brien to climb over the side of the ship with her and said that they would try to catch a raft, as there was no chance of getting into a boat. O'Brien refused, saying *"Don't go!"* Coffey said *"We have no time."* By this time the *Leinster* was listing heavily to port and the deck was at such an angle that it was almost impossible to stand. Coffey went over the side and down a rope to a life raft. When she last saw O'Brien, the latter was at the rail getting over the side of the ship.

Major Charles Duggan, Lieutenant Robert Bassett and Lieutenant Halse had boarded the *Leinster* together, having stayed the previous night at *Rosse's Hotel* in Parkgate Street, Dublin. Duggan and Bassett were British Army doctors. Halse, an officer in the New Zealand Army, had been hospitalised in Ireland for an injured left shoulder. The shoulder was clamped in an iron frame, in order to keep it in position. A newspaper report said that, after the first torpedo struck, Corkman Lieutenant Bassett placed a lifebelt around Halse's neck. Ironically Halse survived, while Bassett and Duggan were lost.

Postal Sorter John Higgins had escaped from the mailroom and had helped his colleague John Ledwidge get out of the exit hatch. Higgins then saw Postal Sorter Thomas Bolster. The latter said that his leg was broken and that he was badly hurt internally. Ledwidge left his workmates and went towards the stern of the ship. Higgins never saw him again. He was later told that Ledwidge had reached a raft, but had died of exposure. Higgins saw Bolster climb over a railing and slide down a rope, in an attempt to reach a lifeboat. But he missed the boat and fell into the sea. He drifted away and Higgins never saw him again. Higgins then climbed over the railing and slid down a rope towards the lifeboat.

Lieutenant J. Craig Carlisle and Anna Ferguson had married five days previously and were going to England as part of their honeymoon. Anna Carlisle was on deck as the first lifeboats were being lowered. She declined to go in these, as her husband was in their cabin. When he arrived they both got into a lifeboat. After the boat reached the water some people jumped aboard from the deck of the *Leinster*. Others clambered on board from the sea. Lieutenant Carlisle was near the front of the lifeboat when a man, according to a newspaper believed to be Postal Sorter John Higgins, fell in on his feet.

Assistant Purser Bill Sweeney had just asked Fireman Percy Lamble for a knife when the second torpedo struck the *Leinster*. Sweeney later said *"I looked up and saw the foremast crashing down and the fore funnel ripped out, as if by a fellow in a bad temper."* He slid over the side of the ship. *"It was quite easy, because she had a good list to port. I slid down and stepped into this lifeboat. We called her 'Big Bertha'."* The lifeboat was crowded. Bill Sweeney, Greaser Philip Connolly and his Cabin Boy son Tom were the only members of the *Leinster's* crew on the lifeboat. Also among those on board was Commander Baggot of the Royal Navy, who was based at Kingstown, Anna and J. Craig

Carlisle, Postal Sorter John Higgins, Cora Daly and *Wrens* Maureen Waters and Miss Barry. The boat, which was certified to carry fifty-two people, was still tied to the *Leinster* by the bow and the stern. Sweeney borrowed a knife from Greaser Philip Connolly to cut the lines. *Wren* Maureen Waters later said that she and Miss Barry also passed penknives to the men in the boat and that they were used to cut the lines and to cut the oars loose. The lifeboat was only a few yards from the ship when the second torpedo struck the *Leinster*. Postal Sorter John Higgins said that the *Leinster* was *"practically blown in two pieces, the whole centre portion being blown sky high."* He said that before the ship sank he saw Postal Sorter Albert MacDonnell on deck, but said that he went down with the ship.

American Captain Hutch Cone was helping to launch life rafts when the second torpedo hit the ship. The explosion lifted him from the deck. Both his legs were severely injured. Looking around, he could see no sign of the lifeboat that had been filled with people on the starboard side. It, and the people in it, had been blown to pieces. Unable to walk, and seeing that the water was now almost up to the deck on which he was lying, Cone lay down and rolled overboard into the sea. He managed to get to a life raft. Unable to climb onto it, he hooked one of his arms into a rope that was looped around the side of the raft. He used his other arm to fend off any debris that came his way. Passenger Fanny Saunders was travelling to Liverpool, where her daughter Janet was seriously ill. On Christmas Eve 1895 Fanny's husband Frank had been lost when the Kingstown lifeboat had capsized while going to the aid of a ship in distress. Almost twenty-three years later Fanny joined Frank beneath the waters of the Irish Sea.

First Officer Patrick Crangle succeeded in getting two of the aft starboard lifeboats filled with passengers and lowered away. *"Whilst lowering the small aft boat on the starboard side, the ship was struck by a second torpedo and immediately afterwards she settled rapidly and all persons including myself, on the boat deck were thrown into the water. I was, with difficulty, hauled into one of the midships boats by Seaman Lacey.* (This was Seaman John Lacey, who had been flung from the ship into the water.) *This boat had been cast adrift and floated off with rafts and other gear. We subsequently hauled on board several ladies, the total complement in the boat being about 25 persons."* After the first torpedo struck the *Leinster* Acting Chief Engineer William Mathias appears to have realised that the lifeboats could not be launched while the ship was still underway. He rushed down to the engine room. Despite the fact that the sea was flooding into the ship, he managed to shut off the engines. His bravery cost him his life, but it enabled some of the lifeboats to be launched.

After following Captain Birch's order to have the rafts on the boat deck launched, Second Lieutenant Hugh Parker went to the saloon deck on the port side, asking the passengers there to remain perfectly calm. A woman, whom he believed to be Lady Phyllis Hamilton, said *"We are quite all right, not a bit excited, don't worry about us."* Parker then went to the starboard side. At this point the second torpedo struck the ship. Parker climbed down a rope into a lifeboat. He later said *"there was some difficulty in getting* (the lifeboat) *free as the lowering ropes, fore and aft, were still attached to the sinking ship. I handed my pocket knife to a sailor who was standing in the bow of the boat and he succeeded in cutting the ropes there. The stern ropes were ultimately got clear and the boat got away just before the ship sank."* These remarks would appear to suggest that he was in the *Big Bertha* lifeboat. As the lifeboat was overcrowded, Parker dived overboard, swam to a raft and climbed onboard. As he watched the *Leinster* sink he realised that someone was clinging to his leg. This turned out to be passenger Maud Marsham Rae. He pulled her onto the raft. A few seconds later she saw her husband, Second Lieutenant Lindsay Marsham Rae, clinging to an upturned boat. Marsham Rae called to Parker *"For God's sake look after my wife."* Also on the raft with Parker and Maud Marsham Rae were four soldiers and two sailors. The group suffered severely from the cold and waves broke over them several times. One of the soldiers let go of the raft and was drowned. Another soldier tried to climb onto the raft and clung to Maud Marsham Rae. Parker ordered him to let go and work his way to a better part of the raft. When the man refused, Parker forced him to relax his grip on the raft believing the man to have gone mad and to be posing a threat to the safety of the others. He threw the man a lifebelt, but he sank. Parker said that he saw four boats get away from the ship, but one overturned and the majority of those on board were drowned. (This was obviously Hugh Owen's boat.)

Because a woman passenger had been clinging to him, Chief Steward Llewellyn Lewis had been unable to go up to the bridge to report to Captain Birch. When a whistle sounded to abandon ship Lewis, with the woman still clinging to him, went over a railing into the sea. Lewis helped the woman into the lifeboat that Michael Joyce M.P. and the stewards had launched. Lewis later said that while still in the water, he helped a postal sorter and one of the *Leinster's* firemen into the lifeboat, before climbing in himself. (The mention of the postal sorter is a bit of a mystery as a newspaper account suggested that John Higgins, the sole surviving postal sorter was in a different lifeboat.) Apart from Michael Joyce M.P. and Chief Steward Llewellyn Lewis, the boat contained Second Mate Harry Addison. The second mate ordered Lewis to cast off. With stewards manning the oars and Michael Joyce M.P. using an oar as a rudder, the lifeboat moved off. According to Lewis *"Immediately after this the second torpedo was fired and the ship disappeared in a few minutes, bow first."* He said that he saw three other lifeboats and several rafts with people clinging to them. From descriptions they gave, it seems likely that Third Stewards Thomas Deegan and John O'Connor were also in Lewis's lifeboat. O'Connor said that when the second torpedo struck the ship *"funnels, coal and wreckage were driven into the air, and the vessel crumpled up and sank almost immediately. As she went down two men were clinging to the propeller."* He said that a young married woman in the lifeboat sang to keep up the spirits of those on board. Michael Joyce M.P. said *"the sea was very rough and breaking, but our crew kept the boat's head up to the sea with their oars, and with the assistance of a sea anchor, which was got out. Although we shipped a good share of water from breaking seas we were always able to bale it out and keep the boat clear."*

Meanwhile, the lifeboat known as *Big Bertha* drifted around the stern of the *Leinster*. Assistant Purser Bill Sweeney saw a group of young British Army soldiers sitting on the rail. He screamed at them to jump. *"But they just sat there."* Finally the ship went down, carrying the soldiers with it. Some of those in the lifeboat spotted an injured man in the water. It was Captain William Birch, who had been blown off the bridge into the sea. Both his legs were broken and he was bleeding from a cut over one of his eyes. He clung to the side of the lifeboat. As waves were splashing into the overcrowded boat Birch shouted: *"Don't let her get waterlogged! Bail her out!"* Sweeney shouted at the passengers to get Birch into the boat. He was partially pulled into the lifeboat. His head rested on the lap of passenger Cora Daly and his feet hung out the side of the boat.

Cora Daly's husband, Major Louis Daly, had been on the bridge with Captain Birch when the second torpedo struck the ship. The bridge was blown up into the air. While Captain Birch ended up in the sea, Daly found himself on the forward deck with both knees out of joint, a fractured leg and numerous cuts and bruises. He saw a civilian trying to push a large wooden grating over the side of the ship. Daly struggled over to help. He later said *"Thanks to my riding breeches, which were tight at the knee, and to my field boots, I was able to use my legs to a certain extent."* By this point the water was level with the top of the ship's rail. The two men got the grating over and floated off with it. Daly said that most of the people who had not got off the *Leinster* were by this time gathered at the stern of the ship. Many of them jumped into the sea at the last minute, so that the water was thick with people, many screaming and shouting for help. Eventually, nearly a dozen people clung to Daly's grating. Every so often a person would try to climb on top of the grating, threatening to overturn it. Eventually Daly spotted a raft floating about fifty yards away. He swam to it. About eight other people joined him.

Stewardess Louisa Parry was trapped inside a cabin with a woman and child. Some of the crew tried to open the door, but they were unable to do so due to the steep angle of the sinking ship and the pressure of water that was in the corridor. Eventually, in order to save themselves, they had to leave. Louisa Parry and the two passengers she had fought to save went down with the *Leinster*.

U.S. Navy Chief Special Mechanic James Mason helped to launch two lifeboats. *"I saw the second torpedo coming directly for the starboard side. This torpedo hit about amidships, in the vicinity of the boilers, which apparently exploded, even though I noticed that the boilers were being blown down through the safety valves from the time the first torpedo hit. The second torpedo and boiler explosion produced an enormous amount of wreckage which fell so thickly in clouds together with steam and debris, that it was difficult to see anything at all. It was impossible to control the people after the second torpedo hit and there was a rush for the boats and rafts. The ship listed to port and went down by the bow."* Mason lowered himself over the stern with a rope and reached a raft. *"There were at least a dozen rafts, which floated clear, but it was very rough and very difficult to stay on the rafts or to hold on when they became crowded."* He tried three different rafts, finding Captain Cone holding onto the third raft. The others on the raft were two U.S. sailors and a civilian.

Maud Elizabeth Ward had been secretary to the Countess of Carysfort, until the latter's death in January 1918. When Lieutenant-Colonel Douglas Proby inherited the Carysfort lands, Ward had continued as secretary to him and his wife. She was travelling to England from the Carysfort estates at Glenart, Co. Wicklow when she was lost on the *Leinster*. Australian Sergeant Francis Coleman and Private Boxer Ware leapt into the sea and swam away from the stricken ship. Coleman later wrote to a mutual friend that as he swam for a raft he heard Ware call his name. *"I turned towards him. He seemed to be going well and not unduly distressed."* Eventually Coleman made it to the raft, and with the help of a New Zealander scrambled aboard. *"On looking back I could not see Boxer and I thought at the time that he might have went to one of the boats."* Private Boxer Allan Ware of 3rd Division Motor Transport Company was lost. His body was never recovered.

Passenger Arthur Lewis helped a young male passenger put on his lifejacket. He later helped an officer from the New Zealand Army with his. When the second torpedo struck, Lewis turned his back to the explosion and bowed his head. He was struck by the water that was thrown up by the explosion. The *Leinster* began to sink quickly. Lewis ran to the stern. There he jumped from the port side, as the deck of the ship on this side was only about twelve feet from the water. He found himself near a small raft and got on to it with a woman and a soldier. Other survivors came along and tried to get on to the raft, causing it to turn over and pitch those on it into the sea. A lifeboat was then spotted and most of those in the vicinity swam for it. Lewis, the woman and the soldier then got back on the raft. They picked up another soldier, but in getting him on board the raft capsized and he was washed off. Lewis held on to him, but the soldier soon became unconscious. When a large wave struck them Lewis lost his grip on the soldier.

Lucy Agnes Plunkett was travelling with her sister-in-law Sheelah Plunkett. Lucy's husband, Lieutenant Leo Plunkett was serving in France with the Royal Dublin Fusiliers. The two women were on deck wearing lifejackets when the second torpedo struck the *Leinster* and the ship keeled over. The women were flung into the sea and became separated. Lucy's lifejacket was insecurely fastened and fell off. She was unable to swim, but a man on a raft caught her before she sank. After a difficult struggle he succeeded in getting her onto the raft. Sheelah, her twenty-one year old sister-in-law, was lost. Recently widowed Fanny Wookey had sold the *Leixlip Woollen Mills* and was going to live with her daughter in England. Like her son Frederick, in 1915, she too was killed by the German armed forces. Lieutenant-Colonel Charles Blackburne travelled with his wife Emily, children Beatrice and Peter and Rose De Pury, the children's governess. Blackburne, a veteran of the Boer War, had served on the Western Front. In 1915 shell fragments had paralysed his left shoulder. No longer fit for active service, he had been assigned to duty in Ireland. Emily Blackburne was the sole survivor of the family group who had boarded the *Leinster* that morning.

*

When the *Titanic* sank in 1912, one of the heroines of the disaster was Molly Brown. She took over the tiller of a lifeboat and kept up the spirits of the boat's passengers. The *R.M.S. Leinster* had its own Molly Brown. Unfortunately, newspaper accounts of the sinking do not give her Christian name. Mrs A. Dudgeon (née Denroche) was the daughter of a Dublin solicitor and the wife of an army lieutenant who was serving in France. *"The Irish Times"* of 14 October 1918 reported: *"Mrs Dudgeon, of Watford, London, daughter of Mr Denroche, solicitor, Dublin states that she was returning to England after a holiday. At the time of the attack by the submarine she was in her berth, and was partly undressed. Putting on an overcoat, she hurried on deck, where she saw a man lowering a boat, which was partly filled with passengers. She jumped into the boat, and when it reached the water she seized a boathook, and kept it clear of the ship. The men in the boat did not seem to know much about rowing, and she had to get the rowlocks and fix them.* (While the crewmen in the boat mainly consisted of stewards, there were at least two men in the boat who would have had knowledge of lifeboats. These were *Leinster's* Second Officer Harry Addison and the four times shipwrecked Michael Joyce M.P., who used an oar as a rudder to steer the boat.) *They ultimately got away from the side of the ship, and rowed about as best they could for over an hour, picking up four or five people who were clinging to the wreckage. There were others whom they could not reach owing to the high seas, and they reluctantly had to be abandoned. One of the men who was in the boat was wounded, and suffered very much from cold. Mrs Dudgeon generously wrapped him in one of the few garments she was wearing."* Speaking of the *Leinster* heroine, another newspaper report said *"Mrs Dudgeon, who appears to have been an expert oarswoman, handled the boat with great skill. The craft was very nearly pulled under when the second torpedo struck the Leinster. The lifeboat was very heavily leaden, and with some difficulty Mrs Dudgeon succeeded in getting some of the passengers to keep the boat's head to the waves. She received great assistance from the Chief Steward, Lewis, who was on board."*

While disaster brings out the best in some people, it brings out the worst in others. According to Assistant Purser Bill Sweeney, four or five of the *Leinster's* crew took off in a lifeboat that didn't contain a single passenger.

*

Josephine Carr from Cork was among those lost. A shorthand typist serving with the Women's Royal Naval Service, she had joined the service on 17 September 1918, just over three weeks previously. So she was probably on her way to take up her first posting. She was the first ever *Wren* to be killed on active service. Canadian Frank Higgerty had been a barrister until March of that year, when he had joined the Canadian Army as a private. Granted a commission in the British Army, he had visited Ireland, the land of his ancestors, before setting out to take up duty. The visit cost him his life. Two fifteen-year-old boys were lost in the sinking. Apart from their age, they had nothing in common. Alfred White Curzon King was the nephew of Press Baron Lord Northcliffe and was returning to Winchester Public School. Gerald Palmer, who had a spinal injury, was travelling from *The Cripples Home* in Bray, Co. Wicklow, to *Barnardos* in London.

Lizzie Healy, Chrissie Murphy and sisters Lena and Norah Galvin, all from Tralee, Co. Kerry, were killed in the sinking. Private Joseph Hill of the Royal Defence Corps was going on leave to his wife Nellie and three sons in Leicester. Wounded on the Western Front, his family thought that he would be safe when he was posted to Ireland. They were wrong. It was not a German bullet, but a German torpedo that took his life.

Lady Alexandra Phyllis Hamilton was travelling with servants Martha Bridge and Ellenor Strachan. Known to her family as Phyllis, she was the daughter of Sir James and Lady Mary Hamilton, Duke and Duchess of Abercorn. Her father was a leading member of the Unionist party and an active campaigner against Home Rule for Ireland. Her parents had attended the launch of the *R.M.S. Ulster* on 26 June 1896, when her mother had christened the ship. Phyllis Hamilton and servants Martha Bridge and Ellenor Strachan were lost in the sinking. None of their bodies were recovered. Lieutenant Sydney Crawford of the Royal Dublin Fusiliers and his sister Letitia Hill were returning from visiting their seriously ill sister. His body was washed up on the west coast of Scotland. Her body was never recovered. Thomas Foley was brother-in-law to world famous tenor John McCormack. The death of Thomas and his wife Charlotte left 10 children orphaned.   Thirty-four year old Violet Barrett was a volunteer nurse, returning to duty in France.   Prior to her leave she had been nursing wounded German prisoners.   Another group of Germans killed her within sight of her homeland.

The Limerick Chronicle of 12 October 1918 told the sad story of the Gould family of 3 Creagh Lane, Limerick, whom it described as *"humble decent people."*   Catherine Gould boarded the *Leinster* with her son Michael and daughters May, Essie, Alice, Angela and Olive.   The children ranged in age from 20 years to 12 months.   The family were on their way to England, where Mr Gould, *"a retired army man,"* was a munitions worker.   The only member of the family to survive the sinking was Essie, the second eldest.   Though the Goulds were the family who suffered the greatest loss in the sinking, their story was not told in any other newspaper.   Like Gerald Palmer, these *"humble decent people"* were doubly forgotten, hardly mentioned in the now long forgotten *Leinster* story.

*

"The Cork Constitution" of 12 October carried accounts of the sinking. *"A survivor said he was watching the postal sorters at work when the first explosion occurred.* (This is a puzzling statement, as the postal sorting room was below deck.)   *Struck forward near the first bulkhead and the forecastle, the vessel withstood the shock.   There was much confusion, especially among the female passengers, who rushed about the deck in a state of alarm. An attempt was made to get the vessel about and make it back to port.   It looked as if it might succeed, so steadily did the vessel ride, despite a heavy swell.   But hopes were frustrated when the second torpedo struck amidships, near the first class saloon.   Immediately there was a violent explosion which shook the vessel from stem to stern and many must have been killed by its force.   The confusion increased as it listed heavily to port. Many men, trusting to their life belts, dived into the sea and most were drowned. The boats were immediately lowered, but some being over crowded capsized before striking the water and their occupants thrown out, while other boats smashed against the sides of the ship.   As the Leinster began to sink the scene became indescribable, and it became apparent that many lives would be lost."*

Another survivor said that: *" he saw the second torpedo coming and knew it was all over with her.   There was a terrible explosion and the boilers were literally blown to pieces.   He jumped headlong into the sea.   At the same moment a little girl of about 5 years did likewise.   The poor little thing was frightened out of her wits. He caught her just as she reached the water and swam with her towards a boat which was struggling in a heavy sea and getting her into the boat, which was already full, she was saved."*

According a third survivor: *"High in the davits, amidships, and overhanging the side of the ship, just about the place where the second torpedo struck, was a large lifeboat with about 70 people in it.   The boat and these people*

67

were blown to fragments in the explosion and scattered in the great clouds of debris that darkened the sky. The whole ship seemed shattered in the awful smash. She was not so much sunk as blown up into the air. Then a moment later nothing was left of her but odds and ends of wreckage and so far as he could make out, only 4 boats crowded with people and several rafts. There was a good supply of rafts but many boats were smashed in the explosion."

*

In the hours following the sinking of the *R.M.S. Leinster* hundreds of people struggled to survive in lifeboats, on rafts, clinging to wreckage and swimming in the rough sea. Many of them lost the grim fight before rescue arrived.

Notes

1   Contemporary newspaper report of Carraher's testimony at an inquest into the death of passenger Georgina O'Brien.
2   Contemporary newspapers.
3   The CDSPCo Crew Agreement Lists for 1918 show Captain Newton's place of birth and give his age as fifty-four. Source: Records from the Maritime History Archives of the Memorial University of Newfoundland. I am grateful to William Byrne for making the records available to me. The *Ulster's* movements: Her Daily Journal for 10 October 1918. (MSS 2854-2886, 33 volumes of the Journals of the *Ulster* in the National Library, Dublin).
4   Sweeney's taped interview with Declan Whelan.
5   Source on UB111 type submarine: Gordon Williamson *U-Boat's of the Kaiser's Navy.*
6   Information on submarine attacks is based on accounts taken from Rear-Admiral Daniel V. Gallery *We Captured a U-Boat*, Wolfgang Hirschfeld *Hirschfeld: The Secret Diary of a U-Boat* as told to Geoffrey Brooks, Rear Admiral William Sowden Simms in collaboration with Burton J Hendick, *The Victory at Sea* and Herbert A. Werner *Iron Coffins: A U-Boat Commander's War.*
7   Captain Birch and the sinking: Contemporary newspapers and Declan Whelan's taped interview with Bill Sweeney.
8   In this paragraph, I have used artistic licence, based on the known facts about World War 1 U-boats, UB-123 and her crew.
9   Australian Red Cross Society Wounded and Missing Enquiry Bureau files 1914-18 War: File 15508050, Lieutenant Francis Patrick Laracy, 1st Battalion.
10   Torpedo that missed: *The Freeman's Journal* 11 October 1918.
11   The sources for the experiences of people on the *Leinster* are given later in the book, when they are quoted in full.
12   The lifeboats were on a deck above the upper deck.
13   Boatswain Jim Carragher testified at an inquest into the death of passenger Georgina O'Brien. Probably under military instructions, he did not mention the shooting of the sergeant by the military policeman. The source for this incident is Bill Sweeney.

Chapter 5

Rescue

"A half dozen tugs steamed forth, followed by torpedo boats and a fleet of assorted trawlers. However, at only three miles distance, a small Manx fishing lugger, the WANDERER, was the craft nearest to the stricken LUSITANIA."

The Lusitania: Unravelling the Mysteries, by Patrick O'Sullivan

Irish Sea, off the south Dublin coast, morning 10 October 1918

Over a period of two and a half hours the sea snatched five of the nine people who clung to the raft. Those who were left were *Leinster* Fireman William Maher, Sergeant (or Private) Duffin of the Suffolk Regiment, Louisa Toppin and her thirteen and a half year old daughter Dorothy. Since reaching the raft, thirty-three year old Maher had supported young Dorothy. At the same time the ex-soldier and father of eight kept up the spirits of the survivors by his cheerfulness and encouragement.

Major Frank Hurndall was travelling on the *Leinster* with his three year old son when the torpedoes struck. Telling the boy that they would play a game, Hurndall managed to get a life raft. He launched the raft as the sea came up to the side of the ship. Placing his son on top of the raft, he gave him a bottle of milk he had been carrying in his pocket. The child sat happily on the raft as his father hung on to the side.

The lifeboat containing Second Mate Harry Addison, Chief Steward Llewellyn Lewis, Michael Joyce, M.P., Mrs Dudgeon and several of the *Leinster's* stewards picked up some people from a raft. Illustrating the confusion that can arise in people's memories during dramatic events, Llewellyn Lewis said that a woman and four men were picked up from the raft, while Michael Joyce said that it was a woman and two men. Third Steward John O'Connor, appears to agree with Joyce in saying that it was a woman *"and two other passengers."* Joyce said that one of the men was a soldier from the west of Ireland, who was returning from leave.

Seaman Hugh Owen had been on the bridge with Captain Birch. The lifeboat in which he escaped from the ship turned over and most of those on board were drowned. Owen then found himself in the sea. While awaiting rescue he kept a young woman afloat. As she could not swim, he supported her by wrapping her long hair around one of his arms.

Having suffered injuries to both of his legs, American Captain Hutch Cone was holding onto a life raft. Noticing U.S. Navy Master Mariner Russell in the sea, he called him and told him to get onto the raft. They were later joined by Chief Special Mechanic James Mason, another member of the U.S. Navy and a male civilian.

*

Irish Sea, north of Dublin Bay, morning 10 October 1918

The destroyers *H.M.S. Mallard,* and *H.M.S. Seal* had left Kingstown at 11 a.m. the previous day and had spent the night at sea.[1] An account by the *Seal's* captain, published after the war, said that both ships were together, in the area between Howth Head and Lambay Island, to the north of Dublin Bay. *HMS Mallard* was under the command of Welsh born Lieutenant Rowland Lloyd, Royal Naval Reserve (RNR).[2] Lloyd had served in the merchant navy before the war. In 1910 he was appointed Sub-Lieutenant in the RNR.[3] On the outbreak of war he was called for service with the Royal Navy. He had been in command of *H.M.S. Mallard* since March 1918. The 350-ton ship had been built by Thornycroft shipyard in 1897. With an overall length of 210 feet, she had two funnels and an armament of one 12 pounder, five 6-pounders and two 18 inch torpedo tubes. The ship had a crew of 63.[4] Due to a fault in its design the front of the ship tended to be wet due to water hitting this area. The *Mallard's* fore bridge was washed away while the ship was steaming to the site of the *Leinster* sinking.

At 8 a.m. on 10 October 1918 the *Mallard's* log recorded a wind force of 6 coming from the south-southwest.[5] 9.42 a.m.: *"S.O.S. received from R.M.S. LEINSTER. Altered course S32W. Full speed."* 10 a.m.: *"Fore bridge washed away by heavy seas."* At 10 a.m. her log also recorded a wind force of 7 coming from the south-southwest.[6] 10.20 a.m.: *"Sighted boats and wreckage."* 10.35 a.m.: *"Lowered whaler, for rescuing survivors, under Sub-Lieutenant Cruikshank R.N.R."* Among those who were picked up by the whaler were *Leinster's* military adjutant Second Lieutenant Hugh Parker, Maud Marsham Rae, two soldiers and two sailors. According to Parker *"I imagine it would be about one and a half hours when we saw two destroyers and a streamer come along. We were picked up by a boat from H.M. Destroyer 'Mallard' into which we managed to get with great difficulty from the raft owing to the heavy seas."* 10.50 a.m.: *"First boat from LEINSTER arrived with survivors. Rescued 19 men. 2 women, 1 succumbed on board."* At 11 a.m. *Mallard's* log recorded a wind force of 7 coming from the south-southwest. Also at 11 a.m. the log recorded: *"Whaler foundered alongside."* 12.40 p.m.: *"Set course for Kingstown."* The damage sustained by the *Mallard* greatly delayed her return to Kingstown. (*H.M.S. Seal* left the scene 10 minutes after the *Mallard*. Yet she docked in Kingstown almost an hour ahead of the latter. *H.M.S Lively*, which left the scene at the same time as the *Mallard*, also arrived an hour ahead of her).

*

Major Louis Daly clung to a raft with about eight other people. *"Probably an hour after the ship had sunk a destroyer appeared and everyone hanging on to the raft became quite cheerful. Owing to the proximity of an enemy submarine, it had to keep on the move as much as possible, but it dodged about and picked up a lot of people before it steamed away, presumably full up. We felt very depressed, but half an hour afterwards another vessel arrived and our spirits rose once more. But the same thing happened again, a few people were rescued and it went away."*

Major Frank Hurndall clung to the side of a life raft on which he had placed his three-year-old son. In the rough sea Hurndall lost consciousness.

*

At 8 a.m. that morning the destroyer *H.M.S Lively* was on patrol near Rockabill, off Skerries, north Co. Dublin. Her log recorded a wind force of 6 coming from the south-southwest. 9.50 a.m.: *"Received signal SS Leinster torpedoed SE of Kish. Altered course to South. Full speed."* 11.12 a.m.: *"2 miles SE of Kish commenced picking up survivors."* Michael Joyce M.P. was in a lifeboat with Second Mate Harry Addison, Chief Steward Llewellyn Lewis, a number of stewards - including Third Stewards Thomas Deegan and John O'Connor - and *Leinster* Heroine Mrs Dudgeon. According to Joyce *"After about two hours a small gunboat, called Lively* (i.e. the destroyer H.M.S. Lively) *came bearing down on us. When she got close we informed the captain that there were a number of rafts down to the leeward of them, and that we were capable of taking care of ourselves while he proceeded to pick up as many as he could find. After some time he came back. I cannot tell the number he picked up, and we then got close to the little gunboat and got all our people safely on board the Lively".* Among those picked up from a raft by *H.M.S. Lively* were Australian Sergeant Francis Coleman and a New Zealand soldier.

H.M.S. Lively also rescued those in the lifeboat containing First Officer Patrick Crangle and Seaman John Lacey. The destroyer later approached the lifeboat known as *Big Bertha*.[7] According to Assistant Purser Bill Sweeney *"There were over seventy in* (the lifeboat) *when the destroyer 'H.M.S. Lively' came along.* (Greaser Philip) *Connolly lifted his son* (Tom) *up from the lifeboat. He didn't bother with ropes or lines. He put his two hands on the boy's hips and raised him up until a blue jacket* (Royal Navy sailor) *caught him. As calm as going up in a lift."* Commander Baggot of the Royal Navy, who was in the lifeboat, told Sweeney that *H.M.S. Lively* would throw a line and asked if he would take it. Sweeney said that he would make it fast to a ring in the back of the lifeboat. The Commander told an American sailor to do the same near the front of the boat. *"The destroyer threw out every line they had. Everyone in the lifeboat made a grab for one, thinking 'That's mine.' The boat keeled over..."* Everyone in the lifeboat was thrown into the sea. According to *The Irish Independent* of 14 October 1918 *"The surge of the vessel on the side lightened by those people taken on board, and the weight of the others still in the boat and those clinging to the gunwale, capsized the lifeboat. A number of the injured and exhausted survivors perished just when relief and safety seemed certain."* Among those lost, so near to rescue, was sixty-one year old William Birch, Captain of the *R.M.S. Leinster*. He had survived his beloved ship by less than two hours.

Also among those flung into the sea from the lifeboat were the newly married Lieutenant J. Craig Carlisle and his wife Anna. According to the previously quoted issue of *The Irish Independent.* *"Mr. And Mrs. Carlyle were thrown in the sea, and the lady sank. It was only by the merest chance that she came to the surface again. Her lifebelt had been so hurriedly and loosely laced that it slipped down and became entangled with her feet, pinioning them so that she could not move, and this tended to keep her head under water. She wore a large fur coat, however, and this appears to have retained the air and floated her head above the surface. She made a desperate grasp, and when she could breath and see, found that she had gripped the tapes at the back of the lifebelt of Mr.* (John) *Hood* (commercial traveller for Millar and Richard.) *A plucky member of the rescuing vessel's crew jumped from his ship on to the keel of the upturned boat. Using his life line as a lasso, he threw the loop over Mrs. Carlyle's head and shoulders and soon she was safely placed on the boat and then on the vessel, where she was overjoyed to find her husband also among the rescued. While struggling in the water, distracted survivors had the additional gruesome experience of feeling dead bodies brush against them, and many were injured by the wreckage."*

Among those rescued from the overturned lifeboat were Assistant Purser Bill Sweeney, John Higgins, Cora Daly and *Wrens* Maureen Waters and Miss Barry. On board the destroyer Sweeney saw Officers Steward Michael Loughlin. The latter had been flung to the deck when one of the torpedoes struck. His head and face had been badly injured. It seems likely that he had been one of the stewards in the lifeboat containing Michael Joyce M.P. Sweeney also found First Officer Patrick Crangle and Second Officer Harry Addison at the stern of the destroyer. Crangle asked after Captain Birch. *"Where is the old man?"* he inquired. *"I'm afraid we've lost him"* replied Sweeney.

H.M.S. *Lively's* Log: 12.40 p.m.: *"Picked up last of survivors. Set course S70W, 18 knots. Rescued numbered 102 men, 24 women, 1 child."* Chief Fireman (Stoker) John Donohoe, who was unable to swim, clung tightly to the ropes on the side of a life raft. A number of British soldiers also clung to the raft. One of them asked the others, in case he didn't survive, to tell his wife that he loved her. The soldier's wife never received his final message. A rescue ship swamped the raft, killing everyone except for non-swimmer John Donohoe.

According to Assistant Purser Bill Sweeney four or five of the *Leinster's* crew took off in a lifeboat on their own. When they were picked up by one of the rescuing destroyers, the commanding officer said that they were very lucky that he hadn't run them down. He put some of his crew into the lifeboat and sent them to pick up survivors from the water.

*

At 8 a.m. on 10 October 1918 *H.M.S Seal's* log recorded that the wind was blowing from the southwest, with a force of 6 to 7. It also recorded *"Very high sea. Ship straining badly."* An entry for 9.45 a.m.: says: *"Altered course S 30 W. Increased to 200 revolutions to position of LEINSTER torpedoed."* 10.30 a.m.: *"Kish altered course E.S.E."* 10.40 a.m.: *"Sighted boats and proceeded to pick up survivors. Skiff* (i.e. ship's boat) *stove in. Whaler badly stove in."* At 12.50 p.m. the *Seal* set out for Kingstown at a speed of 18 knots. She had on board 51 *Leinster* survivors and 2 bodies. A magazine called *"Great War Adventures"* was published in Britain between the two world wars. Issue 7 contains an account by Captain H.N. McGill, R.N.R., of his experiences on board *H.M.S. Seal* at the time of the *Leinster* sinking.[8] *"On the morning when the 'Leinster' left Kingstown with 750 passengers and crew on her last ill-fated voyage my vessel, in company with 'T.B.D.* (i.e. Torpedo Boat Destroyer, now known as destroyers.) *Mallard,' was patrolling between Howth Head and Lambay Island to the Northward of Dublin Bay, in which area a German submarine had been reported. A strong southerly wind was blowing and there was a rough sea, which would have made it impossible for our small low-freeboard craft to keep up with the 'Leinster,' steaming at 23 knots. Unlike the big destroyers, employed with the Grand Fleet and in escorting convoys of merchant vessels through the danger zone, our craft invariably had to reduce to fifteen knots, or less in rough weather."*

"At 9 o clock on the morning in question we intercepted a radio message from the 'Leinster,' saying that she was off the Kish lightship doing her customary 23 knots and zig-zagging, and that all was well with her. A quarter of an hour later we picked up an S.O.S. from the 'Ulster,' coming from Holyhead, saying that she had just met her sister-vessel five miles south-east of the lightship, and that the 'Leinster' was sinking.[9] We learnt subsequently that the first torpedo fired at her brought down the latter's wireless aerial and flooded her mail-room; and that a second one

holed her in the engine-room, with the result that she filled up and sank almost immediately."

"With all hands at their stations and flames pouring from our four funnels, H.M.S. Mallard and my vessel instantly dashed to the rescue. At 9.40 a.m. we reached the position given by the 'Ulster.' But there was no sign of the 'Leinster,' or her survivors. A strong flood tide was sweeping up the coast, so we turned and steamed slowly with it to the northward. A quarter of an hour later we came across the only two life-boats launched from the ill-fated vessel. Packed to the utmost capacity these were submerged almost to the gunwales and closely surrounded by scores of people in the water, who were clinging to their grab-lines. Half a mile further northward the sea was literally black with a mass of struggling, moaning, half drowned humanity, whose cries became more intense and heart-rending when they saw us. Having instructed 'H.M.S. Mallard,' whose commanding officer was my junior, to circle round us and look for submarines, I promptly stopped my engines to do what I could in the way of picking these people up. Except for two small canvas collapsible boats, which were useless in the present circumstances, we had only a whaler and a skiff, which were manned and dispatched to the rescue immediately. Within a few minutes of leaving the vessel's side however, the skiff was literally dragged under water by the scores of people who tried to climb into it, its crew of two extricating themselves and swimming back to the destroyer only with the utmost difficulty."

"The whaler was a little more successful. Having picked up as many people as it could hold it returned alongside, but while the survivors were being taken out of it the boat was stove in against the ship's side, and swamped. I had hove-to about a hundred yards windward of the four or five hundred people in the water to lower our two boats, but now, having lost both boats, I had no option but to get into the thick of them. Lying athwart the rough sea with the struggling mass of human flotsam packed tightly round her, the destroyer began to roll violently, and dozens of the poor wretches were crushed under her bilges. Throwing themselves flat on deck our sailors clutched at the up-flung hands, as the destroyer's port and starboard rails alternately rolled down to the water. Several people were dragged, three times their normal weight in their sodden clothes, slipped from the sailors' grasp, and fell back into the sea, to be swept beyond human aid. While some of our men were thus trying to pull the drowning people straight out of the water, others flung lifelines to them. Had they only known how to, of being physically capable of tying the ends of these lines round their bodies under their armpits many more would have been saved. All they did, unfortunately, was to hold on with their hands, until the lines tautened and slid through their numbed fingers. We shouted ourselves hoarse telling them what to do, but it was to no avail. Finally our men made the lines fast round their own waists, and jumped overboard to the rescue. The few women and most of the men saved owed their lives to this plucky action on the part of the blue-jackets. In the midst of the rescue work the track of a torpedo suddenly shot across the sea, less than a hundred yards ahead of us. The 'Mallard.' instantly opened fire with her twelve-pounder and, steaming full speed for the periscope sighted, dropped a depth-charge,* *whether or not the submarine was destroyed is more than I can say. Taking a chance on this I instructed my colleague to stop his vessel and bear a hand with the rescue work, it being painfully evident by now that the people in the water were near their last gasp. Luckily we were not subjected to another attack."* (Neither his own ship's log nor that of H.M.S. Mallard mentions a submarine attack.)

"Of acts of heroism I witnessed that day I could write at length but where there is disaster and tragedy at sea there is bound to be heroism. I saw one man floating beside a small piece of wreckage, on which he supported his wife. A sailor threw a line to him and having just managed to secure this round the woman's waist he suddenly let go his hold and floated away, face down in the sea. A staff officer with red tabs on his tunic, seated astride a barrel on which he rose and fell with the waves like a man riding a hobby horse, went quickly past our stern as we drifted to leeward. There was something dreadfully pathetic in the spectacle of that brave man riding so coolly to his death. Perched on a broken spar were three American blue-jackets on leave from the U.S. Naval Base at Queenstown. One of them had in his arms a little boy of four whose parents had been lost, and his two shipmates had their arms about his body to prevent him being washed with his precious charge off the spar. As we drifted down to them the blue-jackets handed up the little boy to one of our sailors. Then all three sprang for the rail and vaulted aboard, none the worse for their ordeal. Two young army officers, holding onto a grating, smiled up at me as we drove past them. Realising that I could not save them I made a gesture of impotence, and one of the officers waved back, as if to let me know that they understood. They were doomed, those poor fellows, and they knew it-and were facing the fact like very gallant gentlemen."

"Within half an hour of our arrival on the scene of the disaster we aboard the Seal had picked up fifty-three survivors, (just before docking, the ship's log recorded 51 survivors and 2 dead on board, so, possibly, two of those who were picked up died on the ship) *and the Mallard had picked up twenty-nine.* (Her log records picking up 21, of whom one died on board.) *By then there was no sign of life among the rest of the people in the water. Of the fifty-three persons my vessel rescued, forty-seven were men, five were women, and there was one child-the little boy the American blue-jackets had with them. The procedure with each person we dragged out of the water was the same. Quickly striping them of their clothes we applied artificial respiration. All of them had swallowed a great deal of salt water, and in some cases we had to persevere with the treatment for over half an hour before there was any sign of returning life. After we had wrapped them in blankets, pieces of canvas, newspapers, anything at all to promote warmth, we passed the survivors through the manhole openings to the mess-decks. Subsequently there was a general clamouring for watches, wallets, and sundry articles, which were on their persons, the survivors alleged, when they were rescued. Several weeks elapsed before these things were sorted out and returned to their rightful owners."*

"Two hours after reaching the scene of the disaster H.M.S. Mallard and my vessel were back in Kingstown,[10] *where, in response to my radio message to the S.N.O. there, a long line of motor-cars and ambulances awaited our arrival.*

Meanwhile T.B.D. Sprightly had picked up the Leinster's two lifeboats, with their hundred or so survivors. (In fact H.M.S. Lively picked them up.) *Thus out of the 750 souls who sailed in the ill-fated vessel* (in fact there were 771) *only approximately 182 were saved.* (270 were saved). *Most of the officers and crew went down with their vessel."* (37 died and 40 survived.)

"It was a remarkable coincidence that the Ulster should have sighted her sister-vessel at the very moment when the latter was sinking. But for that very fortunate circumstance there would probably have been no survivors at all, for even the two lifeboats were nearly swamped when the Sprightly (the Lively) found them. The Ulster, packed with passengers herself, dared not stop to render assistance, of course. Had she gone against her strict Admiralty instruction and done so, the toll of life in the Irish Sea that morning might easily have been double what it was."

Motor Launch 154, under the command of Lieutenant Unwin R.N.V.R., arrived at the life raft to which Captain Hutch Cone clung, together with Chief Special Mechanic James Mason, Master Mariner Russell, another U.S. sailor and a male civilian. A line, thrown from the launch, was caught by one of the men on the raft. By this time Captain Cone was unconscious. Due to difficulty in getting him on board, Leading Seaman Alexander Young jumped into the sea and helped to get him onto the launch.

The armed patrol yacht *Helga* was coaling at Traders Wharf in Kingstown harbour when word arrived that the *Leinster* had been torpedoed.[11] The *Helga*, captained by Lieutenant-Commander Henry Stockwell, immediately put to sea. Designed as a fishery protection vessel for Irish waters, the *Helga* had been taken over by the Admiralty on 12 March 1915 and assigned to Kingstown. She was taken into Dublin Dockyard and fitted out as an Armed Patrol Yacht. A twelve-pounder (i.e. 3inch) gun was mounted in the front of the ship. Most of her crew enlisted into the Royal Naval Reserve, many of them continuing to serve on the *Helga*. The following year, during the 1916 Rising, the ship played an often-quoted part in Irish history, when she sailed up the Liffey and shelled the centre of Dublin. Now she was to play a less well-known part in Ireland's greatest maritime tragedy.

Arthur Lewis, Consulting Engineer to the Royal National Lifeboat Institute, was on a raft with a woman and a soldier. He had earlier supported an unconscious soldier, but the sea had washed the man away. *"We drifted near a New Zealand soldier with a large white life-buoy, and pushing some wreckage to him I got him along side the raft. He held on and I talked to him and cheered him up with news of the approaching vessels from Kingstown. Just at the last he was swept away from the raft, but the captain of a patrol-boat had seen him, and getting nearer to him heaved him a line. When he was alongside the patrol-boat he was too weak to save himself, and one of the crew bravely jumped in and rescued him. One other soldier, an Australian, joined us. He was swimming well, and managed to get on the raft without upsetting us. He was a cheery fellow and* had not lost his head. *Two lines were thrown to us from the patrol-boat-the Helga-and with these I soon worked the raft along side the boat, when, as soon as she rolled towards us, we were seized by many hands and lifted over the taffrail, about one hour and a quarter after I jumped from the Leinster."* After picking up survivors the *Helga* set out for Kingstown. In later years comments attributed to Ship's Steward Jim Longmore raised many chuckles when repeated onboard the ship. As he gave blankets to partially clothed women survivors he is supposed to have repeated each time *"Don't mind me ma'am, I'm a married man myself."*[12]

A rescue launch arrived at the life raft to which Fireman William Maher clung with Louisa Toppin, her daughter Dorothy and Sergeant (or Private) Duffin. Maher caught a lifeline from the vessel and helped to get the now unconscious Mrs Toppin on board. Duffin was also taken on board. The launch suddenly started its engines and the life raft was capsized. Young Dorothy was washed away. Despite his exhausted condition, Maher swam after her and saved her. Assistant Purser Bill Sweeney spoke with Maher a few days later. Maher told him that when he finally got on board he had a few choice words to say to the captain of the launch.

Lieutenant-Commander Dillon of the mine-sweeping fleet based at Kingstown testified at an inquest into the death of passenger Georgina O'Brien.[13] He said that he was in one of the first ships to leave Kingstown. He said that they left the harbour at 9.58 a.m. and reached the scene of the sinking at 10.36 a.m. There were destroyers at the scene before them. Bearings showed that they were 12 to 13 miles from Kingstown and 5 miles East South-East of Kish. He said that all the ships from Kingstown were out within 7 or 8 minutes of getting up steam. He said that he could only explain the survivors' belief that they had been in the water a long time as being due to their inability to judge the passage of time. A reason for the delay in picking up survivors was the difficulty of handling a ship in heavy seas. With the water full of people there was a danger of crashing into them. He said that he believed that 10 of the *Leinster's* lifeboats had been lost.

*

The following letter was written five days after the sinking.[14]

Dublin Port and Docks Board
Harbour Master and Pilot Superintendents Office
North Wall

15th October 1918

The Secretary
Dublin Port and Docks Board

Sir,

I have the honour to submit for your information that, in reply to an urgent message from the Naval Base, Kingstown., on Thursday morning, 10ᵗʰ October at 10.30 o'clock--I proceeded in charge of the Board's tugs 'Majestic' and 'Anna Liffey' to the scene of the 'Leinster.' disaster.

I succeeded in picking up 21 bodies but, regret they were beyond human aid. I handed the bodies over to the military authorities at Victoria Wharf, Kingstown, also some bags of mail and passengers' luggage.

Further, I beg to bring under your notice that, on this, as on previous occasions when the Board's tugs were called out in reply to urgent Naval messages for work in waters where the presence of enemy submarines was known to exist-I cannot speak too highly of the conduct of the crews of both tugs: as their anxiety seems to be to carry out my orders and assist me in every possible way.

> I have the honour to be sir,
> Your obedient,
> Louis Brady,
> Asst. Harbour Master

*

Major Louis Daly clung to a raft with eight other people. " One by one the people hanging on to my raft disappeared. I never saw anyone go, probably I was too exhausted to notice much, but I presume they became numbed and unconscious with the cold, let go, and sank. Soon I discovered that I was the only person left. How long I remained I do not know. I just remember seeing a rowboat coming towards me with a man standing up in the bows and trying to wave to him. The next thing I knew was coming to with a great wave of physical pain. I was in the little cabin of a trawler with my field boots off and two men vigorously massaging my legs."

*

It is highly unlikely that either Captain McGill of H.M.S. *Seal* or the *Leinster* survivors he picked up were aware that Laird's had built the *Seal* the year after they had built the mail boat. Neither would the survivors who were picked up by H.M.S. *Lively* have been aware that Laird's had also built their saviour, four years after the *Leinster*.[15]

Notes

[1]   The movements of H.M.S. *Mallard*, H.M.S. *Seal* and H.M.S. *Lively* are from their logs, held at the Public Records Office, Kew Gardens, Surrey.

2   To enable the Royal Navy to rapidly expand its manpower in time of war the Royal Naval Reserve (RNR) was created by an Act of Parliament in 1859. The RNR was comprised of officers and men from the Mercantile Marine (now called the Merchant Navy) who received regular training and were immediately called up in time of war. Rowland Lloyd would have trained with the Royal Navy for four weeks of every year. His training would have covered gunnery, torpedoes, strategy and court-martial procedure. The Naval Forces Act of 1903 established the Royal Naval Volunteer Reserve (RNVR) to supplement the RNR. This force was comprised of volunteers who came from all walks of life apart from the Mercantile Marine. Like the RNR, the men of the RNVR received regular training and were called up in wartime. Ordinary Seaman Fred Hough, one of *Leinster's* three gunners was a member of the RNVR. Leading Seaman George Leatherbarrow, another of the ship's gunners was a member of the RNR. Sources: Royal Navy website, Public Records Office website and the novel *"The Guns of Evening"* by Ronald Basset (London, 1980).

3   Tamsin Bunnay.

4   *Conway's All the World's Fighting Ships 1860-1905.*

5   Wind Force 6: Wind speed 22 to 27 knots, large waves, spray, wave height 8 to 13 feet. Source: Website Wind Speed.htm

6   Wind Force 7: Wind speed 28 to 33 knots, heaped seas, foam from breaking waves, wave height 13 to 20 feet. Source: Website Wind Speed.htm

7   The fact that those in First Officer Patrick Crangle's lifeboat were picked up before those in *Big Bertha* was deduced from Bill Sweeney's statement that when he got on board the *H.M.S. Lively* Crangle was on the ship.

8   *Great War Adventures* was a quarterly publication. Each issue (or "Series" as the cover describes them) contained about 128 pages, with about a dozen stories in each issue. The issues are undated, but publication appears to have started in 1932. The "Seventh Series", containing the account by Captain McGill appears to date from late 1933 or early 1934. My thanks to Ronald Clifton, Historical Information Officer of the Western Front Association who went to a lot of trouble to get me background information on the publication and the account from the "Seventh Series".

9   The passage of time would seem to have affected Captain McGill's memory. His own ship's log records a course alteration at 9.45 a.m. following receipt of the message that the *Leinster* had been torpedoed.

10 According to his ship's log the length of time between arrival at the scene of the sinking and docking at Kingstown was 3 hours and 20 minutes. Due to her damage, it took Mallard 4 ½ hours from arrival to docking at Kingstown.

11 *"The Irish Navy: A Story of Courage and Tenacity"* by Tom MacGinty.

12 Norris Davidson, who served on the *Helga* (renamed *L.E. Muirchu*) after she was taken over by the Irish Navy. Quoted in *"The Irish Navy: A Story of Courage and Tenacity"* by Tom MacGinty

13 *The Cork Examiner* 19 October 1918.

14 National Archives, Dublin.

15 The *Leinster* was the 616th ship built by Lairds, *H.M.S. Seal* was the 628th and *H.M.S. Lively* the 642nd. Source: www.wirral-libaries.net/archives/list_of_vessels_constructed_byc.htm

Chapter 6

Aftermath[1]

"The sea gave up the dead that were in it"
(Revelation 21:13)

Kingstown, Thursday morning 10 October 1918

The *R.M.S. Ulster* docked at Carlisle Pier at 10.14 a.m.[2] News of the *Leinster's* sinking quickly spread through Kingstown. Crowds thronged Royal Marine Road and the approaches to the harbour. From further away people arrived by tram, motorcar and train. The Dublin South Eastern Railway Company put on two special trains to Kingstown. A few hundred yards west of Carlisle Pier, ambulances raced into Victoria Wharf accompanied by doctors, Red Cross nurses and military and naval officers. By noon there were about 200 ambulances lined up at the entrance to the wharf, surrounded by a cordon of soldiers and marines. Police were busy keeping the roadways clear. The crowd had an air of anxious expectancy. The general impression seemed to be that most of those on board the *Leinster* had been saved. People gazed silently seawards. Many scanned the horizon with field glasses. Lieutenant-Colonel Douglas Proby met his cousin, Lady Alice Howard, among the crowd. She was looking for their cousin Lady Phyllis Hamilton. He was trying to find his secretary Maud Elizabeth Ward.[3]

At about 1.30 p.m. the destroyer *H.M.S. Lively* was seen approaching the harbour. The crowd was silent as the ship docked at Victoria Wharf at 1.50 p.m.[4] The *Leinster* survivors on board the *Lively* were 102 men, 24 women and 1 child.[5] After a few minutes those who were able to walk came ashore looking bedraggled and worn. Some limped up the gangway, leaning on the shoulders of men of the St. John Ambulance Brigade. Lastly came the stretcher-bearers carrying the seriously injured. Among those who came ashore from the *Lively* were Australian Sergeant Francis Coleman, Postal Sorter John Higgins, *Leinster's* First Officer Patrick Crangle, Second Officer Harry Addison, Chief Steward Llewellyn Lewis, Assistant Purser Bill Sweeney, Greaser Philip Connolly and his son Cabin Boy Tom Connolly.[6] One of the *Leinster's* firemen strolled out of Victoria Wharf, smoking a cigarette. He was immediately surrounded by anxious relatives, who tearfully embraced him. Two young girls came next, their hair and clothes sea soaked. They were cheered by the crowd, as they walked to the *Royal Marine Hotel*, accompanied by friends. The majority of the surviving crew picked up by the destroyer were firemen. Some of them broke down and wept as they were welcomed by relatives and friends. Some of the female survivors were brought to a rest room on the wharf. Members of the Salvation Army and the Boy Scouts distributed blankets, clothing, tea, sandwiches and cigarettes.[7] As survivors from the *Leinster* were brought ashore, 17-year old Daniel Smyth stood on the quay anxiously looking at the faces of the male survivors. He was looking for his father, Postal Sorter Adam Smyth. Daniel was an assistant steward on the *R.M.S. Ulster*. His ship had passed the *Leinster* that morning and had docked in Kingstown at 10.14 a.m.[8] He did not find his father among the survivors.

At 2 p.m. *H.M.S. Seal* docked at Victoria Wharf near *H.M.S. Lively*. Fifty-one survivors and two bodies were landed from the destroyer. After just 10 minutes, the *Seal* again put to sea, followed 5 minutes later by the *Lively*. Richard Jones, Secretary of the CDSPCo instructed that survivors not in need of hospitalisation should be brought to the *Royal Marine Hotel, Rosse's Hotel* and private hotels on Kingstown's seafront. Ambulances began to leave Victoria Wharf at about 1.45 p.m. Survivors were brought to St. Michael's Hospital in Kingstown, Dublin Castle Hospital, George V Military Hospital near the Phoenix Park (now St. Brickins) and the Rest Camp at the North Dublin Union. The majority of survivors brought to St. Michael's Hospital were civilians, while the majority of those brought to other hospitals were military personnel.[9] A number of American sailors and some of the *Leinster's* crew were brought by ambulance to the *Sailors War Hotel*, 11 Eden Quay, Dublin, only a few doors away from the CDSPCo offices at 15 Eden Quay. After a medical examination they were given warm clothes, a meal and a bed for the night.

Among those picked up from a raft were a three year old boy and his father. As it was believed that the latter was dead, he was placed with a number of bodies on the quayside. Subsequently a nun detected some signs of life and Major Frank Hurndall was brought to St. Michael's Hospital (Kingstown), where his three-year-old son was a patient.

H.M.S. Mallard, under the command of Lieutenant Rowland Lloyd, entered the harbour at 2.53 p.m. and docked at 3 p.m. She had rescued 19 men and 2 women. Unfortunately one of the rescued had died onboard ship. Among the survivors landed by the *Mallard* were *Leinster's* Military Adjutant, Second Lieutenant Hugh Parker and Maud Marsham Rae. Parker's report said *"the survivors were taken to the various hospitals and hotels."* He also said *"Personally I felt none the worse for my experience and proceeded to a hotel."* *Mallard's* damage by the heavy seas had seriously slowed her return to Kingstown.[10] Her log records that after discharging her *Leinster* survivors, dockyard workers came on board to repair the fore bridge. The *Mallard* did not leave Kingstown again until the following day. At 3.11 p.m., after receiving the Admiralty's permission to sail, the *R.M.S. Ulster* left for Holyhead. On board was Assistant Steward Daniel Smyth, who had searched unsuccessfully among the survivors for his father, Postal Sorter Adam Smyth. He would never see his father again.

Patients with influenza occupied most of the beds at St. Michael's Hospital, Kingstown. A virulent form of the illness had swept Europe and the hospital mortuary contained the bodies of people who had died of it. There were only two vacant beds available when news of the sinking reached the hospital. Convalescent patients, and those with minor injuries were discharged and extra beds requisitioned from a woman's refuge next door to the hospital. Among those brought to the hospital was Major Frank Hurndall. His three-year-old son had previously been brought to the hospital. Hurndall was in an utterly exhausted condition. It took three hours of constant attention to revive him. Also among those admitted to the hospital were Maud Marsham Rae, Louisa and Dorothy Toppin, *Leinster* crewman Michael Loughlin, who had a fractured skull and Lucy Agnes Plunkett, whose twenty-one year old sister-in-law Sheelah was lost. Due to the shortage of beds, some of the casualties had to be accommodated in armchairs and seats. Hospital staff were assisted by several VADs. About 20 bodies recovered from the sea were brought to the hospital morgue. Among them was Eileen Hester Campbell, wife of Lieutenant-Commander Colin Campbell, with her dead four and a half year old daughter, Eileen Elizabeth, still clutched in her arms. Colin's father, the Reverend Edward Campbell, identified them at the morgue. Also recovered and brought to the morgue at St. Michael's Hospital were the bodies of Fanny Saunders and Fanny Wookey. People looking for relatives besieged the hospital. The Dublin Metropolitan Police sent a number of men to the hospital to regulate visitors and keep back the crowds.

Father Ryan, Curate at Westland Row Church, Dublin learned of the sinking at about 12.30 p.m. He immediately made his way to Kingstown to give spiritual and temporal assistance to the survivors. He spent the rest of the day at the scene. Having been previously based in nearby Dalkey, he knew many of the ship's crew and local officials. He was active in getting refreshments and accommodation for the survivors. He identified the bodies of several of those brought ashore. He also visited St. Michael's Hospital and helped locate several of the survivors for their relatives. Eleven of the military survivors were brought to Dublin Castle Hospital.[11] These included Captain Hutch Cone of the United States Naval Aviation Service, Sergeant First Class T. F. Denny of the United States Chemical Warfare School, Lieutenant G. Halse of the New Zealand Army, Major Louis Daly of the Leinster Regiment (brought to the hospital sometime after 6.30 p.m.) and

Lieutenant J. Craig Carlisle of the Machine Gun Corps. *Leinster* heroine Mrs A. Dudgeon was treated at King George V Military Hospital in Dublin.

Throughout the afternoon ships continued to arrive in Kingstown harbour with survivors and bodies recovered from the sea. Major Louis Daly was landed from a trawler at 6.30 p.m. and brought to Dublin Castle Hospital by ambulance.[12] As the day wore on more bodies were recovered. By 6.00 p.m. about 70 bodies had been brought ashore. By 10 p.m. over 100 more were recovered. Bodies were laid out in part of Kingstown railway station, adjacent to Victoria Wharf.[13] Many of the bodies were brought to the Dublin City Morgue and the morgue at George V Hospital. Among the bodies recovered was that of Frank Higgerty, the Canadian who had visited the land of his ancestors prior to taking up a commission in the British Army. As described at the beginning of the book, his Dublin relatives telegraphed Ottawa with news of his death. Instructions came back that his body was to be embalmed and sent to Canada.

*

From an early hour the following day hundreds of spectators assembled on Victoria Wharf, hoping that more survivors would be found. They waited in vain. The *R.M.S. Ulster* arrived from Holyhead. Escorted by the U.S. Navy destroyer *Beale*, she carried relatives and friends of *Leinster* passengers from various parts of the United Kingdom. A continuous stream of men and women passed from Victoria Wharf to Kingstown police station on Upper Georges Street, where they scanned the list of survivors. If the names of those sought were not on the list, the searchers went to the morgue at St. Michael's Hospital, to see if their missing relatives or friends were among the bodies there.

Early in the morning eight bodies were brought ashore with dead herrings in their clothing. A newspaper suggested that the fish had been killed when the *Leinster*'s engines exploded. A body was also recovered at the entrance to Kingstown harbour.[14] In St. Michael's Hospital, despite his exhausted condition the previous day, Major Frank Hurndall had recovered so quickly that he was discharged. Before leaving the hospital he visited his three-year-old son, who was still a patient. Lieutenant Rowland Lloyd, captain of the destroyer *H.M.S. Mallard*, was admitted to Hume Street Hospital in Dublin with severe influenza.

In the aftermath of the sinking a number of claims were made regarding the submarine that sunk the *Leinster*. The U.S. Naval Air Service had a station at Ferrybank, Co. Wexford, which became operational in early October 1918. Planes from the station patrolled the Irish Sea on anti-submarine duties. A booklet commemorating the work of the station contains the following entry. *"On October 11ᵗʰ the day after the 'Leinster' was sunk in the Irish Sea off Dublin one of our planes sighted and bombed an enemy submarine in our area. The submarine showed signs of serious distress and had trouble in submerging. Thick, dark coloured oil was seen on the surface of the water in this vicinity for a week after the bombing, proving almost conclusively that the perpetrators of the 'Leinster' crime had been punished."* Naval Historian Dwight R. Messimer says: *"There were nineteen High Seas Fleet U-boats at sea on 11 October 1918 in UK waters. None of those boats reported being attacked by aircraft at any time during their patrols. Only one of the nineteen boats, UB-123 was lost (18/19 October). The other eighteen boats all survived the war, undamaged."*

John Ross, Secretary of the Howth Yacht Club, Co. Dublin, was among those lost. He was on his way to a Scouts Commissioners conference in London. The Commissioner of the City of Dublin Boy Scouts received the following telegram: *"Scouts Commissioners Conference – Heard with deepest regret the death of Commissioner Ross at hands of enemy when on scout service, and tender their warmest sympathy with the Irish Sea Scouts in their loss. Baden-Powell."* When the 8.55 p.m. train arrived at Limerick station Essie Gould, sole survivor of the family who had boarded the *Leinster* the previous morning, descended to be met by a number of friends. Also among the passengers was Michael Joyce M.P., who had survived his fifth shipwreck.[15]

Thomas Foley, brother-in-law to tenor John McCormack, was lost on the *Leinster* with his wife Charlotte. They had been on their way to England to visit Charlotte's brother who had been wounded in France. Christopher Barrett, Charlotte's only brother, died in hospital on 11 October, the day after Charlotte was killed. *The Irish Times* of 12 October reported that, the day the *Leinster* was sunk, four men got a taxi to Westland Row railway station, Dublin. They missed the train connecting with the mail boat. They got another taxi to Kingstown. A wheel came off the taxi at Ballsbridge. They managed to stop a passing taxi. They boarded the *Leinster* at Kingstown. The newspaper said that after the sinking three of the men were missing and one was in hospital.

According to *The Irish Independent* of 12 October 1918 *"The fact that travellers to England had to provide themselves with photographs greatly facilitated the work of identification."* *The Cork Constitution* of 12 October carried an interview with John Folan. It said that he was an Irish sailor, who was travelling as a passenger on the *Leinster*. Under censorship directives, Irish newspapers were not allowed to mention the fact that military personnel, including members of the Royal Navy, were on the *Leinster*. Because Folan was described as being a *"sailor"* and as he mentioned being torpedoed four times, he was almost certainly a merchant seaman. *"I am 28 years of age and have been 4 times on torpedoed ships, once when we were 400 miles from land. I was on deck when the Leinster was struck the second time. A woman handed me a little baby of about 6 months. I was handing the baby up to a man who was on the boat deck when I was knocked over by the second explosion. I saw some men rushing for the boats, and I thought it disgraceful. There were about 100 clambering for one boat. They kept throwing themselves down about 20 feet into her. There was a regular panic among them in every way. There were many cool-headed people on board, but I did not hear any orders given after the first explosion. After the Leinster was struck the second time she took on a list of 45 degrees. A whole batch of passengers, who were on the starboard side, went rolling down the deck in a bunch, into the water. About two thirds of those on board were flung into the water from deck when she listed. They went overboard, mixed up with wreckage and everything. The wreckage fell on them, and I suppose a whole lot were stunned or killed. I fell down where a boat had been lowered, but the boat had gone. She was that loaded when she got to the water that she was below Plimsoll's mark and went under. I was dragged down by the suction about 6 feet. I had hold of a raft all the time. When I was picked up I was well treated. We were given hot drinks and dry clothes and well looked after in Dublin."*

An undertakers strike caused an extra hardship for bereaved relatives trying to arrange burials. The strike was settled on the evening of Saturday 12 October. Widow Fanny Saunders was lost on the *Leinster* while on her way to visit her seriously ill daughter. Her husband Frank had been lost on the Kingstown Lifeboat twenty-three years previously. On 13 October 1918, three days after the *Leinster* sinking, Janet, wife of Ted Owens and eldest daughter of Frank and Frances Saunders, died in Liverpool.

*

On 14 October the Dundalk and Newry Steamship Company vessel *Dundalk* (794 tons) was torpedoed in the Irish Sea off the coast of Anglesey, Wales. Twenty-one of the crew, including the captain, were lost. It has not been definitely established which submarine sank her. Some sources say that it was UB-123. A.J. Tennant in *British Merchant Ships sunk by U-boat in the 1914-1918 War* says that the sinking was carried out by UB-123 and U-90. Between the two world wars, in an attempt to discover how particular submarines were lost and which submarines had sunk particular merchant ships, German Admiral Arno Spindler, examined all available submarine logbooks, radio messages etc. Based on the available information, he thought it unlikely that UB-123 had sunk the *Dundalk*.[16]

On 6 October U.S. President Woodrow Wilson had received a request from Germany for an immediate armistice. He had replied on 8 October seeing clarification from the Germans. Wilson had worked hard to keep the United States out of the war. One of the reasons the U.S. had declared war was the resumption of Germany's unrestricted submarine attacks on merchant shipping. Wilson, who had a deep knowledge of European history, had no desire to destroy Germany, seeking her as a counterweight to

French power in Europe and a profitable trading partner for the U.S. On 8 January 1918 he had laid out his *"Fourteen Points,"* seeking what he called *"peace without victory."* His reply to Germany on 8 October was made without consulting Britain or France. Germany's reply, sent on 12 October, confirmed her acceptance of the *"Fourteen Points."* According to Gregor Dallas in *"1918: War and Peace"* after the *Leinster* sinking *"For days, relatives stood on the shores to identify the corpses as they were washed up. A howl of indignation buried all charitable thoughts in Britain and the United States when Germany's second note was published."*[17] On 14 October Wilson sent a harsh reply to Germany saying *inter alia: "At the very moment that the German Government approaches the Government of the United States with proposals of peace, its submarines are engaged in sinking passengers ships at sea ..."*

Also on 14 October, a service was held at St Mark's Church, North Audley Street, London for Lady Alexandra Phyllis Hamilton, Martha Bridge and Ellenor Strachan. The King, Queen and Prince of Wales were represented. (Lady Hamilton's brother Claude was A.D.C. to the Prince of Wales.) Among the many who attended the service was Irish Unionist leader Sir Edward Carson. Four women from Tralee, Co. Kerry were lost on the *Leinster*. According to Martin Murphy from Steeple View, Tralee, his sister Chrissie was one of the women lost. *"One of my brothers had to travel to Dublin to identify my sister's body. He was charged a shilling to get into the morgue. He recognised my sister from a burn scar on her neck."*[18] At 9.30 p.m. on Tuesday 15 October the body of Nora Galvin was taken from the train at Tralee, Co. Kerry. The following morning the bodies of Chrissie Murphy and Lizzie Healy arrived at the station. The three women were buried at Rath Cemetery. Huge crowds attended their funerals. The body of Lena, sister of Nora Galvin was never recovered.

The body of Maud Elizabeth Ward was identified by Colonel Proby. He arranged for her burial. Funeral arrangements were hindered by the undertakers strike. Maud was buried with her nightdress as a shroud. She was buried at Deansgrange Cemetery, Co. Dublin on 14 October 1918. The following are extracts from a letter dated 19 October 1918, written by Maud's uncle, Reverend Thomas Ward, to his daughter Winnie. *"(Colonel Proby) called yesterday and brought her purse containing seven £1 notes (all stained with seawater), her watch, which was doubtless stopped by the immersion and a little broach . . . . . . It is a great pity she did not stay longer to see Dublin and then she would have escaped. But probably she was eager to get to the Allans at Chester . . . Colonel Proby bought the site of her grave in perpetuity and defrayed all the expenses of her funeral. The headstone, I said we will be responsible for. No doubt her uncle and aunts will wish to bear part of the cost. There is the inscription to be thought of. If you have any suggestions please let me know . . . . . . It would be impossible for anyone to be more kind than Colonel Proby all through. I believe he felt the loss as much as any one of us . . . . . . The sad thing is that the Colonel considered, according to reports of some people in Arklow, that she had been brooding over the possible results of a submarine attack when she used to watch the waves. But this may have been imagination largely, for of course the sea would have been a wonderful fascination for an inland bred person."*[19]

On Wednesday 16 October the 8.55 p.m. train at Limerick station was met by a large crowd. Among them were Essie Gould and her father Mr P. Gould. The body of Catherine Gould was taken from the train. Forty years old, she was the only member of the family whose body was recovered. She was buried in Mount St Laurence Cemetery following a service at St. Mary's Roman Catholic Church.

On Thursday 17 October *The Irish Times* reported that: *"Yesterday a small steamer of the patrol type came in from the sea towing a lifeboat belonging to the ill-fated mail steamer Leinster. It had been found drifting about in the Channel off Dublin Bay. This last recovered relic of the mail boat disaster still had its oars lying in the bottom, with some sodden life-jackets and a small water cask with the bung hole open. The stem* (i.e. the bow) *of the boat appeared to have been a little damaged, but otherwise she appeared to be intact and contained no water. In the newer Custom House Docks are lying two other lifeboats from the torpedoed Leinster, but these are both water-logged and badly damaged, one of them being a virtual wreck, and cut open and away forward down to the water line."*

*

Of all the dangers faced by a submarine, a mine was among the least feared. Mines didn't hunt submarines, as warships did. They didn't bear personal animosity towards submarines, as enemy sailors did. They just sat in one place for days, weeks and, sometimes, years. The crew of a submarine could be blissfully unaware as their boat passed within 2 meters of a mine. But crossing that tiny distance could result in a horrible death for everyone on board. A submarine could travel safely through a minefield 100 times and get caught on the 101st passage. A mine was an unusual weapon. While other weapons tried to strike submarines, mines waited for submarines to strike them. While every other weapon held by the enemy might hit a submarine, they were more likely to miss by some distance and, at worst, inflict some damage on the boat. An encounter with a mine was almost inevitably fatal.

Laying a minefield required much planning, particularly when the objective was to sink or block the passage of submarines, as distinct from surface ships. In the case of the latter it was necessary only to place mines at or near the surface of the ocean. Catching submarines was much more difficult, as they were small targets and could dive. A sparsely sown minefield would have little effect. If all of the mines were near the surface a submarine could dive beneath them. To block the passage of submarines it was necessary to lay a field that was dense, with mines arranged vertically (at different depths) as well as horizontally. This took many mines, knowledge of the topography of the ocean floor and considerable skill in mine laying.

On 3 March 1918, in an attempt to seal off the exit from the North Sea and prevent U-boats from reaching the Atlantic, the American and British navies had begun laying a huge minefield between the Orkney Islands, on the north coast of Scotland and Bergen, on the coast of Norway. The minefield was mostly comprised of the American Mark VI mine and the British H2 mine, both of which had a tendency to explode prematurely. Most of the mines were laid between June and October 1918. The minefield was known as the Northern Barrage. By the end of the war the Americans had laid 56,571 mines and the British 13,546.[20]

*

Friday 18 October 1918, 25 miles north north east of Muckle Flugga, Orkney Islands, Scotland.

At 9.10 a.m. UB-125, outbound from Germany under the command of Oberleutnant zur See Werner Vater, picked up a radio message asking for advice on the best way to get through the Northern Barrage minefield. The sender was Robert Ramm on board UB-123. Extra mines had been added to the minefield every day since UB-123 had made her outward journey. As UB-125 had just come through the minefield, Vater radioed a suggested route. UB-123 acknowledged the message. This was the final contact made with UB-123. Later that day ships of the U.S. navy reported an explosion in the Northern Barrage minefield. The Royal Navy reported an explosion the following day. There is no way of determining which explosion sank the UB-123, but it is almost certain that one of them did. Following the explosion water would have poured into the submarine dragging her to the bottom of the North Sea. In an instant UB-123 would have changed from being a weapon of war to a steel coffin. The crewmen who would have been killed in the initial explosion were the luckiest. The rest would have died one the worst kinds of death imaginable. Robert Ramm's wife and two children never saw him again. Thirty-five other German families were also bereaved.[21]

*

Tenor John McCormack's brother-in-law Thomas Foley was lost with his wife Charlotte. Their deaths left ten children orphaned. On Friday 18

October *The Freeman's Journal* published a cablegram from John McCormack. *"My wife and myself, though stricken to the heart's core by our own great sorrow, wish, through the courtesy of your columns, to convey our profound sympathy to the relatives and friends of the victims in the Leinster catastrophe sacrificed to Germany's brutality. This most cold-blooded murder has brought home to me, as to all true Irishmen, that this is a holy war to save the world from slavery. Advise me how I can help to assuage the sorrows of the other bereaved ones. Already ten of the orphaned children have become mine, but there are others whom we also want to help. John McCormack.*

The editor of *The Freeman's Journal* cabled back advising that the *" Lord Mayor has opened a National Relief Fund. He desires me to thank you for generous offer and say that any help you can secure from America will be most gratefully welcomed. Deepest sympathy is felt for you and Mrs McCormack in your personal sorrow."*

Teenagers Anthony Baker, Anthony Jones and Ralph Murray, students of the Irish School of Telegraphy, Cork were lost on the *Leinster*. The body of Jones was identified by Nurse Catherine Baker of St. Vincent's Hospital, Dublin. The body arrived in Cork on 20 October and was conveyed to St. Patrick's Church by students of the Irish School of Telegraphy. Anthony Jones was buried in St. Joseph's Cemetery, Cork. The bodies of Anthony Baker and Ralph Murray were not recovered. The following poem was written in memory of the three boys.[22]

Les Morts

They sleep in quiet waters where Kish towers,
'Mid sand and slender sea-grass soft and deep,
Through all the sunlit and the moonlit hours
They sleep

They are content, they murmur not, nor weep:
No rushing flotsam hastes to mock their powers;
They are content, and very deep
Their sleep

No tombs enclose them, and they need no flowers,
No mothers' kisses make their fond hearts leap—
'Mid slender sea-grass, bending where Kish towers
They sleep.

"In deep and sorrowing memory of my three pupils, Anthony Baker, Anthony Jones and Ralph Murray, the last-named my son, all aged 17 years, who died the

death of martyrs on October 10th, 1918, torpedoed aboard the R.M.S. Leinster,
during a rough and swift-running sea, and in sight of the Kish Rock Lighthouse.
— Albert Murray"

A day or two after the sinking of the *Leinster*, Assistant Purser Bill
Sweeney was with First Officer Patrick Crangle at the CDSPCo's offices in
Eden Quay. The Irishman who had been in charge of the lifeboat that had
left the *Leinster* with only four or five crewmen – and no passageners - on
board arrived at the office. He said *"Mr Crangle what do you think they will do
now?"* Crangle replied *"If I were you I would go down to the wharf and keep
walking when you get to the end of it."*

On 21 October, eleven days after the sinking of the *Leinster*, Reinhard
Scheer, Admiral of the German High Seas Fleet, signalled his submarines:
*"To all U-boats: Commence return from patrol at once. Because of ongoing
negotiations any hostile actions against merchant vessels prohibited. Returning U-
boats are allowed to attack warships only in daylight. End of message. Admiral."*[23]
The *R.M.S. Leinster* was sunk just eleven days before Germany announced
the end of the U-boat war against merchant shipping.

*

The *Freeman's Journal* of 22 October 1918 reported that: *"In the House of
Commons yesterday the Post Master-General said special provision was made by
means of the Injuries In War (Compensation) Act 1915 in respect of the war risks
incurred by post office servants on the Irish mail boats. This act provides for a
pension to widows in the event of death and a disablement pension in the event of
personal injury arising out of warlike operations, in addition to the ordinary benefits
arising out of the superannuation acts and he did not consider further provision in
the form in the form of a risk allowance to be called for."* Twenty-one post office
staff died in the sinking. Nineteen of those who died were married. Their
deaths left over 100 children without fathers.

Also on 22 October 1918, Police Superintendent James Campbell wrote
the following letter to Canadian Frank Higgerty's widowed mother.[24]

Dublin Metropolitan Police.
Superintendent's Office C Division
22nd October 1918

Mrs Henry Higgery,
54 Somerset St. Ottawa,
Ontario, Canada.

Madam,

As you are already aware your good son Francis Edward Higgerty lost his life on 10ᵗʰ instant in the Irish Sea owing to the torpedoing of the Mail Boat "Leinster" on which he was a passenger. His remains were brought to Dublin, and are at present being embalmed in Trinity College prior to removal to Ottawa.

On the body of your dear son the following property was found by Police:- Cash £1.0.3, a gold finger ring, a wristlet watch, pocket book, fountain pen, penknife, a pair of gloves and some papers.

We have been in communication with your cousin-Mrs O'Keane, 15 Everton Terrace, North Circular Road, Dublin, and she has asked us to forward to you the property of the above mentioned. Same has been carefully packed in a small cardboard box and posted to you on this date. The cost of postage amounted to 2s/4 ½ d. which has been deducted from the total amount leaving a balance of 17s/10 ½d.

On receipt of the property you might please be good enough to acknowledge same.

I beg to tender you my sincerest sympathy for the loss of your dear son, who, I have heard from persons who knew him, was a most exemplary gentleman."

I am, Madam
Yours faithfully,
James Campbell
Superintendent

A Red Cross pageant was held on the streets of Dublin on 24 October 1918. The event was reported in *The Freeman's Journal* the following day. *"Special interest was aroused by two of the lifeboats belonging to the ill-fated 'Leinster' which were drawn on lorries. In the boats were stationed some of the survivors of the vessel including Messrs Philip Connolly, engine room worker, his son Thomas, under steward, William Maher and Laurence Kearns, Firemen. They held out collection boxes to the spectators, who at once responded to the appeal."*

Apart from a brief sortie forth, during the Battle of Jutland in 1916, the German High Seas Fleet had spent the war bottled up in port. Towards the end of October 1918, as peace negotiations were taking place, the higher echelons of the Imperial German Navy, in what they saw they saw as an attempt to restore their honour, planned an all-out attack on the British Grand Fleet. The plan called for twenty-four U-boats to carry out certain tasks before the High Seas Fleet put to sea. On 25 October 1918 submarine UB-116 left Heliogoland under the command of Oberleutnant zur See Hans Joachim Emsmann, friend and classmate of Robert Ramm at the German Naval Academy and brother of Ramm's wife Gerda Emsmann's task was to enter the British Naval Base at Scapa Flow, off the north coast of Scotland, and attack larger ships, so as to weaken the British fleet prior to the attack by the German High Seas Fleet. On 28 October Emsmann's submarine entered Hoxa Sound, Scapa Flow. The British had laid a minefield in Hoxa Sound.

The minefield had underwater microphones called hydrophones, allowing shore-based operators to pick up the sound of an approaching submarine. UB-116 was picked up by hydrophone at 21.21. At 23.32 an electrical cable laid in loops on the seabed sent a signal to a device called a galvanometer, indicating that UB-116 was in the minefield. The operator flipped a switch and a row of mines exploded. *"The next morning the surface was covered with oil and air bubbles were rising steadily. Patrol boats dropped depth charges that brought debris to the surface, including a jacket. British divers visited the wreck on 29 October and on 4 November they returned and recovered UB-116's logbook."*[25] Hans Joachim Emsmann and all of his crew were killed. Within the space of nine days Gerda Ramm had lost her husband and her brother.[26] Due to mutinies on board the ships of the High Seas Fleet the German surface ships were unable to put to sea.[27]

*

The Isle of Man lies in the northern part of the Irish Sea, midway between the east coast of Northern Ireland and the west coast of England. The island is about 48 kilometres (30 miles) long and 16 kilometres (10 miles) wide, with a rocky coastline enclosing a central highland area. In October and November 1918 the sea made a number of grim deposits on the island's coast, when bodies from the *Leinster* were washed ashore. Among them were two women and a number of the ship's crew. Unfortunately it was not possible to identify these bodies. They were buried in churchyards on the island in unmarked graves.[28]

But eleven of the bodies were identified. All were male members of the armed forces. The sole member of the Royal Air Force was Private Cardiff from James's Street, Dublin. He and two soldiers were buried in Douglas Cemetery on the island. The soldiers were Privates Horace Cook, East Kent and West Kent Yeomanry and William Hutchinson (25), Westmoreland and Cumberland Yeomanry. An inquest heard that the bodies of Horace Cook and William Hutchinson were washed up together on the beach at Port St. Mary on 8 November. Cook had been going on leave from his regiment at Ballina, Co. Mayo to his home in Wimbledon. Hutchinson's body was identified from letters in his pocket from his father, sister and brother. He was from Nottingham. Horace Cook and William Hutchinson share the same grave in Douglas Churchyard.

Three men were buried in Patrick Cemetery on the island. Among them was Corporal Michael Carroll, Royal Army Medical Corps, from Dublin. The other two men were Privates A.H. Lott (23), Royal Berkshire Regiment and George Lutton (32), Royal Munster Fusiliers. The bodies of five other soldiers, washed up on the island, were returned home for burial. Lance-Corporal Harold Wilkinson and Private Richard Jones were members of the Royal Welch Fusiliers. Wilkinson's body was found at Port Erin on 2 November and Jones's at Port St. Mary on 15 November. It was mentioned at an inquest that Wilkinson had in his pocket £1-4-0 ½, a silver watch and chain, a special leave ticket and a pass made out for 10 October 1918. He was also carrying a number of photographs (including one of himself) and a copy of Regulations. His remains were identified by his father, as being the youngest of his three sons. He had been on his way home to celebrate his 21st birthday.

The body of Second Lieutenant Victor Frederick Sloper (30) of the Wiltshire Regiment was washed ashore on 15 November. He was returned to Wiltshire for burial. The bodies of two Irishmen were also returned home for burial. Private Michael Biggane of the Canadian Army Service Corps was brought to Waterford, while Private Edward Dunne of the Royal Defence Corps was buried in Dublin. The Isle of Man newspapers reported the tragic findings under headings such as *"Victim of RMS Leinster Outrage,"* *"More Victims Bodies Cast Up,"* *"German Brutality: Seven More Washed Ashore"* and *"Last Victim of German Brutality."*

In separate incidents, the bodies of two Royal Dublin Fusiliers were washed ashore on the west coast of Scotland. The body of Lieutenant Sydney George Crawford (21) was recovered almost a month and a half after the sinking of the *Leinster*. From Foxrock, Co. Dublin, he was buried in Kirkbean Parish Churchyard, Kirkcudbrightshire on 22 November. Private Philip O'Brien from Tullamaine, Fethard, Co. Tipperary was buried in Portpatrick Churchyard. No other bodies were recovered as far from the scene of the *Leinster* sinking as those of the two Irishmen from the Royal Dublin Fusiliers.

"Wreck covers" is the term applied to post recovered from disasters at sea, on land and in the air. Recovered mail is stamped or marked by postal authorities to explain any damage. The stamping or marking can be general or specific e.g. *"Damaged by immersion in water"* or *"Saved from wreck of 'Tararua.'* In December 1918 a bag of mail from the *Leinster* was washed ashore on the Isle of Man. The contents were dried out and subsequently delivered. Before being sent for delivery they were stamped: *'Salved from S.S. Leinster'* in violet. With only three exceptions, the markings stamped on mail recovered from ships sunk during the First World War were of the general type. The *R.M.S. Leinster* was one of the three exceptions. (The others were the *Hesperian* and the *Mongolia*.)[29]

Notes

1   Unless otherwise stated, the details in this chapter are from contemporary newspapers.
2   Details of *R.M.S.Ulster's* movements are from her Daily Journal.

3 *Twilight of the Ascendancy* by Mark Bence-Jones.

4 Contemporary newspapers reported that *"at about 1.30 p.m. a destroyer was seen approaching the harbour."* H.M.S. *Lively's* log for 10 October 1918 shows that she docked at 1.50 p.m. H.M.S. *Mallard* and H.M.S. *Seal* docked later.

5 Details of rescue ships' movements, numbers of survivors taken on board, etc. are taken from ships' logbooks.

6 Bill Sweeney's interview with Declan Whelan, accounts of the sinking by Chief Steward Llewellyn Lewis and Sergeant Francis Coleman and *The Irish Independent.* 14 October 1918.

7 Years later Arthur Haughton from Killiney would remember being on duty that day with the scouts, or, as he still called them, *"the Baden-Powells."* Source: *Holy Trinity Church Killiney 1858-1996: A Parish History.* According to the book, the scouts used to bring refreshments to those coming ashore from ships docked in the harbour. They carried trays with cigarettes, tobacco, sandwiches and tea with milk and sugar added.

8 Details on Daniel Smyth: *The Sunday Express* December 1963.

9 Newspapers and a partial list of survivors in the National Archives, Dublin.

10 After picking up survivors the *Mallard* set out for Kingstown at 12.40 p.m. The *Lively* left the rescue scene at the same time. She docked at Kingstown at 1.50 p.m., the journey having taken 1 hour and 10 minutes. The *Seal* left the rescue scene ten minutes after the other two ships and, like the *Lively*, also made the trip in 1 hour and 10 minutes. The journey took the *Mallard* 2 hours and 20 minutes.

11 Partial list of survivors in the National Archives, Dublin.

12 Daly's account of the sinking and aftermath.

13 The late Robbie Brennan, local historian.

14 *The Irish Independent.* 12 October 1918

15 The 8.55 p.m. train: *The Limerick Chronicle* 12 October 1918.

16 U-boat archives, Cuxhaven.

17 *1918: War and Peace* by Gregor Dallas. Dallas is one of the few authors who seems to be aware of the scale of the death toll for the *Leinster.* In saying that 527 were lost, he exceeds the official death toll of 501. My own research indicates that the actual loss of life was closer to the figure quoted by Dallas. The article *"When submarine UB-123 attacked the ferry Leinster, it torpedoed Germany's last hope for a 'soft peace' in 1918"* by Ann B. Sides in Military History, October 1998 is interesting. However, from my reading of a number of authors' accounts of President Wilson in October and November 1918, it appears to somewhat exaggerate the importance of the *Leinster* sinking on his thinking.

18 *Tralee's Old Stock Reminisce: An Oral History of Tralee and Its Surroundings* by Mick O'Neill. Thanks to Kate Healy Coburn for bringing this to my attention.

19 Thanks to Dr Margaret Elmes for a copy of the letter.

20 *Find and Destroy: Antisubmarine Warfare in World War 1* by Dwight R. Messimer, *Verschollen: World War 1 U-Boat Losses* by Dwight R. Messimer, *The Macmillan Dictionary of The First World War* by Stephen Pope & Elizabeth-Anne Wheal, *Battle Beneath the Waves: U-boats at War* by Robert C. Stern and *Business in Great Waters* by John Terraine.

21 *Verschollen: World War 1 U-Boat Losses* by Dwight R. Messimer, *The German Submarine War 1914-1918* by R.H. Gibson. and Maurice Prendergast, *The Victory at*

Sea by Rear Admiral William Sowden Sims and Burton J. Hendrick and the U-Boat Archives, Cuxhaven, Germany

[22] Thanks to Declan Jones for the poem.

[23] *Business in Great Waters* by John Terraine.

[24] Thanks to Will Lockhart for the letter.

[25] *Verschollen: World War 1 U-boat losses* by Dwight R. Messimer. Details on the operation of the hydrophones and the shore-controlled mines are from *Find and Destroy: Antisubmarine Warfare in World War 1* by Dwight R. Messimer.

[26] Hans Joachim Emsmann captained UB-5, UB-10, UB-40 and UB-116. On ten patrols he sank twenty-seven ships, totalling 9,221 tons. During World War Two the 5th U-Boat Flotilla was named *Flotilla Emsmann* in his honour. Source: uboat.net

[27] Information on the plan for the attack by the 24 U-boats and the German High Seas Fleet kindly supplied by Naval Historian Dwight R. Messimer. His sources were D. Gross *Der Krieg zur See: Der Krier in der Nordsee, Vol. 7* and Arno Spindler *Der Krieg zur See: Der Handelskrieg mit U-booten Vol 5.*

[28] Margery West *Some Corner of an Off-Shore Island* Bulletin of The Western Front Association No. 42 (June 1995).

[29] Page from untitled and undated philately journal held by Dún Laoghaire Heritage Society.

Chapter 7

From then to now

"In this generation we redeem their memory, acknowledging their service and the pain of those who loved them."

President Mary McAleese remembering Ireland's First World War dead, Messines, Belgium, 11 November 1998

The *R.M.S. Munster* had been taken out of commission on 5 October 1918 and did not return to service until 26 October 1918. The sinking of the *Leinster* meant that the *Ulster* had to cover the Holyhead-Kingstown route on her own for over two weeks. The final two and a half weeks of the war saw the *Munster* and the *Ulster* covering the route. The Daily Journals of the ships show that they were escorted for nearly every journey over the next few weeks. Some sources say that towards the end of October 1918 the *Ulster* was struck by a torpedo that failed to explode. However, neither the *Ulster's* Daily Journal nor the *"British Merchant Vessels damaged or molested by the enemy but not sunk"* section of the H.M.S.O. (1919) publication *"British Vessels Lost at Sea 1914-18"* mention this attack.

On 11 November 1918 the *R.M.S. Munster,* under the command of Kingstown born Captain James Penston,[1] left Holyhead at 7.00 a.m. She docked at Kingstown at 10.30 a.m. Half an hour later the guns fell silent on the Western Front. The war was over. The *R.M.S. Ulster* left Kingstown at 8.46 a.m. that morning. Commanded by Birkenhead born Captain Robert Newton,[2] she was carrying troops among her passengers. Presumably, there was a celebration on board when news of the armistice was announced. The ship docked at Holyhead at 11.50 a.m. The peace was almost an hour old. Shortly before the *Ulster* docked at Holyhead the town's church bells tolled. Ships in the harbour sounded their sirens. Young Edward Anthony was playing with his friend Sam Williams. Edward was the son of Lamp Trimmer Robert Anthony, who had been killed in the *Leinster* sinking. Someone told the boys the reason for the excitement. They ran to Edward's home and shouted to his mother: *"The war is over!"* Mary Anthony said sadly: *"The war ended a month ago, for me."*[3]

On 10 October 1918 Dublin bookmaker Richard Duggan had seen off some friends on the *Leinster*. They were traveling to England for the Cambridgeshire, one of the last big races of the flat season. In the aftermath of the sinking the Lord Mayor of Dublin opened a relief fund. Richard Duggan set out to raise £1000 for the fund. He set up a lottery with a prize of £100 and tickets selling at a shilling each. Tens of thousands of tickets were sold. Many dependants of *Leinster* victims received support that winter because of Duggan's lottery. The combination of a deserving cause coupled with the chance to win money proved irresistible to the public. It was a lesson that was not lost on Duggan. He went on, with two others, to establish the world famous *Irish Hospitals Sweep Stakes*.[4]

A general election for Great Britain and Ireland was called for 14 December 1918. As part of his re-election campaign for Member of Parliament for the city of Limerick sixty-seven year old *Leinster* survivor Michael Joyce M.P. held a rally on 25 November.[5] The execution of the leaders of the 1916 Rising and an attempt to introduce conscription into Ireland caused an upsurge in support for the Sinn Féin party.[6] Joyce's election rally was disrupted by Sinn Féin supporters. As feelings were running high, Joyce decided not to contest the election, in order to save the city of Limerick from further turmoil. His parliamentary career was over. He retired from Limerick Harbour Board in January 1920 and from the post of President of the United Kingdom River Pilots' Association in 1923. Over the next two decades he maintained his interest in social and cultural affairs. During his political career he rubbed shoulders with the leading parliamentarians of his day. T.P. O'Connor, Nationalist M.P., introduced him to Mark Twain, saying that he was introducing *"the Shannon Pilot to the Mississippi Pilot."* On 9 January 1941, in his ninetieth year, Michael Joyce died at his home, *The Moorings*, O'Connell Avenue, Limerick.

A letter from the Admiralty was read out at a Kingstown Urban District Council meeting on 5 December 1918.[7] It proposed that one of the German submarines surrendered at the end of the war make a visit to Kingstown and that the Urban District Council would be allowed to charge the public a fee for *"inspection"* of the submarine. It was proposed by Councillor Devitt and seconded by Councillor Murray *"That the thanks of the Council be conveyed to the Admiralty for deciding to allocate one of the ex-German submarines to Kingstown, and for allowing a charge for inspection to be made. That they be requested to allow interior inspection and the Council suggest that the proceeds be allocated equally between St. Michael's Hospital and the Monkstown Hospital, Kingstown and that if possible the submarine which sunk the 'Leinster' be sent to Kingstown."* The motion was carried. Councillor Smyth drew attention to the bravery of Fireman William Maher, following the sinking of the *Leinster*. It was proposed by Councillor Smyth and seconded by Councillor Kennedy *"That the attention of the War Office, the Admiralty, the 'Leinster' Fund, the Royal*

Humane Society, and the Carnegie Hero Fund be directed to the action of Mr. William Maher, and that the Town Clerk be directed to communicate with these bodies on the subject." The motion was carried.

On 14 January 1919 the committee of The Royal Humane Society discussed the War Office referral of *Leinster's* Military Adjutant Captain (as he now was) Hugh Parker.[8] The committee's records say that at 9.45 a.m. on 10 October 1918 the *Leinster* was struck by a torpedo. Captain Parker and Mrs M. M. Rae, aged 26 were thrown into the sea, which was rough. Captain Parker supported Mrs Rae for one and three quarter hours, when they were rescued in a state of collapse. The committee decided to award a silver medal to Captain Parker. The Royal Humane Society's annual report for 1919 said that *"Mrs. M. M. Rae and her husband were passengers on the ship and when the second torpedo was fired both were thrown into the sea and parted, the lady being unable to swim. Captain Parker, who had practically only the use of one arm, owing to wounds received in France swam to her assistance."* On 20 March 1920 the British High Commissioner in Cairo presented Acting Captain Hugh Love Parker with the Order of the British Empire (OBE) for *"valuable services in connection with the war."* Hugh Parker O.B.E. rejoined the army at the outbreak of the Second World War. On 1 April 1941 he was mentioned in despatches for distinguished services in the Middle East during the period August 1939 to November 1940.[9] There were at least two other O.B.E.'s awarded to men involved in the rescue of *Leinster* survivors. Lieutenant Rowland Lloyd R.N.R., captain of *H.M.S. Mallard* was given the award, as was Gunner Ernest J.A. Gale from the destroyer *H.M.S. Lively.*

In January 1919 the Lord Chamberlain received the following letter at his office in London.[10]

Kilniddery,
Woodurne Avenue,
Streatham,
London S.W.
16/1/19

Dear Mr Trendall,

I am anxious that the heroic conduct of Stoker William Maher should be brought to the notice of the proper authorities and I should be much obliged if you could do anything in the matter.

On 10ᵗʰ October last, I was a passenger with my daughter (aged 13 and a half years) on the ill-fated R.M.S. Leinster. As the world knows she was torpedoed and out of 777 people on board only 164 were saved and entirely owing to the gallant conduct of Stoker Maher, my daughter and I were among the latter number.

On being hurled into the sea we both swam for and succeeded in reaching one of the ship's rafts where we were helped by Maher. For two and a half hours we clung to this raft and five out of nine people were washed away from it by the heavy seas. Had it not been for Maher's encouragement and cheerfulness which helped us immensely we should, without doubt, have also perished.

He held on to my daughter the whole time and assisted me, but when help arrived in the way of a motor launch I lost consciousness, but he caught the lifeline and helped me to get on to the launch. During this operation the raft capsized and my daughter was washed away, but not withstanding his exhausted condition he swam for her and succeeded in getting her also hauled on board.

He also helped and saved Private Duffin of the Suffolk Regiment, who was beside us all the time. Maher is an old soldier having been some years in the Royal Irish Fusiliers in which regiment he fought through the Boer War, since which he has been a stoker on the Irish boats. He is the father of eight children and most respectable in his mode of life.

If any further details should be required I shall be pleased to supply them, as I strongly feel that his case should be considered for the Albert Medal.

Yours sincerely,
Louisa Toppin

The Royal Humane Society held a committee meeting on 8 April 1919.[11] Among the topics discussed was case number 44724, W.A. Downing, Patrick D. Starrs and William Maher. The committee's records said that after the *Leinster* was sunk *"a number of persons were in the sea, which was rough. All three sailors at great risk succeeded in saving life."* The Admiralty had referred Downing and Starrs to the Royal Humane Society. This appears to suggest that they were members of the Royal Navy on board the rescue ships. William Maher was referred by the Board of Trade. The committee decided to award a silver medal to Maher and bronze medals to the other two. Maher's medal was sent to the Board of Trade on 11 August 1919. The Royal Humane Society's annual report for 1919 gives the circumstances for which Maher was awarded the silver medal. Unfortunately, the society does not have a record of why the bronze medals were awarded to Downing and Starrs.

The Lord Mayor of Dublin presided at a meeting of the Local Marine Board at Eden Quay on 29 September 1919.[12] He read out the letter Mrs Toppin had sent to the Lord Chamberlain. He presented William Maher with the Silver Medal of the Royal Humane Society. Edward Watson, Managing Director of the CDSPCo said that he was proud of William Maher. He said that Maher and himself had served in the same regiment during the Boer War. He said that during his time with the CDSPCo nothing had caused him so much grief and sorrow as the loss of the *Leinster*. The company had done everything they could to protect their vessels and he felt that if those responsible for the safety of the *Leinster* had done their duty very few lives would have been lost. He felt that, either there should be an investigation into the loss of the ship, or pensions should be paid to the widows and dependants of those who were lost. He said that if Germany were responsible for the loss of the ship they should be made to pay reparations. Watson said that 501 lives had been lost and that had it not been for the bravery of William Maher, the figure would have been 504.

Young Dorothy Toppin gave William Maher a watch in appreciation for his saving her life. An inscription on the watch reads *"To William Maher From Dorothy Toppin. As a small token of gratitude for saving her life. Leinster disaster 10th October 1918."* Maher greatly treasured the watch and wore it into old age.[13] Bill Sweeney said that he often saw Maher wearing his medals at the head of Armistice Day parades. William Maher died in 1954. He is buried in Deansgrange Cemetery, Co. Dublin.

In the final days of 1918 Gerald Palmer's' father wrote to the matron of *The Cripples Home*, Bray, Co. Wicklow.[14]

Dec 29th 1918

Dear Matron,

I received your letter today with the sad news of Gerald's end. My poor boy, how I would have liked to have seen him. Matron I know and deeply regret I have not written to him often but Matron the position I have been placed in, God knows, hindered me. But I never forgot him as you may think. I am sorry my boy William who lives in Derbyshire has not written. I often asked him. Matron, do you really believe he is drowned? If he is I trust he is in heaven now with his poor dear mother where I trust and hope in God I will meet them both. When one's home is broken up what a separating. I know it all. I hope Gerald will forgive me and Matron that you will. I will often regret it, Matron. A few months ago I went to see my boy William who lives 50 miles from here and we talked it over and Willie was going to get him on the railways along with him as soon as he would leave your home. He got married six months ago and had a home to bring him to but what a great disappointment. If the Great War had not been on Willie would have been over to see him long since. Matron I have been in a very poor way of living and not in good health. I have no money. If I had I would send something to the Home for all the trouble and kindness to poor Gerald.

I enclose a ten shillings postal order for a cake for tea for the boys of Gerald's class. Please accept the same as a small token of my fond love for poor Gerald and pray and all the boys pray, that God will forgive me for all my neglect to him. I am truly sorry, may God forgive me. If you know anything about his end kindly let me know. Matron, did Gerald ever say he loved me or did he ever ask for Willie? I suppose Gerald never had his photo taken. If you have one I would be grateful for same.

I am your obedient servant,
P. Palmer---Poor Gerald's Father.

No obituary was written on the passing of Gerald Palmer. His name is not on any memorial. His story was lost in the mists of time until Bray historian Francis Loughrey came upon his name and details in a minute book for *The Cripples Home*. Thanks to Francis Loughrey, Gerald Palmer can finally be remembered.

The death of Thomas and Charlotte Foley left 10 children as orphans. Thomas's sister Lily was married to tenor John McCormack. The McCormacks made provision for the rearing and education of the children. Nine of the children went to live with Lily's mother and an older sister. John and Lily McCormack adopted the youngest child, 16- month-old Kevin.[15] On 30 November 1919 an Australian who had served in a Queensland battalion wrote to Irishman Will Copeland. He had met Will when he visited Ireland with Will's cousin, Australian soldier Richard Kelly-Healy. The letter contains the following lines. *"Like yourself I am not likely to forget the 10th 10th* (i.e. 10 October) *and how lucky we were not being on the Leinster but if the old saying is true 'luck is a fortune' I should have been a millionaire a dozen times over."* The letter is signed *Barney*. So it appears that at least two Australian soldiers were lucky enough to have missed getting on the *Leinster*.[16]

An entry in the Vestry notes of St. Brigid's Church of Ireland, Stillorgan, Co. Dublin for 1920 reads *"Mrs Crawford was allowed to erect a Mural Tablet in memory of her son and daughter, both lost by the sinking of H.M.S. (sic) Leinster."* On the north wall of the church there is an elegant memorial in the form of an open book. It is inscribed: *"In loving memory of Letitia Harriet eldest daughter of Wm. Henry and Elizabeth Crawford of Stillorgan, Co. Dublin and wife of Captain V. Hill, R.F.A., aged 34 years. Also her brother Sydney George Crawford Lieutenant R.D.F. aged 21 years. He was buried in Kirkbean, Kirkcudbright Scotland 22nd November. Both drowned on the R.M.S. Leinster when torpedoed in the Irish Sea 10th October 1918."*[17]

In 1920 *The Victory at Sea* by William Sims, Commander of the U.S. Naval Forces operating in European Waters was published. The book mentions that Captain Hutch Cone had been on the *Leinster*. *"In September 1918, Captain Cone's duties took him to Ireland; the ship on which he sailed, the Leinster, was torpedoed in the Irish Sea; Captain Cone was picked up unconscious in the water, and, when taken to hospital, it was discovered that both his legs were broken. It was therefore necessary to appoint another officer in his stead."* Captain Cone was awarded the U.S. Distinguished Service Medal with the citation: *"For exceptional meritorious service in a duty of great responsibility as Commander of the U.S. Naval Aviation Forces, Foreign Service, and later as Aide for Aviation on the staff of the Commander, U.S. Naval Forces in European waters."* He received two letters of commendation from Rear-Admiral Sims, one for his service in command of the U.S. Naval Aviation Forces Foreign Service and one for his assistance in saving lives during the sinking of the *Leinster*. For his war service he received the Victory Medal and Overseas Clasp. The French government made him an Officer of the Legion of Honour. The British government conferred him with the Distinguished Service Order and, in recognition of his saving of lives on the *Leinster* they made him an Honorary Companion of the Military Division of the Order of the British Empire. The Italian government conferred him with the Cross of Officer of the Order of St. Maurice and St. Lazarus, and the Order of Mariziane with the Rank of Ufficale.[18]

In December 1918 Cone returned to the United States for hospitalisation. After discharge he attended the Naval War College, Newport, Rhode Island and later took command of the armoured cruiser *Huron*, flagship of the U.S. Asiatic Fleet. Having served as Chief of Staff to the Commander in Chief of the Asiatic Fleet, he returned to the United States in February 1922. The injuries he sustained in the sinking of the *Leinster* had resulted in permanent physical disability. On 11 July 1922 he was retired with the rank of Rear Admiral. Following his retirement he took up various posts in shipping and aviation. On 12 February 1941 Hutch Cone died in Orlando, Florida, two and a half months before his 70th birthday. On 18 August 1945 the United States Navy commissioned the destroyer *U.S.S. Cone* (DD-866) in his honour.[19]

The CDSPCo continued to operate the mail service with the *Munster* and the *Ulster*. In 1920 the firm finally lost the mail contract to the London North Western Railway. The Irish members of parliament at Westminster had always represented the interests of the CDSPCo. As they often held the balance of power in the parliament, their support was very beneficial to the company. By 1920 the Irish Party had been replaced by Sinn Féin, who refused to sit at Westminster and set up a parliament in Dublin. The loss of the Irish voice at Westminster hindered the cause of the CDSPCo when the mail service contract came up for renewal. At 7 p.m. on Saturday 20 November 1920 the *R.M.S. Munster* left Kingstown harbour for the final time. Commanded by Captain James Penston, she didn't carry any passengers. At 8 p.m. the *R.M.S. Ulster* bade her final goodbye to Kingstown. Under the command of Captain Robert Newton, she carried one hundred and fifty seven and a half passengers. (Children were counted as half passengers). The *Munster* docked at Holyhead at 10.10 p.m. The *Ulster* arrived fifty-eight minutes later, at 11.08 p.m. By 11.39 p.m. her passengers and luggage were landed.[20] The incredible story of *The Provinces* had come to an end.

The *Munster* and the *Ulster* remained at Holyhead for almost three-and-a-half years. Gerard Crangle, son of *Leinster's* First Officer Patrick Crangle, remembers playing on the ships during visits to Holyhead. In March 1924 they were sold to German ship breakers and towed away. In the years following the First World War many Irish soldiers died as the result of wounds sustained in the war. Bill Sweeney would have included the

102

remaining two *Provinces* in this category. On tape he said: *"The Germans got the four of us. They sank two and they bought the other two for scrap."*

In 1919 the services operated by the CDSPCo to Liverpool and Manchester were taken over by the British & Irish Steam Packet Company (B&I). On 1 January 1922, under the terms of a treaty signed in London on 6 December 1921, The Irish Free State was established as an independent country within the British Commonwealth. *The Freeman's Journal* of 4 April 1922 carried the following report. *"When the City of Dublin Steam Packet Company's Bill for Winding-Up came before a Select Committee of the House of Lords yesterday, the question was raised whether the Committee had jurisdiction following the passing of the Irish Free State Act. Serjeant Sullivan contended that the jurisdiction remained and the Committee proceeded with the Bill."*[21] The select committee would probably have been unaware that they were winding up a company whose founder, Charles Wye Williams, had died 56 years and one day earlier.

The CDSPCo was finally wound up in 1924. According to Maritime Historian Hazel P. Smyth it was *"one hundred years after its first ship, the 'City of Dublin,' had gone to sea."* The only remaining visible symbol of the company's existence is the fine CDSPCo crest that still adorns the face of 15 Eden Quay, Dublin. At the time of winding up, the following were on the company's board of directors. Edward Watson, J.P., Managing Director, W. H. Litchfield, Managing Director, Richard Jones, Secretary, Wilfred Fitzgerald, S .D. Lambert, John Murphy and The Most Hon. The Marquess of Ormonde. Among the last captains of the CDSPCo ships were John Theodore Rogers, Daish, Knight, Mahon, Perkins and Redmond.[22] (All/most of them would appear to have operated on the Dublin to Liverpool and Manchester routes).

Leinster's First Officer Patrick Crangle died on 8 August 1925. He was only 48 years old. The injuries he sustained in the sinking had probably shortened his life. He is buried in Deansgrange Cemetery, Co. Dublin.[23]

Army Order 78, of 11 March 1922, disbanded most of the Irish regiments in the British army. Among them was Major Louis Daly's regiment, the Leinster Regiment. Daly remained in the British army. He served as a General Staff Officer with the Waziristan Force 1920-23 and was twice mentioned in despatches. In 1924 he joined the Devonshire Regiment. In the same year he was conferred with the O.B.E., becoming the third *Leinster* survivor to receive the award. (Though his award was not related to the loss of the *Leinster*). His account of the *Leinster* sinking was published in 1927. He joined the Kings Own Yorkshire Light Infantry the same year. He was promoted to Lieutenant-Colonel in 1932, commanding 1st Battalion Kings Own Yorkshire Light Infantry from 1932 to 1935. From 1936 to 1940 he commanded 147th (Second West Riding) Infantry Brigade, Territorial Army. He retired in 1940. He and his wife Cora had one son and one daughter. Cora Daly died in 1947. Louis Daly died on 10 June 1967 at Leighcroft, Hoddesdon. He was 83.[24]

Bill Sweeney said that Chief Stewardess Mary Coffey did not return to work with the CDSPCo after the sinking. She never married. She became a travelling companion/governess to a Spanish or Venezuelan family. Her family became involved in Ireland's War of Independence and weapons were stored in the family home. Her family took the anti-treaty side in Ireland's civil war. During the Second World War she hid the German spy Hermann Goertz in her home in Dún Laoghaire. Goertz had come to Ireland to make contact with the I.R.A. After Goertz was arrested, the Irish Government interned Mary Coffey. She died in 1953.[25]

Seamen Hugh Owen was on the bridge of the *Leinster* with Captain Birch. In later life he rarely spoke of the sinking and never mentioned the fact that he saved the life of a young woman. As she was unable to swim, Hugh kept her afloat by wrapping her long hair around his arm. In later years Hugh took a shore job at the Marine Department in Holyhead, where he was responsible for supervising the docking of the ferries which crossed the Irish Sea. He died in 1992.[26]

A plaque in the club commemorates John Ross, Secretary of Howth Yacht Club, Co. Dublin.[27] In the church at the Diocesan Training College, Derby a memorial window was dedicated to Maud Elizabeth Ward, Secretary to Lieutenant-Colonel Proby.[28] The window, showing the Annunciation, was by church artist Eadie Reid. An office block called *The College Business Centre* now stands on the site of the Diocesan Training College at Uttoxeter New Road, Derby. Maud Elizabeth Ward is buried in Deansgrange Cemetery, Co. Dublin. The gravestone is a simple granite cross with the inscription *"Maud Elizabeth Ward. Born 12 June 1874. Drowned on S.S. Leinster 10 October 1918."* At the base of the cross are the words *"He sent from above, He took me, He drew me out of many waters."*

After the war Rowland Lloyd, captain of *H.M.S. Mallard*, returned to work with his previous employer, the Royal Mail Steam Packet Company (RMSPCo). He took a shore job in Southampton, as he was not well enough to go to sea for any length of time. However, in the late 1920's he travelled once or twice to South America with his wife and daughter. A founder member of the Southampton Master Mariners Club, he was a keen fisherman and held several records in the 1920's for trout fishing. After surviving several bouts of pneumonia and a serious hit and run accident, he retired from the RMSPCo in 1931 with the rank of Assistant Marine Superintendent. He lived the rest of his life in Southampton, where he died in 1940.[29]

Mervyn Wall was a young boy living in Dublin in October 1918. A female cousin from Cork came to stay with the Wall family. She feared that her brother, Matthew Murphy, an army officer, had been on the *Leinster*. Mervyn's eldest brother went into Dublin with his cousin to search the hospitals and the City Morgue. They found the young officer's body among many others laid out on the floor of the City Hall. Mervyn Wall became a writer in later life. In his novel *"Hermitage"* young Tony Langton's brother Malcolm joins the army. He travels to England on the *Leinster*. When the Langtons learn of the sinking, Tony and his father travel to Kingstown seeking news of Malcolm. The book gives what appears to be a very realistic account of the scenes at Kingstown harbour following the sinking. Malcolm's body is eventually found, laid out on the floor of the City Hall, Dublin.[30] The real life Malcolm, Captain Matthew Murphy, was a member of the Royal Army Medical Corps. He is buried in Cloyne (St. Coleman) Cathedral Churchyard, Co. Cork.

During the late 1930s Father Joe Ranson began to write down the songs that were sung by ballad singers on the Co. Wexford coast. On 26 August 1946 he took down the words of the following song from Patrick Doyle of Kilmacoe, Co. Wexford.

The Mail Boat Leinster.

You feeling hearted Christians all in country or in town,
Come listen to my doleful song which I have just penned down.
'Tis all about that German act, that awful tragedy,
When the Dublin Mail Boat Leinster was sunk in the Irish Sea.

On the tenth day of October, Nineteen eighteen, the year,
This mail boat on her passage went, I mean to let you hear,
With six hundred and ninety passengers and seventy of a crew,
She sailed away from Kingstown Quay and for Holyhead bound to.

In pride and stately grandeur did the Leinster plough her way.
And all on board were of good cheer with spirits light and gay;
Not fearing that the U-boat lay hid beneath the wave,
That would send them soon unto their doom, and give a watery grave.

The German monster came on them when they did least expect,
And fired torpedoes at the boat, which quickly took effect.
Her boilers burst; the flames ascend with fury to the sky:
Mid the echo of the deafening din you could hear the women cry.

Oh, the Leinster now is sinking fast; she's going down by the head,
And many too, while in their bunks are numbered with the dead.
The passengers, their life belts on, unto the boats repair,
While cries for help do rend the skies in sad and wild despair.

Now to conclude and finish – my doleful lines to close;
May the Lord have mercy on their souls and grant them sweet repose.
Beside the mail boat, Leinster, they quietly now do sleep,
In the cold and changeless waters of the Irish Sea so deep.

Patrick Doyle sang the song to the air of another local ballad, *"The Poulshone Fishermen."* Father Joe Ranson subsequently published the ballad in *Songs of the Wexford Coast* (1948). As the *Leinster* was long forgotten at the time Patrick Doyle sang the song for Father Ranson, it was unlikely to have been recently written. This would appear to suggest that the song was probably written shortly after the sinking, when the composer knew the details of the tragedy. Historians and musicians owe the late Father Ranson a debt of gratitude for recording a *Leinster* song that would otherwise have been forgotten in the mists of time.

On 30 March 1951 Rector Conor Collins conducted a funeral service in *Rocklands,* a private house at Bullock Harbour, Co. Dublin. Then, in accordance with her final wish, the coffin containing the body of seventy-two year old Mrs Agnes Louise (Lola) Toppin was brought by hearse to a nearby pier and put on board the fishing launch *Ability.* Mrs Toppin's three sons, relatives and friends embarked on the boat. With the Irish national flag flying at half-mast, the *Ability* travelled beyond the three-mile limit to the open sea. Rev. L. Stuart, Chaplain to the Missions for Seamen, conducted a service, following which the lead weighted coffin was lowered into the sea.[31] Lola Toppin was finally at rest with the passengers and crew of the *R.M.S. Leinster.*

The foremast of the *Leinster* was recovered and towed to the Irish Lights boat yard at Kingstown. Bill Sweeney gave £1 to an Irish Lights employee to cut a piece of the mast for him. He had the piece mounted. But he later gave it to a friend of Captain Birch, from Dalkey, Co. Dublin, then living in London. After the *Leinster* was sunk Bill Sweeney served on the *Munster* and the *Ulster,* mostly on the latter under Captain Newton. He later worked for a ventilation equipment company in London. The company made the propellers for the *Queen Mary.* He married and had a family. Later in life he worked in the gift shop of the *Cutty Sark* at Greenwich. He worked until he was 67 years old. He started to research the history of the CDSPCo at the Maritime Museum, Greenwich. He wrote up his findings in the park behind the museum. Unfortunately, his research was never published.

Bill Sweeney was predeceased by his wife. He spent his final days in the *Holy Family Home,* a nursing home on Roebuck Road, Dublin. While at the nursing home he became friendly with Declan Whelan, who lived nearby. Whelan arranged a trip to Holyhead for Sweeney and one of his mates from the nursing home. He brought them to the ferry at Dún

Laoghaire (previously Kingstown) and saw them off. That evening he went to Dún Laoghaire to collect them. The two elderly gentlemen stumbled off the ship somewhat the worst for wear. During the trip over, word had been sent to Holyhead that a survivor of the *Leinster* was on his way. Upon arrival the two men were taken on a tour of Holyhead's fine hostelries and didn't have to put their hands in their pockets for the entire the visit!

Bill Sweeney died in the *Holy Family Home*. When it became obvious that Sweeney was dying, Declan Whelan requested, and was granted, permission to move a camp bed into his room so that the elderly man would not have to die alone. Bill Sweeney died in October, the same month in which his beloved *Leinster* was sunk. He departed this life on 16 October 1979, less than a week after the 61st anniversary of the sinking. He is buried in Deansgrange Cemetery, Co. Dublin.[32] Declan Whelan recorded a number of conversations with Bill Sweeney on tape. The tapes provided a very valuable source for this book.

On 30 September and 14 October 1960 the *Dublin Post* published photographs and information on *Leinster* survivors John Brown, (77), Jim Carraher (78), Tom Connolly, Laurence Crowe (72) and Christopher Hynes. The paper reported that Carraher and Crowe had been picked up by *H.M.S. Lively*. It said that Carraher had retired seven years earlier *"after a full seafaring life."* Crowe had served on the mail boats up to the previous year when, he was quoted as saying, *"they kicked me into retirement."*[33]

Cabin boy Tom Connolly served with the Canadian Pacific Line for some time before settling down in his hometown. In 1934 he married Sheila Gaffney from Dalkey, Co. Dublin. He went into business. In 1961 he opened one of the first supermarkets in Ireland at Patrick Street, Dún Laoghaire. It was often referred to as *"Cut-Price Connolly's."* A model of the *Leinster*, made for the CDSPCo, ended up on display in O'Hara's, Chancery Street, Dublin. Connolly offered £100 for the model but the owner would not sell it at any price. Later the premises changed hands. By a twist of fate it was bought by a friend of Tom Connolly's, who gave him the model as a present.[34] For many years the model was on display in his shop.[35] When he retired he gave the model to the Maritime Museum in Dún Laoghaire. It is still on display there and alone is worth the price of admission.

On 10 October 1968, the fiftieth anniversary of the sinking of the *Leinster*, Tom Connolly hosted a dinner for five other survivors at the *Ross Hotel*, Dún Laoghaire. Those invited were Mary Buckley, Thomas Deegan, Florence Enright, Christopher Hynes and Thomas T. Richards. The event was reported the following day in the Dublin newspaper the *Evening Press*. Mrs Mary Buckley (née Hoare), of Randolf, Massachusetts, said that, at the time of the sinking, she had been travelling to England as a passenger. *"I was downstairs when I heard a terrible bang. I thought it was thunder, but the boat swayed and shook. I went out into the aisle and saw the steps awash with water. I* managed to get out into the water and onto a life-raft. *There was a soldier from France with me. We prayed together all the time. The life-raft was overturned and I passed out. I woke up in Dún Laoghaire. A local family looked after me for three months. They re-united me with my mother."* Mrs. Florence Enright (77) said that, at the time of the sinking, she was travelling to Liverpool to meet her husband. *"I jumped into the water, but I could not swim a stroke. I hung onto a piece of driftwood and my lifebelt. I was picked up three hours later."* Thomas Deegan was a Saloon Steward on the ship. *"I was finishing my work in the saloon when I felt a bump as if we had struck a stone wall. I made for the deck to the lifeboat station and we managed to get a lifeboat in the water. It was very difficult to persuade anyone to get in along with us. We filled her up with people and we drifted for more than two hours in the rough seas, before we were picked up."* Christopher Hynes said that he was a greaser on the ship. *"I was in the engine room when the torpedo struck. We rushed to the lifeboat station and managed to get a lifeboat afloat. We drifted for about three hours before being picked up."* Thomas T. Richards was a passenger. *"I came to work in Ireland in 1916 for the Western Union Cable Company in Valentia, Co. Kerry. I was on deck when the torpedo struck. I took off most of my clothes, put my money in my hip pocket and dived over the side. I must have been swimming in the water for about two and a half or three hours before I was picked up."*

Labour T.D. (member of parliament) Seán Dunne sometimes wrote articles for the English newspaper *The Sunday Express*. In December 1963 the paper published an article on the *Leinster* sinking by *"Seán Dunne T.D. in association with Raymond Foxall."* On 9 December 1964 Daniel Nolan of *The Kerryman* newspaper wrote to Dunne about a book the newspaper were considering publishing for him. The letter mentioned in passing that Dunne was considering a book about the *Leinster* sinking.[36] However, the book had not been published by the time Dunne died in 1969.

British merchant ships during World War 1 were insured by the British Government under a war risk policy. The CDSPCo were eventually compensated for the loss of the *Leinster*. The British government then became owners of the wreck. Eventually Sydney Wignal bought the wreck. He later sold it to Des Brannigan.[37] In 1991, on behalf of Des Brannigan, divers Noel Brien, Fred Hick, Billy Owens and Brian Whelan recovered the *Leinster's* starboard anchor. The anchor was cleaned up and placed near the Carlisle Pier, from where the *Leinster* had set out on her final journey. On 29 January 1996 the anchor, with a plaque commemorating the 501 who died, was formally dedicated by the Minister of State for the Marine Eamon Gilmore T.D. The ceremony was attended by a large group of people. To coincide with the dedication ceremony, a commemorative leaflet was produced in memory of the postal workers who died.[38]

William Byrne is the great-grandson of *Leinster* survivor Chief Fireman (Stoker) John Donohoe. In childhood William was told the story of the sinking of the *Leinster*. As he got older he couldn't understand why the tragedy of the sinking wasn't better known. He decided that something had to be done to further lift the fog of amnesia that had been partly cleared by the dedication of the *Leinster* anchor. In October 1998, on the eightieth anniversary of the sinking, he and *Leinster* wreck owner Des Brannigan arranged to have a commemorative mass said in St. Michael's Church in Dún Laoghaire, followed by a wreath laying ceremony at the *Leinster* anchor. William was subsequently interviewed on a number of radio and television programmes. Also in 1998, the first book about the sinking was published. *"Death in the Irish Sea: The sinking of the R.M.S. Leinster"* by Roy Stokes places the sinking in the context of the First World War and Ireland's part in the war. There is a detailed account of events surrounding the sinking and of the subsequent press coverage. The book also raises a number of questions about the circumstances of the sinking.

On 10 October 2001 the 82nd anniversary of the sinking was marked by a memorial service at the recovered *Leinster* anchor. The service was organised by William Byrne and myself. The event was marked by poetry and music. William Byrne sang Patrick Doyle's 1946 song *The Mail Boat Leinster*. Members of the crowd read out a representative sample of twenty names of those who died in the sinking. Roger Imes, grandnephew of Corporal John Williams, Royal Defence Corps, travelled over from Wales with his girlfriend Anthea Cull especially for the ceremony.

The destroyer *H.M.S. Mallard*, commanded by Lieutenant Roland Lloyd R.N.R, rescued some of the survivors from the *Leinster* sinking. On 24 February 2002, Tamsin Bunnay, great-granddaughter of Roland Lloyd, visited the Maritime Museum in Dún Laoghaire. There, in front of the museum's model of the *R.M.S. Leinster*, she met with Anne O'Bróin (granddaughter of *Leinster* passenger Michael Joyce M.P.), William Byrne (great-grandson of *Leinster* Chief Fireman John Donohoe), Des McCloskey (grandson of Private James Ratcliffe, Royal Army Medical Corps), Roy Stokes (author of *Death in the Irish Sea*) and myself. By chance, also in the museum at the time was Des Brannigan, owner of the *Leinster* wreck. As far as is known, it was the largest gathering of people with *Leinster* connections since Tom Connolly's reunion of *Leinster* survivors on 10 October 1968.

While researching this book I became determined that the sinking should, for the first time ever, be jointly marked in the towns of Dún Laoghaire and Holyhead and settled on the 85th anniversary as the year in which it should occur. Father Patrick J. Mangan PP enthusiastically agreed to hold a commemorative service in St. Michael's Church, Dún Laoghaire and through the structures of the Holyhead-Dún Laoghaire Link Organisation *Friends of the Leinster* committees were established in Holyhead (chaired by John Cave) and in Dún Laoghaire (chaired by myself).

Shortly before 9 a.m. on the morning of Friday 10 October 2003 the Irish naval vessel *L.E. Aoife* left Dún Laoghaire harbour under the command of Lieutenant-Commander Peter Twomey. On board were members of the media, relatives of those who sailed on the *Leinster's* final voyage, John Moore, *Friends of the Leinster* committee member, Father Seán Cassidy and myself. Just before 10 a.m., following a course plotted by Lieutenant Martin Tarrant, the *Aoife* approached the site of the *Leinster* wreck. Just then four RAF Hawk jets, from Valley, Anglesey, flew overhead in tribute to those who died in the greatest ever loss of life in the Irish Sea. They were flown by Lieutenant-Commander Jamie Harms RN (Formation Leader), Flight Lieutenant Nick Foster, Flight Lieutenant Rich Homer and Flight Lieutenant John McCullagh. It truly was an historic occasion, being the first time ever that the RAF and the Irish Naval Service took part in a joint commemoration. The jets then flew low over the incoming ferry from Holyhead with its large contingent travelling to Dún Laoghaire's commemorative services.

On board the *Aoife* Pauline Farrell had come to remember her grandfather, Postal Sorter Adam Smyth and Marilynn Hearn was there with her husband John to commemorate her grand uncle, army doctor Lieutenant Robert Bassett. Jim Honan had travelled all the way from Canada to remember his grandfather James Honan of the Royal Defence Corps. With him was his brother-in-law Liam Lundon. Frank Coffey had come to remember his aunt, Chief Stewardess Mary Coffey, who survived the sinking. Billy Byrne was there with his wife Phyllis and son William (Secretary of *The Friends of the Leinster*), to remember his grandfather Chief Stoker John Donohoe, who also survived the sinking. The Dún Laoghaire Lifeboat *Anna Livia* was already at the site of the *Leinster* wreck. On board were Honorary Secretary RNLI Dún Laoghaire Lifeboat Stephen Wynne, Coxwain Ken Robertson, Mechanic Kieran O'Connell and crewmen David Branigan, Wayne Farrell and Stuart Kane.

The group on board the *Aoife* assembled on the bow of the ship. Lieutenant-Commander Peter Twomey stood at attention with some of his officers and crew. I gave a short address on why we were there, concluding by quoting President Mary McAleese's words at Messines, Belgium on 11 November 1998: *"In this generation we redeem their memory, acknowledging their service and the pain of those who loved them."* Father Seán Cassidy led us in prayers from a booklet he had specially printed for the occasion. William Byrne and I then cast a wreath into the sea, followed by a wreath from the men on the *Anna Livia*. Having paid an historic tribute to those who died on the *Leinster*, the *Aoife* and the *Anna Livia* returned to Dún Laoghaire.

As I walked into St Michael's Church in Dún Laoghaire I was overcome by a wave of emotion on seeing all of the people who had come to remember the greatest ever loss of life on the Irish Sea. The No 1 Army Band was playing *Gabriel's Obo*. Among the congregation were relatives of those who were on the *Leinster's* final voyage, committee members of *The Friends of the Leinster* from Dún Laoghaire and Holyhead, nuns and nurses from St Michael's Hospital, Dún Laoghaire (where some of the injured from the *Leinster* had been treated), local *Gardaí* (police), including Inspector Tom Lundon and Garda Cian Long, who both professionally and personally contributed so much to make the commemorations a success, the aide-de-camp to An Taoiseach Bertie Ahern TD, the Cathoirleach and members of Dún Laoghaire-Rathdown County Council, Albert Owen MP for North Wales, postal workers from Belfast, Dublin and Holyhead, teachers and school children from St. Joseph's National School, the Dominican Convent, St. Nicholas Montessori School, St Kilian's German School and the Park School Holyhead, Lieutenant-Commander Peter Twomey and crew from the *Aoife*, the mayor and members of Holyhead Town Council, local TDs, retired members of the Royal Welch Fusiliers, diplomatic representatives from Australia, New Zealand, Canada, Great Britain and the United States. Also there were members from the Dún Laoghaire Borough Historical Society, the Genealogical Society of Ireland and the Royal Dublin Fusiliers Association. With members of the Reserve Army and Naval Defence Forces providing a colour party at the altar, Rev. Father Patrick J. Mangan PP, the earliest supporter of *The Friends of the Leinster*, gave a very moving eulogy for those who died on the *Leinster* and submarine UB-123. He then led an inter-church prayer service with Rev. Canon John Nice from St Cybi's Church Holyhead, Rev. Canon Victor Stacy, Rev. Derek Poole and Pastor Chris Hudson. The service included William Byrne performing *The Mail Boat Leinster*. The song, sung by Patrick Doyle and written down by Father Joe Ranson in 1946, is now available to a new generation of listeners. Among the most moving parts of the service was a reading by local school children of a random sample of names of people who died on the *Leinster* and by children from St. Kilian's German School reading names of some of the crew of UB-123.

At the conclusion of the prayer service the congregation paraded to the *Leinster* anchor near the Carlisle Pier. There, following addresses by Councillor Denis O'Callaghan (former postal worker) and Albert Owen MP (former merchant seaman), wreaths were laid at the anchor. *Leinster* relatives then attended a reception at the County Hall, hosted by *The Friends of the Leinster* with the support of generous sponsors. At the reception RTE's (Irish television and radio) Marine Correspondent Tom McSweeney launched a commemorative booklet. He later interviewed a number of people for his radio programme *Seascapes*. At 6.45 p.m. a plaque was unveiled by *An Post* (the Irish Post Office) at Dún Laoghaire Post Office in memory of the postal workers who were lost on the *Leinster*. Present for the unveiling were relatives of postal workers who died, my wife Kate and myself. I had researched the names of the postal workers and had proposed the erection of the plaque. Holyhead members of *The Friends of the Leinster*

111

and William Byrne, Secretary of the Dún Laoghaire Committee also attended.

On Sunday 12 October 2003 St Cybi's Church in Holyhead was packed for a commemorative service conducted by Rev. Canon John Nice. Many people from Dún Laoghaire and Dublin travelled over for the service. Lessons were read by Air Commodore M.J. Milligan C.B.E. RAF (retd.) and Major Stephen B. Hunt, Royal Welch Fusiliers (Retd). The latter was also a very hardworking member of the Holyhead branch of *The Friends of the Leinster*. A choir from The Park School sang at the service, as did a combined choir from St Joseph's School/The Dominican Convent School and St Nicholas Montessori School Dún Laoghaire. Monsignor Thomas Fehily represented Father Patrick J. Managan PP at the service and William Byrne performed the haunting ballad *The Mail Boat Leinster*. Afterwards wreaths were laid at Holyhead's cenotaph in memory of those who died on the *Leinster* and a reception was held for those who attended the services.

Diver Noel Brien, one of the team who recovered the starboard anchor of the *R.M.S. Leinster,* composed the following poem for the commemorations.

Leinster

Ascended from a dark watery grave
Where time seems to have stood still,
To gaze once more upon a heavenly sky
Where the stars still shine at will,
To feel again the soft gentle sea breeze
And the softness of the morning mist,
To watch the seagulls soar on high
Through heavenly bliss and yet,
Sadly this world was not for them
For they were victims of a warring past.

Jeff Evans, Joint Chairperson of the Holyhead-Dún Laoghaire Link Organisation, composed and recited the following poem at both commemorative services.

R.M.S. Leinster

Thursday 10th October 1918 and the end of World War One was nigh,
And of 771 passengers aboard the RMS Leinster, 501 were today to die.
At the end of that fateful day, as the true horror of the tragedy unfurled,
We learned of the loss of crew, of military personnel from around the world.

From Ireland, Wales, Scotland, England, New Zealand, Australia,
America and Canada,
For in World Wars our men and women bravely came from so near and far.
This was the greatest ever loss of life in the Irish Sea, and there is no denying,
A terrible waste of life, children, mothers, families left distraught and crying.

The Leinster had been hit, struck by torpedoes, and not just one but two,
A German submarine UB-123, its torpedoes fired so accurately and true.
We do not look back in anger, for the young German crew there is no shame,
For in War, troops fight in the belief and orders, and attributed can be no blame.

Later, returning home, the German submarine struck a mine in the North Sea,
The 35 crew were killed, now just memories, for family and German history.
The RAF, Royal Welch Fusiliers, Navy, Army, the forces lost fine young men,
And in Josephine Carr from Cork, on active service was lost the first WREN.

Who could have foreseen, sailing from Kingstown Dún Laoghaire to Holyhead,
That so many civilians, postal workers and crew, would also be injured or dead.
Now hands extended via the Holyhead and Dún Laoghaire Link, across the Irish Sea,
Result in "Friends of the Leinster" holding a memorial service, to their memory.

The commemoration not to just the 501, many still in their watery graves,
But also to honour those who assisted the survivors, ensuring that 270 were saved.
In St. Michael's & St. Cybi's the congregation will hear the peal
of the church bells ring,
And hear the pupils of St Joseph's Dún Laoghaire and Park School, Holyhead sing.

We will never forget our forefathers who perished in war, on land, in air or at sea,
For it is they who ensured we are here today, living in peace, freedom and liberty.

God Rest Their Souls.

Exactly one month later, on 10 November 2004, a commemorative plaque was unveiled at The Park School Holyhead (Ysgol Parc, Caer Gybi) in memory of a former teacher and former pupils from the school who were lost on the *Leinster*. The plaque was erected following representations by

John Cave, Chairperson of the Holyhead committee of *The Friends of the Leinster*.

As this book goes to print a team of divers are working on another *Leinster* project, conceived by the dedicated and hard working Holyhead Historian John Cave. The divers are searching for the second anchor of the *R.M.S. Leinster*, with the objective of placing it as a memorial in Holyhead. Des Brannigan, owner of the *Leinster* wreck has given the project his wholehearted blessing. Hopefully the project will be successful and those who died on the *R.M.S. Leinster* will be commemorated on both sides of the Irish Sea.

*

At last the *Leinster* tragedy is beginning to be remembered. It's as if, after all this time, the ship has begun to force parts of her story to the surface of the sea of forgetfulness in which history has buried her. Hopefully, this book will be another step in restoring the tragedy to memory. Hopefully too, Ireland will soon remember her sons and daughters who lost their lives in the country's greatest maritime disaster. When she does remember, then Ireland can address the relatives of those from Britain, Australia, New Zealand, Canada and the United States who died in the sinking. She can speak by borrowing from the beautiful words of Turkish Prime Minister Kemal Ataturk, after the end of the First World War. Addressing the people of the former Allied countries, who had suffered huge casualties while attempting to invade his country during the war, he said: *"You the mothers who sent their sons from far away countries wipe away your tears. Your sons are now lying in our bosom and are in peace. After having lost their lives on this land they have become our sons as well."*

Captain William Birch[39]

William Birch was born in 1857, the second son of Edwin Birch, Woollen Merchant and Eliza (née Worn) of 1-3 Molesworth Street, Dublin. Like many ship's officers of the early twentieth century, he began his seafaring career in sailing ships. Among the ships on which he served were the *Singapore* and the coastal steamer *May Pocha* (Pacific Navigation Company). He received his mate's ticket at the age of twenty-four and served as mate on the *Emulation*, the *Valencia* and the *Iran*. After he married, he decided to serve in home waters. He started work with the CDSPCo on 11 September 1902; three days after the *Leinster* sank the Kish Bank lightship *Albatross*. He soon rose to the rank of Captain on the company's Dublin-Liverpool route. From there he moved to the Kingstown-Holyhead route. Eventually becoming the senior captain on the CDSPCo mail boats, he held the honorary rank of Commodore. He settled in Holyhead. He, his wife Louisa and family lived at *The Sycamores* on Gors Avenue, off South Stack Road.

In his youth Birch had a keen interest in shark fishing. On one occasion he caught a shark when he was fishing from a ship off the west coast of America. The line broke and the shark swam off. Birch jumped into one of the ship's boats and chased the shark until he regained the end of the line. He managed to tow the shark for some distance. Unable to get back to his ship, he refused to give up his catch. His crewmates brought the ship around and returned to pick him up. He got his crewmates to pass him a harpoon. He killed the shark and had it hoisted on to the ship.

During the First World War a captured German submarine captain was brought on board the *Leinster* for transportation to a prisoner-of-war camp in England. Birch later spotted him walking on deck. He called Assistant Purser Bill Sweeney. *"Is that a German submarine commander I see walking around my deck?"* asked Birch. *"Yes"* answered Sweeney. Birch said: *"Go down and tell his escort I want him locked up."* Sweeney found the escorting officer drinking a whiskey in the smoking room. He conveyed Birch's order. The escort replied: *"Nonsense old boy! He's an officer."* Sweeney returned to Birch and told him. Birch said *"Go back down and tell him that if he doesn't lock him up, I'll lock the two of them up!"* Years later a newspaper ran a series of interviews with German submarine commanders. One told how a young army officer took him from Ireland to Britain. While crossing the Irish Sea his escort allowed him to walk around the deck of the ship. Suddenly he was taken below and locked up. He said that he was very nervous during the rest of the trip.

The editor of *Lady of the House* magazine was in Holyhead during the First World War. He was surprised to see the *Leinster* arrive escorted by an American destroyer. He had often crossed by the mail steamer and had never before seen it under escort. As the *Leinster* came into the harbour she passed a minesweeper carrying crewmen from an oil tanker torpedoed just outside Holyhead. The editor travelled on the *Leinster* for the return journey. Despite the obvious danger, the ship was not escorted. The editor spoke with Captain Birch, who pointed to an outgoing Atlantic liner, with seven or eight escorts. The editor asked how such a level of escort could be provided for the other ship, while none was provided for the *Leinster*. *"Ah"* said Birch. *"We are only an Irish Steamer."*

In his book *Airship Pilot No. 28*, Captain T.B. Williams said that during the First World War he flew airships from Anglesey on patrol over the Irish Sea. *"Captain Birch and I had become friends as we were on and over the Irish Sea so often together. I took him for a flight in* (Airship) *SSZ-35 on the 1st June* (1918), *and he arranged with the Triplex Company, of which he was a shareholder, to send me some flying goggles, which I still have."* (Williams's book was published in 1974).[40]

Blown off the bridge of the *Leinster*, Birch was picked up by the *Big Bertha* lifeboat, but was lost when the boat overturned. His body was never recovered. He is commemorated on the memorial to merchant seamen at Tower Hill, London. His home, on Gors Avenue, Holyhead is still called *The Sycamores*. Bill Sweeney described Captain Birch as *"a very silent type."* His silence concealed at least two secrets. After Birch's death, his wife Louisa contested a will that he had drawn up at their home in Holyhead on 14 December 1917. Newspaper accounts of Louisa Birch's legal challenge reported that while the will left *"certain portions of his property"* to his wife and family, it also bequeathed stocks and shares to *"a Miss Caroline Barnard, who was a friend but no relative of his."* Any doubts as to the nature of the friendship were removed by the fact that William Birch left the residue of his assets to Caroline Barnard of Monkstown, Co. Dublin in trust *"for his son Charles."*[41]

"Disclosed after 50 years: Arms for Ulster Volunteers came through Dublin" was the headline of a front-page article in *The Irish Times* of 31 July 1964. The report said that Mr Knollys Stokes had contacted the paper's editor following the publication of an anniversary article on the landing of guns for the Irish Volunteers at Howth, Co. Dublin in July 1914.[42] Stokes (61), of Summerlodge, Wellington Road, Cork told the editor that he was surprised that historians of the period had never mentioned the landing of arms for the Ulster Volunteer Force (UVF) at Kingstown, also in July 1914. He said that the weapons *"were carried over on the mail boat and Captain Burchill* (sic), *who was afterwards torpedoed in the Leinster saw to their discreet landing."* Stokes said that the guns were stored in his family home at 14 Brighton Vale,

Monkstown, Co. Dublin by his father Frank. He said that he was aged ten at the time of the event. While he did not know how the weapons were carried to the house, he said that there were 600 rifles and 300 pistols that had been brought from Germany. He named Sir Simon Maddock and Solicitor William Vernon Sedall as having been involved in the gunrunning with his father. His sister Miss Ruby Stokes of Donnybrook, Dublin, supported Stokes's story. She said *"While I never saw the guns, I knew that they were in our house. My mother used to tell me to keep away from the place where they were hidden and to keep quiet."*

The Irish Times interviewed Historian Dr Hayes McCoy and Mr G.G. Duggan, who had been an official at Dublin Castle in 1914. Both said that while a few weapons may have been smuggled in, they doubted the numbers cited by Mr Stokes. *The Irish Times* said that Mr Stokes was *"a man of many interests. He is one of the greatest experts in the country on antique clocks. His knowledge is not merely theoretical, as he is able to manufacture missing parts for many time-pieces and make them go again. In his lifetime he has made a study of old Cork glass and of silver and his expert knowledge of them is recognised by museum authorities and others. To those who follow the vintage car races, Mr Stokes is a well known figure. He has a considerable number of old models and has competed in some of the veteran car races."* All in all, with an interest in things requiring precision, Mr Stokes sounds like he would have been a good witness. Another point in his favour was the fact that he had absolutely nothing to gain – and possibly something to lose – in the Ireland of 1964, from a claim that his father had run guns for the UVF in 1914.

So was Captain William Birch running guns for the UVF? It is beyond doubt that *"Captain Burchill, who was afterwards torpedoed in the Leinster"* was William Birch, as the other captains on the route were named Newton, Penston and Thompson. If Birch did smuggle guns, they were not carried on the *Leinster*, as the ship was commanded by Captain Robert Newton in 1914. During 1914 William Birch commanded the *Munster*.

First Officer Patrick Crangle

Patrick Crangle was born in 1877, the youngest of five children and the only boy born to Patrick and Catherine Crangle of Killough, Co. Down. The senior Patrick was captain and owner of the sailing ship *Amaranth* (1,248 gross tons). On 11 April 1890 the vessel left Belfast bound for Quebec. Two months later, on 9 June, following an accident on board the *Amaranth*, Captain Crangle was taken ashore at Quebec. He died the following day and was buried in locally.[43] His father's death didn't deter Patrick junior from going to sea. He served his time on the brigantine *Cave Hill*, from which he was shipwrecked. He later joined the CDSPCo. In 1915 or 1916 he married Anne Clancy from Kingstown.[44] Patrick and Anne had two boys, Patrick Gerard and Frank. The family lived at *Cosy Nook*, 4 Summerhill, Sandycove, Kingstown. Bill Sweeney said that: *"Crangle was decent. You could talk to him."*

On 10 October 1918 Patrick Crangle was first officer on the *R.M.S. Leinster*. By then he had served with the CDSPCo for approximately 23 years. He survived the sinking but both his legs were injured. The next day, from his home, he sent a report to Edward Watson, managing director of the CDSPCo.

Copy

> *"Cosy Nook",*
> *Summerhill,*
> *Kingstown.*

> *11th October 1918.*

Sir,

> *S.S. "Leinster."*

I beg to report as First Officer of above that we left Kingstown in the usual course at 8.53 a.m. on the 10th inst., and were abreast of the Kish Lightship at 9.23. Captain Birch and Mr. Addison were on the bridge. I was in my cabin making up the pay sheets.

I heard an explosion about 9.50 and immediately rushed on the forward boat deck. The ship at this time was settling by the head. The boats were being got out by Captain Birch's orders and I proceeded to have the starboard forward boat out and lowered her level with the deck. The Captain said that he would see to these boats and ordered me to look to the boats aft.

The passengers had gathered round the boat deck and I assured them that the ship would not sink, as I observed she had stopped settling.

I managed to get the two starboard boats on the after boat deck out and lowered away filled with passengers. Whilst lowering the small aft boat on the starboard side, the ship was struck by a second torpedo and immediately afterwards she settled rapidly and all persons including myself, on the boat deck were thrown into the water. I was, with difficulty, hauled into one of the midships boats by Seaman Lacey. (This was Seaman John Lacey, a native of Wexford.) *This boat had been cast adrift and floated off with rafts and other gear. We subsequently hauled on board several ladies, the total complement in the boat being about 25 persons.*

The last time I saw Captain Birch he was with others clinging to the bow of one of the large boats, about this time the ship was stern in the air, propellers clear of the water. I may mention that my watch stopped at 9.55.

As far as I can gauge, we were picked up after an interval of about two hours and with about one hundred survivors landed at Victoria Wharf by Destroyer D.55 (H.M.S. Lively).

I am at present confined to bed and under the care of Dr Merrin, Kingstown., whose certificate I have already forwarded.[45]

I am,
Sir,
Your obedient servant.

E. Watson Esqr.

Patrick Crangle's eldest son, Gerard, holds the letter quoted. It is a copy and does not have his father's signature. Not mentioned in the report is the fact that, despite injuries to both his legs, First Officer Crangle gave up his place in the lifeboat so that a woman could be taken on board. Patrick Crangle died on 8 August 1925. He was only 48 years old. The injuries he sustained in the sinking had probably shortened his life. He is buried in Deansgrange Cemetery, Co. Dublin.

Assistant Purser William Sweeney

Bill Sweeney was born on 27 April 1897, two months to the day after the *Leinster* made her trial voyage.[46] At the time of his birth, his family lived at 60 St. Albans Road, off South Circular Road, Dublin. Sweeney was educated at Rathmines National School and Synge Street School, Dublin. His father worked for the CDSPCo for forty years. In 1912, as was the custom in the company, Sweeney was offered employment with the CDSPCo when his father died. He started as a junior clerk at 6/- per week at the company's office at the North Wall, Dublin. In 1916 he was transferred to the *R.M.S. Leinster* under the command of Captain William Birch. He became Assistant Purser on the ship. Shortly before his death in 1979, he was interviewed by Declan Whelan on tape. The following is based on his account of the sinking of the *Leinster*.

On 10 October 1918 Assistant Purser Bill Sweeney (21) was on deck after the *Leinster* left Kingstown. *"There was a bit of a swell, but you wouldn't say it was dirty weather."* He spoke with passenger Arthur Adshead, Irish agent for the Midland Railway Company. Adshead pointed to a faraway ship and asked if it was the incoming mail boat. Sweeney confirmed that it was the *Ulster* coming from Holyhead. *"Sometimes they were very close together when they passed each other in the morning. But I had never seen the other boat so far north. She seemed to be hugging the coastline at Howth"* (on the north side of Dublin Bay). Sweeney later spoke with Officers Steward Michael Loughlin, before going to the saloon. He was on the port side of the ship, in the corridor between the saloon and the ladies cabins. Stewardess Louisa Parry called to him: *"Wait a minute Bill, I'll give you your watch back."* He had lent it to her the previous evening. Sweeney said: *"I'll be back in a second, I've a call to make."* He had only gone a few yards when he *" heard this almighty crash and a shattering of glass. I looked into the saloon just before I went upstairs and the whole mantelpiece above the fireplace was fallen down. I didn't know what it was. I got up on deck.* (Harry) *Addison, the Second Mate, shouted to me 'We've been torpedoed!' He'd been torpedoed in the 'Connaught,' the sister ship of this one in the English Channel. I went up to* (First Officer Patrick) *Crangle's room. He always kept a lifebelt under his chair. But there wasn't any there. Someone had got there before me. I wasn't going to go down to my room to look for one. There were no VC s in our family. But Old Birch called me up and told me to go down and get his confidential papers out of the chart room. When I got down, the ship's adjutant, a fellow called Parker, was already there. I said ' What are you doing?' 'I'm getting the codes. They're supposed to be thrown over the side if anything happens.' 'Well' I said: 'You'd better carry on. Bring them up to him.' He brought them up and I don't know where he went* (then). *I went up to Birch. We tied them* (the codes) *up and dumped them over the side.*

There was a small lifeboat under the bridge on the starboard side. Birch said: 'Get that boat down in the water!' And I, a bloody clerk! I called lamp trimmer (Robert) *Anthony and we put her in the water beautifully. Just as I was going to slide down into her, Old Birch called me again. 'Go down and get that accommodation ladder out.' The bloody thing was lashed to the side. I called to* (Fireman Percy) *Lamble 'Have you got a knife?' He was pulling up his little monkey jacket and the next thing she got the second one"* (i.e. the second torpedo struck). *'Says I 'To hell!' I looked up and saw the foremast crashing down and the fore funnel ripped out, as if by a fellow in a temper. I couldn't wait any longer. I slid over the side. It was quite easy, because she had a good list to port. I slid down and stepped into this lifeboat. We called her 'Big Bertha'. She was certified to carry fifty-two souls. That was stamped into one of the seats.*

As Sweeney stepped into the lifeboat he saw that both the bow and stern were still tied to the *Leinster.* "*She was bobbing down with the big ship pulling her down.* (Greaser Philip) *Connolly loaned me the big tobacco knife he was carrying. I slashed all the lines and she bobbed up nicely. There was a naval commander on board.* (This was Commander Baggott of the Royal Navy, who was based at Kingstown). *When he saw me in uniform he said ' Are you in charge of this boat?' I said: ' No. You are!' Our lifeboat, I suppose, drifted around the stern and at this time she* (Leinster) *was nearly gone. Quite a lot of young Tommies were sitting on the rail and I was shouting at them to 'Jump!' and signalling to them to jump, because it was the only chance they had of getting hold of something. But they just sat there.*

The mail boats had a very nice crest on the stern. It wasn't just a plain 'R.M.S. Leinster,' it was more like a scroll, a coloured thing. And then you had these lovely bronze propellers. There was a little bit of light from somewhere and it caught them with a shaft of sunlight. Anyway, she finally went under with this hissing sound. The air whistled through the propeller shafts I'd imagine. I was only a young lad. I loved ships and I loved the old 'Leinster'. I'd been in her so long. (I felt) *a sense of loss. You had lost something, an old friend. Ah, it was a great sadness for me. But when I looked back on it afterwards, I suppose it was a proud way for her to leave the stage.*

I couldn't get this soldier from Northumberland into the boat. I put a line under his arm pits. And didn't I tie it around my own thigh!. Every time he bobbed down, my thigh was struck. I was black and blue. He was o.k. (He was saved). *In the lifeboat with me were* (Cabin boy Tom) *Connolly and his father* (Greaser Philip Connolly), *the rest were passengers.* (Tom) *Connolly was only a kid. He was wearing a short white jacket. He was frozen. I kept him between my knees to keep him warm.* Some of those in the lifeboat spotted Captain Birch, in the sea. Sweeney shouted at the passengers to get Birch into the boat and he was partially pulled on board. We were in the lifeboat for over two hours before the destroyers came. *It wasn't easy to bail out. I bailed from my cap into a pail and then over the side. The lifeboat was packed at this time. There were over seventy in her when the destroyer 'H.M.S. Lively' came along.* (Philip) *Connolly lifted his son up from the lifeboat. He didn't bother with ropes or lines. He put his two hands on the boy's hips and raised him up until a bluejacket* (Royal Navy sailor) *caught him. As calm as going up in a lift.*

Commander Baggot told Sweeney that *H.M.S. Lively* would throw a line and asked if he would take it. Sweeney said that he would make it fast to a ring in the back of the lifeboat. The Commander told an American sailor to do the same near the front of the boat. *"The destroyer threw out every line they had. Everyone in the lifeboat made a grab for one, thinking 'That's mine.' The boat keeled over and that's how Captain Birch was lost."* Sweeney was among those rescued from the sea. He saw Officers Steward Michael Loughlin on board *H.M.S. Lively.* Loughlin had been flung to the deck when one of the torpedoes struck. His head and face had been badly injured. Sweeney found First Officer Crangle and Second Officer Addison at the stern of the destroyer. Crangle asked after Captain Birch. *"Where is the old man?"* he inquired. *"I'm afraid we've lost him"* replied Sweeney. *"The 'Lively' landed us at Queen Victoria wharf in Kingstown. The place was full of Red cross and Salvation Army."*

Chief Steward Llewellyn Lewis

Llewellyn Lewis (38). Born Holyhead. Brother of William John Lewis, who was travelling as a passenger. Brother-in-law of Acting Chief Engineer William Mathias. Left the following unsigned account of the sinking on CDSPCo headed paper.[47]

Holyhead. 30th January 1919

On the morning of the 10th October 1918 when the "Leinster" was about an hour out of Kingstown., everything was being carried on as usual in the cabin, breakfast about finished and dining saloon cleared. I was standing at the saloon entrance talking to my brother Mr. W. J. Lewis (William John Lewis, CDSPCo Superintendent Steward at Holyhead) *when I heard a crash which I realized to be a torpedo. I immediately brought off my passengers, and issued life-jackets to all at hand. Mr W. J. Lewis assisted me as far as No 20 cabin, then he asked me for a life belt which I helped him fasten on himself, he then went up on deck. I continued clearing the cabin. Owing to the rush of people going up the after companion I was unable to reach the Ladies Cabin. I returned to my room when I saw Thomas Doyle the luggage guard* (for the London North Western Railway) *badly injured about the face seeking a life jacket. I eventually found him one and followed him up on deck to report to Captain Birch that all was clear down below. On my way I met Mr Parker the Adjutant* (Second Lieutenant Hugh Parker, Captain Birch's liaison officer with the military on the ship) *who also was seeking a life jacket. I opened (with a skeleton key) one of the Directors cabins and brought out two jackets. I handed Mr Parker one and held the other in my hand. My attention was drawn to a one legged officer and I immediately transferred through another officer the belt to him, as I was anxious to reach the Captain. A lady now clung frantically to me and further impeded my progress. At last I managed to shout to the Captain that all was clear down stairs. He did not answer, but on second calling the 2nd mate* (Harry Addison, who was on the bridge with Captain Birch) *answered "all right." Then the whistle sounded. With the lady still clinging to me we both went over the rail and fell on to the rubber. I managed to get her in to the port side life boat which had already been launched, I then got a fireman and a letter sorter into the boat* (This is puzzling as a newspaper reported that sole surviving Postal Worker John Higgins was in a different lifeboat) *and then got in myself. The 2nd mate in charge of the boat* (i.e. Harry Addison) *ordered me to cast away. Immediately after this the second torpedo was fired and the ship disappeared in a few minutes, bow first. I noticed three other boats afloat and several rafts with people clinging to them. Our boat was able to rescue one lady and four men off a raft, a dangerous and difficult task in such a sea. The boat, now riding at sea anchor, awaited rescue. A destroyer appeared in about an hour's time a long distance off and was soon on the spot. Their first attention was given to those on rafts and wreckage. Meanwhile other rescue ships were busy and after about three hours we were picked up and safely on board the destroyer H.M.S. Lively and landed at Kingstown."*

Under Steward (Cabin Boy) Thomas Connolly

Tom Connolly, Tivoli Terrace, Kingstown. Son of Christina and Greaser Philip Connolly.

The CDSPCo employed twelve cabin boys on the Kingstown to Holyhead route. All were between 16 and 19 years old. At the time of the sinking Connolly had only been employed by the company for a few months.[48] He told a newspaper reporter that *"Breakfast was being served when the first torpedo struck the ship at about 9.50 a.m. Three torpedoes were fired at her, the first one missing."* On the 50th anniversary of the sinking he told another reporter what had happened to him on that fatal day.[49] Unfortunately, some confusion is created by the report interspersing Connolly's verbatim account with references to him in the third person. *"It was 10 a.m. on the morning of October 10, 1918. The s.s. Leinster was just off the Kish lightship on her way to England with troops and some passengers. A 16-year-old boy was making his way into the saloon to begin work there when the ship shivered and shook to begin a nightmare four hours for the boy, Tom Connolly. They had been torpedoed by a German U-boat and the boy knew what to do."* The report then quotes Connolly: *"The whole ship seemed to open from end to end and close again. The first torpedo went in through the post office sorting office on board the ship, and she began to sink quickly. I ran to number 8 lifeboat station and my father* (Philip Connolly), *who was a greaser was also there at the same station. There was general panic as we began to get the women and children into the lifeboat."* The report continues: *"The ship was sinking, bows first, and her propellers were high in the air. As the lifeboat was being lowered, Mr Connolly jumped overboard and missed the boat. His father managed to free the lifeboat from the ship and it began to drift out from the stricken vessel."*
Unfortunately the newspaper does not explain why, having arrived at the lifeboat station before the lifeboat was launched, and his father having got on board, Connolly found it necessary to jump overboard in order to catch the lifeboat. On a minor point, there is a disagreement between the newspaper's comment that Philip Connolly (46) *"managed to free the lifeboat from the ship,"* with Bill Sweeney's statement: *" Connolly loaned me the big tobacco knife he was carrying. I slashed all the lines and she bobbed up nicely."* The report again quotes Tom Connolly: *"I was in the water with a life jacket on. My father must have never lost sight of me for when the lifeboat came my way, he shouted for me to get in. The Germans sent a second torpedo into the ship and it hit near the stoke hold. The sky rained a shower of hot cylinders on me and I was slightly burned. The injured and panic stricken people in the water screamed. It was terrible."*

"The lifeboat picked up young Tommy Connolly, but he had to sit in it with one leg dangling over the side. It was crammed full and very few of the people knew how to row. They threw the captain, named Birch, a line, but he was lost in the raging gale that was blowing. But it was only the beginning of Tom Connolly's nightmare. He was in a lifeboat crammed mostly with women and children along with his father. They only had two oars out, and they were fighting to keep the boat headed into the wind. About noon, a cargo vessel owned by the London North West Railway Company passed them but it could not stop for fear of being torpedoed. The shouts of joy in the lifeboat faded as quickly as they had risen in the throats of the survivors. 'I thought we would all die' said Tom. The boat was filling with water rapidly and it was almost impossible to bail out the incoming sea. The water was around their knees when they sighted a destroyer approaching. The destroyer circled around the little lifeboat, protecting it from the winds. The sailors on board began to throw lines to the boat. 'My father shouted; "Tom get a rope" as we were floundering in the water. I don't know how long it was, but a big chap with a head of curly hair reached down from the destroyer and hoisted me aboard. I lay exhausted on the deck among injured people. I could only think of my father out there in the sea' Mr Connolly added. "The exhausted boy was lowered down a hatch to receive attention. 'My father had been pulled in and he was lucky enough to have been able to catch a rope. We were reunited on board the destroyer. I'll never forget the name of that ship. It was the Lively-D55.' Said Tom. At about 2 p.m. on October 10, the Lively brought in the last of the survivors. Tom Connolly, and his father, were reunited with his mother (Christina). For her it had been a heart-rending vigil with hundreds of others at the jetty at Dún Laoghaire. In the nearby railway station a temporary morgue held the bodies of the less fortunate." The newspaper doesn't mention that Captain Birch was picked up and was only lost when the rescue ship arrived. It wrongly suggests that he was lost because of a "raging gale that was blowing." It is interesting that the errors and omissions in the article occur at those points where Tom Connolly is not being quoted and the reporter was giving a general account of the sinking.

Captain Birch's crew

On 12 October 1918 the *Irish Times* reported that they had asked the CDSPCo for a crew list for the *Leinster*. The company told them that the list would not be published until every name had been verified and they were not yet in a position to do this. In an undated entry in the *Leinster's* Daily Journal Edward Watson, Managing Director of the CDSPCo recorded the total number (but not the names) of crew and passengers on the ship. He also gave the numbers who survived. Watson recorded that, including the captain; there were 77 crew on the ship, of whom 40 survived. Thus 37 died.

On 16 October 1918 newspapers published the ship's crew list. The reports, however, only give the names of 40 survivors and 36 casualties among the crew, including the captain. As Watson's figures are undated, it is not clear whether Owen Richard Hughes is included among the survivors. Although rescued, he subsequently died of injuries received in the sinking. So my list (including Captain Birch) has 39 survivors and 37 casualties, one less than Watson's number of survivors and equal to his number of casualties. The only explanation I can suggest for the difference is that Watson may have include the ship's military adjutant Second Lieutenant Hugh Parker as one of the crew. I have listed him among the military totals.

Abbreviations:
+ = killed in the sinking. * = mentioned in the main text. B. = birthplace. Where one of the parents are described as "late", this means they were deceased at the time the Commonwealth War Graves Commission records were compiled in the 1920's. Female names followed by address = name and residence of crewman's wife. s. = son of. dau.= daughter of. Tower Hill = Commemorated on memorial near the Tower of London to merchant seamen whose bodies were not recovered. Maeshyfryd Cemetery = Holyhead (Maeshyfryd) Burial Board Cemetery. Where known, locations of graves are given. Ages of survivors calculated from 1918 Crew Agreement Lists.

Addison*
Second Officer Harry J. (38). Certificate number 002685. B. Hastings. On the *Leinster*, in Kingstown harbour during the 1911 census. Records him as aged 30, married, two children. Second officer on the *R.M.S. Connaught* when she was sunk in the English Channel in 1917. Only officer to survive sinking of *Connaught* and *Leinster*.

Anthony +*

Lamp Trimmer Robert (55). Mary, 6 Bath St, Holyhead. Maeshyfryd Cemetery: 2. 1568. His father, also named Robert, served with CDSPCo. Aged 12, Robert junior joined the company as Captain's Boy to Captain Kendall. Years later in Dublin he met Mary Rigelli. From Milan, Italy, Mary's family had moved to Dublin, where they opened a confectionary shop. Robert and Mary married and settled in Holyhead. Bill Sweeney said that Robert Anthony and himself lowered one of the *Leinster's* lifeboats. Unfortunately, Anthony was lost.[50]

Baker

3rd Steward Richard (28), 7 Harcourt St.?? Kingstown. b. Kingstown.

Brennan+

Seaman William John. (35). B. Kingstown. s. Richard & Fanny. Anne (née Kinch), 135 Lower Georges St., Kingstown. Tower Hill.

Brett

3rd Steward N.

Brown*

Fireman John, 2 Sarsfield St., Kingstown. Photograph of Brown (77) in *Dublin Post* 14 October 1960. Then living in Sallynoggin, reported to have survived the sinkings of *Connaught* and *Leinster*.

Carraher*

Boatswain James (36). Per article *Dublin Post* 30 September 1960 Carraher (78), then living at 21 Findlater Street, Glasthule.

Cody+

Fireman Thomas (39). B. Kilkenny. s. Thomas & Bridget (née Curran). Mary (née Malone), 13 Clarinda Park North, Kingstown. Tower Hill.

Coffey*

Chief Stewardess Mary (40), 1 Charlemont Avenue, Kingstown. Employed by CDSPCo for 18 years at time of sinking. Third eldest of nine children, born Co. Kildare 1878. Brother Private James Coffey died Calcutta, India 1901, serving with the Royal Irish Rifles. Brother Sergeant Thomas Coffey, Royal Dublin Fusiliers, killed at Passchendaele August 1917.[51]

Connolly*

Greaser Philip (46), Tivoli Terrace, Kingstown. Husband of Christina. Father of Tom.

Connolly*
Under Steward (Cabin Boy) Tom.

Crangle*
First Officer Patrick. See separate entry.

Crispin+
4th Engineer John David (49). B. Holyhead. Mary Elizabeth (née Evans) 38 Maeshyfryd Road, Holyhead. Tower Hill.

Crowe*
Seaman Lawrence (30). *Dublin Post* 30 September 1960 published his photograph, together with his granddaughters Jacqueline and Rosanna. Said that Crowe (72), then of 2 Northumberland Place, Dún Laoghaire, had been picked up by *H.M.S. Lively.*

Deegan*
3rd Steward Thomas (30). B. Dublin. Gave an interview to a newspaper years later.[52] See account of 1968 reunion dinner.

Donnelly
3rd Steward Thomas (26). B. Dublin.

Donohoe*
Leading Fireman John (43). B. Dublin. Joined CDSPCo upon leaving school.[53] His daughter Madeline remembered that he often took her on board ship for the *"turn around."* CDSPCo ships would dock at Kingstown with Carlisle Pier on their port and their bow pointed towards land. In order for the ships to make their next trip to Holyhead, they needed to do a 180-degree turn, docking on the other side of the pier with their bow pointed seawards. Madeline remembered her father coming home after the sinking. *"He was wearing a tight little jacket and a balaclava. I think two or three men came home with him. There were no buses or taxis in those days, so they walked all the way up from Dún Laoghaire."* But poor Donohoe did not get much rest that night. According to Madeline: *"I was very bad myself that night, because it was the time of the big flu and I was threatened with meningitis. After he came home he had to get up at three o'clock to get a doctor for me."*[54]

Flood*
Second Steward John (42). B. Crooked Wood, Co. Westmeath. Worked as a butler in St Columba's School, Rathfarnham subsequent to the sinking. Spent all his working life in service. Worked as a waiter in *Woodenbridge Hotel*, Co. Wicklow and the *Gresham Hotel*, Dublin. But his most interesting

employment must have been that of butler in the Vice-regal Lodge, home of the Lord Deputy of Ireland, in the Phoenix Park, Dublin. The only one of *Leinster's* three Second Stewards to survive. In the water for a few hours. Picked up from the sea, he was landed in Kingstown. Went home and changed his clothes. He then went to CDSPCo offices, Eden Quay, Dublin and reported for work! [55]

Griffiths
Under Steward (Cabin Boy) William (17). B. Holyhead.

Harvey+
Fireman Michael (24). s. Cornelius & late Julia (née Hobson), 30 Tivoli Terrace East, Kingstown. Next-door neighbour, Greaser James Hickey and Postal Sorter Adam Smyth, 24 Tivoli Terrace East also killed. Tower Hill.

Hickey+
Greaser James (28). B. Kingstown. s. Bridget & late James. Alice (née Kenny), 29 Tivoli Terrace East, Kingstown. Tower Hill.

Horan
3rd Steward Patrick (35). B. Co. Kildare.

Hughes+
Crew's Cook Owen Richard (29). Second s. Owen Thomas & Margaret, 9 Boston St., Holyhead. Maeshyfryd Cemetery: 2. 1570. Had served with the CDSPCo for eight years at the time of the sinking. Survived sinking but severely scalded. Brought to King George V Hospital, Dublin (now St. Bricins), where he died.

Hughes+
3rd Engineer Richard George (36). Certificate number 44051. B. Holyhead. s. Sarah & late Robert. Laura (née Jones), *"East Lynne,"* Rhosygaer Avenue, Holyhead. Tower Hill.

Hynes*
Greaser Christopher (29). Survived sinking of *Connaught* and *Leinster*. *Dublin Post* 14 October 1960 published a photograph of Hynes (living at Begnets Villas, Dalkey) with his grandsons Alan and Brendan.

Inglis+
Second Steward Joseph (41). B. Dublin. s. late Robert & Sarah Ida (née Plant), 7 Newry Fawr St., Holyhead. Captain Birch and he were the only Dublin born crewmen living in Holyhead. Tower Hill.

Jeffries+
Radio Operator Arthur Henry (27). B. Cambridge. s. Richard. Margaret (formerly Torkington, née Smith) and stepson Charlie, Monastir Lodge, Glenageary Road, Kingstown. Buried 15 October Dean's Grange Cemetery, Co. Dublin: SW. T1. 90. Bill Sweeney said that whenever the *Provinces* passed each other the radio operators would give a tap on the key to say *"hello."* "*Paddy Ryan* (Radio Operator on the '*Ulster*')[56] *was telling me a couple of days afterwards that he gave the usual tap on the key and got a reply back, and then immediately, very faintly, he got this 'S.O.S. S.O.S. S.O.S. Torpedoed. Torpedoed. Torpedoed. And the name of the ship.' So Paddy broadcast it. He knew there was something wrong with the Leinster's wireless mast and he broadcast it immediately."* Jeffries died in the sinking. Stepson Charlie died in a shooting accident at Holyhead 1923.[57]

Jones+
Fireman Hugh (45). B. Gaerwen, Anglesey. s. late Hugh & Elizabeth. Jane, 34 Lainfain, Holyhead. Tower Hill.

Jones+
Greaser John (37). B. Holyhead. s. late Evan & Jane. Alice (née Eaton), 41 Teal St., London Road, Holyhead. Tower Hill.

Jones+
Second Steward Owen John (48), 5 Roberts St., Holyhead. b. Holyhead Maeshyfryd Cemetery: 2. 1553.

Jones
Fireman Robert (43). B. Holyhead.

Jones
William Thomas (37), 5th Engineer. b. Caernarvon. *"The Chronicle"* (Holyhead.) 18 October 1918 described Jones as *"fourth engineer."* Other newspapers, the crew agreement list for 1918 and a partial list of survivors and casualties said that he was *"fifth engineer."* "*The Chronicle*": "*Mr Jones, Orton Road, Holyhead, said he was in the stokehold when the vessel was first struck. Realising what had occurred, he instructed the firemen to leave. It was his intention to see to the engine, but suddenly, changing his mind, he followed the firemen, which proved fortunate for him as less than a minute later the vessel was again struck and a terrific explosion followed, which practically wrecked the ship from stem to stern. Mr Jones jumped into the water, and got hold of a raft on which were a number of other persons. After clinging to the raft in the icy cold water for over an hour they were picked up by a destroyer and taken to Kingstown.*"

Kearns*
Fireman Laurence (36). B. Kingstown.

Kehoe+
Seaman Frank (25). B. Wexford. s. Catherine (née Murphy) & late John, 2 Eden Terrace, Kingstown. Family left Wexford when he was young.[58] Very able at mathematics, he sat an examination to become a clerk with Kingstown Corporation. Family tradition says that, though he did well at the examination, he wasn't offered a position due to religious bigotry. As his family had a seafaring background Kehoe became a seaman with CDSPCo. In 1914 his father, John, who worked on a pilot boat out of Dublin, died following illness, aged 49. Frank was 25 when killed on *Leinster*.

Lacey*
Seaman John (32). B. Wexford.

Lamble*
Fireman Percy (30). B. London. Treated in George V Hospital.

Lewis*
Chief Steward Llewellyn. See separate entry.

Lewis
Second Cook Robert James (29). B. Holyhead.

Longmore+
Seaman Henry (32). B. Kingstown. s. Thomas & Margaret. Mary (née Dondall), 50 Convent Road, Kingstown. Tower Hill.

Loughlin+
Seaman John (45). B. Kingstown. s. William & the late Elizabeth. Mary (née Foy), 105 Patrick St., Kingstown. Tower Hill.

Loughlin*
Officers Steward Michael (27). Paradise Row, Kingstown. B. Kingstown.

Loughlin
Seaman Patrick (34), 117 Georges St., Kingstown. B. Kingstown. Brother of Michael Loughlin.

Maher*
Fireman William (33), Desmond Avenue, Kingstown.

Mathias+*
Acting Chief Engineer William (52). Certificate number 29426. B. Holyhead. s. Jane & late John. Elizabeth (née Lewis), 33 Newry St., Holyhead. Brother-in-law to Llewellyn and William John. Lewis. Chief engineer on the *Connaught*, probably on board when she was sunk. As the junior ranking chief engineer, he had to revert to the position of second engineer after *Connaught* was lost. When *Leinster's* chief engineer became ill, he was appointed acting chief engineer. Tower Hill.

Merrigan
Seaman John. From Kingstown.

Michael
Robert (45). Different sources describe him as 2nd or 3rd Engineer. Certificate number 35270. B. Holyhead. He gave a newspaper interview shortly after the sinking.[59] *"We left Kingstown about the usual time, 8.50 a.m., with passengers and mails, and all went well until we had cleared the east side of the Kish, when the Leinster was struck by the first torpedo on the port forward, and almost ripped her, followed a couple of minutes later by the second, which took effect full amidships. Efforts were made after the first attack to lower the boats, but they were not all launched when the second torpedo struck. There were ten boats altogether, in addition to the lifebelts, with which all on board had been supplied soon after leaving. There was a large number of women and children on board. When the attack was made I was in my room, and was knocked unconscious. How long I remained in this condition I do not know, but it was the icy cold water that brought me to, and I then found I was bruised all over, and my right arm was very painful. I struggled to my feet and got clear of the wreckage. How I got on to the deck I do not know, but I managed to do so, and made for my boat, feeling quite dazed. There were some women in our boat, which was full. We noticed two men clinging to a raft some distance away, and they seemed as happy as the day is long, as the saying goes. They did not appear to realize their position. We were drifting about for two hours before we were picked up by a destroyer and taken to Kingstown, where we were attended to with great kindness by the St. John Ambulance and a number of ladies."* Hospitalised after rescue.

Moors+
Engineers Steward Edward Salisbury (48). B. Birkenhead. Mary (née Richards), 9 Edmund St., Holyhead. Tower Hill.

Murphy+
Fireman Bernard (23). B. Kingstown. s. Margaret (née Farren) & late Bernard, 1 Adelaide Cottage, Kingstown. Member of Glasthule Mitchels, G.A.A. Football Club. Tower Hill.

Nicklin+

Third Officer Leslie Benjamin (31). Certificate number 006866. s. Benjamin & late Clara. Athena (née Henri), 6 Park St., Holyhead. Smethwick (Uplands) Cemetery, Staffordshire: 5. NC. A. 314.

O'Connor*

3rd Steward John (19). Magenta Place, Kingstown. B. Kingstown. Told *Irish Independent* reporter that he was at the bottom of the stairs *"in steerage"* when he heard the ship's propeller stop. *"He rushed on deck to see what was wrong, and as he got on top of the stairs the first torpedo entered the vessel. The explosion threw him on his back on the deck. He got up at once, and went below to the first class cabins to look for a lifebelt. As he was at No. 2 cabin, a lady stood at No. 1 and laughed at the rush of passengers. She evidently did not realise the seriousness of the situation. When he secured a lifebelt she asked him how to put one on. He fixed the lifebelt for her, and told her to rush on deck at once. When he returned to the deck he heard the captain shouting orders in a cool voice to lower the boats. He tried to get to the boat decks, but owing to the action of a certain section of the passengers, who scrambled for the boats, he and some others of the crew could not get near them. He heard two of the disorganised passengers trying to restore order, but to no effect. He then went to the boat on the bridge, which the captain ordered them to lower. They succeeded in getting it down to the water without any mishap, and put off with a number of passengers. This was the only boat, he said, which got clear of the vessel. When they reached the water a young married woman in the boat sang to keep up their hearts, and continued to do so right through the whole agonising scene. Just as they got away a second torpedo struck the ship. Funnels, coal, and wreckage were driven into the air, and the vessel crumpled up and sank almost immediately. As she went down two men were clinging to the propeller. When the lifeboat got clear they picked up a lady and two other passengers from a raft. They were taken on a vessel after being two hours in the ship's boat."*

O'Toole+

Fireman Patrick (22). B. Kingstown. s. James & Catherine (née Dent), 26 Stockton St., Middlesbrough, Yorkshire and 1 Summerhill Avenue, Kingstown. Member of Glasthule Mitchels, G.A.A. Football Club. Tower Hill.

Owen*

Seaman Hugh (31).

Owen+*

Second Stewardess Hannah (36). B. Holyhead. dau. William & Mary, 2 Tower Gardens, Holyhead. Maeshyfryd Cemetery: 2. 890. Left school at 14. Stayed with aunt, Blackfriars, London. Subsequently returned home. Went into service with Mrs Forcer Evans at Forcer Hill, Holyhead. Later employed at Mill Road Infirmary, Liverpool, the Home for Incurables, Parliament St, Liverpool and New Highfield Hospital, Knotty Ash. Subsequently employed by CDSPCo. Served on all the *Provinces*. Employed by CDSPCo for 12 years when lost on *Leinster*.

Parry+*

Louisa (22), Second Stewardess. b. Holyhead. Fourth daughter of Owen & Katherine (née Williams), 5 Fair View, Holyhead. Known to family and work colleagues as Louie. Lively, active, good-humoured person, who in childhood was a leader among her peers, never allowed shortcomings to deter her from any course of action to which she set her mind. The only tone-deaf member of an exceptionally musically talented family, she was determined to join a children's choir. She went for audition with her sister Margaret. True to form Louie was the one who was accepted by the choir! Leaving the Park School, Holyhead at 15, she worked as a nurse probationer at The College, Morton-in-Marsh, Gloucester. Then worked in Mexborough, Yorkshire. In the autumn of 1914, having completed her training, she was employed by the CDSPCo as a stewardess. Bill Sweeney described Louie Parry as *"a lovely girl."* He said that she was one of three sisters employed by CDSPCo. (The others were Margaret and Jane). Engaged to be married at time of her death. Louie's body was never recovered. Her mother mourned Louie for the rest of her life. For many years she would not allow the doors of the house to be locked in case Louie came home. But her grief was so great that she never spoke of Louie or allowed her name to be mentioned. Hannah Owen and Louisa Parry. are included among the names on a memorial in York Minster to the women who lost their lives in the 1914-1918 war.[60]

Pritchard
Fireman William (42). B. Holyhead.

Roberts+
Fireman Richard (44). B. Llechcynfarwy, Anglesey. s. Owen and Ann. Tower Hill Memorial. Father agricultural labourer at local mill. Family later moved to village of Llandrygan, Anglesey. Roberts married Catherine Williams. They had seven children and lived at 55 London Road, Holyhead, where Catherine's mother owned a shop. Roberts was employed as van man with Llewellyn Jones, Denbigh House, bakery and shop. Firm often supplied ships at Holyhead. Perhaps due to his contact with ships, Roberts later joined CDSPCo. Working for them for about nine years when lost on *Leinster*. Name occurs in several books on history and music that were funded by local subscription. Accomplished musician and conductor of a children's choir. All of the Roberts children had musical ability.[61]

Roberts+
Seaman (Cook) William (46). B. Amlwch, Anglesey. s. late George & Jane. Mary, 14 Wian St., London Road, Holyhead. Tower Hill.

Rowlands+
Purser Hugh (43). B. Holyhead. s. late David & Mary. Tower Hill. Family had lengthy seafaring tradition.[62] All of his direct paternal male ancestors, back to his great-great-grandfather, went to sea. Great-grandfather, coxswain of the Holyhead lifeboat, known as William *"Life Saving"* Rowlands, due to heroic rescues. Grandfather, John, First Officer on original *Munster*. Father, David, steward on CDSPCo ships. So, people must have been surprised when Hugh commenced his working life as a teacher at Park School, Holyhead. But the ghosts of his ancestors called and he soon took to seafaring. Started as steward on White Star Line's *Gothic* sailing between Liverpool and Australia. Decided to settle for shorter voyages, joined CDSPCo. With them for 21 years when lost on *Leinster*. A branch of the Rowlands family had settled in Kingstown. Hugh's cousin John was on duty as pier master the day *Leinster* was sunk.

Smith+
John William (49), Greaser. B. Leeds. s. Hannah & the late John. Mary (née Maguire), 17 Desmond Avenue, Kingstown. Buried 14 October Deansgrange: West 11, P4.

Sweeney*
Assistant Purser Bill. See separate entry.

Thomas+
Greaser Robert (35). B. Holyhead. s. William & Elizabeth. Jennie (née Jones), 20 Rock St., Mill Bank, Holyhead. Tower Hill.

Thomas
Under Steward William R. (16). B. Holyhead.

Tyrell+
Quartermaster Henry (57). B. Arklow, Co. Wicklow. s. late Michael & Elizabeth. Bridget (née Blanch), 2 Jane Villa, Tivoli Road, Kingstown. Dean's Grange: North K1: 92. The Quartermaster was the crewman who steered the ship. There were two Quartermasters on board *Leinster*. Presumably they were to take turns at the wheel. Both were lost. Tyrell aged about 50 when he married Bridget Blanch, CDSPCo stewardess, in 1911 or 1912.[63]

Warren+
3rd Steward William (35). B. Kingstown. s. Job & late Catherine. Charlotte (née Archbold), 6 Wellington St., Kingstown. Tower Hill.

Whelan+
Quartermaster Dennis (48). B. Kingstown. s. Michael & late Mary (née Connell). Catherine (née Berry), 29 Lower George's St. Kingstown. Brother Joseph (25) lost 4 September 1915 on the *Hesperian*, sunk by same submarine that sank R.M.S. *Lusitania*. Both brothers on Tower Hill.[64]

Williams
Seaman Elias R. (25) Seaman. b. Caernarvon.

Williams+
Fireman Griffith (49). 4 Gilbert St., Holyhead. b. Holyhead. Maeshyfryd Cemetery: 2. 28.

Williams
Hugh (33), Seaman. b. Holyhead.

Williams
Under Steward (Cabin Boy) John Joseph (16). B. Kingstown.

Williams
3rd Steward John (29). B. Holyhead.

Williams+
Fireman John (29). B. Gwalchmai, Anglesey. Mary (née Hughes), 9 Summer Hill, Holyhead. Tower Hill. Coal miner in Aberfan, south Wales. As wife was afraid of the danger of his work, he went to CDSPCo. Lost on *Leinster*. Family were told that he saved a woman passenger and had gone downstairs to save another when he was killed.[65]

Williams+
Seaman Richard (52). B. Holyhead. s. Jane & late Richard. Catherine (née Lewis), 9 Rock St., Holyhead. Tower Hill.

Williams+
Carpenter Robert John (49). B. Holyhead. s. William & late Jane Louisa (née Murphy), 1 George St., Holyhead. Tower Hill.

Williams+
Leading Fireman Thomas (63), b. Hilton Leigh, 18 Cybi St., Holyhead. Maeshyfryd Cemetery: 2. 1564.

Sources: Contemporary newspapers. Records of the Commonwealth War Graves Commission. Crew agreement records from the Maritime History Archives of the Memorial University of Newfoundland. Relatives of the crew.

Leinster's Military Adjutant

Scotsman Hugh Love Parker had worked for a tobacco company in Egypt before the First World War.[66] On 27 June 1917 he was commissioned Second Lieutenant in The Queen's Own Cameron Highlanders and posted to the regiment's 7th battalion in France.   In 1918, he was hospitalised, evacuated home and reassigned to the 3rd battalion of his regiment.[67]

Although the *R.M.S. Leinster* was a civilian passenger ship, the majority of her passengers on the day she was sunk were military personnel. Towards the end of 1917 military personnel began to travel on CDSPCo ships in large numbers.[68] Many of them were going on leave, others were returning to duty after a period of leave. Due to the large number of military travelling on the *Leinster*, at the end of June 1918 Second Lieutenant Parker was assigned to the ship, with the role of adjutant. This meant that he was responsible to Captain Birch for all military personnel on the ship. He told the military of any areas of the ship that were out of bounds to them and any behaviour considered unacceptable in front of civilians. He informed them of any special orders from Captain Birch. He would probably have kept records of the numbers travelling and any difficulties experienced.   Bill Sweeney described Parker as *"youngish, a nice fellow."*

The following is Parker's report on the sinking of the *R.M.S. Leinster,* written the day after it was lost.[69]

"I have been employed as Ship's Adjutant of 'R.M.S. Leinster' since 28th June 1918, having been placed in that capacity during convalescence, after five months in hospital, through being incapacitated in France.

Yesterday morning the ship started from Kingstown at 8.50 a.m. with a full complement on board. I was at the entrance to the saloon, where I had been talking to Mr (William John) Lewis, Shore Steward of the C. of D.S.P.Co. and his brother (Llewellyn Lewis) the Chief Steward of the 'Leinster.' I had just left them when the ship was hit on the port side forward at about 9.37 a.m. In compliance of my duties I made for the bridge to report to the Captain. I reached the upper deck on the port side where I found one of the boats being lowered by several members of the crew. Two civilians, I believe one was a priest, were getting into the boat, so I immediately caught one who was partially in and threw him back and told him it was women and children first on this boat and if he tried to get in again I would kill him. Both apologetically explained that they were only helping and that they were not trying to get into the boat. I am absolutely confident this statement was quite untrue. I stayed there for a few minutes until the boat was out of their reach and lowered down, then rushed on the bridge where I found Captain Birch standing talking to

Captain Cone of the U.S. Navy. I noticed the forecastle of the ship was well down, but not completely submerged, and the ship maintained a perfectly even keel.

I said to Captain Birch 'I have come to report Sir, what are your orders?' He replied, 'Just wait one minute, Mr. Parker.' He then gave some orders to Captain Cone and turning to me said 'The wires are gone, so we have not been able to send a message. I am sure the ship will float.' I said ' I think it extremely probable they will come back and hit us again, Sir'. He then put his hand in his pocket and withdrew a bunch of keys, selected one, told me to go down to the Chart room, open the top chart drawer and bring him the weighted books. I did as instructed and noticed his revolver in a case in the same drawer. I took up the two books and the revolver and going on to the bridge again handed them over to Captain Birch. He then told me to go back to the Boat Deck and give orders for the rafts to be let loose. I did this and again returned to the bridge. I asked him if he had any further orders and he replied ' No, Mr. Parker, I have to thank you very much, you have done your duty, there is nothing more to do, it is now everyone for themselves.'

I wish at this point to pay a tribute to the perfectly cool manner in which Captain Birch conducted himself. He was absolutely calm and collected and a Britisher through and through in every sense of the term, reminding me as he did, of the many stories I had previously read of the traditions of the British seamen. I feel proud to have known and sailed with him.

Having completed my duties I saluted him, descended to the saloon deck on the port side, and requested all the passengers to keep perfectly calm and not to get excited. One lady who, I am positive, was Lady Phyllis Hamilton, daughter of the Dowager Duchess of Abercorn, turned around smiling and said to me ' We are quite all right, not a bit excited, don't worry about us.' There was no panic or confusion whatever. I can truthfully say I did not see one excited person. The ladies were absolutely magnificent. I then proceeded down the saloon deck on the starboard side. Then the second torpedo hit her amidships and nothing more could be done as the whole interior of the boat seemed to be blown into the air. Many of the passengers were blown up with the explosion and many more were killed and injured by the falling debris. I was certainly on the last boat to leave the ship after she was hit the second time. I climbed down a trailing rope into a boat which had been lowered but there was some difficulty in getting it free as the lowering ropes, fore and aft, were still attached to the sinking ship. I handed my pocket knife to a sailor who was standing in the bow of the boat and he succeeded in cutting the ropes there. The stern ropes were ultimately got clear and the boat got away just before the ship sank. The boat into which I had dropped was well crowded so I dived overboard and swam to a raft about 20 yards off.

On arriving there I looked around and saw the stern of the 'Leinster' high in the air and at that moment realised some person was clinging to my leg; this I found to be a lady and I pulled her alongside on to the raft. (The woman was Maud Marsham Rae). On looking round again the ship had disappeared. A few seconds later the lady whom I had got hold of recognised her husband (Second Lieutenant Lindsay Marsham Rae) clinging to an upturned boat; simultaneously he *recognised his wife. He shouted to me 'For God's sake look after my wife' and I promised to do so as long as I survived. I had the good luck to support her until we were ultimately rescued.*

On the raft with me were two sailors, four soldiers and a lady. The sea was very rough indeed and a moderate gale was blowing. At times the wind seemed to increase and seas broke over us several times. We suffered severely from cold and stiffness, and one of the soldiers hanging on to the raft evidently went mad; he let go, slipped off and was drowned. Another soldier had a similar experience and tried to climb on to the raft. I ordered him not to do so as it was positively going to mean the loss of us all, but he clung on to the lady and refused to let go. I ordered him to let go and work round to a better position on the raft but he cursed me and kept dragging the lady down. All the time he seemed to be quite mad, so realising the danger to the others, I forced him to relax his grip and pushed him off with my foot. I threw him a grating and another lifebelt but he sank.

I imagine it would be about one and a half hours when we saw two destroyers and a steamer come along. We were picked up by a boat from H.M. Destroyer 'Mallard' into which we managed to get with great difficulty from the raft owing to the heavy seas. However, we were ultimately taken on board the destroyer where we received and met with very great kindness from the officers and crew who did everything possible to make us comfortable. Altogether, I would say we were two hours in the water. The lady I managed to support during that period is the wife of Second Lieutenant Marsham Rae, Second Yorks Dragoons. I regret to state that her husband has been lost.

I saw four boats that had got safely away from the ship filled with passengers, nearly all civilians, although one was upset by a big sea a few minutes later. A number succeeded in clinging to the upturned keel but the majority were swept away and drowned.

I saw many dead and drowning with lifebelts on and properly adjusted and this was undoubtedly due to the heavy seas breaking over the survivors. Had the sea been calm, many more would have been saved. In my opinion the rafts were safer and did greater service than the boats.

We reached Kingstown about 3 p.m. and the survivors were taken to the various hospitals and hotels.

Personally I felt none the worse for my experience and proceeded to a hotel."

The report is signed: *H.L. Parker*
Second Lieutenant. Adjutant, R.M.S. Leinster.
3rd Cameron Highlanders.

Post Office staff on the *R.M.S. Leinster*

There were 22 postal workers on the ship, only one of whom survived.

Abbreviations: b. = birthplace. Twenty-four (1911) = age at time of 1911 census. 14 years = Number of *"completed years"* served with the post office at the time of death. Glasnevin = Glasnevin Cemetery, Dublin.

Charles Joseph Archer, 1 Enniskerry Road, Phibsborough, Dublin. b. Dublin. Twenty-four (1911). Wife Anne. Four children. Replaced ill colleague. 14 years.

Jennins Attwooll, 15 Norman Terrace, Jones's Road, Drumcondra, Dublin. b. Easton Village, Portland, Weymouth, Dorsetshire, England. Forty-nine (1911). Twin brother John. Father, John, customs officer transferred, with family, to Dublin when Jennins was five. On mail boat four years at time of death. Wife Edith Jane (née Earls. b. Dublin 1887, died 1954.) Ten children. Two sons in army. 39 years.

James Joseph Blake, 167 Clonliffe Road, Dublin. b. Dublin. Forty-two (1911). Wife Catherine seriously ill when James lost. Eight children. 29 years.

Tom Bolster, Member Davis Hurling Club. Club comprised of post office employees. 15 years.

Joseph Henry Bradley, 3 Pretoria Villas, Clontarf, Dublin. b. Dublin 1865. Forty-five (1911). Wife Margaret Alice. Nine children. (Edith Elizabeth, William George, Victor Henry, Gladys, Frederick, Winifred, Walter, Herbert and Dorothy Louise). 33 years.

Matthew Brophy, 27 St. Patrick's Road, Drumcondra, Dublin. Widow and infant child. 17 years.

Peter Paul Daly, 23 Richmond Road, Dublin. Widow and three children. Member Davis Hurling Club. 21 years

John Dewar, 9 Carnew Street, North Circular Road, Dublin. b. Scotland. Twenty-nine (1911). Wife Agnes. Three children. 19 years.

John Dolan, Ruthville, Philipsburg Avenue, Fairview, Dublin. Wife Jane. Three children. 15 November 1918 Jane granted permission by probate court to assume husband's death. Postal Sorter John Higgins testified that Dolan was near him when first torpedo struck. Believed he was killed immediately. 18 years.

Patrick Forbes, 103 Clonliffe Road, Dublin. Single. Mother and two sisters as dependents. Joined Postal Service 1893. 25 years.

John Joseph Higgins, 17 Prospect Square, Glasnevin, Dublin. Married. Only postal sorter to survive sinking.

Michael Hogan. Member of Davis Hurling club. 21 years.

John Ledwidge, *St. Joseph's*, 4 Coliemore Road, Dalkey, Co. Dublin. b. Dublin. Forty-two (1911). Wife Ellen. Seven grown up children. Glasnevin: Grave Bi 166 1/2. 32 years.

Albert T. MacDonnell. Replaced ill colleague. 22 years.

William Maxwell (46), *Devenish*, 132 Connaught Street, Phibsborough Road, Dublin. b. Inishmore, Lisbellaw, Co. Fermanagh. Family home was local post office. Brother Michael was local postman and postmaster. William worked in Glasgow, before returning home. Later worked Post Office Dublin. Married Mary Ann O'Toole in Fairview in 1898. Eleven children. 21 years.

Patrick Murphy, 1 Iona Road, Glasnevin, Dublin. Wife Esther May. Per newspapers buried Glasnevin Cemetery unable to locate record. 40 years. The longest serving postal sorter.

William John Pasker, 2 Brooklyn Terrace, South Circular Road, Dublin. b. Dublin. Thirty-five (1911). Wife Kathleen. Two children. Replaced ill colleague. Buried 16 October 1918 from Dublin City Morgue to Mount Jerome Cemetery, Dublin. 23 years.

Richard Patterson, Assistant Superintendent of Postal Sorters, Class 11, 9 Leahy's Terrace, Sandymount, Dublin. Grown up family. Three sons in army. President & Treasurer of Dolphin Rowing Club, Ringsend, Dublin. 38 years.

Joseph G. Robinson, 1 Whitworth Road, Dublin. b. 28 May 1875, Killimore, Co. Galway. Married Elizabeth Quinn 25 July 1904 Dublin. Seven children. Eldest child Kathleen died of influenza 3 June 1912. 21 years.

Adam Smyth, 24 Tivoli Terrace East, Kingstown, Co. Dublin. Born 21 May 1875 at 19 Sandycove Road, Kingstown, Co. Dublin. Son of Daniel, boot maker, from Dalkey and Ellen (née Magee) Rathdrum, Co. Wicklow. Second eldest of three brothers and seven sisters. Married Elizabeth Bergin 1900. Nine children. Son Daniel (18), Under Steward on the *Ulster.* Buried Deansgrange Upper North, Row Y3, No. 119. 24 years.

William Henry Wakefield, 162 Botanic Road, Dublin. b. Newtownforbes, Co. Longford to Church of Ireland family. Mother converted to Roman Catholicism, bringing William and his brother into this faith. William lived with wife Agnes and four children Botanic Road, Dublin. 14 years.

James Alfred Warbrook, (known to his family as *"Jem"*), 2 Woolsey Street, South Circular Road, Dublin. b. Co. Offaly. Forty-four (1911). Wife Annie (née Dunne). Three children. *Jem* played banjo, often accompanied by daughter Emily on piano. 31 years.

Sources: Contemporary newspapers. 1911 census records for Dublin. Relatives of some of the men. Patrick Forbes's first name and the date he joined the Post Office supplied by Stephen Ferguson, Heritage Director, *An Post.* Length of service from letter by H. V. Tipping, Dublin Postal District, to the Secretary of the Post Office 14 October 1918.

Postal Sorter John Joseph Higgins

Postal Sorter John Higgins was married and lived at 17 Prospect Square, Glasnevin, Dublin. On 14 October H. V. Tipping of Dublin Postal District sent a report to the Secretary of the Post Office. This said *"Mr Higgins, who is under the care of the Medical Officer, is not able to resume duty at present and I, therefore called to see him on the 12th instant. He told me that he had sustained no physical injury as a result of his experiences except for a couple of blisters on one hand which he thought were due to grasping the electric wires to haul himself out of the Post Office but which looked to me like welts produced by rowing in the ship's boat and which he agreed might have been caused in this way. He stated, however, that his nerves were shaken and that the Doctor had ordered him complete rest for some days. His appearance was undoubtedly haggard and worn and as I did not consider he was in a fit condition to write out a statement I made notes of his experiences which are embodied in a separate paper."*

Tipping also said *"So far 26 bags (of post) have been recovered – 24 letter and 2 parcel. All the contents are in sodden condition and a portion of them are in fragments. They are, however, being dried and will, as far as possible, be forwarded to destination. I have already made a proposal for relieving the immediate needs of the dependants of the deceased officers in a paper sent to the Secretary on the 11th instant and a relief fund, which is being generously subscribed to, has been started by the Sorting staff of this office."*

I have come across three accounts by Postal Sorter John Higgins of his experiences during the sinking. These were a statement made to H. V. Tipping, testimony in a probate hearing regarding Postal Sorter John Dolan and an article he wrote years later for the *Postal Worker*. Understandably perhaps, the later article does not have the immediacy and drama of the earlier accounts. Indeed it does not mention any of the other postal sorters. To save needless repetition the following piece combines all three accounts, as each account leaves out items that are mentioned in one or both other accounts.

"On the morning of the 10th October 1918, the R.M.S. Leinster left Dún Laoghaire on her last voyage. The weather was somewhat blustery and a heavy sea was running. In the post office on the vessel work was going on as usual, and as it was the fourth year of alarms the staff had become somewhat hardened to the danger of submarines, especially in a rough sea. I was working beside Patrick Murphy and Jennins Attwooll. The three of us were working at registered letters in a small office which was partitioned off in a corner of the post office. Mr Patterson was seated at his desk outside the Registered Letter enclosure.

When the first torpedo hit the bow of the mail boat it penetrated the port or left hand side of the bow, burst with a terrific noise inside and blew a large piece out of the opposite side of the bow. It left two sides of the post office open to the sea and wrecked the interior. The force of the explosion knocked me down and partly stunned me. When I recovered I found that the corner of the office where I was escaped the full burst of the torpedo. All lights were extinguished by the explosion, except for a faint glimmer from the port lights which were mostly under water. We were left in the dark, while the sea water was rushing in. I called out to Patrick Murphy that we were torpedoed and to come with me, but he appeared to be dazed by shock and I do not know if he heard or understood what I said in the noise and confusion. (The statement that he called to Murphy was made at the probate hearing. In his statement to H. V. Tipping he said that it was Attwooll to whom he spoke.) I passed by him and stepped out into the sorting office and was immediately over my waist in water. I looked around and saw none of my colleagues – I saw nothing but falling beams and the twisted iron of the sorting divisions. I heard no sound but the roaring of water. I clambered over some bags in the centre of the office with the water rising higher as I advanced and reached the stairway with wood floating around my face. To this day I vividly recall a sea of white letters which were floating on top of the water. When I reached the place where the stairs should be I was horrified to find that they had been blown away, leaving only a large hole through which a pale glimmer of daylight was shining.

I observed a couple of strands of electric wire hanging loose from the roof and grasping these I held on until the rising water brought me under the opening. After several vain attempts to grasp something solid I succeeded in getting hold of the upper edge of the opening. I clambered up onto the roof of the post office. (He was now in the area known as "The Mail Shed.") The stairways from the Mail shed to the deck were intact and I went on deck. I stood there for a minute and then went back to the Mail shed for a life belt. They were not worn by the staff as they could not do their work with them on. There were about thirty of them intended for the use of the postal staff kept hanging in a rack just over the roof of the post office, so that each man could get his jacket on the way to the main deck. I put on my life jacket. This was less than two minutes after the first torpedo had struck. The water was over my ankles in the shed.

I then saw John Ledwidge coming up the opening (of the post office roof). I believe that he escaped in the same way I did, by the electric wires. I told him to get a life belt. This he did and I tied it on him and tied my own – I did not think anyone could have got out of the Post Office after me. I next went amidships to look for a coat, as I had been working in shirt and trousers, but didn't get one. The ship was very much down by the head and looking aft I saw that all the passengers had gone to that portion of the ship. Coming forward again John Ledwidge had hold of Tom Bolster and was tying a life jacket on him. Tom Bolster got me to take off his boots as one of his legs had been hurt in the explosion and he told me that he was badly hurt internally. He then jumped clear into the water (according to the account to Tipping. Or Bolster "crossed the rail at the side of the boat and slid down a rope, *intending to reach a lifeboat alongside. But he missed the boat and fell into the sea. I saw him drifting away on his back in the water. I never saw him again."* (According to the account to the probate hearing.) *John Ledwidge left us and went towards the stern of the ship. I never saw him again, but I was told that he reached a raft and died on it after about an hour's exposure.*

I saw the forward lifeboat, with about 20 to 25 people in it, in the water and a rope training down. I then went over the rail and with the help of the rope I got into the lifeboat alongside, arriving there just as she was being shoved away from the ship. I saw Albert MacDonnell on the deck, get over the rails. Then the second torpedo struck and I did not see him again. We were only a few yards away when the second torpedo struck the Leinster and she was practically blown in two pieces, the whole centre portion being blown sky high.

The lifeboat, being so near the sinking ship, was in great danger of being drawn into the vortex and it was only the good seamanship of the crew that saved the boat. After being adrift for some hours we were rescued by a British destroyer. (H.M.S. Lively). *The rescue boats picked up people in the water and on the rafts before those in boats. The British sailors did everything possible for the people they had taken aboard and after some hours searching for further survivors we were landed at Dún Laoghaire, where a sailor who knew me exclaimed: 'You are the only Post Office man I saw coming ashore yet.' That was a bad shock, as up to this time I thought that some others might have got clear and been taken on some of the other ships. I was taken to the Red Cross station at Dún Laoghaire where I received every attention, being fitted with some dry underclothing and a jacket and afterwards rode in a military lorry to the G.P.O.* (General Post Office) *where I got down as I did not wish to go to hospital. At the G.P.O. I borrowed an overcoat and reached home about 3.45 p.m. I am not likely to forget the happenings of that day, but one particular occurrence which is burned in my memory is when the Leinster plunged to her last resting place to see hundreds of people who could not get off in time being brought down with the ship."*

Bill Sweeney, Assistant Purser on the *Leinster*, referred to John Higgins in a taped interview. He said that when Higgins reached O'Connell Street in Dublin (Location of the G.P.O.) he insisted on going to wash up in a public toilet, to prevent his wife being upset by his appearance. Sweeney said that Higgins was in a state of shock.

Charles Wye Williams, founder of the City of Dublin Steam Packet Company.

The Crest of the City of Dublin Steam Packet Company is still on the wall of No. 15 Eden Quay, Dublin.

The R.M.S Leinster at Carlisle Pier, Kingstown Harbour. Note the spire of St. Michael's Church in the background. (Contemporary Post Card.)

The R.M.S Connaught at Carlisle Pier, Kingstown. (Courtesy of the Maritime Museum, Dún Laoghaire.)

Aerial photo of the R.M.S. Leinster in dazzle paint camouflage. Assistant Purser Bill Sweeney said that the picture was taken from an airship a few months before the ship was sunk. Possibly taken by Captain Birch's friend Captain T. B. Williams. (Courtesy of the Maritime Museum, Dún Laoghaire.)

A contemporary drawing showing the sinking of The R.M.S Leinster.

Unfortunately no photo of UB-123 is known to exist.This is a photo of her sister submarine UB-122. (Courtesy of the U-Boat Archives, Cuxhaven).

Oberleutnant zur See Robert Ramm (Courtesy of the U-Boat Archives, Cuxhaven).

A photo of Robert Anthony (Lamp Trimmer). Believed to have been taken when he joined the CDSPCo.

Captain William Birch, Master of the R.M.S. Leinster.

Boatswain Jim Carraher.

Chief Stewardess Mary Coffey. The photo was taken after she had left the CDSPCo and was working as a governess. The child is one of her charges.

Greaser Philip Connolly. His son Tom was a cabin boy on The R.M.S. Leinster.

First Officer Patrick Crangle.

John Donohoe, one of the Leinster's two Chief Firemen (Stokers).

Fireman hero William Maher.

William Maher in later life. On the chain is the watch given to him by Dorothy Topping.

Engineers Steward Edward Salisbury Moors. (Lost).

Stewardess Hannah Owen. (Lost).

Seaman Hugh Owen was on the bridge with Capt. Birch. Photo shows him in later life.

Second Lieutenant Hugh Parker, Military Adjutant on the R.M.S. Leinster.

Stewardess Louisa (Louie) Parry, lost while trying to save passengers.

Assistant Purser, Bill Sweeney (left) and – believed to be – Purser Hugh Rowlands (right). Rowlands was lost in the sinking. (Courtesy of the Maritime Museum, Dún Laoghaire.)

Fireman Richard Roberts (Lost). Taken with his wife Catherine and six of their seven children.

Cabin Boy Tom Connolly several years after the sinking.

Postal Sorter Joseph Henry Bradley (Lost).

John Higgins, the only Postal Sorter to survive the sinking.

Postal Sorter Joseph Robinson (lost), shown here with his wife Elizabeth.

Postal Sorter Adam Smyth who was lost on the Leinster while replacing a colleague who was ill.

Lieutenant Robert Bassett, Royal Army Medical Corps (Lost)

Captain Hutch Ingram Cone Commander of the U.S. Naval Air Service, Europe.

Passenger Elizabeth Ellam (Lost).

Passenger Elizabeth (Lizzie) Healy. One of four women from Tralee, Co. Kerry who were lost in the sinking.

Private Joseph Hill, Royal Defence Corps (Lost).

Canadian Frank Higgerty was on his way to take up a commission with the British Army, his visit to Ireland cost him his life.

Michael Joyce, Member of Parliament for Limerick, had survived four shipwrecks before surviving the Leinster sinking.

Australian Lieutenant Francis Patrick (Sonny) Laracy and the Military Cross sent to his mother Johanna in 1919.

Captain Robert Ernest Lee, Royal Army Medical Corps (Lost).

Private Philip (Philly) O'Brien, 6th Battalion, Royal Dublin Fusiliers (Lost). Body washed ashore on west coast of Scotland. Buried Portpatrick Cemetery.

Sergeant George Phillpott, lost with his wife Margaret.

Passenger Fanny Saunders.(Lost).

Private Ezekiel Thomas, 3rd Battalion Royal Welch Fusiliers with his wife and infant son. Thomas, who had joined up in June 1918 was training in Limerick. He was travelling to attend the funeral of his father Evan on 11 October, when he was lost on the Leinster. He is buried in Grangegorman Military Cemetery, Dublin.

Corporal John Williams, Royal Defence Corps. (Lost).

Passenger Maude Marsham Rae. Rescued by H.M.S. Mallard. Her husband Second Lieutenant Lindsay Marsham Rae was lost.

Passenger Clare McNally. (Lost).

160

Three Royal Navy and three U.S. Navy sailors who travelled as passengers on the Leinster and survived the sinking. Back row: Left to right: Leading Seaman Patrick Foley H.M.S. Cumberland, Carpenters Mate J. M. Rafferty U.S.S. Whitby Island, Seaman William O'Sullivan H.M.S. Carysford. D.J. Murphy, Stoker McCarthy H.M.S. Marlborough, Frank A. Martin. Rafferty, Murphy and Martin were U.S. Navy sailors. Murphy is wearing what is possibly a borrowed British Army uniform. The open uniform and the hat give him a casual look similar to an Australian soldier. (Photograph courtesy of Christine O'Sullivan)

Lieutenant Roland Llyod RNR, Commander of the destroyer H.M.S. Mallard. (Courtesy of Tamsin Bunnay).

Irish First World War Researcher Conor Dodd at grave of Canadian Sergeant Gavin Francis Andrew, Grangegorman Military Cemetery, Dublin. Conor is holding Gavin Andrew's memorial plaque. These plaques were given to the relatives of men and women killed on active service. (Photo Liam Dodd).

Children from the Park School, Holyhead (Ysgol Parc, Caer Gybi) at the Leinster anchor, Dún Laoghaire with (left) Albert Owen MP for North Wales and Author Philip Lecane 10 October 2003.

This map of the North Sea and British Isles shows the arena in which the tragic stories of the R.M.S. Leinster and UB-123 were played out. UB-123 was lost in the minefield between the Orkney Islands and Norway. A cross marks the sinking position of R.M.S. Leinster. (From maps drawn by Dwight R. Messimer).

List of Civilian Passengers

Unlike the military on the ship, who came from many different countries, the civilians were natives of Ireland and Great Britain. As far as I can discover, a full list of passengers was never produced. Whereas the Commonwealth War Graves Commission has recorded most military deaths, no similar record was produced for civilian deaths. For these I have had to depend on newspaper reports and relatives. There were instances where newspapers named people believed to have been on the *Leinster*, only to correct themselves in later editions. I may have missed some corrections.

Edward Watson, Managing Director of the CDSPCo recorded that 180 civilians travelled on the ship, of whom 65 survived. Thus 115 died. It is not possible to say, however, whether he included as passengers, CDSPCo employees Edwin Ferber, William John Lewis and Philip Michael, who travelled on the ship. Unfortunately, further confusion is caused by the fact that Watson's figures are undated. Thus it is not possible to say whether passengers Margaret Cooke and Alice Fleming who were rescued but died in hospital, are recorded as survivors. It is possible, though unlikely, that the unidentified woman wearing a gold ring inscribed *"Marion Stephen"* was someone I have already listed as a casualty under a different name. This list is the best that could be compiled given the information available. The list contains 187 names, as against Watson's 180. I have 134 casualties (53 survivors), as against Watson's 115 casualties (65 survivors).

Abbreviations: Number in front of name means that it refers to more than one passenger. + = Killed in the sinking. * = mentioned in the main text. b. = born. First name on its own is the name of the person's spouse. Dau. = daughter/daughters of. s. = son/son of. Wife Robert = wife of Robert. Col. = Colonel. Lt. = Lieutenant. Deansgrange = Deansgrange Cemetery, Co. Dublin. Glasnevin = Glasnevin Cemetery, Dublin. Grangegorman = Grangegorman Military Cemetery, Dublin.

Adshead+*
Arthur (51), 4 Villiers Rd, Rathgar, Dublin. General Traffic Agent for Ireland, Midland Railway Co. (England). Travelling to Derby for Midland Railway meeting. Survived by wife & dau. Body conveyed North Wall-Holyhead. Buried Bradshaw, near Bolton, Lancashire.

Alexander+
Robert Jocelyn, known to family as *Joc.*[70] b. 1852, s. Rev. William and Frances (née Humphries). Dublin born mother wrote hymns *"All Things Bright and Beautiful," "There is a Green Hill Far Away"* and *"Once in Royal David's City."* Father Archbishop of Armagh and Primate All Ireland for 15 years. Robert educated Winchester and Brasenose College, Oxford. 1874 awarded Newdigate Prize for poetry. (Oscar Wilde was also awarded the Newdigate Prize). Married cousin Anne Humphries 1876, lived London. Only s. died eight months. H.M. Inspector of Schools. Survived by wife and dau. Betty. Buried Derry.

Allen+
Mrs. Allen (or Allan), Sligo. Identified by son-in-law Mr Hackett, Cork.

(2) Archer+
Marjorie (or Margaret) (4 or 7), Cork. Also mother Mrs. Norah (née Desmond), Cork. Crossing to England.

Baker+
Anthony. Teenagers Anthony Baker, Anthony Jones and Ralph Murray, students of the Irish School of Telegraphy, Cork, going to work with the Commercial Cable Company, London. All lost.

Barlow+
Miss Emily E. (42), Mostyn, Cheshire, England. Youngest dau. late John, Riverstown, Co. Sligo. Buried 14/10/18 Deansgrange, South West Row 01, 91. Headstone: *"Emily E. Barlow, lost on the Leinster 10/10/1918."*

Bartley+
Rev. J.R., LL.B. Trinity College Dublin. Presbyterian Church, Tralee, Co. Kerry. Travelling to severely wounded eldest son in military hospital, Tooting. Buried 15/10/18. (Son, Sergeant William Bartley (24), Canadian Infantry, died 16/10/18.)

Billington
James, Wexford. Member Wexford Harbour Board.

(2) Blackburne+*
Charles Bertram (known as Peter) b. 3/9/1911. Buried with father. Officers Burial Ground: 67, Royal Hospital Kilmainham, Dublin. Also Beatrice Audrey b. 24/6/1907. Body never recovered. Children Lt.-Col. Charles Harold.

Blackburne*
Emily Beatrice second dau. Rev. Canon H.D. Jones, Chichester. Wife Lt.-Col.
Charles Harold. Mother Beatrice & Charles. Sole family survivor.

Blacker-Douglas
Alice, Belle View Park, Killiney, Co. Dublin.[71] Only child Robert McGeough,
Silverbridge, Co. Armagh. Uncle Captain Ralph MacGeough survived
sinking of *H.M.S. Birkenhead* off coast South Africa 1852. 1906 husband
Maxwell Blacker-Douglas D.L. elected a director of Royal City of Dublin
Hospital (Baggot St.). 1907, was appointed trustee. 1/2/15 s. Lt. Robert St.
John Blacker-Douglas (22) No. 4 Company, 1st Bn. Irish Guards killed near
Cuinchy, France. Posthumously awarded Military Cross 10/3/15. Buried
Cuinchy Communal Cemetery, Pas de Calais: 11.B.32. Commemorated Holy
Trinity Church of Ireland, Killiney. Maxwell Blacker-Douglas moved to
Seafield, Millbrook, Jersey, Channel Islands early 1920's.

Bowen Green (or Ball Greene) Miss H., Greystones, Co. Wicklow.

Bower+
Two and a half year old s. Mrs Bower, Rathgar Rd, Dublin.

Bowers+
Marion (or Mary Anne), 34 Dudley Road, Waverly Liverpool. (Probably the
mother of the above child, surname misspelled in one instance and that the
Dublin address was where she stayed.)

Bridge+*
Mrs Martha. Cook to Dowager Duchess of Abercorn, 112 Gloucester Place,
London.

Burleigh+
Alex, Florencecourt, Enniskilling, Co. Fermanagh. Travelling to seriously
wounded brother.

Butcher+
Alice, 8 Phelix Rd, London.

Callingham+
Mrs Doris Natalie, Chiltern Lodge, Beaconsfield. Ronald.

(2) Campbell+
Eileen Elizabeth (4½), only dau. Also Eileen Hester, 3rd dau. of Lt-Col. Knox Browne of Aughentaine Castle, Co. Tyrone. Wife Lt-Comm. George. Mother Eileen. Grangegorman: CE Officers 29.

Campbell+
Rev. Henry O.S.B. St. Mary's, Coventry. s. late John, Mountjoy Square, Dublin. Stayed with friends 27 Pembroke Rd, Dublin.

Carlisle*
Mrs Anna (Nano), wife Lieutenant J. Craig Carlisle. Younger dau. Mr. A.O. Ferguson, 49 Brighton Rd., Rathgar, Dublin. Married 5 October 1918 at Christchurch, Rathgar, Dublin.

Cavill
B.W. Cavill?, Whitecroft, Kent.

Clarke+
Elizabeth. Elderly. Native Blackwater, Co. Wexford. Dau. late Captain O'Connor. Widow late Dr. Clarke, *The Nook*, Cosby, Liverpool. Returning Liverpool, visited sister-in-law Mrs Flynn, Blackwater. Survived by son, sisters and niece. Buried Carrig-in-Bannow, Co. Wexford.

Cohen
Arthur, Gerber Bros. & Co., 127 Argyll St., Glasgow.

Cooke+
Miss Margaret (30), Ardfinnan, Co. Tipperary. Housekeeper Capt. McDonald, 40 Ailsbury Rd., Dublin. To have been married England 15 Oct. Thrown into sea. Swam about. Rescued. Chatted in hospital, but died after few hours. Body brought to Cahir, Co. Tipperary by train. Large funeral. Buried Whitechurch.

Costello
Miss Elizabeth, Dunmore, Co. Galway. Clung to raft for about hour before becoming unconscious. Taken onto another raft, from where subsequently rescued.

Cramshaw
Mr A.W., Army Contracts Department, War Office.

Cropper
Mr J.H., Clent House, Maghull, Lancashire, England.

Crystal+
Fred, Grange, Co. Sligo.

(2) Daft+
C.F., Nottingham, former champion hurdle racer, nephew of cricketer Richard Daft. Also son C.F.

Daly*
Mrs. Cora, wife Major Louis Daly, Pier View, Blackrock, Cork.

Davey
Arnold.

Davey
Mrs Dorothy N.

(2) Davoren+
Sisters Delia (37) and Norah (35). Nurses. C/o Claureen House, Ennis, Co. Clare. Both nursed ten years, England. Returning to Nottingham after holiday, Ennis. Newspaper said sisters got on train, Ennis 8 October. Got off to check luggage on luggage van. Train pulled out. Got later train, missed original sailing.

De Burg Dwyer+
Ella. Only child late John. Ballyguirk, Carrigahorig, Co. Tipperary. Large landowner. Employed many locals. Body brought to Birr railway station, Co. Offaly, 15 October 1918. Buried same day.

Dee
Miss Hannah, 7 Camden Buildings, Dublin. *Irish Independent* 12 October 1918 said she went on deck when first torpedo struck. Flung into water by second explosion. Leg injured by wreckage. Tried to cling to raft, twice washed off by waves. An officer shouted to those on the raft to help her and she was pulled aboard. Hospitalised for injuries.

De Molens
Mr. Fractured arm. Treated Royal City of Dublin Hospital.

Dene+
Mrs Elsie Beatrice. Wife Lt.-Col. A. P. Dene D.S.O., Berkshire Regt. Youngest dau. Major Gen. F. W. Koe C.B. C.M.G., Commissioner of Salvage, East Africa. The Lodge, Currabawn, Nenagh, Co. Tipperary. Two children. Buried Charlestown Cemetery.

Donnelly*

Minnie. See separate entry.

Donohoe

Edward, Manchester, England.

Doyle+

Margaret Evelyn (29). Eldest dau. Fred, 8 Lindsay Rd., Glasnevin, Dublin.

Doyle+

Thomas, luggage guard London North Western Railway. 22 Upper Grand Canal Street, Dublin. Body never recovered. Rose., six sons, three daughters.

Dudgeon*

Mrs A.

Earlie

Cathleen, Drewsbury. A child.

Ellam+.

Mrs. Elizabeth (60). W.H. Ellam, Sunnyside, George Lane, South Woodword, Essex. Visited dau. Mrs Townsend, Crosshaven, Co. Cork. Buried 15 October 1918 by 2nd Lt. Townsend Royal Welch Fusiliers. Deansgrange Southwest R. 85. Headstone: *"In loving memory of my mother Elizabeth Ellam. Killed in the Leinster 10/10/1918."* (Dentist son-in-law identified her by her teeth).[72]

(2) Ellis+

Office Keeper Ruben, DORE (Cork). Civilian. Elderly. Formerly Sergeant, Army Hospital Corps. Also grandson Ruben. Both identified by Fr. Fitzmorris of Cork. Body Ruben senior brought to military barracks Cork. Commemorated Hollybrook Memorial, Southampton.

Enright*

Mrs Florence. See separate entry.

Enthwistle

John, Old Trafford, Manchester. Pig salesman Manchester Market.

Esmonde+

Thomas L. (53). J.P., Ballycoursey, Enniscorthy, Co. Wexford. Only s. late Col. Thomas Esmonde V.C., Kilgibbon, Meemine, Co. Wexford. (Father awarded the Victoria Cross during the Crimean War). Married. Chairman Board Wexford Bacon Factory, founder of Farmers' Union, Chairman County Committee of Agriculture. Travelling to London on business. Lady Esmonde, wife of cousin Sir Thomas, identified body Dublin morgue. Funeral from University Church, St. Stephens Green 14 October 1918. Glasnevin: GH 42.

(3) Evans+*
Charles, Ella and only child Charles Gregory (13). Osborne Terrace, Balmoral, Belfast. He: Employee of Guinness. Travelling to take up post in company's London branch. She: Dau. Mary (d. 17/7/1930) & Colonel David Beamish, Northumberland Fusiliers (d. 29/6/1915. Age 73.) Bodies not recovered. Commemorated on headstone of Beamish grave in Deansgrange: Row K, Grave 69. Headstone: " . . . *his daughter Ella, her husband Charles Evans and their only child Charles Gregory age 13 who were lost on the torpedoing (Sic!) of the Leinster 10/10/1918.*"

Fahy
Miss Susan, Castlerea, Co. Roscommon.

Fennessy+*
Dr. Thomas, Grangeville, Waterford, Ireland. Buried Ballygunner church, townland Knockboy, 3 miles from Waterford city. s. Lilian Agnes (née Rance) of Liverpool. Older brother, Frederick, died 1914.[73]

Ferber+
Edwin George. Superintendent Engineer CDSPCo.[74] Wife Ellen. Joined CDSPCo as youth. From Liverpool, lived 41 Dartmouth Square, Leeson Park, Dublin. Twenty-two years previously, newspapers listed an E.G. Ferber among those who attended the launching of *Leinster*. Seems likely it was same man. If so, he was present at the birth and the death of the ship. 24 September 1917, drew up will at CDSPCo offices, Eden Quay. Will mentions Ellen second wife. Specified to be buried in Anfield Park Cemetery, Liverpool. At funeral minister said that Ferber fastened lifebelt on one of the stokers after first torpedo struck ship. Said to stoker *"Now Ted, we shall be alright."* On coffin was simple wreath from stoker. Buried Anfield Cemetery, Liverpool. Wife paid compensation by Board of Trade.

Fife-Miller
Mrs. Wife Lt. Fife-Miller.

Fleming+

Miss Alice (approx 34), 4 Stanhope St., Hyde Park Gardens, London. Niece of Miss Fleming, Dalkey. Rescued, died 17 October St. Michael's Hospital, Kingstown.

Foley+*

Thomas and Charlotte (née Barrett), 12 Leinster Rd., Rathmines, Dublin. He: Clerk Dublin Corporation. Sister Lily married to world famous tenor John McCormack. Body never found. 29 November 1918 sister Miss Margaret Foley, Melford, Westfield Road, Harold's Cross, Dublin granted order to presume death. Left life insurance policy of £390 and household furniture of about £70. She: Travelling to England to visit her brother, who had been severely wounded in France. Buried Glasnevin.

Frend+*

Miss Louisa, Boher, Caherconlish, Co. Limerick. Dau. late William, Lacrough, Co. Limerick. Left Co. Limerick home 4 October. Travelling to visit relatives Eastbourne. Stayed with Mrs Wilson, Rathgar, Dublin. 8 October wrote to sister Arabella in Chester, saying she intended to cross 10 October. Evening 9 October travelled to Kingstown with Mrs Wilson. After they said goodbye, went on board *Leinster,* where she had booked berth for night. 22 November 1918 sister Arabella Frend, Chester, granted order to presume death. Limerick Historian Patrick J. McNamara believes Louisa Frend was sister or cousin of Second Lieutenant John Frend, Royal Artillery, killed France 17/1/17.

Frizzell+*

Virginia Maud (24), Husband Robert, Newry St., Holyhead., Wales. Youngest dau. Thomas Carter, Teignmouth, Devon.

(2) Galvin+*

Miss Lena and Miss Norah, Perry Buildings, Strand Road, Tralee, Co. Kerry. Dau. Garrett. Buried Rath Cemetery, Tralee, Co. Kerry.

Gibson+

Miss Mary, Listowel, Co. Kerry. Eldest dau. late Thomas, Listowel. Sister Dr. Gibson, 74 Merrion Square, Dublin.

Glynn+

Mrs. Marion, Sundridge Park, Bromley, Kent. Widow.

Goodman+
Christine Sophia (63), 177 Upper Parliament St., Liverpool. Single. Buried 12 October Deansgrange South, 97, A.

(5) Gould+*
Alice, Angela, May, Michael, Olive.

Gould+*
Catherine Gould (40), 3 Creagh Lane, Limerick. Mother of previous and next. Wife P. Gould.

Gould*
Essie Gould

Graham+
George, Parnell Place, Cork.

Hackett
Mrs Ann, St Peter's Vicerage, Belsize Square, Hampstead, London. Wife Dean Hackett, formerly Dean of Waterford. *Waterford News* 18 November 1918 said she spent six weeks with relatives in Ireland. Dean Hackett went Euston Station to collect her. Arriving late, presumed he missed her. Not finding her at home, telephoned railway station asking if there was later train. Told of *Leinster* sinking. Spent anxious time with daughter-in-law. 8.30 p.m. telegram arrived, one word: *"Safe."* Telegram from wife. Treated St Michael's Hospital, Kingstown.

Hall
Miss May.

Hamilton+*
Lady Alexandra Phyllis, known to family as Phyllis.[75] b. London on 23 January 1876, dau. Sir James & Lady Mary (née Curzon-Howe), Duke & Duchess of Abercorn. Father leading member Unionist party, active campaigner against Home Rule for Ireland. Mother launched *Ulster* 26 June 1896. Brother Captain John Hamilton, Irish Guards killed France 6 November 1914. Brother Lord Claude Hamilton DSO, Grenadier Guards, A.D.C. to Prince of Wales. Only sister, Mary Gladys, married Ralph Francis Howard 7th Earl of Wicklow. Mary died 12 March 1917, aged 37. October 1918 Phyllis and mother stayed with widower Ralph Howard, Shelton Abbey, Arklow, Co. Wicklow. Phyllis seeing local man on leave from British army. When mother returned to London Phyllis stayed another week with family cook, Mrs Martha Bridge and servant Ellenor Strachan. Phyllis,

Bridge, Strachan lost. No bodies recovered. Phyllis's family told by survivor that as ship going down she gave her life jacket to servant, saying: *"I'm a strong swimmer."'*

Healy+*
Elizabeth ("Lizzie"). Brogue Makers Lane, Tralee, Co. Kerry, second youngest nine children Matthew and Hanoria (née Sullivan) Healy. *"In Brogue Lane were a gathering of Shoemakers, Tailors, Dancers, Musicians, Comedians and Singers."*[76] (Lizzie's father Matthew was a baker.) Buried Rath Cemetery, Tralee, Co. Kerry.

Healy
Patrick, Fair St., Mallow, Co. Cork. One of six brothers who joined army during war. One killed. Patrick and brother invalided home. Both obtained work in munitions factory, England. Patrick returning to work, survived.

Hearn+
John J.P., Bawn James, New Ross, Co. Wexford. Star Iron Works, Wexford. Member urban council since 1899. Represented district on Wexford County Council. One of five brothers. Only son official in Army Training School.

Hearn
John William, Methallah Lodge, Kildare.

(2) Hearn+
Mr. And Mrs parents of previous.

Henry
Nora, Temple Bay, Sligo.

Hill+*
Mrs Letitia Harriett. Travelling with brother Lt. Sydney Crawford.

Hoare*
Mary J. Survived. As Mrs Buckley, attended 1968 reunion organised by Tom Connolly. Died 1996.

(2) Hobson+
Richard (10) and Elizabeth, his aunt. 28 Northumberland Ave., Kingstown.

Hoey
Rev. James. Brother Parish Priest Aughrim, Co. Wicklow. Returning to Liverpool diocese.

Hood
John, *Neidpath,* Northfield Road, King's Norton, Leicestershire.

Horgan
Tim, Dromkeen, Innishannon, Co. Cork. Lifeboat capsized after launching. (Same lifeboat as crewman Hugh Owen?). Rescued.

(2) Howell+
Henrietta Alice and Ida Wigmore, Lislee, Courtmacsherry, Co. Cork.

Hurndall*
Hurndall (3). Son Major Frank Hurndall.

(2) Hynes+
James. Businessman returning to Manchester from Tulla, Co. Clare. Lost with daughter Clare.

Irvine+
Miss Edith, All Saints Vicerage, Blackrock. Eldest dau. late Capt. W.H., (The Buffs) 27 Bramham Gardens, London.

Jameson+
Mrs. Helen Maude, Windfield, Menlough, Co. Galway. Widow Major James, 4th Battalion Connaught Rangers. Member whiskey distilling family.

Johnson+
Mrs. Mary Ann, Highfield, Hythe, Kent. Mother of Ethel Lethbridge, Glenageary, Dublin.

Johnson+
Sarah L., 31 Marlborough Mansions, Portobello, Scotland. Body recovered.

Jones+*
Anthony (17). Third son William Jones, Cable Station, Waterville, Kerry. See Anthony Baker.

Joyce*
Michael M.P. for City of Limerick. See separate entry.

Kelleher
Patrick, 26 Corporation Buildings, Cork. Treated St. Michael's Hospital.

Keown+
Robert (67), 41 Southwood Ave, Highgate, London. Native Rathfriland, Co. Down. Managing Director Messrs Apperley, Carson & Co. Ltd, London. Returning from business in Ireland. Mount Jerome Cemetery, Dublin.

King+*
Alfred Curzon White (15). See separate entry.

Kingsmith+
Mrs Alice, Westward Hotel, Worthing, Sussex. Visited Mrs Baylis, Dublin Castle. Buried 14 October 1918. Mount Jerome Cemetery, Dublin.

Kirwan+
Henrietta. Second dau. late Dennis J.P., Dalgin, Tuam, Co. Galway. Buried 15 October from Milltown.

Kirwan+
Nora, London. Dau. late Dr. W. Kirwan, Spiddal, Co. Galway. Sister Capt. F. Kirwan (RAMC), 15 Oaklands Park, Ballsbridge, Dublin.

Lalor
Laura, 27 Holybank Avenue, Sandford Row, Clonskea, Dublin.

Lastuck
Miss Ivy, 75 Bees St., Manchester.

Lewis*
Arthur Wilfrid. See separate entry.

Lewis+*
William John., CDSPCo Superintendent Steward, Holyhead. Newry Street, Holyhead. Brother Chief Steward Llewellyn Lewis and brother-in-law Chief Engineer William Mathias. Bill Sweeney (letter dated 14 October 1918 to CDSPCo Secretary Richard Jones), said he last saw Lewis assisting launch forward lifeboat *Leinster's* port side. Lewis subsequently lost.[77] Board of Trade paid compensation to widow.

Lynch+
Patrick, 2 Cross Green, Cork. Member Amalgamated Society of Tailors. President Cork Trades Council. Wife & six children.

(2) MacDonald+
Mrs Edwin (approx 30 years), Hailsham, Streatham Hill. Husband serving Mesopotamia. Visiting husband's parents Almeda Ave, Kilmainham, Dublin. Dau. Flora (3) also lost.

McManus+
James, 69 Ranelagh Road, Dublin and Walsall. Husband S.E. MacManus. s. late Dr. MacManus.

Mallin
Mrs. Wife Capt. Mallin, 615 Motor Transport Company, Army Service Corps, Dublin. Hospitalised.

Malone+
Norah T., 11 Strand St., Tralee.

Marsham Rae*
Mrs. Maud, Ross Castle.

Maxwell+
Harriett Fanny, Hampton Court Palace. Widow Col. Robert J. Eldest dau. Col. Middleton C.B. Memorial service Royal Hampton Court Chapel 2.30 p.m. 23 October.

McCarron+
Alderman James, Derry. Prominent Trade Unionist. Amalgamated Society of Tailors and Tailoresses (ASTT), with largely male membership and British headquarters, organised the Irish clothing trade. Had strong centres in Cork and Dublin, but most prominent figure was Derry tailor James McCarron. President of ITUC three times.[78] Buried Derry.

(2) McCarthy
Brothers John and Thomas, Kinsale, Co. Cork. Survived.

McDermid
Mrs. *Belle View*, Beverly Road, Driffield.

McGrath+
Jonathan, Rockborough House, Cork. Manager, Cork Gas Works. Body brought by train from Dublin. Buried Templebrady, Crosshaven, Co. Cork.

McKenna+
Violet Adeline, eldest dau. Albert Haxby, Allhallowgate, Ripon, Yorkshire.
Wife passenger Regimental Quartermaster Sergeant Samuel McKenna.

McLynn+
Lizzie, 6 Pound St., Sligo.

Michael+
Philip Thomas (38). Elizabeth (née Tyrell), 51 Newry St., Holyhead. Four
children. Apprenticeship with CDSPCo, Holyhead. Junior engineer *SS
Ramazan*. Joined *William Thomas and Co., Liverpool* shipping line. Served 4
years on their *SS King*. Returned to CDSPCo. Body conveyed from North
Wall, Dublin to Holyhead. Maeshyfryd Cemetery: 2. 1546.

Morley+
Nurse Mollie, Firvale House, Sheffield. Dau. Michael & Margaret, 4
Annaville, Ballinlough Road, Cork.

Morrison+
Mr. R.W. Native Sligo. Successful businessman Capetown. Returning to
Africa. (Photo *Freemans Journal*. 19 October 1918.)

Mosse+
Mrs Ellen (Nellie) (58), Woodware, Earlsfort Terrace, Dublin. Wife
passenger Col. Mosse, Royal Munster Fusiliers. Dau. late Daniel, Grimsdale,
Uxbridge. Grangegorman: CE Officers 20.

Mulhall+
Philip, Newry St., Holyhead. (Duplication of Philip Michael?).

(2) Murphy+*
Miss Amy Isabel. Eldest dau. passenger Eliza Jane & late Benjamin, Prior
Park, Clonmel. Plans to travel 8 October prevented when Amy developed
cold. Chief Stewardess Mary Coffey testified at probate hearing two berths
reserved for Mrs Murphy. Morning 10 October Murphys, *"An elderly woman
and a middle aged woman came on board the Leinster. Both lay down in their berths
shortly afterwards."* Mrs Eliza Jane. Mother passenger Amy. 15 November
1918 probate granted to Thomas Murphy, Brewer, Mountain Lodge, Clonmel
in wills of mother & sister. Considerable assets, some in Germany, which it
was hoped would be realised in time.

Murphy+*

Chrissie, Tralee. One of family 7 boys, 3 girls living Steeple View, named because of proximity of church with a high steeple.[79]

Murray+*

Ralph (17). See Anthony Baker.

(2) Musgrave+

Miss Florence Sophia (Known as "Margaret") and Miss Frances Anne (known as "Fanny"). Dau. late Sir Richard, Tourin and 63 Cadogan Gardens, London. Sisters Sir Richard, Cappaquin, Co. Waterford. Both buried 16 October from Cappaquin Church to Affane Cemetery, Co. Waterford.

O'Beirne (or O'Brien)+

Maggie (40), 7 Camden Row, Dublin.

O'Brien+

Miss Georgina, 45 St. Augustine's Road, Camden Square, London.

O'Connor+

Patrick, Charleville, Co. Cork.

(2) O'Grady+

Nurses Margaret and May. Dau. Francis, Manse, Quin, Co. Clare. Returning from holidays, to nursing duties (Margaret at the Isolation Hospital, Mitcham, England. May to England).

O'Rowe+

May T., 298 Kew Road, Richmond, Surrey.

Osborne

Francis Paget, Smithstown, Drogheda. Judge of high court Sudan.

O'Shaughnessy+

Nurse Julia, 32 Upper Baggot St., Dublin. Buried 14 October Glasnevin.

Palmer+*

Gerald (15). b. 4 June 1903. Mother died by time he was four. Partially paralysed, due to injury to spine. Spent much of early years in Cottage Home for Children, Kingstown and the Infirmary, Shankill, Co. Dublin. 1907 application made for admission to Cripples Home, Bray, Co. Wicklow. Due to skin disease, which doctors feared might be transmitted to other children, was not admitted until early 1909. In teens, as was the usual practice of the home, matron applied for place at Dr Barnardo's Home, London. Barnardos. trained young people with disabilities for employment. Minutes of governors' meeting of Cripples Home 9 October 1918 recorded *"The Matron's report was read and correspondence from Barnardo's Home accepting Gerald Palmer who was to leave for London on Oct 10th."*[80]

Phillpott+
Mrs. Minnie. Wife passenger Sergeant Alfred George Phillpott.

Plunkett*
Mrs Lucy Agnes Plunkett. (née Harrington).[81] b. Bedford, England 11 December 1887. Husband, Lieutenant Leo Plunkett. serving France with Royal Dublin Fusiliers.

Plunkett+*
Sheelah Isabel Mary (21). Youngest dau. late John. 18 Landsdowne Road, Dublin. Sister-in-law to Lucy and Dr. Patrick Dempsey, 7 Merrion Square, Dublin. Buried Glasnevin.

Prendergast
Miss Nellie. Dau. James, Strand St., Tralee, Co. Kerry. Treated St. Michael's Hospital.

Richards
Thomas T.

Riordan+
Miss Lizzie, Milleenanaig, Dunmanway.

Roberts+
James M.A. LL.B. Barrister, 32 Marlborough Road, Dublin. Eldest s. late John. Formerly of Farmore, Strokestown, Co. Roscommon. Educated Trinity College Dublin. Entered Inner Temple, called to English bar. Author various works English law. Became ill following strenuous legal work various parts of England in connection with war. Recovered. Returning to London. Buried Mount Jerome, 15 October.

Ross+*
John, *Erndene*, 10 Conquer Hill, Clontarf, Dublin. Secretary Howth Yacht Club. Going to scouting conference in England.

Rowe+
Mary Thirza Osmond, Kew Gardens, Surrey. Eldest dau. Rev. W.

Ruddel+
Alfred. Transit Section W. and R. Jacob & Co. Ltd.

Saunders+*
Mrs Francis (*Fanny*) Elizabeth (51).

Scroope+
Miss, 7 Ashbourne Terrace, Leeson Park, Dublin. Buried Glasnevin.

Shaw Jones+
J. (37 approx), 85 Surbiton Road, Southend-on-Sea, Essex. Auditor, Ministry of Munitions, London. Native of Galway?

Southam+
Leslie. Senior Partner Pig Sales firm. Bordsley St., Birmingham. Wife & three children. Son-in-law of John McCandless, Lisroan, Coleraine, Co. Londonderry.

Sparks+
Miss Margaret Sparks, Farquar Road, London. Only dau. late Richard, Carlow.

Stephen+
Unidentified woman with gold ring inscribed *"Marion Stephen, 14th December 1900."*

Strachan+*
Ellenor. Servant to Dowager Duchess of Abercorn, 112 Gloucester Place, London.

Thompson+
Professor Sir William Henry. b. 17 August 1860, third s. William Thomson, Ballynulty House, near Granard, Co. Longford. Educated Dundalk. Institution, entered Queens College Galway 1879, studied medicine. Won Peel Prize in mathematics, first in university's medical exams four consecutive years. Graduated first class honours 1883. Appointed demonstrator of anatomy Trinity College, Dublin. Further studies London, Paris, Leipzig, Marburg and Heidelberg. 1893 appointed first Dunville Professor of Physiology Queens University Belfast. 1894 married Isabel Redfern, eldest dau. Professor Peter Redfern, Queens University Belfast and Templepatrick House, Donaghadee. One son, four daughters. Lived 14 Hatch Street, Dublin. 1899 elected honorary member Imperial Military Academy of Medicine, Petrograd. 1902 appointed King's Professor of the

Institute of Medicine School of Physic, Trinity College Dublin. Fellow Royal College of Physicians, Ireland and Royal College of Surgeons, England. 1914 appointed scientific advisor Ministry of Food. 1917 published *Food values, with a note on Irish food supplies*. Knighted 1918. Travelling to London for meeting at Ministry of food. 1935 Lady Isabel Thompson, presented Trinity College Dublin with portrait of her late husband.[82]

Thornton+
Mrs Pugia

(2) Toppin*
Miss Dorothy and Mrs Louisa.

Tordoff?
Denis

Tuzard
Miss M., 47 Charlesworth St., Weymouth.

Vaughan+
Frank, 1 Neville Road, Liscard, Liverpool.? Engraver, The Technical Schools, Bolton St., Dublin. Remains brought via North Wall, Dublin for burial family plot, Wallasey.

Vereker
Fred W.

Walsh+
Joseph, Tourlestrane, Co. Sligo.[83]

Ward+
Sergeant Owen, No. 59102, Royal Irish Constabulary. b. Monaghan 1879. Joined R.I.C. 1 September 1899. Roman Catholic, occupation farmer. Served in Donegal, Derry, Belfast, Sligo, Galway and Clare. Married 3 April 1907. Promoted Acting Sergeant 1 March 1910, Sergeant 1 February 1912. In charge of Ennis district, Co. Clare. Was travelling to Birmingham on official business.[84]

Ward+*
Miss Maud Elizabeth, Elton Hall, Peterborough. b. 12 June 1874, dau. Joseph & Jemima Jane (née Terrell), 34 Severn Street, Birmingham. Mother seems to have died when Maud young. 1881 census describes her father as widower, Maud living with grandfather. Educated King Edward's High School &

Mason College, both in Birmingham. Further education St. Stephen's College, Cleever and Ecole Normale d'Institutrices, Chateuroux, France. April to December 1898 employed as Junior Mistress Allen Olney Private High School, Hampstead. January 1899 took teaching post at Diocesan Training College, Derby, specialising in French. Secretary to the Countess of Carysfort 31 December 1913. Carysfort seat Elton Hall, near Peterborough, Cambridgeshire. Family also had estates in Ireland at Glenart, Arklow, Co. Wicklow and near Ballycastle, Co. Antrim. Earl of Carysfort died 1909. From then, until her own death in January 1918, Countess of Carysfort lived at Glenart, Co. Wicklow. Following death of Countess, Carysfort lands inherited by Lieutenant-Colonel Douglas Proby, who had served in Irish Guards. Maud became secretary to the Colonel and his wife. Was travelling to England from Glenart.[85]

Webb+
Miss Lydia Maria (76), Sprout Farm, Rotherfield, Sussex. Dau. late James. Buried Friend's Burial Ground, Temple Hill, Blackrock, Co. Dublin 14 October.

Wilde+
Robert. Works Manager Great Northern Railways, Dundalk. Joined Dublin. Railway Company 1876. Continued when amalgamated with G.N.R. Appointed chief draughtsman Dundalk 1881. Appointed works manager 1892. Seen by Chief Steward Llewellyn Lewis just before first torpedo struck the ship.

Wilkes+
Mrs. Edith Catherine, Watford, London. Wife of passenger Lt. Percy Wilkes.

Wilson-Smiley+
Mr J., Liverpool.

Woodhouse+
Elizabeth, 49 Grafton St., Dublin. English. Supervised the purchase of hay in Co. Wicklow on behalf of British government for several months prior to sinking.

Wookey+*
Mrs Fanny, Weston Lodge, Leixlip, Co. Kildare. Widow late Frederick J.P,. owner of Leixlip Woollen Mills (died 1918). Son, Second Lieutenant Frederick Wookey (27), "C" Company, 1st Battalion Royal Irish Regiment, killed 19 March 1915 Western Front. Fanny sold woollen mills. After

number of delays, set out on *Leinster* to move to England to live with daughter. Buried Leixlip.

Sources: Unless otherwise indicated, details were taken from contemporary newspapers.

Stop Press!

The following information was received from Peter Wood as the book was going to press. My thanks to Peter for same. There wasn't time to include the information among the figures for civilian casualties cited at the start of this section.

Kerr+
Robwert. Braemar Cottages, Ingatestone, Essex. Second s. Daniel of Greenock NB. Buried Fryerning (Essex) Cemetery.

Passenger Minnie Donnelly

Miss Minnie Donnelly, Lady-in-Waiting to Lady Keppel, was returning to London after a visit to Kilmeaden, Co. Waterford. On 18 October 1918 the *Waterford News* published an interview with her.

'Looking fresh, roseate and cheery Miss Minnie Donnelly of Kildermody, Kilmeaden did not, with the exception of an almost imperceptible limp in the left foot, look as though she had gone through one of the greatest tragedies of modern times, the sinking of the Leinster. She arrived in Waterford last Saturday (i.e. 12 October) *from Kingstown'. She was returning, after a holiday, to Lady Kepple in London, with whom she is a Lady-in-Waiting.*

'We left Kingstown at 9 a.m. The boat was packed and I may say that there was a big number of women and children also. The sea was very rough at the time the affair happened-about an hour and a quarter after we left. I was in the salon when the first torpedo struck and at once there was a shout and general commotion. Several people saw the submarine and the wake of the torpedo. I rushed on deck at once and secured a lifebelt which I immediately put on. There was not much panic at the time, until the second torpedo struck. As soon as the first torpedo struck the vessel in the front part the order was given to lower the boats and this was being done with the greatest haste and the passengers were putting on lifejackets. I was very fortunate to be able to get into the first lifeboat thanks to an American soldier who handed me into the boat. (He looked Irish. He must have been Irish, added Miss Donnelly with a smile). There were about thirty in our boat, though there were only a few women and children. (She commented adversely on the conduct of certain men who paid no heed to the motto 'Women and children first'). We had just shoved off from the Leinster, which was settling down by the head, when the second torpedo struck. The result was terrific. It was as if the whole place had been rent asunder. Dense black clouds of smoke went up. Pieces of the steamer were blown into the air including the two funnels and some of the passengers were also blown up with the force of the explosion. Debris fell all around and there were agonising screams and cries for help. After the first torpedo struck, people who could not get into a boat threw themselves over the side of the vessel into the water---men, women and children. When the second missile struck terrible panic prevailed. We could see the people jumping into the water in hundreds. Some of them – mostly women – appeared to have been in bed below, or to be suffering from sea sickness, for I could see them rushing about the decks very scantily clad and their hair flying loose. In about four minutes after the second torpedo struck, the Leinster split up and sank. I was a bit stunned with the shock. We could see another lifeboat full of people being capsized, and the sight of the occupants struggling in the water and their cries for help were heart rending. When the boat capsized many of them clung on to the keel and sides of the overturned craft until the nails of their fingers were absolutely torn

away. All around us floated all sorts of wreckage to which were clinging women and men. All about us, struggling in the water were hundreds of persons crying for help. Numerous dead bodies were floating all round. One thing I saw particularly impressed me. It was a sailor in the water with a baby in his arms whom he was trying to save. It was over an hour before we were rescued by a war vessel and brought to Kingstown.

Miss Donnelly was lucky to have her trunk saved also, for it was left behind at Kingstown by mistake. She was wearing in her blouse an Irish Volunteer badge, which she was also wearing on board the vessel. When the 'News' man humorously suggested that it was that which helped to save her, she smiled and said 'I believe it was a badge of the Little Flower of Jesus that saved me. For I always wear it. A strange thing is that a week ago a gentleman told her fortune and said that within six days something terrible would happen in which she would be concerned."

Passenger Florence Enright

On 12 October 1918 *The Freeman's Journal* published an interview with Mrs. Florence Enright, 55 Mountjoy Street, Dublin. She had been crossing to Liverpool to meet her husband, who worked on the continental mail service. *"She had a life belt. She did not put it on, but sat on her box on deck."* The report continued with Florence Enright's account of what happened next. *"I saw a thing coming along. A long grey thing with red marks, but I did not know that it was a torpedo. It crashed into the engine room and some of the stokers ran up on deck bleeding. They then tried to lower the boats and the best part of them turned over. Only one boat lowered went right and got away. I was still on deck when the second torpedo came along in less than ten minutes. Pieces of iron and wood flew about hitting various people, many of whom were wounded, blood flowing freely from them. The boat immediately listed and the deck went perpendicular, so that we could not stand. I jumped off into the water and was sucked underneath the sinking vessel. On coming to the surface I swam away until I got hold of an upturned boat. Shortly afterwards something struck me on the head and I was rendered unconscious. I don't remember anything else until I awoke in the bunk of a ship, the engineer of which must have rescued me as he was very attentive to me when I recovered. I am sure from what I saw that a great number must have gone down. I could see all the people sinking. I saw one man trying to save two save two children but they were swept away and I suppose lost. In the water I saw two little girls with their mother in an exhausted state. There were a large number of women on board and everything was going smoothly and calmly until the second torpedo came. This seemed to blow half the boat away, knocking everything into smithereens."* The report said that Mrs Enright was the mother of two children, whom she had left in Dublin. At the time of interview she was a patient at St Michael's Hospital, Kingstown. She attended the 50th reunion organised by Tom Connolly in October 1968.

Passenger Michael Joyce M.P.

Michael Joyce was the Member of Parliament for the City of Limerick.[86] He was on his way to London, to go the Admiralty with a deputation of river pilots the following day. Born on 4 September 1851 at Merchants Quay, Limerick, he was educated by the Christian Brothers in Bridge Street, Pery Square and Sexton Street. At the age of 14 he went to sea on the barque *Red Gauntlet*. Though he only spent five years at sea, they were very eventful years. He was shipwrecked four times, each time losing all he possessed. In November 1869 he was on board the *Herald*. About 150 miles west of the Bay of Biscay it ran into a hurricane and began to take on water. An Italian barque sank within sight of the *Herald* and her crew were drowned. Eventually a French brig saved Joyce and the survivors from the *Herald*. He had another narrow escape from death while serving on a sailing boat, which capsized during a gale in the Atlantic. For five days Joyce and the surviving crewmembers clung to the waterlogged ship, until picked up by another boat. He was twice shipwrecked in the North Sea. On one occasion his ship was blown ashore by a storm. On another voyage his vessel went aground due to the removal of all buoys and light-ships during the Franco-Prussian War.

Possibly due to his unfortunate experiences, Joyce returned to Limerick in the early 1870s and began an apprenticeship as a river pilot. Following examination by the Pilot Committee of Limerick Harbour Commissioners on 8 March 1878, he was granted a pilot's licence. The committee recorded that he was 26 years old, had spent five years at sea, had made several foreign voyages and was enrolled in the Naval Reserve. He played an active part in sport and politics. He was a founding member of the Sarsfield Branch of the National League in Limerick. He occupied the chair at the founding of Garryowen Rugby Football Club, and played in the first fifteen for Garryowen and for Limerick County. In the 1900 general election, standing as an Irish Parliamentary Party candidate, he was elected M.P. for Limerick. He was twice Mayor of Limerick. A member of Limerick Harbour Board and its Pilotage Committee, he became active in the United Kingdom Pilot's Association. In 1910 he became President of the Association. His second eldest son, Joseph, died prematurely shortly after the outbreak of the First World War. His eldest son, Richard, who had immigrated to America, fought in France with the 165th United States Regiment.

An interview with Michael Joyce was published in *The Freeman's Journal* of 11 October 1918. His family also holds an account he gave of the sinking.

Both accounts agree in most respects, with the newspaper account being longer. The following combines both accounts:

"*I was a passenger on the 'S.S. Leinster' on Thursday 10th October 1918, and left Dún Laoghaire at 9 that morning. We were about an hour at sea and were then about seven miles east of the Kish lightship. Everything was settled down at the time. The ticket collectors had been around, and I was seated in the smoking room reading a book. Suddenly, and without any warning, there was a terrific crash that shook the ship from stem to stern. I knew at once that the ship had been struck by a torpedo. I had my lifebelt alongside me and I put it on immediately and stepped out on deck. As a nautical man I thought it my duty to give a hand at the lowering of the boats.*

Looking forward, I saw the deck on the forepart of the ship all torn up and the vessel was sinking by the head. There was no confusion at the time because, I think, the passengers did not realize their danger. Attempts were being made to get out the boats on both sides. Having looked over the situation, I made my way to the bridge boat deck and saw the chief officer of the 'Leinster' (**Patrick Crangle**) *endeavouring to launch a lifeboat on the starboard side of the ship. I also saw a number of stewards launching the port lifeboat and, crossing over to them, I assisted in the lowering of this boat. There was some difficulty in getting the ladies into it. One woman, who had apparently lost her nerve had to be forced bodily into the boat while it was being lowered. I was assisting to get her into it and in order to get her over the rail I went over myself and took her bodily into the boat. The boat was being lowered away all the time and I was lowered with it naturally. While it was being lowered another torpedo struck the ship on the starboard side, where several boats were being lowered at the time.*

The lifeboat, which I assisted in lowering, got clear of the ship after a struggle and the stewards manned the oars while I steered the boat with an oar, because no rudder had been shipped. At this time it was blowing fresh from the south-west and the sea was very rough and breaking, but our crew kept the boat's head up to the sea with their oars, and with the assistance of a sea anchor, which was got out. Although we shipped a good share of water from breaking seas we were always able to bale it out and keep the boat clear. After the first torpedo had struck the ship , and when I went out on deck from the smoking lounge, I saw several steamers some distance away but they dared not come near to help us as they would have been torpedoed. Of course, a wireless message was sent to Dún Laoghaire when the first torpedo struck us, and we naturally knew that help would be forthcoming as soon as possible. I think there were six or seven small gunboats coming to our assistance within an hour after we were struck.

After a while we found that there were people in the water, some of them quite close to us, but we found it impossible to get them aboard. Some of them were within the oars distance of us, but were washed out of our reach. It was heartbreaking to be in such a helpless position, but absolutely helpless we were in the circumstances. While we were waiting to be picked up we saw a life raft drifting towards us with two men and a woman clinging to it. One of the men was a soldier, from the west of Ireland, and was going back to the front after being on furlough. We picked up these two men and woman, and I fancy we then had about forty people in the boat. After about two hours a small gunboat, called 'Lively' (i.e. the destroyer H.M.S. Lively) *came bearing down on us. When she got close we informed the captain that there were a number of rafts down to the leeward of them, and that we were capable of taking care of ourselves while he proceeded to pick up as many as he could find. After some time he came back. I cannot tell the number he picked up, and we then got close to the little gunboat and got all our people safely on board the 'Lively.'*

When we got on board we found that some of the people already there were in a bad way, some injured by the explosion and some were in a bad way from exposure. I understand from inquiries I made subsequently that there were 109 rescued people aboard. Of these twenty, including the three we took off the raft belonged to our boat. (This part of the account, made to the newspaper, is the only area in which the statement differs from the statement held by his family. The latter contains the already quoted statement that he estimated that there were about forty people in his lifeboat.) *The chief steward of the Leinster* (i.e. Llewellyn Lewis) *was among the survivors on our boat. The gunboat then proceed to Dún Laoghaire. When we landed at the pier, there were hundreds of motor cars and scores of doctors waiting to give all the assistance that was necessary. I escaped so well that, with the exception of small bruises and cuts to my legs and arms, I was able to slip ashore quietly and get a couple of wires away to my wife and friends at home to let them know that I was safe. The passengers and crew of the 'S.S. Leinster' that day numbered 791, and out of this number there were only 191 or 193 saved. The rest were drowned."* (CDSPCo Managing Director Edward Watson's figures said that there were 771 people on board, of whom 270 survived. The figure of "191 or 193" survivors is one that appeared in newspapers the day after the sinking.) His daughter Maureen's memory of Joyce speaking about the sinking is: *"Poppy was helping to lower boats to save people. He was lowering a woman into a boat when she pulled him into it. His boat was so full they moved from the ship. However, he saw a young girl, who had drowned, with beautiful blond hair floating in the water."*

Passenger Alfred Curzon White King[87]

Alfred Curzon White King (15). Known to family as Bob. Educated Winchester College. Youngest child (twin) of Sir Lucas White King, (Indian Civil Service Retired, 1856-1925) and Geraldine Harmsworth (1866-1945). Bob's elder brother Lucas, known to the family as Luke, had been killed in action on the Western Front.[88]   Geraldine's brothers Alfred (Viscount Northcliffe) and Harold (Viscount Rothermere) owned several British newspapers, including *The Times* and *The Daily Mail*. Northcliffe, who had huge influence on the British Government, was much hated in Germany. It was he who had first in print referred to the Germans as *"The Hun,"* thus establishing the term in common usage.[89]

Bob's elder brother Cecil, known to the family as Snow, had returned to Winchester school a day ahead of Bob. Within a couple of days he received the following letter, written on 11 October 1918.

My Darling Snow,

After all our talks, plans & jokes about submarines, the worst has happened. Our dear Bob, I am afraid has been drowned in the 'Leinster.' We have had hours & hours of anxiety mixed with hope and now must give up.....Enid (an older sister) by a fortunate chance did not travel with Bob as she had arranged........ Consult Mr Blather as to what you would like to do for the next few days. Would you like to go for walks with him or perhaps a chum. I am quite stunned. Our noisy jokey boy gone. . . .

My love to you dear. More precious than ever if possible, now you are our only son left.

Your heartbroken Mother

On 15 October 1918 his father wrote:

My Darling Boy,

In the midst of my grief I cannot help feeling for you as you must be so lonely with no one to comfort you. My heart goes out to you dear son and I wish I could comfort you.........

Of course I feel it much more than Luke's death who fell on the field of glory but this. Oh! The pity of it . . . It was the merest chance that we have not lost two . . .

All my love dear boy
Your heartbroken Dad

On 18 October 1918 Bob's maternal uncle Harold (Viscount Rothermere), who had lost two sons on the Western Front, wrote to his sister Geraldine (Bob's mother).[90]

My Dear Dot,

Enid's letter has plunged me once more into the blackness from which I was emerging. It is terrible and I feel for you more than I can say. You and I have had blows rained down on us and the unfairness of it all makes me hate this world.

I am thinking of you both very much and of the four young lives sacrificed thank God not in vain.

Always your devoted brother,
Harold

In an undated letter to his sister Geraldine, Alfred, Lord Northcliffe, wrote: *"It was not till Sunday night* (probably 13 October 1918) *that I heard a rumour about the Sea Boy. I had read the lists with anxiety, but did not see his name. His dear sacrifice is one of those that are bringing vengeance on the Brutes for you will see that President Wilson specifically mentions this horrible crime."*

According to Ruth Dudley Edwards[91] *"Bob's death, like those of Vere and Vyvyan, exacerbated the ailing Northcliffe's loathing of Germany, about which he was becoming increasingly irrational. The demands of his newspapers for punitive reparations and the hanging of the Kaiser militated against making a reasonable peace."*

Passenger Arthur Lewis

Arthur Wilfrid Lewis, 10 Whitecroft Way, Beckenham, London, was a member of the firm of Lewis and Duvivier, consultant engineers to the Royal National Lifeboat Institution. His account of the sinking was published in the Institution's magazine shortly after the sinking.[92] *"As it was in the course of my duties as Engineer to the Institution that I was returning from Ireland on board the Leinster on Thursday morning, October 10th, a short account of my experience will not be out of place in the Life-Boat Journal. My story will not be a full description of the disaster, but merely an abridged record of what I saw and what befell myself and a few other passengers.*

I was sitting on the deck on the starboard side of the ship a little way aft of amidships, when, at 9.32 a.m., the first torpedo struck the Leinster on the port side.[93] I had a momentary warning from a man who ran across from the port side to the starboard side, saying as he passed my seat, 'A torpedo coming!' The shock of the explosion was not very great. The ship shivered and began to dip slightly forward. I think that no one on deck was in any way hurt. Men of the crew ran at once to the upper deck and began lowering the life-boats. There were calls for 'Women and children first' and cries of 'Steady, men, steady' from some officers. I saw no panic or cowardice among those around me. There seemed little for one to do but wait. I realized that there was no chance of getting into a life-boat. A lad of seventeen or so passed me carrying his life-belt in his hand, and I stopped him and fixed it on him. A New Zealand officer was standing near me, and he said 'I can't swim a yard.' I told him he had not got his belt on correctly, and took it off him and put it on right. I was myself wearing a Kapok waistcoat and had put on a life-belt also immediately the torpedo struck the ship.

I observed a life-boat on the starboard side about amidships being lowered, with only a few men in her. Others jumped in or slid down the davit ropes. The official who had examined my ticket at Kingstown Quay was on board her, and I think in charge. I do not know the fate of this boat, but there were women on deck. (The mention of the ticket checker suggests that he was possibly referring to Bill Sweeney's lifeboat "Big Bertha." The comment that there were only a few men in her, until others jumped in or slid down on ropes, coupled with the remark about women on deck, appears to suggest that the boat was almost empty. However, every account by those on "Big Bertha" say that she was overcrowded and Cora Daly, Maureen Waters and Miss Barry got into the lifeboat before it was lowered. Lewis could have been referring to the lifeboat in which 4 or 5 of the *Leinster's* crew left the scene, but for the mention of the man who checked his ticket. Tickets would have been checked by Purser Hugh Rowlands, who was lost in the sinking, and Assistant Purser Bill Sweeney.) *Almost immediately after noticing this boat, and*

I should say about twelve minutes after the first torpedo, a second one struck us, and a tremendous explosion amidships followed. I turned my back to it and ducked my head. Nothing, however, struck me except water, and I found myself unhurt but very wet. The ship started to sink very quickly, and the deck was so aslant it was difficult to stand. There were cries of 'Jump!' and the water alongside was at once full of struggling men and women. I ran aft before jumping, and left it to the very last chance. I jumped from the port side near the stern, being about twelve feet or so above water, and saw no more of the ship. I found myself close to a small raft about four feet square, and got on to it with a woman and a young soldier. Others came along and tried to get on. The raft was upset and we were all in the water again. There was a life-boat near with only a few on board, and most left and made for the boat. I stuck to the raft and got on again with the same woman and young soldier.

There was a very big surge, but fortunately not much wind to break the crest of the waves. We appeared to rise and fall about six to twelve feet, and the young soldier was helpless with sea-sickness. The woman lay on her face across the middle of the raft, the soldier on her right side and I on her left. She was very plucky. We drifted away from the life-boat and came across another exhausted soldier. I got him partly on to the raft, which nearly capsized again, and I regret to say he was washed off. I then held on to him in the water, but he was soon unconscious. He never spoke, and when a rather bigger wave came along, I lost hold of him. We drifted near a New Zealand soldier with a large white life-buoy, and pushing some wreckage to him I got him along side the raft. He held on and I talked to him and cheered him up with news of the approaching vessels from Kingstown. Just at the last he was swept away from the raft, but the captain of a patrol-boat had seen him, and getting nearer to him heaved him a line. When he was alongside the patrol-boat he was too weak to save himself, and one of the crew bravely jumped in and rescued him. One other soldier, an Australian, joined us. He was swimming well, and managed to get on the raft without upsetting us. He was a cheery fellow and had not lost his head. Two lines were thrown to us from the patrol-boat-the Helga-and with these I soon worked the raft along side the boat, when, as soon as she rolled towards us, we were seized by many hands and lifted over the taffrail, about one hour and a quarter after I jumped from the Leinster."

Military Personnel on the *Leinster*

Edward Watson's figures give 489 military personnel on the ship (67 military officers and 422 other ranks). Of these, 163 survived (34 officers and 129 other ranks). This means that 326 were killed (33 officers and 293 other ranks). Watson did not include the *Leinster's* Royal Naval Gunners among his military totals.

The following list, which I compiled from Commonwealth War Graves Commission Records, the Australian War Memorial website, a partial list of survivors and casualties from the Public Records Office, Kew Gardens and some personal contact with researchers, has 491 military personnel on the ship, of whom 339 were killed and 152 survived.

To compare:

	Edward Watson.	Philip Lecane
Total:	489	493
Killed:	326	340
Survived:	163	153

It is not known whether Watson recorded military nurses and VADs (volunteer nurses serving in military hospitals) as military personnel as I have. If he did, there is no way of knowing whether he recorded them as officers or other ranks. As mentioned at the start of the crew listing, it is possible that Watson included the *Leinster's* military adjutant Second Lieutenant Hugh Parker as one of the crew. I have listed him among the military. It is probable that Watson's military figures do not include Francis Higgerty, who had been discharged from the Canadian army and was on his way to take up a commission in the British army. I put him on my military list because he is recognised by both the Canadian and British as a military casualty. I have put him with the Canadians. It is possible that Anderson from the U.S. Navy, mentioned in a list of Americans compiled by the U.S. Consul in Dublin – and so on my list – is in fact Gunner Andorsech, who is not mentioned on the list. If so, I have counted him twice. Watson recorded the *Leinster's* three Royal Navy Gunners separately. Rather than having a separate list for three men (two of whom were killed), I have included them with the Royal Navy men on this list. Finally, as will be seen in the

Appendix 4, 18 soldiers boarded the *Leinster* without their names being recorded. As military authorities were anxious that this fact would not become known, it is possible (though not probable) that Edward Watson was unaware of it.

Comparing Watson's overall figures with mine:
(First figure = Total. Figure in brackets = Casualties.
Military figures include the *Leinster's* Gunners)

	Edward Watson.	**Philip Lecane**
Captain & crew	77 (37)	76 (37)
Postal Sorters	22 (21)	22 (21)
Civilians	180 (115)	187 (134)
Military	492 (328)	493 (340)
Total	771 (501)	778 (532)

Abbreviations: Pte. = Private. Cpl. = Corporal. L/ = Lance. Sgt. = Sergeant. D.C.M. = Distinguished Conduct Medal. D.S.O. = Distinguished Service Order. M.C. = Military Cross. * = More details in the text. + = Killed. More details on those killed are available on the Commonwealth War Graves Commission Internet site www.cwgc.org

A.A.C.?
Gunner W. Brennan

A.S.V.
Pte. M. Barnes

Air Force
Flight Sgt. Barton
Cadet Knox
Pte. Rugmer
Pte. T. Walker

(The partial list of survivors and casualties in the Public Records Office, Kew Gardens, does not say whether these men are British or American. They are probably British. The Americans didn't have an *Air Force*. They had an *Army Air Service* and a *Naval Air Service*.)

Argyll & Sutherland Highlanders
Second Lieutenant C. Emmett
L/Cpl. Gavagan
Second Lieutenant Green
Pte. Maigan

Army Pay Corps
Pte. K. Galbraith

Army Veterinary Corps
Pte. Jack Williamson+

Australian Army
Pte. Joseph Barnes+
Pte. Edwin Carter+
Sgt. Francis Coleman*
Pte. Joseph Gratton+
Driver Frederick Hopkins
L/Cpl. Frederick Knuckey*+
Lieutenant Francis Laracy M.C.*+
Pte. John Meigan
Pte. James Moore
Cpl. John Murray
L/Cpl. Michael Roach*
Pte. Michael Smith+
Driver Boxer Ware*+

More details are available on the Australian War Memorial website
(www.awm.gov.au/) as well as the Commonwealth War Graves
Commission website.

Australian Nursing Staff
Sister Winifred Starling*+

Ayrshire Yeomanry
Cpl. J. Burt
Pte. James Duller+
Pte. John Phillips+

Berkshire Regt.
Pte. A. Lott+

Black Watch
Pte. William Duncan+
Cpl. McIsaacs
Pte. John Nixon+
Sgt. J. Robinson+

Cameron Highlanders
Pte. Thomas Limbert+
Pte. Robert Mack+
Sgt. Donald Macleod+
Second Lieutenant Hugh Parker (*Leinster's* Military Adjutant)*

Canadian Army
Sgt. Gavin Francis Andrew+
Pte. Michael Biggane*+
Gunner William Burns+
Pte. James Finleon+
Pte. W. Galls
Lieutenant Donald Gwyn M.C.*+
Cadet Francis Higgerty.*+
Pte. T. Higgins+
Pte. C. McArdel
Pte. G. McDower
Capt. Edward Milne M.C., D.C.M. and bar.*+
Pte. William Mooney+
Signaller Pearson
Major Reynolds
Pte. Elmer Skinner+

Canadian Army Medical Corps
Nursing Sister Henrietta Mellett.*+

Cheshire Regt.
L/Cpl. Harold Hanna+
Second Lieutenant or Lieutenant Sargent
Pte. Sidney Singleton+

Connaught Rangers
Pte. J. Dillon
Pte. Michael Dolan+

County of London Yeomanry (The Sharpshooters)
Pte. Alfred Horner+
Pte. Frederick Laws+

Dorset Yeomanry
Cpl. Thomas Kellaway+
Pte. John Oakleigh +

Duke of Cornwall's Light Infantry
Cpl. Joseph White+

Duke of Lancaster's Own Yeomanry
Pte. A. Owens
Pte. Richard Pearson+
Pte. George Walker

East Riding Yeomanry
Pte. Frederick Auty+
Pte. Edward Barradell+
Pte. Ernest Bugg+
Pte. Emerson
Pte. Albert Hunt+
Pte. Nicholas Stephens+
Pte. Thomas Turner+
Pte. Claude Whitlam+

Essex Regt.
Pte. Charles Bennett+
Pte. Cyril Boon+
Pte. George Cannell+
Pte. John Cummins+
Pte. Albert Dean+
Pte. S. Frampton
Pte. Alfred Gordelier+
Pte. William Hedges
Pte. William Standing+

Essex Yeomanry
L/Cpl. F. Budgeon
Sgt. Edmund Freeman+
L/Cpl. A. Morgan
Pte. Percy Thurston+

Hampshire Yeomanry
Pte. A. Lewis+
Pte. Thomas White+

Irish Guards
L/Sgt. James Brady+
L/Sgt. Michael Cooke*+
Pte. Martin Flaherty+
Pte. Patrick Halligan
Pte. Kane
Pte. Joseph Lyons
Pte. William Murphy+
Pte. Hugh Sheerin+
Pte. Joseph Verner (served as *"Pte. Joseph Pendleton"*)*+

King's (Liverpool Regt.)
L/Cpl. A. Beckett
Pte. Henry Chater+
Sgt. Hayes
Lieutenant Nathaniel Hobson+
Second Lieutenant Frank Horton M.C.+
Cpl. Peter Howard+
Sgt. E. Jackson
Second Lieutenant Alexander Lamont+
Pte. Joseph Larner+
L/Cpl. Lawler
Lieutenant Percy Leatherland+
Pte. James Lee+
Sgt. D. McVeigh
Capt. Samuel Rozelaar +
Pte. Charles Sweeney+
Sgt. James Thomas+
Sgt. John Unsworth+
Pte. Percy Whalley+

Kings Own Scottish Borderers
Pte. John Alexander+
Pte. J. McCormack
Cpl. Alfred Myles+

Kings Own Yorkshire Light Infantry
Sgt. Calvert
Major Newton

Labour Corps
Pte. James Canavan+
L/Cpl. James Coughlan+
Pte. John Coyne+
Pte. Frank Crompton+
Cpl. John Docherty+
Pte. John Dysart+
Pte. James Elliott+
Rifleman Felix Gartland+
Pte. E. Gibbs
Pte. Arthur Hampton+
Pte. William Kerrigan+
Pte. Augustine McCarthy+
Rifleman Robert McMullan+
Pte. Michael O'Connor+
Pte. Robert Quinn +
Pte. W. Scully
Pte. David Smith+
Pte. J. Smith+
Pte. J. Woods

Lancashire Hussars (Yeomanry)
Pte. James Bowen+
Pte. Edmund Hailwood
Pte. W. Hampson
Pte. Albert Lewis+
Pte. George Rayner+
Pte. William Till+
Cpl. Thomas Tolladay+
L/Cpl. George Wood+

Leinster. Regt.
Pte. Edward Colon+
Major Louis Dominic Daly D.S.O.*
Pte. Patrick Faughlin+
Pte. Edward Finnion+
Pte. B. Hall

Lincolnshire Regt.
Lieutenant Thomas Harrison+
Sgt. Alfred Patch+
Pte. F. Smith

London Yeomanry
L/Cpl. G.P. Finch
L/Cpl. Pannett?

Loyal North Lancashire Regt.
L/Cpl. Harry Burrell+
Sgt. W. Demaine+
Pte. Arthur Double+
Second Lieutenant F. Heyes

Lincolnshire Regt.
Sgt. Arthur Brassington+
Lieutenant Thomas Harrison+
Sgt. Alfred Patch+

Machine Gun Corps
Lieutenant J. Craig Carlisle*
Pte. John Hayes+
Pte. John McDonnell+
Pte. J. Moore

Middlesex Hussars (Yeomanry)
Pte. Albert Baker+
L/Cpl. Charles Beaumont+
Pte. Charles Bryant+
Pte. David Fisher+
Pte. Thomas Elkins+
Pte. John Hogan+
Pte. George More+
Pte. William Salton+

Middlesex Regt.
Pte. Samuel Probert+

Military Police Corps
L/Cpl. C. Billings*+
L/Cpl. Arthur Hewitt*+

M.S.C.
J. Monc?*

Navy (not known whether Royal or U.S. Navy)
Trimmer William Henry

New Zealand Army
Second Lieutenant Henry Doyle*+
Rifleman P.J. Fahey*
L/Cpl. Peter Freitas+
Lieutenant G. Halse*
L/Cpl. J. Keen
Gunner W. Olliver
Pte. Richmond

Norfolk Yeomanry
Second Lieutenant Cecil Ford+

Northumberland Fusiliers
Second Lieutenant Harry Bentley+
Regimental Quartermaster Sgt. Samuel McKenna*+

North Somerset Yeomanry
Squadron Quartermaster Sgt. Duncan McKellar+

Queen Alexandra's Imperial Nursing Service
Nursing Sister Mary Murphy

Queen Mary's Army Auxiliary Corps
Assistant Administrator May Westwell+

Queen's Own Yorkshire Dragoons
Second Lieutenant Lindsay Marsham Rae*+

Rifle Brigade
Lieutenant Anchital Boughey*+
Sgt. T. Reynolds

Royal Air Force
Cpl. Harry Alderidge*+
Boy Alfred Boucher+
Pte Cardiff*+
Pte. Second Class John Corrigan*+
Cpl. Dennis Creedon*+
Air Mechanic Second Class William Crichton*+
Lieutenant Christopher Patrick Domegan*+
Pte. Patrick Gilligan+
Second Lieutenant Hume
Pte. Second Class Edward Kelly*+

Lieutenant Norman Mellor+
Pte. Second Class Robert O'Grady+
Pte. Thomas Reilly+
Capt. George Swanson+
Pte. Thomas Woodgate*+

Royal Army Medical Corps
Capt. R. Ball
Lieutenant Robert Bassett*+
Pte. Thomas Bernard+
Pte. Roy Black+
Capt. Digby Burns+
Cpl. Michael Carroll*+
Pte. Danby
Major Charles Duggan*+
Pte. James Gambles+
Capt. Robert Ernest Lee*+
Cpl. T. Lewis
Cpl. T. Lucas
Cpl. Thomas McAuley+
Sgt. Clarence McDermid+
Capt. Matthew Murphy*+
Pte. Alfred O'Halloran+
Pte. James Joseph Ratcliffe*+
Pte. Albert Thomson+

Royal Army Ordinance Corps
Pte. William Bradley+
Pte. Leslie Burnett+
Pte. Angus Galbraith+
Pte. N. Jackson+
Staff Sgt. Frederick McGroff+
Pte. Varley
Pte. J. Woods+

Royal Army Service Corps
Driver Edwin Butt+
Pte. M. Byrne
Pte. Joseph Cronin+
Company Quartermaster Sgt. Alfred Ford+
Cpl. (Wheeler) James Gilbert+
Pte. Gillard (Gulland)
Pte. Thomas Kelly+

Pte. T. Prinket
Pte. E. Roberts
Second Lieutenant Percy Wilkes+
Pte. W. Wood

Royal Berkshire Regt.
Second Lieutenant Douglas Aldworth+
Lieutenant Col. Aveline
Lieutenant Basil Haye+
Pte. A.H. Lott*+

Royal Defence Corps
Pte. Joseph Barraclough+
Pte. Thomas Blackhurst+
Pte. William Chaldecott+
Pte. George Cole+
Pte. Alexander Cruickshanks+
Pte. Samuel Donnelly+
Pte. J. Doyle
Pte. Edward Dunne*+
Pte. Frederick Emblein+
Cpl. William Finch+
Pte. Frank Gyde+
Pte. Craven Harling+
Pte. Robert Henderson+
Pte. Leonard Hewitt+
Pte. Joseph Hill*+
Pte. James Honan+
Pte. John Kinsella+
Pte. George Lee+
Pte. John Loughlin+
Pte. Henry Maddock+
Pte. Charles Marsh+
Sgt. George Mole+
Lieutenant Rupert?
Pte. Leslie Storer+
Pte. James Sullivan+
L/Cpl. John Sutton+
Pte. Thomas Walker+
Sgt. John Whittaker+
Cpl. John Williams*+

Royal Dublin Fusiliers
Lieutenant Sydney Crawford*+
Pte. Philip O'Brien*+
L/Cpl. William O'Mahony*+
Pte. Thomas Thompson*+

Royal East Kent & West Kent Yeomanry
Pte. Horace Cook+

Royal Engineers
Pioneer Patrick Boyle+
Sapper Edward Carew+
L/Cpl. S. Doyle
Cpl. Robert Gilmore+
Sapper Patrick Lane+
Pte. J. Leonard
Pte. B. McDermott
Sapper John Riordan+
Sgt. Charles Self+
Pioneer Edward Travis+
Sapper Frederick Watkins+
Sapper B. Vesper

Royal Field Artillery
Driver Pearcy Beardon+
Gunner Thomas Cahill+
Pte. (Shoeing Smith) James Matthews+
Driver McCabe+
Driver Thomas Monaghan+
Driver Robert Thompson+

Royal Fusiliers
Capt. Frank Winterbourne+

Royal Garrison Artillery
Gunner Michael Barry+
Gunner Patrick Earley+
Gunner Edward Hayes+
Bombardier Abraham Herman+
Company Sgt. Major Thomas Prosser+
Bndmr. B. Scott

Royal Irish Fusiliers
Pte. Dennis O'Driscoll+

Royal Irish Rifles
Pte. Crawford
Pte. J. Donoghue
Pte. Young

Royal Irish Regt.
L/Cpl. Thomas Dooley+
Cpl. John Gallivan+
Pte. James Hickman+
Pte. Thomas Kearney+
Capt. Harold Locke+

Royal Marines
Pte. J. Gryce
Petty Officer W. Penney
Pte. Thomas Williams+

Royal Munster Fusiliers
Pte. George Lutton*+
Pte. John Lynch+
Col. William Mosse*+
Pte. C. O'Shea
Pte. H. Roche
Pte. Maurice Roche+

Royal Navy
Commander W.T. Baggott*
William Bunday+
Lieutenant-Commander George Campbell*+
Signalman John Christy+
Sick Berth Attendant Arthur Eade*+
M. Flaherty
Leading Stoker Patrick Foley
Stoker Gallagher
Seaman A. B. Hartnett (Believed to be one of the *Leinster's* Gunners)*
Ordinary Seaman Fred Hough RNVR (One of the *Leinster's* Gunners)*+
Able Seaman James Hughes+
Leading Stoker Michael Joyce+
Seaman Martin Langley+

Leading Seaman George Leatherbarrow RNVR   (One of the *Leinster's*
Gunners)*+
Stoker McCarthy
Petty Officer Stoker James Nyhan+
Leading Seaman William O'Sullivan*
Seaman C. Pelew?
Chief Petty Officer Herbert Pilgrim*+
Petty Officer Stoker George Stokes+
Second Engineer? H. Twidale
Able Seaman David White*+

Royal Scots Fusiliers
Lieutenant Fife-Miller

Royal Sussex Regt.
Pte. Arthur Colgate+
Pte. George Ellis+
Pte. Vincent Knight
Pte. Thomas Pritchard+
Pte. Alexander Promfret+

Royal Warwickshire Regt.
Sgt. (Gym Instructor) Alfred George Phillpott*+

Royal Welsh Fusiliers
Pte. J. Bedall
Sgt. John Brennan+
Cpl. W. Dudley
Sgt. William Fishwick+
Pte. W. E. Frost
Lieutenant T. Gadd
Pte. Robert Henry Hall+
Pte. Robert Arthur Hendry+
Second Lieutenant B. Jennins
Sgt. R. Jones
Pte. Richard Jones*+
Pte. Samuel Langfield+
L/Cpl. John William Lundy+
Lieutenant Francis McIntosh*+
Cpl. Page*
Pte. Harold Pickles+
Pte. David Rowlands+
Lieutenant William Singleton*+

Pte. Ezreiel Thomas*+
Pte. William Walker+
Cpl. Harold Wilkinson*+

Royal Wiltshire Territorials
Pte. G. Somers

Royal Wiltshire Yeomanry
Pte. Edward Argent+
Pte. Tom Hiscock+
Pte. Richard Moore+
Pte. Harry Sheerman+

Scottish Horse
Pte. Ernest Akehurst+
Pte. Harry Bishop+
Lieutenant J. Campbell
Pte. Robert Cross+
Pte. William Dillingham+
Pte. R. Dowdle+
Pte. William Gardiner+
? Maighall
Pte. Henry Page+
Pte. V. Rennis
Pte. Alexander Robertson+
Pte. Runnung?
Pte. William Smith+
Pte. Percy Taylor
Pte. Cyril Wiggins+
L/Cpl. R. Woodhouse+

Scottish Womens Hospital, Royamont
Nurse J. M. (Teresa?) Fannin+

Shropshire Light Infantry
Sgt. James McLean+
Pte. Ridway
Pte. Walter Watson+

Shropshire Yeomanry
Pte. Andrew McCartney*+
Sgt. Walter Rogers+

South African Engineers
Sapper Thomas Curtis+

South Irish Horse
L/Cpl. Augustus Doyle+
Cpl. (Shoeing Smith) Timothy Heenan+
Pte. Nevin
Pte. Henry Quinsey+

South Lancashire Regt.
Sgt. Robert Askew+
Lieutenant John Fitzgerald+
Lieutenant William Hall+

Suffolk Regt.
Pte. P. Duffy
Sgt. or Pte. Duffin*
L/Cpl. John Wells+

Suffolk Yeomanry
Second Lieutenant Arthur Gray+

Surrey Yeomanry
Pte. George Earrey+

The Cameronians (Scottish Rifles)
Second Lieutenant Samuel Barclay+

U.S. Army
Sgt. 1st Class T. Denny*
Sgt. Eugene O'Connor*
Sgt. John A. Rose*+

U.S. Medical Reserve attached to British Forces
Lieutenant Joseph Furlong*+

U.S. Naval Air Service
Capt. Hutch Cone*

U.S. Navy
Anderson. Mentioned in a telegram by U.S. Consul Adams. Possibly refers
to Andorsech, who was not mentioned in the telegram.*
Gunner E. Andorsech*

Seaman P. Barnier
Gunners Mate Second Class John Balmer Black*+
Daniel Dwyer
Quartermaster Second Class Joseph Leo Hogan*+
Seaman Frank A. Martin*
Chief Special Mechanic James B. Mason*
D.J. Murphy
Carpenter's Mate J. Rafferty
Master Mariner G. Russell*
Chief Machinist's Mate Roderick Perry Taylor*+
Yeoman Third Class John James Valentine*+

Unknown
Lieutenant Col. Crosbie
Pte. Lawson
Reporter? K. Lynton. R.N.R.F.

V.A.D.
Sophia Violet Barrett*+
Anna Maude Barry+
Margaret Dillon+
Dorothy May Jones+
Clare McNally+
Birdie O'Connor

Welsh Regt.
Cpl. Samuel Eddy+

West Kent Yeomanry
Pte. E. Dane

Westmoreland & Cumberland Yeomanry
Second Lieutenant William Adey+
Sgt. James Albeson+
Pte. James Birch+
L/Cpl. Thomas Black+
Pte. A. Corner
Pte. James Gibson+
Pte. Owen Hughes+
Pte. William Hutchinson+
Pte. Percy Power+

West Yorkshire Regt.
Pte. Patrick McBrien+

Wiltshire Regt.
Second Lieutenant Victor Sloper*+
Second Lieutenant John Wallis+

Worcestershire Regt.
Pte. William Colwill+
Pte. Charles Evans+
Second Lieutenant Thomas Hedworth*+
Pte. George Hyett+
Cpl. M. Jones
Pte. A. Yates

Wrens
Miss Barry*
Josephine Carr*+
Maureen Waters*

Yorkshire Hussars
Pte. Thomas Ball*+
Pte. Henry Barlow*+
Pte. Joseph Bowers*+
Pte. B. Clapham
Sgt. Major Foghill
Staff Sgt. Major Frank Hullay*+
Pte. Isaac Hustwitt*+
Squadron Quartermaster Sgt. Vivian Mildred*+
Second Lieutenant or Lieutenant Morton
Pte. George Mullholland*+
Pte. James Sheldon*+
Pte. Arthur Sumner*+

1st Reserve Cavalry Regt.
Pte. Cantler+
Pte. Spacey

5th (Princess Charlotte of Wales's) Dragoon Guards
Lieutenant Col. Charles Harold Blackburne D.S.O.*+

7th (Queens Own) Hussars
Pte. J.G. Delaney

12th (Prince of Wales's Royal) Lancers, 1st Reserve Cavalry
Pte. William Bennison+

14th/20th Hussars
Major Frank Hurndall M.C.*

20th Hussars
Trooper T. Regan

Blackburne

Lieutenant-Colonel Charles Harold (42). D.S.O. 5th Bn. Dragoon Guards (Princess Charlotte of Wales's). b. 20 May 1876, third son Charles Edward of Oldham. Tonbridge School, Kent (1890-1893). 11th Bn (West Kent) Imperial Yeomanry throughout Boer War. Promoted Capt. Awarded Distinguished Service Order. Three times mentioned in despatches. Queen's Medal (Three bars) King's Medal (Two bars). Secretary to Transvaal Repatriation Dept. after the war. 1902-1906 General Manager of Transvaal Stud Farm at Standerton. 1903 married Emily Beatrice Jones. Returned to England, purchased estate at Tyddyn, near Mold, North Wales, in 1910. In livery and motor components business in Liverpool.[94] Children Beatrice Audrey and Charles Bertram (known as Peter).

On the Special Reserve of officers, he was attached to 5th (Princess Charlotte of Wales's) Dragoon Guards on the outbreak of the First World War. He took part in the battles of Mons and Le Cateau and the retreat, which followed. When the Allies counter attacked, he took part in the Battle of the Aisne and the First Battle of Ypres. In November 1914, under very heavy shellfire, he and five others carried four seriously wounded men from the trenches, near Ypres, Belgium. One of the party was killed and another wounded. Captain Blackburne was mentioned in despatches for this action.

On 13 May 1915 the trenches held by Captain Blackburne's men were under heavy shellfire during the Second battle of Ypres. He constantly exposed himself to fire in order to direct the rebuilding of parapets. Eventually he was wounded in his left shoulder by shell fragments. He was evacuated to England on 19 May. In spite of several operations, his arm was permanently disabled. He was unfit for further active service. On 22 June 1915 Field Marshal Sir John French mentioned him in despatches for services prior to 5 April of that year. He was made Brevet Major on 23 June 1915, in the 1915 Birthday Honours List. On Friday 28 April, towards the end of Easter week 1916, he was posted to the Curragh, Co. Kildare, Ireland. He was appointed principal officer to General Lowe, who had commanded the British troops in Dublin during the 1916 Rising. On 1 January 1917 he was promoted to Brevet Lieutenant-Colonel. He subsequently served on the staffs of General Sir John Maxwell, General Sir Bryan Mahon and General Sir Frederick Shaw. At some point the Blackburnes sold the Tyddyn estate to J. Graham Reece. On 10 October 1918 the family and the children's governess, Rose De Pury, were on board the *Leinster* on their way to visit friends in the vicinity of their old home.

On 14 October 1918 the Church of Ireland Primate of All Ireland held a funeral service in the chapel of the Royal Hospital, Kilmainham, Dublin. The choir of St. Patrick's Cathedral, Dublin were in attendance. The hospital cemetery had not been used for many years. It was opened that day by order of the Viceroy, Field-Marshal Sir John French. General Sir Frederick Shaw, the commander of the British army in Ireland, his staff, and many officers and friends were present. Lieutenant-Colonel Charles Harold Blackburne D.S.O. and his son, seven-year-old Charles Bertram (known as Peter), were buried in grave number 64 of the officer's burial ground. The body of eleven-year-old Beatrice Audrey Blackburne was never recovered. Emily Blackburne was the only member of the family to survive. She had lost her husband and two children.

The following three items appeared in *The Times* (London).

12 October: *"One gallant man, highly stationed and very popular in Dublin, was last seen swimming with his little child on his back. He and his two children have perished but his wife was saved."*

15 October: Death notice: *"On the 10ᵗʰ October, Lieutenant-Colonel Charles Harold Blackburne D.S.O. 5ᵗʰ Dragoon Guards aged 42, foully murdered by a German submarine on the Irish mail boat Leinster, with his two children. Beatrice Audrey Blackburne aged 11. Charles Bertram aged 7."*

19 October: Death notice: *"De Pury- On the 10ᵗʰ October Rose De Pury passenger on the Irish mail boat 'Leinster,' the beloved governess of Audrey and Peter Blackburne."*

Soldiers Stories

The majority of passengers on the *Leinster* were military personnel. Of these, the majority were soldiers in the British Army. This section tells some of their stories.

McKenna

Regimental Quartermaster Sergeant Samuel McKenna, C Company, 25th Battalion Northumberland Fusiliers (2nd Tyneside Irish), from Dundalk, Co. Louth was travelling with his wife Violet.[95] They had been married the previous week, on 2 October at Ripon, Yorkshire. McKenna (26) had brought Violet to visit his relatives in Dundalk. As his battalion were in France, presumably he had married while on leave. The *Dundalk Democrat* on 12 October 1918 published the announcement of their marriage at the Wesleyan Chapel, Ripon. On the same page was a news item reporting their deaths on the *Leinster*.

The Royal Defence Corps

The Royal Defence Corps, similar in many respects to the Home Guard of the Second World War, was formed in August 1917. It was made up of soldiers who were beyond the age set for combat service, fighting men who had been medically downgraded and men with slight disabilities, which prevented front line service. They were put on guard duty at important points such as railways, tunnels, pumping-stations, certain military establishments, roads and ports. They thus freed up combat ready troops for front line service. The Corps were formed into *Protection Companies*, of which there were over 500 by the end of the war.[96] There were 29 men from the Royal Defence Corps on the *Leinster*.

Joseph Hill from Leicester married Nellie Clarke in 1910.[97] A barman at *The Grapes* public house, Joseph is said to have been easy-going, very good looking and a bit of a dandy. He was a teetotaller, but smoked a pipe. A socialist, he knew Ramsay McDonald when he was politically active in Leicester.[98] Nellie was a cigar maker. Like her husband, she was a radical, being a member of the suffragettes. The Hills had two boys, Joseph junior and Kenneth, when Joseph joined the army in September 1914. In a surge of patriotism the Hills called their next child, born in 1915, Albert Kitchener.

Joseph served in France with 1/5th Battalion Lincolnshire Regiment. Wounded on the Somme, he was posted to 462nd Protection Company, Royal Defence Corps. When he was posted to Ireland, his family were relieved that he was away from the firing line. He was going on leave when he was killed on the *Leinster*. Meanwhile, Nellie left a twist of Joseph's favourite tobacco in the coolest place in the house, under a metal bread bin. She then went to Leicester railway station to meet her husband. When Joseph wasn't on the expected train, she stayed all night at the station, meeting every train. Early next morning a newsvendor came along the platform shouting that the Irish mail boat had been sunk. Nellie collapsed. She never got over Joseph's death. She was left to bring up their sons, aged seven, five and three. The eldest son Joseph Frederick died at the age of 19, of what is believed to have been meningitis. He was a reserve for the English schoolboys rugby team.[99]

Forty-year-old Corporal John Williams, 412th Protection Company, Royal Defence Corps., was born in Old Colwyn, Denbighshire, Wales.[100] Prior to joining the army he was manager to Mr D.O. Williams, Church Walk, Old Colwyn. He joined the Royal Welch Fusiliers in 1915 or 1916. He served on the east coast of England for a time. In 1917 he was transferred to the Royal Defence Corps. He was stationed at Liverpool and in Ireland. While in Ireland he spent some time in hospital. He was going on leave when he lost his life on the *Leinster*.

The Irish Guards

There were nine Irish Guards on board. Eight of them were lost. Lance-Sergeant Michael Cooke had been in the Royal Irish Constabulary (R.I.C.) before the war.[101] Most members of the R.I.C. who served in the war joined the Irish Guards. Born in Sligo in 1882, Cooke had joined the R.I.C. in 1902 from Galway, West Riding. He served in Kerry and Galway, East Riding. He joined the Irish Guards on 30 December 1914 in Dublin. At the time, he was living in Gort, Co. Galway. He was lost on the *Leinster*.

Twenty-eight year old Joseph Verner may have had something to hide. Born in Co. Down, he enlisted in Limerick under the alias Joseph Pendleton. His residence at the time of enlistment was Rosythe, Fifeshire, in Scotland. Commonwealth War Graves records show his wife Annie as living in Dublin. If he was trying to hide something, it was lost with him on the *Leinster*.

Phillpott

Alfred George Phillpott, known to his family as George, was born in Leicester.[102] He was descended from an old Kent family, one of whom, Sir John Phillpott, Lord Mayor of London, was instrumental in putting down *"The Peasants Revolt"* in 1385. George left school at the age of thirteen and began his working life as a shoe clicker. This job involved cutting leather to the shapes required for making shoes. At the age of 21 he joined the Birmingham Police force and, as PC 126, was based at Ladywood, Birmingham. His eldest brother, Ernest, was a regular soldier who served as a Colour Sergeant in the Boer War, on the North West Frontier in India and in Mesopotamia. On the outbreak of war Ernest was one of the *"Old Contemptibles."*[103] Commissioned in the field, he was badly wounded in October 1914. George probably hero-worshipped Ernest. At any rate he joined the army in 1915, becoming a gym instructor. On 16 February 1918, while stationed at Parkside Camp, Prescot, Lancashire, he married Margaret (known as *Minnie*) Bowles at St. John's Church, Ladywood, Birmingham. His brother, Captain Ernest Phillpott of the Northamptonshire Regiment was best man. By October 1918 George was a Sergeant and was attached to 3rd Battalion Royal Warwickshire Regiment. At the time of the *Leinster's* sinking the 3rd Battalion were stationed at Dover. George and Minnie were travelling together on the *Leinster* on 10 October 1918. It is not known why they were on the ship. They appear to have visited the Curragh army camp in Co. Kildare. Perhaps George's army duties took him there, or perhaps they were visiting relatives or friends. In any event the visit cost both of them their lives.

The Rifle Brigade

Lieutenant Anchital Boughey had been an officer before the war.[104] He resigned his commission in 1913 and went to Canada. He settled in Montreal, where he was on the staff of the Bank of Montreal. On the outbreak of war he returned to England and joined up. On 14 September 1914 he was gazetted Second Lieutenant in 8th Battalion Rifle Brigade. He served on the Western Front from May 1915. Wounded at Hooge in July 1915, he was invalided home. On recovery, not being fit for active service, he was appointed Instructor to an Officers' Cadet Battalion. Subsequently given a post at the War Office, he went to Ireland on recruiting work. He was on his way back when he was killed. A few days before his death his appointment as Staff Captain was recommended and approved. He was single.

The Territorials

On 1 April 1908 Britain set up a new army intended for home defence.[105] Called the Territorial Force (nicknamed *The Terriers*), the force was made up of part-time volunteer soldiers. Men enrolled for four years. They attended regular drills and a 14 to 18 day camp annually. There were no units in Ireland, the force being confined to England, Scotland and Wales. The Territorials were only liable for home service. They could not be ordered to go overseas, but could go if they volunteered. The organisation of the Territorial Force was similar to that of the regular army. There were infantry battalions, artillery, engineers, supply and medical formations. Its cavalry were known as Yeomanry.

On the outbreak of war many Territorial units volunteered to serve abroad. Many of the soldiers on the *Leinster* were *Terriers*. Among them were twelve men from the 2/1st Yorkshire Hussars.[106] Formed in 1914, the unit was kept on home duties. In July 1916 they became a cyclist unit. In May 1918 they were sent to Ireland, where they remained until the end of the war. Part of the unit was stationed in Fermoy, Co. Cork and the other part in Fethard, in Co. Tipperary. Nine of the 12 men aboard the Leinster were lost. *"Several more (men from the unit) had embarked on the Leinster, but were taken off before she started-one of the latter, through some staff mistake, being officially notified as drowned."*[107]

According to Yorkshire Hussars Researcher John Liffiton *"All ranks subscribed a day's pay to erect a cross in Dublin Military Cemetery* (i.e. Grangegorman Military Cemetery). *The inscription on the memorial is as follows: 'Sacred to the memory of following Warrant Officers, Non-Commissioned Officers and men of 2/1 Yorkshires Yeomanry who lost their lives through the torpedoing of the RMS Leinster on the 10th October 1918.' On the bottom part of the memorial are the following names; SSM Hullay F, SQMS Mildred VL, Pte Ball TC,* Barlow HS, Bowers J, Huswitt IJ, *Mulholland G,* Sheldon J *and* Sumner A.*"*[108]

The Territorials: Shropshire Yeomanry

There were two men on board from the 2/1st Shropshire Yeomanry. Formed in 1914, they became a cyclist unit in July 1916. In early 1918 they were sent to Ireland with 6th Cyclist Brigade and stationed at the Curragh Camp, Co. Kildare. Private Andrew McCartney (34) was born in Belfast.[109] In 1901 he joined the East Lancashire Regiment in Preston. He married Annie Moran there in 1906. Wounded on the Western Front, he was reassigned to the 2nd/1st Shropshire Yeomanry. On 10 October 1918 he was travelling to visit his mother, who was seriously ill. Because of this, he may have forgotten that the day was a significant one for him. He had joined the army in

Preston on 10 October 1901, exactly 17 years earlier. 10 October was also the day on which he lost his life.

Machine Gun Corps

There were four men from the Machine Gun Corps on board. Lieutenant J. Craig Carlisle was from Ballybay, Co. Monaghan. Five days previously he and Anna Ferguson of Rathgar, Dublin had married. They were on the *Leinster* on their way to honeymoon in England. According to *The Irish Independent* of 14 October 1918 "*They were among those saved from the lifeboat in which Captain Birch was attended to. Mrs Carlyle was on deck when the first lifeboats were being lowered, but declined to go in either the first or second, preferring to await her husband, who was in the cabin at the time. It is believed both of these first boats were swamped or smashed subsequently. She and her husband got into the third boat, and as it was lowered, and after it was launched, it was crowded with people many of whom clambered in from the water and were helped on board, while others jumped from the sinking ship. Mr Carlyle was seated near the gunwale, wedged in closely by the crowd and a man - -believed to be Mr. Higgins, the sole survivor of the Packet Post Office staff – fell in upon his feet. The two oars in the lifeboat broke when put in use, and the frail craft, burdened with the great number of people who were packed into her, and by those clinging to her sides or held up by those at the gunwales was awash with and almost submerged by the heavy seas. Absolutely helpless to move away it remained under the shelter of the ship's side when the vessel was slanting her beam ends. This kept the boat out of the direct 'line of fire' when the second awful explosion tore the ship in two and flung her amidships portions high into the air in one huge burst of fragments. In the debris parts of the funnels, machinery, platings, bridge, decks, saloon, and storeroom furniture and fittings, coal, cinders, bunkers etc., could be seen. Like stones thrown from a sling portmanteaux, suitcases, and even large heavy trunks fell in terrifying crashes for a distance around. When a rescue vessel rushed up it circled close to this boat and sheltered it on its lee, and the brave crew hauled up several occupants with ropes. The surge of the vessel on the side lightened by those people taken on board, and the weight of the others still in the boat and those clinging to the gunwale, capsized the lifeboat. A number of the injured and exhausted survivors perished just when relief and safety seemed certain. Mr. and Mrs. Carlyle were thrown in the sea, and the lady sank. It was only by the merest chance that she came to the surface again. Her lifebelt had been so hurriedly and loosely laced that it slipped down and became entangled with her feet, pinioning them so that she could not move, and this tended to keep her head under water. She wore a large fur coat, however, and this appears to have retained the air and floated her head above the surface. She made a desperate grasp, and when she could breath and see, found that she had gripped the tapes at the back of the lifebelt of Mr. (John) Hood* (commercial traveller for

Millar and Richard.) *A plucky member of the rescuing vessel's crew jumped from his ship on to the keel of the upturned boat. Using his life line as a lasso, he threw the loop over Mrs. Carlyle's head and shoulders and soon she was safely placed on the boat and then on the vessel, where she was overjoyed to find her husband also among the rescued. While struggling in the water, distracted survivors had the additional gruesome experience of feeling dead bodies brush against them, and many were injured by the wreckage. Mr. Carlyle was severely crushed in this way, and is at present a patient at the Castle Hospital. Mrs. Carlyle received attention also, though happily not of a severe kind."*

Worcestershire Regiment.

1st (Garrison) Battalion Worcestershire Regiment had been formed at Portsmouth in January 1916. In June 1918, just four months previously, they had been posted to Dublin. There were six men from the battalion on the *Leinster*, of whom one was an officer. Second Lieutenant Thomas Hedworth had been a revenue clerk before the war.[110] He had been a member of the Territorials, for whom he had trained the boys of Worcester Royal Grammar School. On 10 October 1918, the thirty-three year old Hedworth was going on leave to his wife Ada, daughter Doreen and sons Thomas and Selby in Worcester. He and three of his men were lost.

The prisoner and the military police

The Freeman's Journal of 12 October 1918 carried the following item. *"An extraordinary escape from death was that of a military 'absentee' or deserter who under the escort of two or three soldiers was being sent back to England on the mail boat. When the vessel sank, the deserter was rescued from the water and brought ashore, but of his escort he saw no further trace."* Unfortunately, the prisoner's name is not recorded. He was being escorted by Lance-Corporals Charles Billings and Arthur Hewitt of the Military Police Corps. Charles Billings (48), from Sussex, was married to Mahalia. They lived in Brighton. No background details have been found for Arthur Hewitt.[111]

King's (Liverpool Regiment)[112]

There were 17 men from the King's (Liverpool Regiment) on board. Most were from the 3rd Battalion, which had been stationed in Cork since late 1917.

Twelve men from the regiment were killed. Second Lieutenant Alexander Lamont (29) was a member of the 9th Battalion. On 1 November 1914, he went to France with the London Scottish, a Territorial battalion. At Messines Ridge, south of Ypres, the London Scottish became the first Territorial battalion to go into action in the war. In *"First Ypres 1914"*, David Lomas says that *"German attacks were pressed all along the Messines-Wytschaete ridge, and facing them the London Scottish, who became the first Territorial infantry unit to go into action. Advancing in short sharp rushes to the eastern slope of the ridge at Wytschaete, 750 strong, they were reduced to little more than 400 at nightfall."* Lamont subsequently spent some time in England. In 1916 he was commissioned in the King's (Liverpool Regiment) and in May 1917 he again went to France. Nine months later he was attached to the County of London Yeomanry at the Curragh, Co. Kildare, Ireland. In March 1918 he married Elizabeth Drummond of Anfield, Liverpool. He was on his way to take up a staff appointment overseas, when he was killed. Although attached to the County of London Yeomanry at the time of his death, Commonwealth War Grave Commission records list him as being a member of the 9th Battalion, The King's (Liverpool Regiment).

Lieutenant Nathaniel Hobson of the 5th Battalion The King's (Liverpool Regiment) had received a French decoration for his war service. He was from Kingstown, Co. Dublin, *Leinster's* place of departure. He had visited Kingstown to collect his ten-year-old son Richard and bring him back to school in Liverpool. Richard had been staying with Nathaniel's parents at 28 Northumberland Avenue, Kingstown. As Nathaniel's sister, Elizabeth, ran a school from that address, the boy had probably received some education there.[113] Elizabeth travelled on the *Leinster* with her brother and nephew. All three were lost.

The Royal Welch Fusiliers

Apart from their shared Celtic heritage, the Royal Welch Fusiliers had another reason for affection towards Ireland. The first ever Victoria Cross to be awarded to a soldier was given to an Irishman serving in the regiment. Sergeant Luke O'Connor from Elphin, Co. Roscommon was awarded the V.C. for bravery in the Crimean War. He went on to achieve the rank of Major-General. He was knighted and appointed Colonel of his old regiment. His portrait hangs in the officers' mess of the Royal Welch Fusiliers at Caernavon.[114]

3rd Battalion Royal Welch Fusiliers were based in Limerick from November 1917. The poet Siegfried Sassoon was based there from 7 January to 8 February 1918. Between 22 to 27 January he went to Cork on an *"anti-*

gas" course.[115] There were 21 Royal Welch Fusiliers on board the *Leinster*, four officers and 17 men.[116] Two of the officers and 12 of the men were lost. At the outbreak of war Francis McIntosh was Assistant Master at a boys school at Tamsworth. He enlisted immediately. He served with the Royal Welch Fusiliers in Flanders for a year and a half. He was then invalided home with trench fever and shell shock. He recovered and after further training at Oswestry he was promoted to Lieutenant. At the time of his death he was serving with the 3rd Battalion, based at Limerick. Prior to joining the army, William Singleton (30) was Assistant Master at The Park School, Holyhead. One of the founders of the local Boy Scout Movement, he was a prominent member of the local amateur orchestral society. He was severely wounded while serving with the 20th Battalion of the Royal Welch Fusiliers in France and was transferred to the 3rd Battalion at Limerick as an instructor.

Corporal Page was a gardener to Mr Buckley, of Beech Holme, Holyhead before the war. He was gassed in France in August 1917. At the time of the sinking he was attached to the musketry staff at Limerick. He spent an hour and a half in the sea, clinging to a life raft. Suffering from shock and an injury to the face, he was treated at George V Hospital, Dublin and survived.

Private Ezeciel Thomas (23) was born at Llanrwst, Denbighshire. Employed as a teamsman at Glyn Farm, Colwyn Bay, he enlisted at Colwyn Bay on 17 June 1918, less than four months before the sinking. He was sent to Limerick for training. He was crossing on the *Leinster* to attend the funeral of his father, Evan Thomas of Brynymaen. He was lost in the sinking and left a widow and a 12-month infant. Buried in Grangegorman Military Cemetery, Dublin, Colwyn Bay researcher Myra Thomas, no relation of his, said that he is commemorated in Glan Conway Cemetery. *"All local men from the Parish of Glan Conway who fell in the war each have an individual detailed stone which line the main path in the cemetery – it really is quite a remarkable sight."*

Royal Irish Regiment

There were five men from the Royal Irish Regiment on board. All of them were lost. In 1955 the fortieth annual report of the Royal Munster Fusiliers Old Comrades Association published an item headed *"A curious story."*[117] While the item is incorrect on several major points and totally unclear on others, it is reproduced here for two reasons. Firstly there is possibly some tiny kernel of truth in the story. Secondly it is an example of some of the confused stories that have been published about the *Leinster* sinking.

"On October 10ᵗʰ, 1918, S.S. Leinster was torpedoed outside Kingston (Sic) Harbour. Amongst those reported missing believed drowned was Pte. James Hickman who, being under age (16 ½) was claimed out by his mother, Mrs Hickman, of Tralee. He was then serving with 2ⁿᵈ Bn. in France, and was sent home, acting as escort to a prisoner. Before the ship sank a man of the 18ᵗʰ Royal Irish gave his overcoat to the young lad. In the pocket were certain papers, which led to the identification of a body, which was buried, with military honours as the R. Irishman. This man last year came home, met his own mother and visited his 'own grave.' The body it seems was wrongly identified, and appears to have been that of a young Munster, a brother of one of our members."

It seems unlikely that a young lad being send home from the front as under age would be asked to escort a prisoner. The item suggests that Hickman was coming home to Ireland from France. In fact the *Leinster* was travelling from Ireland and many of its passengers were travelling to France. Hickman is described as being in the 2ⁿᵈ battalion. As the item was published in a Royal Munster Fusiliers publication, presumably it means to suggest that he was a member of that regiment. In fact he was serving in 4ᵗʰ battalion Royal Irish Regiment, stationed at Larkhill, England. However, records show that he had previously served with the Royal Munster Fusiliers. The rest of the story appears to suggest that a member of the *"18ᵗʰ Royal Irish"* gave his overcoat to Hickman, *"a young Munster"* who was later buried as the man from the *"18ᵗʰ Royal Irish."* Records show that Hickman is commemorated on the Hollybrook Memorial in Southampton. The memorial commemorates military personnel lost at sea who have no known grave. This would appear to suggest that he could not have been buried under another name. (However, Sophie Violet Barrett and Ruben Ellis, also commemorated on the memorial are buried in Ireland.) As none of the men from the Royal Irish Regiment on the *Leinster* survived, the man who visited his own grave could not have been from that regiment. However, three men from the Royal Irish Rifles did survive. Interestingly, their 18ᵗʰ battalion was stationed at Larkhill, England, where Hickman was based. Another reason for supposing that there might be even a tiny grain of truth in the story is that the source of the story appears to be Hickman's brother. Private James Hickman (18), 4ᵗʰ Battalion Royal Irish Regiment was the son of John and Catherine Hickman of 3 Waterloo Place, Tralee, Co. Kerry.

Royal Dublin Fusiliers

The four Royal Dublin Fusiliers on the *Leinster* were lost. Lieutenant Sydney Crawford boarded the ship with his sister Letitia Hill.[118] He was twenty-one, she was thirty-four. From Stillorgan, Co. Dublin, they had come home to visit their sister, who was seriously ill. Sydney joined the South Irish Horse in September 1914, aged seventeen. In January 1915 he was discharged as medically unfit. Two months later, in March 1915, he enlisted in 7th Battalion Royal Irish Rifles. He served on the Western Front from December 1915, in the Loos and Hulloch sectors. He later fought at the Somme and was present at the capture of Guillemont and Ginchy. He was commissioned as a Second Lieutenant in the Royal Dublin Fusiliers. He served through the Battle of Paschendaele with their 11th Battalion. At some point he seems to have been reassigned to the Royal Dublin Fusiliers 3rd Battalion, which was stationed in the Grimsby area. On 9 October 1918, the day before sailing on the *Leinster*, he was promoted to Lieutenant.

On 16 February 1915, at St Brigid's Church of Ireland, Stillorgan, Co. Dublin, Letitia Harriett Crawford of Stillorgan Cottage, Stillorgan, married Second Lieutenant Valentine Hill of the Royal Field Artillery.[119] His address was Brewery Road, Stillorgan and he was the son of a gamekeeper. On 10 October 1918 she boarded the *Leinster* with her brother Sydney. They both lost their lives in the sinking. On the headstone on the family grave, in Deansgrange Cemetery, Co. Dublin, Letitia Harriett is remembered as *"Harry, eldest daughter."*

Lance Corporal William O'Mahony (33), 1st Battalion Royal Dublin Fusiliers was single. He was the second son of Michael O'Mahony of 36 St. Thomas Terrace, South Circular Road, Dublin. Philip O'Brien was one of eight children born to Blacksmith Philip O'Brien and his wife Winifred of Tullamaine, Fethard, Co. Tipperary.[120] Always called *"Philly"*, he and his brother Jack joined the Royal Dublin Fusiliers. But it was not Gallipoli or the Western Front that brought about *"Philly's"* death. At the outbreak of war *"Philly's"* brother Paddy and his wife sent their daughter Winnie from Liverpool to stay with her grandparents in Tullamaine, Co. Tipperary for the duration of the hostilities. The war was nearly over when Jack asked *"Philly,"* who was on leave, if he would bring Winne from Tullamaine back to Liverpool. However, Winnie refused to leave and *"Philly"* boarded the *Leinster* on his own. Private Philip O'Brien, 6th Battalion Royal Dublin Fusiliers was among those lost on the *Leinster*. His body was washed up on the west coast of Scotland. Private Thomas Thompson from Co. Derry had formerly been a member of the Black Watch. The son of Thomas and Susan Thompson of Melrose Terrace, Derry, he had been Secretary of Derry Y.M.C.A. He joined the army in Derry. Wounded a short time previously, he was returning to duty after have spent a few weeks leave with his parents.

Medical Personnel

Army Doctors

Many doctors flocked to join the British Army on the outbreak of war. They were assigned to the Royal Army Medical Corps (R.A.M.C.) and given temporary officer rank for the duration of the war. Of the 18 R.A.M.C. members on the *Leinster*, six were doctors.[121] The rest were orderlies.

Major Charles Duggan and Lieutenant Robert Bassett had stayed at *Rosse's Hotel* in Parkgate Street, Dublin the previous night. Duggan was fifty-one and had served in the Sofa expedition of 1893-94. He had been mentioned in despatches. Married, with a home address in Hampshire, he was probably going on leave from duty in Ireland. Because he had stayed in a Dublin hotel the previous night, it is unlikely that his army posting was in Dublin. Twenty-eight year old Lieutenant Robert Bassett was probably returning from leave, as his family home was in Cork city. Like Duggan, he had stayed at *Rosse's Hotel* the previous night. Also staying at the hotel was Lieutenant Halse of the New Zealand Army, who had been hospitalised in Ireland for an injured left shoulder. The shoulder was clamped in an iron frame, in order to keep it in position. A newspaper report on the *Leinster* sinking said that, after the first torpedo struck, Lieutenant Bassett placed a lifebelt around Halse's neck.[122]

Captain Robert Ernest Lee was known to his family as Ernest.[123] His mother Annie was a relative of Ernest Shackleton, the polar explorer. His father Edward was owner of a large drapery firm, with branches in Kingstown, Rathmines, Dublin, and Bray, Co. Wicklow. Edward Lee was a very progressive employer. He was the first in Ireland to introduce half-day working on Wednesdays, for which his employees had presented him with an engraved scroll. During the 1913 industrial dispute in Dublin Lee was one of only two employers to publicly break ranks with the tactics used by employer leader William Martin Murphy.[124] The high Victorian infant mortality rate affected even well off families like the Lees. Three children, including the family's only girl, died before reaching the age of 6 months. Four sons survived into adulthood. On the outbreak of war Ted, the eldest son, stayed at home to work in the family business. The three youngest joined the army. A newspaper photograph early in the war, captioned *"Three sons serving at the front,"* showed the three in uniform. Lieutenant Joseph Lee, the third son, was killed at Gallipoli on 8 August 1915, while serving with 6th Battalion Royal Munster Fusiliers.

Ernest Lee, the second eldest son, was a graduate of Medicine at Trinity College Dublin. He obtained his M.B. in 1910 and his M.D. in 1911. He served as a student doctor at the *Royal City of Dublin Hospital* (now called Baggott Street Hospital.) According to the previously mentioned newspaper item he had been Resident Medical Officer of the *Royal Hospital for Incurables*, Donnybrook, Dublin and Senior House Surgeon *"in one of the principal hospitals in England."* He joined the army on the outbreak of war. On 15 August 1914 he was appointed Lieutenant in the R.A.M.C. On 10 September 1915 *The Freeman's Journal* newspaper published an article headed *"Captain Ernest Lee: How he won promotion at Hill 60."* The lengthy article told how Lee and Methodist chaplain O.S. Watkins had gone to a first aid post under heavy fire. At the post Lee had tended to the wounded. The chaplain and he then went back under heavy shellfire, in an attempt to get stretcher-bearers.

Ernest Lee spent the rest of the war serving on the Western Front. He appears to have been on leave at the time *Leinster* was sunk. Family tradition says that he was travelling to England to stand as godfather to the child of a friend, before returning to France. Ernest Lee was lost on the *Leinster*. In the aftermath of the sinking, his grief stricken father wrote the following letters to his youngest son Tennyson, the only survivor of the three brothers who had joined the army.

Bellevue,
Blackrock.
Co. Dublin.

Oct 11th 1918

My own dear Boy Tennyson,
You will have seen no doubt from the papers the terrible tragedy which occurred to the Mail Boat yesterday. I fear our very dear and loved son Ernest is no more in this world. There is no account of him dead or alive. He left by the boat. The Leinster was torpedoed on Thursday morning and she was sunk inside an hour. Oh the horror of it. Your poor mother is bearing up as well as can be can be expected but God alone knows the sorrow that we feel. I sent you two wires late last night when I could get no tidings at all "that Ernest would not be in London tomorrow," one to Plymouth and one to the Waldorf Hotel, London. I also wired you this morning "Mail Boat lost Ernest missing." – Of course I don't know if you if you got them. – May the good Lord pity my dear Boy. – You will be very desolate as we are. – While I write this (4.45 p.m. Friday). I am expecting possibly a "wire" from them. I fear you will not get this 'til Sunday morning. I am sending you the Irish Times of today. Will "wire" if any good news comes to hand. We fear the worst as we can get no news at all today. Mother and Ted join in unified love to our dear boy.

Your loving and affectionate father.
Edward Lee

Ernest Lee's body was recovered. On 15 October 1918 he was buried in the family plot in Deansgrange Cemetery, Co. Dublin. His father sent the following letter to Tennyson a month later.

Bellevue,
Blackrock.
Co. Dublin.

2 Enclosures

10.11.18

My dear Tennyson,
I was glad to see from your letter to mother that you were feeling very fit. – Just a month today our dear boy Ernest lost his life so tragically. Oh we do feel so terribly poorer for the loss of our brave boys. – You no doubt feel the same way. – They died as they lived bravely and unselfishly giving inspiration to us all – but their spirit lives and can never die. I enclose two extracts from letters received, one only yesterday – how many others he helped to save God alone knows. – Mother bears up wonderfully. We are very proud but very very sad – I will just go now with Ted to visit his grave. Love from Mother and Ted with my own.

Your very affectionate father.
Edward Lee

The two enclosures were extracts from letters received by the family. They were copied out in beautiful copperplate writing. While it is not clear whether they were copied by Edward Lee or another member of the family, their beautiful style make them miniature memorials to Ernest.

Extract from letter of a Dublin Doctor

"I heard the other day in the Castle Hospital that your son just before losing his own life was instrumental in saving a brother officer's, who, with his arm in a metal splint, would have been quite helpless had not your son taken care to fit on his life belt for him after the ship was first struck."

Extract from letter of a Lady

"He was the man that did all Earthly power could do to save my life. He adjusted my life belt with a smile on his face, when the ship was actually sinking. He spoke to me encouragingly, fastened my belt securely, and wished me luck."

The war ended the day after the letter was written. The next letter was sent two weeks later. *"our babes"* refers to the family's two boys and the girl who died as babies. *"Joe"* refers to Joseph Bagnall Lee, who was killed at Gallipoli. Even though he had lost two sons in the war, and wanted Tennyson home as soon as possible, Edward Lee could still think of the needs of other families when it came to demobilization of the troops. He could also think of the rights of the striking staff at Arnotts Department Store.

Bellevue,
Blackrock.
Co. Dublin.
Sunday
November 24th 1918

My dear Boy Tennyson,

I was greatly pleased to get your letter and it gave your mother and myself great comfort. Surely Ernest died the noblest death a man can die in trying to save the lives of others but our sorrow for him is very great indeed. We only trust in God that when our time comes we may meet our babes and our dear Joe and Ernest with all our loved ones where there shall be no more partings or death or sorrow. — May we prove ourselves worthy — We hope soon to have you back with us again but we know you will do the right thing no matter how irksome it may be, but the long service men we hope will be fairly treated when matters come to be arranged. You may well conjure up the anxious time your mother and I have had in the past few months but thank God we seem to feel relieved now. God in his infinite wisdom was pleased to take our two beloved sons to himself, but we say "His will be done." I have really no news to tell you and I am sure mother keeps you well posted — possibly you have heard of the strike at Arnotts' the place is closed since Wednesday night. — I fear the firm are wrong as they refused to discuss matters with the union — that day is gone and the workers are determined to get a place in the sun, which I think is quite as it should be — I have no doubt there are faults on both sides — Mother and Ted join me in best love.

Your very affectionate father.
Edward Lee

When Edward and Annie Lee died, it seems as if they wanted to ensure that all their children were included in their embrace. The Lee family plot in Deansgrange Cemetery has two headstones. The left headstone, in the form of a cross, is inscribed *"In loving memory of Robert Ernest Lee, Captain R.A.M.C. Lost in the sinking of R.M.S. Leinster. Oct 10 1918. Aged 35 years. Faithful unto death."* The headstone is inscribed on the base: *"Edward Lee J.P. (Father) Died 14th February 1927. Aged 73 years."* The other headstone, commemorating the children who died in infancy and Joseph who was killed at Gallipoli, is inscribed at the base: *"Annie Lee, (Mother), Died 6th March 1938, Aged 79 years."*

The Orderly

Rehoboth Avenue, South Circular Road, Dublin. Early morning 10 October 1918.

It was time to leave. Private James Ratcliffe of the R.A.M.C. walked to the door of his home accompanied by his wife Margaret. Another parting. They stood at the door together, the twenty-four year old wife and her thirty-three year old husband, who had gone to war as a volunteer. They had shared so much joy and sorrow in their eight years of marriage. Their son, William was now seven. They had lost a beloved daughter to diphtheria, at the age of three. Now, Margaret was expecting another baby. James hugged his wife. Then he set off down the avenue. He stopped, came back and hugged her again. Several neighbours witnessed the scene. The more superstitious among them considered his turning back to be a bad omen.[125] Whether or not it was, Margaret never again saw her husband, alive or dead, as his body was never recovered.

The nurse

> *"Mid the war's great curse*
> *stands the Red Cross nurse*
> *She's the Rose of No Man's Land."*

(Words by Jack Caddigan
Music by James A. Brennan)

Elizabeth Barrett had travelled to Dublin to meet her sister Violet, who was on leave from her nursing duties in France. After she saw Violet off at Kingstown Harbour she returned home to Longford. When she got off the train at Longford she heard that the *Leinster* had been sunk.[126]

*

Before the First World War, the War Office introduced a system to supplement army medical structures. Volunteers were drawn from the British Red Cross Society and the St. John Ambulance Brigade. They served in units called Voluntary Aid Detachments (V.A.D.s). The V.A.D.s supplied auxiliary nurses, ambulance drivers and stretcher-bearers. Sophia Violet Barrett, known to her family as Violet, served as a volunteer nurse during the war. Violet's aunt, Marcella, married William Wilson of *Carrickmines House*, Foxrock, Co. Dublin. Violet, originally from Galway, must have gone to live with them, as she joined the Carrickmines, Co. Dublin, V.A.D.

The first requests for V.A.D.s came from military hospitals on the home front in early 1915 and from France in May of the same year. From January to April 1915 Violet served at Monkstown House Auxiliary Hospital, Monkstown, Co. Dublin. This was a private home, donated by its owner for use as an hospital for wounded officers. Later Violet was transferred to the Second Northern General Hospital, Leeds until 1916, when she was posted to France. From April 1916 to August 1918 she served at No. 6 General Hospital, Rouen. On 24 December 1917 she was mentioned in despatches. This entitled her to wear two red stripes on her uniform. From August to October 1918 she was attached to No 2 Stationary Hospital, Abbeyville, France. Her last month on duty was spent nursing wounded German prisoners. She spent her final days on leave at *Carrickmines House*, Foxrock, Co. Dublin. Violet Barrett was lost in the sinking of the *R.M.S. Leinster*. She was thirty-four. Her body was recovered and brought to Dublin City Morgue. From there it was brought to *Carrickmines House*, Foxrock. On Monday 14 October 1918 her funeral procession, headed by a party of Hussars, left *Carrickmines House* for Kilternan Churchyard, Co. Dublin. Her coffin was carried in an ambulance loaned by the Royal Irish Automobile Club. The mourners included officers and members of the St. John Ambulance Brigade and the British Red Cross Society.

In 1919 a silver chalice in memory of thirty-four year old Volunteer Nurse Violet Barrett was presented to Tully Church, Foxrock, Co. Dublin, where she had worshipped while living in Dublin. An inscription on the base reads *"To the glory of God and in memory of Sophia Violet Barrett, torpedoed in R.M.S. Leinster October 1918, when returning to duty in France. Presented to Tully Church by her fellow members of Carrickmines St. John Ambulance Nursing Division."* The chalice is used for communion every Sunday.[127] On the outside wall of the church, Violet is commemorated on a memorial to parishioners who were killed in both wars. Hers is the first name and the only female on the memorial. She is also commemorated on a memorial in the Church of Ireland, Kenagh, Co. Longford and on the Holybrook memorial in Southampton, even though the latter is a memorial for recording the names of those lost at sea and who have no known graves.

Clare McNally worked as a volunteer at a hospital in London. The daughter of the late Major James McNally, 4th Battalion, Connaught Rangers, she was engaged to Lieutenant Lindop of the Royal Innskilling Fusiliers. She was returning to London after a visit to Bantry and Kinsale in Co. Cork. Lost on the *Leinster*, she was buried at Prospect Hill, Galway. Her coffin was taken to the grave between two files of Connaught Rangers, followed by their band playing the funeral march. The Marchioness of Londonderry wrote to Mrs McNally about Clare's war service work *"In appreciation of the good work voluntarily done by your daughter at my hospital at Londonderry House for more than two years."*[128]

*

The Civilian Doctor[129]

In 1947 Mary Fennessy (née Hearne) wrote the following account of her brother-in-law's death on board the *Leinster*. Thomas (Tommy) Fennessy from Grange, John's Hill, Waterford was a doctor in practice in London. His brother Arthur, who had joined the Australian Army, was Mary's husband. Another brother, Edward (Eddie), a doctor in the R.A.M.C., was stationed at Ballykinler, Co. Down.

"Late in September 1918, Tommy Fennessy, Arthur's brother, came over on a holiday from London to see his parents. He took Lilla (his younger sister Lilian) *and myself for a few drives on the old side-car. One afternoon we went to Dunmore* (Dunmore East, on the estuary of the River Suir). *I remember well* (that) *Councellor's Strand was strewn with huge dead dogfish. We walked through the village and down to the beautiful pier, looking across to the Hook* (Hook Head, the Wexford side of the estuary); *we could see two poles sticking up out of the water. They were* (there) *to mark the place where a German submarine had been sunk. It was the 8th October 1918, a beautiful clear, sunny day. Poor Tommy, I often wonder if he had a presentiment at all, his turn was so soon to come!*

He went to Dublin (the) *next day, and on the 10th was crossing to Holyhead on board the Leinster, when a few miles out from Kingstown she was torpedoed. It was the last ship sunk before the Armistice on 11th November 1918. His brother Eddie was on duty at Ballykinler, Northern Ireland. So he went at once to Kingstown on hearing the sad news.*

The poor fellow (Tommy) *was very brave. He and another young doctor on board the Leinster worked until the last, helping the wounded, and getting the women and children away in the boats. He did not save himself, but his body was found, and Eddie took him home to Knockboy to the family burial place* (in the cemetery at Ballygunner church in the townland of Knockboy, 3 miles from Waterford city). *The sorrow at Grange* (his home) *was terrible, especially for his poor mother. Her one consolation was that Tommy had been to confession and Holy Communion the day before he left."*

The Colonials

Britain's declaration of war in 1914 automatically meant that her colonies were also at war. New Zealand, Australia and Canada sent troops to assist the motherland. On 10 October 1918 each of the three countries had soldiers on board the *R.M.S. Leinster*.

New Zealand

New Zealand is comprised of two major islands and several smaller islands. Until 1841 it was a dependency of the Australian colony of New South Wales. It then became a colony of Great Britain until 1907, when it was given Dominion status. In 1911 the country was divided into four military administrative districts, Auckland and Wellington on the North Island and Canterbury and Otago on the south island. On the outbreak of war William Ferguson Massey was prime minister. Born in Limavady, Co. Derry, Ireland on 26 March 1856, his family immigrated to New Zealand in 1870. New Zealand made an extensive contribution to the allied war effort. From a population of 1,090,000, more than 100,000 served abroad, virtually half the eligible male population. Almost 58,000 casualties were sustained, of whom more that 17,000 were killed.[130] The were seven New Zealanders on board the *R.M.S. Leinster*. Two were officers and five were other ranks.[131]

Lieutenant Halse of the New Zealand Army had been treated in an Irish Hospital for an injured left shoulder. To keep it in position, he had his left side clamped in an iron frame. On the night of 9 October 1918 he stayed at *Rosse's Hotel*, Parkgate Street, Dublin. Also staying at the hotel were Lieutenant Robert Bassett (28) from Cork and Major Charles Duggan (51) from Hampshire. Bassett and Duggan were doctors and members of the Royal Army Medical Corps. The three men embarked on the *Leinster* the following day. *The Irish Times* of 12 October 1918 reported that Lieutenant Bassett put a lifebelt around Lieutenant Halse's neck after the first torpedo struck. *"Then the second torpedo exploded on the ship, and Mr Halse said to Mr Bassett 'The only thing to do is to jump at once.' Mr Bassett hesitated for a moment. Then he said to Mr Halse 'Good luck' and jumped off. Mr Halse immediately followed and the three gentlemen became separated. Mr Halse could not swim, but somehow he managed to float for about twenty minutes when a life-boat came along, crowded with people. For nearly three-quarters of an hour Mr Halse held on to the boat with his uninjured hand. He was then becoming exhausted, and told the seamen who seemed to be in charge of the boat that he could hold on no longer. Ropes were fastened around his body, and he was hauled in, suffering such agony with his wounded arm that he became unconscious. He recovered consciousness on the journey to Dublin, and is now in the Castle Hospital."* Lieutenant Bassett and Major Duggan were lost.

Two sources, however, appear to suggest that the exact circumstances of Lieutenant Halse's survival might have been slightly different from the newspaper report. Major Louis Daly mentioned Halse in his account of the sinking. However, he said that Halse jumped into the water with his servant *"and, though he could not swim, his servant kept him afloat until they reached some wreckage, to which they clung until they were picked up."* It is course possible that both accounts are true and that Halse was accompanied by a servant/batman as well as by Bassett and Duggan. A letter sent to businessman Edward Lee, by a doctor at Dublin Castle, would appear to suggest that that the officer who put the lifebelt around Halse's neck was Captain Robert Ernest Lee. Like Lieutenant Robert Bassett, Captain Lee was a R.A.M.C. doctor. Like Bassett, his first name was Robert. So it is possible that the authorities confused the two. It is of course possible Lee and Bassett both assisted soldiers who had their arms in splints. Wounded arms are common in wartime. What is certain is that Major Duggan, Captain Lee and Lieutenant Bassett died and Lieutenant Halse survived.

The other New Zealand officer on board did not share Lieutenant Halse's luck, being killed in the sinking. Second Lieutenant Henry Doyle (28) of the Wellington Regiment was from Auckland.[132] He was the only New Zealand soldier to die on the Leinster.

One of the surviving New Zealanders was involved in an interesting incident. On 12 October 1918 the *Dublin Evening Mail* published an account by a reporter who visited Dublin Castle Hospital. He met an Australian who had been plucked from the sea by a New Zealander on a raft. His rescuer had provided him with whiskey. The reporter expected that the two would have become friends for life. But no! After they landed at Kingstown, the two men walked up Marine Road. The Australian set off in search of a hospital. The New Zealander said *"Goodbye Aussie"* and jumped onto a Dublin bound tram in his wet clothes. (As Australian Sergeant Francis Coleman was pulled from the sea by a New Zealander on a raft, he would appear to be the Auzzie in the story.)

Canada[133]

Great Britain declared war on Germany on 4 August at 11 p.m. Greenwich mean time. On 6 August Canadian Premier Sir Robert Borden ordered the mobilisation of a Canadian Expeditionary Force (C.E.F.) to serve in Europe. Men from the Canadian regular army and militia volunteered to serve, as did thousands of civilians. Among those who joined up were many from

Britain and Ireland who had immigrated to Canada. A huge mobilisation centre was built at Valcartier, Quebec. Here 32,000 volunteers were assembled and began training. On 3 October 1914 the CEF sailed for England in one of the largest convoys ever assembled up to that time. After further training in England, the 1st Division landed in Continental Europe in February 1915. The 2nd Division arrived in September 1915. Both divisions formed the Canadian Army Corps. The 3rd Division arrived between December 1915 and March 1916 and the 4th Division in August 1916. More than 595,000 men enlisted in Canada, of whom 418,000 served overseas. In all, 258 battalions of the CEF were formed during the war. Conscription was introduced in the winter of 1917/18, but this accounted for fewer than 86,000 of the men who served. Canada sustained 210,000 casualties in the war, including more than 56,500 dead. Canadian soldiers were paid almost 5/- (five shillings) per day, as against British troops who were given 1s. 2d. (one shilling and two pence). The Canadians were excellent soldiers. In April 1917 they secured the first major allied victory on the Western Front when they captured Vimy Ridge, probably the strongest of the German positions in northern France. The last allied soldier to be killed in the First World War was a Canadian. Private Price was shot by a German sniper at 10.58 a.m. ib 11 November 1918, two minutes before the agreed cease-fire, while holding flowers given to him by Belgian civilians.[134] There were 14 Canadian soldiers and one nurse on the *Leinster*. Only five of them survived.[135]

Captain Edward Milne, on his way for a consultation at a London hospital, came on board the *Leinster* on crutches. Known to his family as Ned, Milne was born in Scotland.[136] His family moved to Galway when he was six. Later in life he was a junior reporter on the staff of the *Galway Express*. Around 1909 he moved to Canada. Joining his brothers who had already settled there, he went into farming in British Columbia. On the outbreak of war he and his brothers joined the army. He joined the Mounted Rifles. He later transferred to an Alberta Regiment and sailed for England on 3 October 1914 as part of the first Canadian contingent. After further training in England, he landed in Continental Europe in February 1915 as a private in the 1st Division. He served on the Western Front throughout the war, rising to the rank of Captain and being awarded the Distinguished Conduct Medal for bravery. Recovering from wounds, he came back to Ireland. Having survived the battlefield he was lost while travelling on the *Leinster* for a consultation at a London hospital. His body was recovered and taken to Galway for burial.

The *Galway Express*, the paper for which he had worked before moving to Canada, reported his death. *"Born at Montrose Scotland on 27 February 1888, Edward Ramsay Milne had just passed his thirtieth year when he met his untimely death on Thursday of last week by the torpedoing of the Leinster. There was an infinite touch of pathos in the tragedy, for it occurred on the eve of the first anniversary of his marriage and at a time when he could only walk by the aid of crutches and was therefore unable to make any fight for his life."* The report said that the Connaught Rangers took part in the burial service and that *"all the recruiting offices in Ireland were closed from twelve to two during Captain Milne's funeral. The officers and staff of the Galway offices joined in the cortege. The funeral was attended by his wife Mrs E.R. Milne, mother Mrs W.N. Milne and sister Rose Milne."* The fact that all the recruiting offices in Ireland closed for the funeral and that the officers and staff of the Galway office attended the funeral would appear to suggest that the wounded and decorated Captain was engaged in recruitment in Ireland.

Lieutenant Donald Gwyn (22), from Sherbrook, Quebec was a member of the Royal Canadian Dragoons. The regiment went to France with the 1st Division in February 1915. Gwyn was awarded the Military Cross for bravery. Having survived the horrors of the Western Front, he died on the *Leinster*. Private Michael Biggane of the Canadian Army Service Corps came from Bonmahon, Co. Waterford. He was probably among those who joined up following emigration to Canada. His mother lived in Waterford. So it was likely that he was visiting her while on leave. He was killed returning to duty. Nursing Sister Henrietta Mellett (39) was a member of the Canadian Army Nursing Corps.[137] Known to her family as *Marion*, she was from Co. Mayo. Her records show that she joined the Nursing Corps on 22 January 1918, was 5 ft. 7 ins. in height and weighed 130 lbs. She had previously served with the Red Cross in Egypt (18 months) and Tunbridge Wells, Kent, England (10 months). On 4 February 1918 she was posted to the 15th Canadian General Hospital, Taplow. She died on the *Leinster*. Her death notice in *"The Irish Times"* said that she was *"murdered by the huns."*

There was another Canadian on the ship who had recently been discharged from the Canadian Army.[138] The ancestors of Francis Edward Higgerty had come from Ireland, where their surname was probably Hegarty. A barrister by profession, he joined the 2nd Battalion, Eastern Ontario Regiment of the Canadian Army on 28 March 1918. The battalion was an Officer Training Corps and he started with the rank of private. He was 5ft. 10 ins. In height, had blue eyes, black hair and a ruddy complexion. At some point during 1918 he applied for, and was granted, a commission in the British Army. He was discharged from the Canadian Army and sailed for England. Before taking up his commission he decided to visit the land of his ancestors. His mother's cousin lived in Dublin. The visit cost him his life.

Frank Higgerty liked to write poetry. The emotional effect of visiting Ireland, the land of his ancestors, is shown in the following poem, written on 8 October, two days before the *Leinster* sinking.

"From Canada my home land, to Ireland my Sireland
From Ottawa to Dublin, some three thousand miles away
The call of one's relations, above the din and war of nations
Conserves the one green spot in memory forever and a day.
And when back o'er the sea I wander to the land that lies there yonder
I'll bring tidings from dear old Ireland to the land I adore,
To Canada my homeland, From Erin my own Sireland,
Stretch fond memories and emotions for ever and evermore."

The poem was found on his body.

Australia[139]

On 1 January 1901 the Commonwealth of Australia was formed by the coming together of the self-governing colonies of New South Wales, Queensland, South Australia, Tasmania, Victoria and Western Australia. On the outbreak of war Prime Minister Andrew Fisher said that Australia would *"pledge our last man and our last shilling to see this war brought to a successful issue."* Volunteers poured into staging camps. They came from town and country: clerks, solicitors, shop assistants, drovers, shearers and boundary riders. 332,000 troops served overseas as the Australian Imperial Force (AIF). Of these, approximately 60,000 were killed and over 212,000 were wounded. This was the highest proportion of casualties sustained by any army during the war.

The AIF eventually comprised of five infantry divisions with a total of 60 battalions.[140] It also included a mounted division made up of light horse regiments.[141] There were supporting arms: artillery, engineers, transport and medical. Each state tended to supply units as formations were raised.[142] For instance when the 1st Division was raised New South Wales furnished the 1st Brigade (1st to 4th Battalions), Victoria the 2nd Brigade (5th to 8th Battalions), and the four smaller states the 3rd Brigade (Queensland, 9th Battalion, South Australia, 10th Battalion, Western Australia, 11th Battalion and Tasmania, Western Australia and South Australia 12th Battalion). The same pattern was generally followed in almost all infantry divisions, supporting arms and branches. There were 13 Australian soldiers known to be on the *Leinster*.[143] Nine of their units are identified. As they came from different units, it seems unlikely that they were in Ireland on official duties and were probably on leave.

Lieutenant Francis Laracy was the only Australian officer on board. Known to his family as *Sonny*, he was studying to be a chemist at the University of Sydney when he enlisted in the Australian Army in August 1914.[144] Sent overseas in October 1914, he fought at Gallipoli, where he was wounded in May 1915. He was promoted to Sergeant in March 1916 and to Second Lieutenant in August 1916. He was wounded in France in October 1916 and in December he was promoted to Lieutenant. In July 1918 he was again wounded in France. After four years of war, instead of returning to Australia with his battalion, he decided to visit Ireland to meet his relations. He then sent a cable to his family, telling them that he was coming home. On 10 October 1918 he lost his life on the *R.M.S. Leinster*. His body was never recovered. In 1919 his mother Johanna received the following letter.

Base Records Office A.I.F.
7 March 1919

Dear Madam,

I have much pleasure in forwarding copy of extract from Third supplement, No. 30950 to the London Gazette, dated 15 October 1918, relating to the conspicuous services rendered by your son, Lieutenant F. P. Laracy 1st Battalion.

AWARDED THE MILITARY CROSS

'His Majesty the King has been graciously pleased to approve of the above award to the under mentioned officer in recognition of his gallantry and devotion to duty in the field: -

Lieutenant Francis Patrick Laracy

For conspicuous gallantry and leadership. With a small patrol of four other ranks he surprised and captured various enemy posts, capturing twenty-eight prisoners and four machine guns. He then reported the situation to his company commander, and during the main operation, he rendered assistance in co-operation by making a further advance, capturing seven prisoners and a machine gun. With the aid of re-enforcements he then linked up with the unit to his right, while the position gained was consolidated. Thanks to his splendid patrol work, valuable ground was won with slight casualties and with considerable loss to the enemy.'
The above has been promulgated in Commonwealth of Australia Gazette, No. 23, dated 12th February 1919.

Yours faithfully,

For Officer i/c Bn.

The Military Cross was presented to Johanna Laracy in March 1920.
Lance-Corporal Frederick Knuckey enlisted in the Australian Army signal school on 14 February 1916, at the age of 35 years and 4 months.[145] A

bank manager at the time of enlistment, he was of the Presbyterian faith, had fair complexion, brown hair and blue eyes. He sailed for Britain and disembarked at Plymouth on 10 August 1916. Attached to the 38th Battalion of the AIF, he arrived in France on 22 November 1916. Almost a year later, on 14 November 1917, he was a casualty of a gas attack. He was hospitalised in France until 26 January 1918. Following discharge, he spent a few weeks leave in England and rejoined his unit in France on 25 February 1918. He was probably on further leave when he died on the *Leinster*. Official records show that in all theatres of war twenty-two Australian soldiers died on 10 October 1918.[146] Of these, seven died on the *Leinster*.

There was an Australian born nurse on board the *Leinster*. *De Ruigneys Roll of Honour* contains an entry for her. As it mentions *"active service"* this, and the fact that she served in two hospitals where war wounded were treated, would appear to suggest that she was either a military nurse or a VAD. *"Nursing sister Winifred Starling was born at Petersham,* (a western suburb of Sydney) *the daughter of John and Elizabeth Jane (née Dudley) Starling. She was educated at Ardnaree, Burwood and the Girls' Church of England Grammar School, Sydney. She trained as a nurse at the Children's Hospital, Chelsea, London and at the Royal Prince Alfred Hospital (General), Sydney, New South Wales. In August 1915 she went to London and volunteered for active service. She was appointed Nurse, and later Sister, at Sutton-Veny (Warminster) Hospital and at the* (No 2) *New Zealand* (General) *Hospital, Walton-on-Thames. She was returning from Ireland when killed on the Leinster. She was unmarried."*[147]

The Americans

The United States Naval Air Service

The U.S. Navy showed an early interest in the military use of aeroplanes. When America declared war on Germany, on 6 April 1917, the U.S. Naval Air Service had 48 officers, 239 men, 54 training aircraft and one air station at Pensacola, Florida. On 24 October 1917 the United States Naval Aviation Forces, Foreign Service was established under the command of Captain Hutch Cone, with headquarters in Paris. It began to build air stations in Europe. Sixteen stations were built in France, 5 in Ireland, 2 in England and 2 in Italy. The Admiralty did the initial work on the 5 Irish stations. The Americans took over and finished the stations. The Irish bases were a kite balloon station at Berehaven, Co. Cork and seaplane stations at Whiddy Island, Co. Cork, Queenstown, Co. Cork, Ferrybank, Co. Wexford and Aught Point, Co. Donegal.[148] Captain Hutch Cone was returning from an inspection of the U.S. Naval Air Service bases in Ireland when he boarded the *Leinster* on 10 October 1918.

Hutch Ingham Cone was born in Brooklyn, New York on 26 April 1871.[149] He graduated from the United States Naval Academy in 1894 and was commissioned Assistant Engineer on 1 July 1896. He subsequently served on a wide range of ships. In October 1907 he took command of the Second Torpedo Flotilla. On board the *U.S.S. Whipple*, he took the flotilla, which also comprised of the *Hopkins, Hull, Lawrence, Stewart* and *Truxton* from Norfolk, Virginia through the Straits of Magellan at the tip of South America to San Francisco on the west coast of the United States. President Teddy Roosevelt wrote to him commending him on his achievement. In June 1908 he was assigned to the battleship *Connecticut* at San Francisco. The ship, accompanied by 15 other U.S. battleships, had partly completed a round-the-world voyage. As Fleet Engineer, Atlantic Fleet, Cone served on the remainder of the cruise. The voyage showed that the United States was now a world naval power.

On 21 April 1914 Cone had temporary command of the *Utah* when, during an intervention in a Mexican civil war, 3,000 soldiers and marines were landed at Vera Cruz. On 1 September 1915 he was appointed Marine Superintendent of the Panama Canal, a post he held until August 1917. The United States had declared war on German on 6 April 1917. In September Cone arrived in London and reported to Vice-Admiral Sims, Commander of U.S. Naval Forces in Europe. He was given command of the United States Naval Aviation Forces, Foreign Service, with headquarters in Paris. Shortly afterwards the Service was reorganised. Cone was reassigned to London, at the headquarters of Vice-Admiral William Sims. Soon after his posting to London Cone went on a tour of inspection of the U.S. Naval Air Service bases in Ireland. On 10 October 1918, his inspection finished, he boarded the *R.M.S. Leinster* in Kingstown., Co. Dublin. He was injured in the sinking and was brought to the Red Cross hospital at Dublin Castle, from where he made the following report.

Dublin Castle Hospital

Dublin, Ireland.
20th October 1918.

Memorandum

"*My experience on board the Irish Mail Steamer Leinster on October the 10th 1918, when that vessel was torpedoed off Dublin Harbor.*

I boarded the Leinster at the dock at Kingstown about twenty-five minutes of nine. I went in the smoking room, sought out a seat, deposited my overcoat in it, got a life preserver from a package there, put that in the seat next to me, deposited my grip in the smoking room and my steamer rug on top of the life buoy. Thus having my personal belongings disposed of, I went out on deck, the smoking room being on the upper deck and, as I remember it, fairly well aft.

On deck I found people coming on board in large numbers, especially British soldiers returning from leave. Among these British were a large number of Australian and New Zealand soldiers. I sat down on a bench just outside the smoking room watching the embarkation of the different passengers. I noted several women with children come on board and one in particular, a beautiful little girl about two years old, with blond curls. Naturally, I did not learn these people's names. One very attractive girl with a V.A.D. uniform sat next to me on the bench. (V.A.D.s were volunteer nurses). *I noted during this time that several American bluejackets* (i.e. sailors) *with white hats boarded the steamer, I should estimate that about five or six came under my observation. They were all in good spirits and nice clean looking boys. Before the steamer left things began to look crowded on deck. A woman with a child and basket evidently needed my seat, so I gave it to her and went back into the smoking room where I occupied the seat I had reserved for myself, got out of my grip a Saturday Evening Post and settled myself to read a story.*

I paid no particular attention as to when the ship steamed out of the slip, but things seemed to be going normally and I had been reading for probably half an hour or more when someone rushed into the smoking room door, and at exactly the same time the ship felt as if she had hit something forward a terrific blow. Of course I knew that it was a torpedo – so I got up. The first thing I did was to carefully put on and adjust my life belt and securely tie it to my body outside of my uniform coat.

My overcoat, grip and steamer rug I left in the smoking room and went out on deck. Up to the time the Leinster was hit and I came out of the smoking room I had not noticed that there was any particular sea running, as I don't remember that the ship had any unusual motion on her, but when I came out of the smoking room and started forward I noticed with dismay that there was a very heavy sea running, which, of course greatly added to the complications. By this time there was some excitement, many women were crying. Of course, the obvious thing to do was to try to assist these excited people and also get the boats lowered. I noted aft that they were just as many people working with the boats as could, so I went forward, as the vessel was sinking by the head and it seemed advisable to get out the boats as soon as possible. In going forward I met a few of the crew who had come up from the engine room. Among them a fireman who was in pitiful state – he evidently had both legs broken by the explosion and was otherwise mutilated about the face and bleeding profusely. This man was, of course, very much excited and begging everyone to save him.

I went in the bridge first and there found the Captain perfectly calm and clear headed. He told me that he was very much distressed, he was afraid that the wireless had not gotten through that we had been torpedoed, as the wireless was one of the first things damaged. I asked him, if he thought that the forward bulkheads would hold, in which case we should be able to get the boats and passengers away if there were sufficient boats to hold them, but observed that the German would probably hit us with another torpedo before we could do this, with which opinion the captain was in agreement. The captain also stated that he did not have enough lifeboats to hold anywhere near all the passengers. Upon my offering my services, he suggested that I assist in getting out the forward boats on the bridge deck. At that time there was a boat immediately under us swung in and two or three men trying to get it rigged out. One of the ship's officers, myself and six or eight men succeeded in rigging it out. In the meantime one of the boats on the port side had been rigged out and lowered into the water, but was nowhere near filled with people. As soon as we got the boat on the starboard side rigged out I saw that there was a sailor at each fall and lowered it down level with the main deck and women and children principally, but some men, climbed into it until it was full. In the meantime I went back up on the bridge and remarked to the captain that the boat from the port side was nowhere near full and he called it back along side and I believe that the people in the boat made an honest effort to get back and get more passengers. At any rate they made some effort.

I then went back down the ladder to the bridge deck and was casting off the lashings of the small box life rafts when a second torpedo hit, which seemed to be to be directly under me. Of course, it could not be absolutely under me, as I was very near the middle of the ship, just abaft the chart house. At any rate, it took the deck upon which I was standing up with it, and it seemed to me that I went up a mile high, but of course went only a few feet. In coming down I got entangled in the signal halyards hanging along the after side of the pilot house and I have a distinct recollection of the trouble I had in disentangling myself from these halyards while at the same time water from the column of water thrown up by the torpedo seemed to be coming down for an interminable time. Finally, when that was cleared away I found the deck practically disrupted where I had been standing and also that I could not bear any weight on the left leg. In fact, my right leg, when I put it down on the deck just doubled up under me and I could not bear any weight on the left leg. I also noted that the water was just about level with the bridge deck. I saw no signs of the boat and its occupants that we had just loaded at the starboard side.

When I saw that the bridge deck was actually getting down to the level of the water and that the seas were coming over, and I found I could not walk to the edge, I simply laid down and rolled overboard. When I got into the water I found that it bore my legs in a perfectly comfortable position. I immediately made efforts to swim away from the ship as it was evident that she would stay afloat only a few seconds longer. When I kicked my legs I found that they were perfectly useless and I realized that it would be doing them bad service by kicking them around. I attempted to paddle away with my hands, but had not succeeded in getting further than a few feet away, not more than twenty or twenty-five at a maximum, when the ship went down, her stern cocked up in the air. My last impression of the ship was a lot of people sliding down the hull from the stern to get into the water. I don't believe that there was any particular suction. If there had been, it most assuredly would have affected me for I was at this time being supported by a life belt only and a small grating. There seemed to be ample floating material around of all descriptions, including a small type of life raft built exactly like a box, and in my judgement perfectly worthless for lifesaving purposes. However, I spied one of these rafts and went to it and found that due to the condition of my legs I could not pull myself up on top of it, so I simply hooked my arm into the rope lanyard that was looped around its side and determined to fight it out in that position. This left my other arm free to push away any heavy timbers and debris that the sea might bump against me.

At this early time there were a great many lifeless bodies floating around. They must have been killed by the explosion because I particularly noted the large number of dead bodies afloat only a few minutes after the sinking of the vessel. I had been on the life raft only a short while when I spied an American bluejacket who proved to be a boy named Russell from Whiddy Island, floating in a white circular life buoy. (This was U.S. Navy Master Mariner G.W. Russell, based at Whiddy Island, Bantry Bay, Co. Cork.) *I motioned to him and he came over to me. I suggested that he get up on the life raft, as it was better than the way he was rigged. He climbed up on the life raft, taking his circular buoy with him and he seemed to fair pretty well. At this time a civilian dressed very scantily and whose name I have not been able to learn, swam up and climbed up on the other end of the raft. These two young men were very considerate and fine to me.*

I had been clinging to this rope in the water for only a few minutes when it carried away and I had to hook my arm into another rope. The boys on the raft continuously tried to cheer me up and at this time attempted to pull me up on the raft, but the thing was so small that it only resulted in turning it over. In fact, it was nothing like large enough for three people to sit on and would immediately turn over if they tried it. I waited as patiently as I could for any signs of craft coming out to rescue us and kept asking the fellows on the raft, who could see much further than I, as with a heavy sea running I could see no distance away. Finally one of them sent up a lusty cheer and said there certainly was a torpedo boat coming. This cheered me up greatly and I made up my mind to stick it out, although I was getting pretty weak. As there were a large number of life belts floating around, I took one of these and jerked the lanyard off. I used the lanyard to lash my left arm to the rope around the life raft and then looped the life belt itself under my right arm so that in case I went unconscious my head would be a little more secure in floating above the water line. Things began to get a little hazy to me about this time. But finally a destroyer was close and the two boys on the raft were pointing out the boat to me and cheering me up. I finally saw her myself, but the sight of the destroyer is the last thing I remember, as my next conscious moment was when I woke up in a bunk in the officers' quarters of the motor launch that finally rescued me.

When I came to I was in one of the officers' bunks of motor launch number 154 Royal Navy. I was covered with blankets and absolutely freezing. I was watched over with the greatest of care by a bluejacket who when I regained consciousness was forcing a little Scotch whiskey out of a bottle between my lips. He gave me a big drink and got some peacoats and piled a couple of them on top of my blankets. I still was practically frozen and had a succession of very severe chills. There were two or three women in the compartment, sitting on bunks opposite me, who had been taken from the water and who were wrapped up but apparently not much the worse for their experience and were talking and sympathizing with me in my predicament. I asked the bluejacket how long they thought we would be getting in and where we were bound for, and he told me we would be in Kingstown at the dock in about ten minutes. He watched over me constantly until we arrived at the dock. Then it was only a very few minutes before I was taken out of the bunk, helping myself up through the hatch as much as I could, laid on a stretcher and thoroughly wrapped up in blankets.

There was a doctor in a British khaki uniform who attended me here. He made a cursory examination, made some notes and put me into an ambulance where I was the only person and started me post haste for the hospital. I was in a semi-conscious state during the trip, but it seemed to take an interminable time to reach the hospital. I remember their pulling me out of the ambulance but do not remember much more until I regained consciousness while lying on a bed in the ward that I am now occupying in the Dublin Castle Red Cross Hospital. There were a number of doctors and nurses around me attempting to get my clothes off. After much exertion during which I did my best to help them, they finally they got my clothes off, wrapped me in blankets galore, gave me large drinks of whiskey and rolled my bed in front of a roaring fire. While attempting to get off the deck of the ship, I had the distinct impression that both my legs were broken, as I could not bear the slightest weight on either. In fact the right one had simply doubled up under me when I attempted to stand. On examination at the hospital the doctors told me that I was suffering from the worst kind of shock and that I had the right leg badly broken with a compound fracture between the knee and the ankle, and the left leg probably had the bone cracked in the ankle. *This diagnosis turned out to be practically correct when the X-rays were taken.*

*

"**Note**: *The following information was gleaned from Lieutenant Edward* Unwin, *R.N.V.R. Commanding Officer of* H.M. Motor Launch 154, *who picked me out of the water.*

It seems when the motor launch got up near me they noted that I was practically unconscious and would soon pass away, so they threw a line to one of the men on our raft and pulled it over alongside of the motor launch. I was noticed to be between the raft and the motor launch with the launch rolling very heavily, making it almost impossible to get me from the water. Lieutenant Unwin was informed by one of the men on the raft with me that both of my legs were broken and hence he instructed them to use as great care as possible in getting me on board. He expressed the opinion that they never would have gotten me on board had it not been for the fact that one of his crew, Leading Seaman Alexander Young, jumped overboard, passed a line around me under my arms and assisted in numerous ways in getting me on board the motor launch. When on board they were confronted with the problem of getting me down the very small hatch to a bunk, with my legs dangling as they were and the boat rolling so deeply. The crew of the launch finally succeeded in accomplishing this and made me as comfortable as possible when I regained consciousness. Lieutenant Unwin states that once when he visited me in the cabin of the motor launch I was delirious and was asking in a wild voice if I were alive, or words to that effect, all of which, of course, is beyond my memory."

*

"In order that my recollections may be of possible value to someone else, I am going to record here the things that I noted that it appears to me could have been better on board the steamer Leinster than proved to be the case.

1. Life belts were not sufficient in number to hold anywhere near all the passengers.

2. The boats were not rigged out, but were rigged inboard over the deck and in my opinion should have been rigged out as they are in crossing the Channel.

3. There were a large number of life rafts about the deck in my vicinity, all of which were held down by lashings and the lashings secured by pelican hooks. I was engaged in going around casting off these pelican hooks when

244

the second torpedo blew up. These rafts were very unhandy as a life saving appliance, although I am bound to say one of them saved my life. In the first place, they are a perfect box shape, about six or seven feet long, three feet broad by twelve or fifteen inches deep, and with a small rope lanyard along the side half way of its depth all the way around, with a little piece of cork in the middle of the loop. The first loop that I caught on the life raft that I secured carried away and the rope was undoubtedly rotten. I must say, however, that I noted no case where rotten falls or ropes in other parts of the ship caused any accident.

4. *There were large numbers of life preservers on board, of the type that you stick your head through and then lash around your body so as to keep your head well out of the water. This proved with me to be a most excellent type. The rule that all people should wear their life belts was not carried out and naturally caused some confusion by all hands putting on life belts at the last moment. As a matter of fact, I saw several officers of the ship using their valuable time in showing excited passengers how to put on their life belts after the torpedo had blown up.*

5. *In addition to the life belts, life rafts and boats there was a large amount of wreckage of all kinds, boxes, gratings, timbers, etc. floating around — ample to support the weight of every person on board if properly distributed. I fear that this wreckage caused the death of a good many people in the water by striking them on account of the high sea that was running. My most vivid recollection was the large number of dead bodies that were floating around in the water very soon after the explosion of the second torpedo and I firmly believe that a large percentage of those lost were killed by the explosion of the two torpedoes."*

*

The United States Navy[150]

On 4 May 1917, less than a month after America's declaration of war, the U.S. destroyers *Wadsworth* (flagship of Commander Joseph Taussig), *Conyngham, Davis, McDougal, Porter* and *Wainwright* arrived at Queenstown (now Cobh), Co. Cork. By the end of the war there were 92 U.S. ships in the harbour and 17 in Bantry Bay, West Cork. The ships in Bantry Bay, including the battleships *Nevada, Oklahoma* and *Utah,* were sent to prevent German surface attacks on ships carrying U.S. troops to France. There were twelve or thirteen U.S. Navy sailors on the *Leinster,* of whom four were lost. Master Mariner G. W. Russell, who was attached to the U.S. Naval Air Station at

Whiddy Island, Bantry Bay, Co. Cork, shared a raft with Captain Cone. He survived the sinking.

Gunners Mate Second Class John Balmer Black, from Darby, Pennsylvania, had enlisted in the U.S. Navy at Philadelphia on 15 December 1914.[151] A minor puzzle is caused by the fact that The American Battle Monuments Commission database records him as being assigned to the _H.M.S._ Leinster at the time of his death. The Royal Navy didn't have a ship of that name, and as he died on the _R.M.S_ Leinster, presumably the record refers to the mail ship. As he was a gunner, does this mean that he was one of Leinster's gunners? It doesn't seem likely that the United States Navy would assign one of their men to an Irish merchant ship. CDSPCo managing director Edward Watson recorded that Leinster had three gunners, of whom two were killed. The Commonwealth War Graves Commission record two Royal Navy gunners who died on Leinster. So it seems likely that the recording of Black being _"assigned to H.M.S. Leinster"_ was due to a clerical error.[152]

Quartermaster Second Class Joseph Leo Hogan, from Mechanicsville, New York, had enlisted in the U.S. Navy on 15 December 1917 at Albany, New York. Like survivor Master Mariner G. W. Russell, he was attached to the U.S. Naval Air Station at Whiddy Island, Bantry Bay, Co. Cork at the time of his death. Chief Machinist's Mate Roderick Perry Taylor was from Orlando, Florida. A member of the U.S. Naval Reserve Force, he had rejoined the navy on 6 September 1917 at Jacksonville, Florida. He was attached to the U.S. Naval Air Station at Queenstown at the time of his death. Also lost was Yeoman Third Class John James Valentine from New Briten, Connecticut.

The Cork Constitution of 12 October 1918 had an interview with American Seaman Frank A. Martin. _"The first torpedo struck the mail boat on the portside forward. Several passengers on the portside said they saw the torpedo about forty yards off before it struck. It seemed to go through the ship, as I saw splinters flying out of the starboard side. Then there was a regular panic and confusion on board. One boat was lowered, but too many got into it – they were jumping on top of each other. The bow of the boat hit the water first and capsized, and all in it were thrown into the water. Myself and some other Americans tried to lower other boats, but they would not work. During this time the mail boat did not seem to settle much, but she had stopped, and was not moving at all. From the noise I thought the pumps were working, but it may have been that the water pipes were broken. Anyhow, the vessel did not seem to settle down, but just to stand still. Then there was a second shot about 3 to 5 minutes after the first. That shot struck on the port side forward._ (This was a surprising mistake for a sailor to make. In fact the Leinster had turned around and was now facing back the way it had come. The second torpedo struck the ship on the starboard side.) _It seemed to cut the ship in two. Everything flew, debris of all kinds. The boilers and everything_ went, there seemed to be an explosion. The mail boat listed to port and flung down everyone on board. It did not take 5 minutes from the time the second shot was fired until the ship sank. Then everyone was scrambling in the water and grabbing whatever they could."

The Reporter asked Martin: "Where were you when the second torpedo struck?" Martin: "I was in the aft end of the vessel. The women and children were mostly forward and amidships." Reporter: "How many boats had been got away before the second torpedo struck?" Martin: "I saw about 5 or 7 men put out in one boat and get away from the ship. I did not see them making any attempt to save anyone. Every effort was made by the Americans with me, including D. Dwyer, J. Hogan, D.J. Murphy, J.M. Rafferty and G.W. Russell, to get boats out to save people, but we did not succeed in getting any of them clear before the second shot. There was an American captain on board – Captain H. Cone- and he did his best to direct the people. He shouted orders from the bridge deck, and did all he could to establish order out of the prevailing confusion. We only managed to lower the boat tackles about 5 feet and the boats were then some 10 to 15 feet from the water. Then people clambered into the boats and one end of the boats would dip. I suppose the people thought they would be saved that way, but when the boats dipped they were all pitched into the water. I would say the vessel was travelling about 18 knots when she was first struck, she was not going at top speed. When the second torpedo struck, the whole ship seemed to be torn in two amidships. The decks were all covered with steam and water. The people ducked down to avoid the flying stuff. Many of them were stuck. Everyone was then thrown into the water and we grabbed what we could. The ship sank very fast. It was surprising there was not more suction. I was in the water and I thought everyone would be sucked under. I had no life belt. Hardly any of my party had life belts. It was our own fault and risk. We did not put them on. I saw 8 or 9 people hanging on to one raft near me. Everyone was fighting for life. The cries of the women and children in the water were heard. There were no boats about and no vessels in sight. We were somewhere between 2 and 3 hours in the water. Then the destroyers and mine sweepers came along and we were picked up. We could not have been better treated than we were after being rescued."

Reporter: "How many had gone down when the first rescue vessel arrived?" Martin: "Very many and many others were floating about dead, with their life belts on them, their faces black and blue. The rafts that are kept on board and floated off when the ship sank were the only things the people had to cling to. When the Leinster went down bow first I saw her propeller in the air. It was not working and the ship had been crippled from the first explosion." The report said that Frank Martin and several of his countrymen were taken to the Sailors War Hostel, Eden Quay, Dublin.

*

U.S. Navy Chief Special Mechanic James Mason made a report of the sinking.[153] The report was typed. At the start of the report Mason's middle initial is mistakenly given as *"D."* He signed the report James B. Mason. Base Six, mentioned in the report, was at Haulbowline, near Queenstown, (now Cobh), Co. Cork.

U.S. Naval Forces operating in European Waters,
Destroyer Flotillas,
Torpedo Repair Station.

Base Six.
12 October 1918.

From: J.D. Mason, Chief Special Mechanic, U.S.N.
To: Officer in charge.
Subject: Report of sinking of S.S. Leinster.

(1)   *I took passage, going on leave, on the S.S. Leinster leaving Kingstown, Ireland, sailing about 9.00 a.m. At about an hour from Kingstown I was sitting on the starboard side aft when I heard one of the soldiers shout: 'A torpedo.' Immediately afterwards a shock shook the vessel, of a torpedo which apparently hit the vessel in the vicinity of the mail which was blown out. I proceeded to the top of the after upper deck with about a dozen men, one of whom kept the remainder from rushing up. This was one of the ship's crew apparently stationed at the ladder for this purpose. We hoisted out two boats on the portside, both of which were just reaching the water with the regular crews in them when I saw the second torpedo coming directly for the starboard side. This torpedo hit about amidships, in the vicinity of the boilers, which apparently exploded, even though I noticed that the boilers were being blown down through the safety valves from the time the first torpedo hit. The second torpedo and boiler explosion produced an enormous amount of wreckage which fell so thickly in clouds together with stream and debris, that it was difficult to see anything at all. It was impossible to control the people after the second torpedo hit and there was a rush for the boats and rafts. The ship listed to port and went down by the bow. I left the upper deck and lowered myself over the stern with a rope. I swam to a hatch and then to a raft. I looked back and saw the ship sink. At the time there were not more than four or five lifeboats right side up in the water and I believe all of them must have capsized. There were at least a dozen rafts which floated clear but it was very rough and very difficult to stay on the rafts or to hold on when they became crowded. I tried three different rafts, staying on the last one until taken off by the ML 154. As I went up to the third raft Captain Cone was holding on and in reply to my question as to how he was doing he told me both his legs were broken. The Captain, two U.S. Naval enlisted men (I think Aviation Quartermasters), one civilian and myself were the only one's holding on to*

248

this raft. The raft capsized twice and the sea was so high that we could do nothing but hold on to it and pieces of passing wreckage in an effort to hold the raft steady. I was in the water holding on to this raft about an hour and I would estimate that we were not picked up until two hours from the time the ship was torpedoed. There was considerable difficulty in getting the Captain aboard the motor launch, each of us in turn trying to hold him up. Finally one of the crew jumped overboard and made a line fast to him and he was hoisted aboard. The Captain, officers and crew of the ML 154 treated us with great consideration and did everything possible for us which could be done. This little boat with only half the crew on board picked up altogether twelve or fourteen and by promptly leaving the scene when no more people could be found alive undoubtedly saved those they had rescued who were the most seriously injured and exhausted. The crew of this boat deserve great credit for gallant and untiring action and for the apparently excellent condition of their machinery when run at utmost speed. Fortunately the ML 154 had some whiskey aboard which, in the absence of medical attendance, under the conditions was very much appreciated. Captain Cone was so exhausted that he could not drink but when his lips were moistened with a little whiskey his condition was perceptibly improved.

(2)   I know that there were at least three other U.S. Naval men on board, one Chief Petty Officer, whom I saw in the distance and two enlisted men who were shipping over from the UTAH and I saw them on a raft afterwards but do not know whether they were saved. There were also several American soldiers on the ship, three or four of which I believe were saved, possibly more.

(3)   When the torpedo hit I do not think there were any ships in sight but the smoke of the mail steamer, which we had passed, was on the horizon astern. A British destroyer was the first to reach the scene followed shortly by other destroyers, motor launches and trawlers.

Lieutenant E. Unwin of the ML 154, who was at the wheel and to my mind handled the little boat excellently, took me up to his house after landing at Kingstown and was extremely generous and considerate in his treatment. The entire part taken by the ML 154 during this accident cannot be too highly praised.

                                                                                        /s/   James B. Mason.

*

The United States Army[154]

Chief Special Mechanic James Mason's account said that there were "*several American soldiers on the ship.*" On 11 October 1918 a columnist for the *Dublin*

Evening Mail reported that he had met an American soldier, named Denny, at Dublin Castle Hospital. From Massachusetts, the man had dislocated his shoulder in the sinking of the *Leinster*. Denny said that he was sitting in the stern of the ship with another American soldier named Rose. When the ship was struck, Denny heard people say that it was a torpedo. The shock was so slight he got up to see if in fact they had been torpedoed. He and Rose were helping a girl when the second torpedo struck. The next thing he remembered was being in the water, swimming. He had no idea how long he'd been there. He was rescued by a destroyer. He said that he would be very grateful for information on his colleague, Rose. A partial list of survivors and casualties shows that Denny was Sergeant 1st Class T. F. Denny, Chemical Warfare School.

On 12 October 1918, *The Cork Constitution* carried an interview with T. F. Denny., 266 South Main Street, Gardner, Massachusetts, who had boarded the *Leinster* following a visit to the home of his family in Kerry. The interview makes no mention of Denny and Rose helping a girl. *"I was standing near the stern of the ship. Immediately after the explosion there was considerable confusion and scrambling around among the passengers. An attempt was made to lower the boats, but there appeared to be a good deal of panic around about. Instead of waiting, some passengers scrambled into one boat. I saw a couple of Australians behaving very well indeed. One of them got a life preserver for a very young girl. I do not think there were enough life preservers to go around, not amongst those in the stern, anyway, because I hunted looking for some. There were a couple of Americans who had no life preservers, and I remember looking for them. I saw one girl on board without any lifebelt on. She was quite calm, and was waiting to get a place in a boat. I had started going down a rope to get into the water when there was a second explosion, and I remember nothing after that for some time. My first impression afterwards was that my lungs had burst. I was under water and must have been drawn down by the sinking of the ship. When I got to the surface and was able to get my breath back, I caught hold of a spar. I found that my right shoulder was dislocated and my arm useless. Fortunately, I had done some swimming before, so I managed to cling on to the spar. I saw at least twenty people die in the water around me. I could do nothing for them. Then I remember seeing destroyers coming up. Of course I do not know how long that was afterwards, but my own impression was that it was from two and a half to three hours. I would like to know when these rescuers came up, as I am wondering if I can judge time. There was a very high sea running, and I found it exceedingly difficult to cling to the spar. I do not remember getting on board the vessel that rescued me. I must have been in a semi-conscious condition. The first thing that I remember is a man trying to make me sit up. He caught hold of my injured shoulder and the pain roused me. I did not see any vessel in sight at the time of the first explosion. When I was in the water I remember seeing two destroyers. The first explosion on the Leinster was not very violent at all. I don't know how violent the second explosion was, as it threw me overboard. Then, when I was in the water, I was trying to get as far away from the* suction of the ship as possible. I called to a friend of mine, an American named John Rose, who had never done much swimming, and I don't know what happened to him. It seems to me now that just before the ship went down I saw hundreds and hundreds of people clinging to the deck and to the rails and some of them diving into the water, but that is not clear in my mind. The boat must have gone down very quickly after the second explosion. The first explosion seemed near the bow and the second near the stern. I did not see the Leinster sink. When I rose to the surface she was gone." Sergeant Denny mentioned his friend John Rose to both reporters and told the first reporter that he would be very grateful for information about Rose. Sergeant John A. Rose, Base Section, U.S. Army was killed when the *Leinster* was sunk.

An American soldier who survived the sinking was mentioned in a telegram sent by the American consul in Dublin. This was Sergeant Eugene O'Connor, 108th Engineers, U.S. Army. Another American soldier on the ship was Lieutenant Joseph Furlong (28). The millennium (year 2000) edition of *The Wexford People* said that he was from the U.S. Medical Reserve and was attached to the British Forces. It said that he was the eldest son of Michael Furlong, St. Louis, Missouri, formerly of Lough, Duncormick, Co. Wexford. Lieutenant Furlong was returning to duty after paying his first visit to his father's native district. The trip cost him his life.

*

The American consul in Dublin sent the following telegram to Washington on 10 October 1918.[155]

"I have the honor to report that the British unarmed steamship LEINSTER was sunk by torpedoes on October 10th at 10 a.m., about 15 miles from Kingstown. The LEINSTER left Kingstown on October 10th at 9 a.m., for Holyhead. It was struck by two torpedoes without warning and sunk in about fifteen minutes. The total dead and missing is estimated at about 500. About 200 survivors were rescued by Naval and other vessels and landed at Kingstown and Holyhead. The sea was rough. It is believed that there were about fifteen Americans on board. Among those reported to be Americans are: Anderson, U.S.N., Sergeant Eugene O'Connor, 108th Engineers, United States. Army, T. F. Denny, 266 South Main, Gardner, Massachusetts, Captain Himicone, American naval officer, was saved and is now recovering in a Dublin hospital, Frank A. Martin, J. M. Rafferty, D. J. Murphy, G. W. Russell, Hogan and Dwyer whose addresses are not yet learned are reported among the survivors. The vessel was not convoyed. A United States Naval Officer is investigating. Affidavits have not been obtained by this office."

Adams, American Consul.

"Anderson, U.S.N." may possibly be Gunner E. Andorsech from the *U.S.S. Utah,* who survived the sinking. Apart from this, referring to Captain H. I. Cone as *"Himicone"* and including Hogan among the survivors, the information in the telegram is remarkably accurate. (It may suggest that Quartermaster Second Class Joseph Hogan survived the sinking, only to die in hospital.)

*

Vice-Admiral William Sims, Commanding U.S. Naval forces in Europe sent the following telegram.

From: London
To: OPNAV

6740. Ireland mail steamer LEINSTER torpedoed Thursday morning about 500 missing. Captain Cone saved and now in Dublin Castle Hospital with leg broken. Doctor Irvine sent from Queenstown and Cones nephew, Doctor Rhodes from here. He is apparently in no danger. Mrs Cone express my sincere sympathy. The torpedoing of LEINSTER published in British press but no names of survivors mentioned.

10-11-18

The following messages were sent from the U.S. Navy base at Queenstown to Vice-Admiral Sims in London.

U.S. Naval Forces Operating in European Waters
Destroyer Flotillas, Torpedo Repair Station
Base Six, 12 October 1918

From: Officer in Charge
To: Force Commander

Subject: MASON, J. B., C.S.M. – On board S.S. Leinster

Mason's information as to this disaster is told by him without any reference to his own conduct. It would appear that he is largely responsible for the successful launching of two boats, that he sought his own safety without a life preserver as the ship sunk swimming from one raft to another until he found one not so crowded,

252

*that he aided Captain Cone as far as was possible and that until exhausted he
assisted the crew of ML 154 to perform their very creditable work.*

(S) Radford Moses

*U.S. Naval Forces Operating in European Waters
Destroyer Flotillas, Torpedo Repair Station
Base Six, 13 October 1918*

*From: Senior Officer Present
To: Force Commander*

Subject: Report of James B. Mason, Chief Special Mechanic, U.S. Navy

*Particular attention is respectfully invited to the gallant conduct of the officers and
men of H.M. Motor Launch 154. The skilful handling of this motor launch and the
untiring efforts of the crew resulted in saving the lives of Captain H. I. Cone, U.S.
Navy and Chief Special Mechanic James B. Mason, U.S. Navy.*
    It is recommended that proper acknowledgement of these services be made.

(S)   H.B. Price

Vice-Admiral Sims sent the following memo to the Secretary of the Navy.

14 November 1918

*From: Force Commander.
To; Secretary of the Navy (Bureau Of Navigation)*

*Subject: Commendable conduct of J.B. Mason, Chief Special Mechanic, U.S. Navy,
      in connection with loss of S.S. Leinster.*

   *(1) Forwarded, inviting particular attention to the conduct of Chief Special
      Mechanic J. B. Mason on duty at the Torpedo Repair Station, Queenstown, it
      is recommended that Mason receive the Department's commendation.*

   *(2) Copy of a letter addressed by the Force Commander to the British Admiralty
      concerning the conduct of officers and crew of the British Motor Launch No.
      154 is attached for the Department's information.*

The memo was rubber stamped *WMS*. (i.e. William Sims.)

29 November 1918

From: Force Commander.
To: Secretary of the Admiralty.

Subject: Meritorious conduct of Leading Seaman Alexander Young H.M. Motor Launch 154.

1. I am informed by Captain H. I. Cone, who has been in charge of U.S. Naval Aviation in Europe, of the meritorious conduct of Leading Seaman Alexander Young in rescuing Captain Cone after the sinking of the Leinster.

2. Captain Cone had very serious injuries, one leg being broken. He was found lashed to a raft in practically an unconscious condition.

3. Captain Cone states that it is very doubtful if it would have been possible to get him aboard the motor launch if it had not been for the prompt action of Seaman Young who, in a cold and rough sea, jumped overboard and swimming around Captain Cone succeeded in passing a line under his arms. He remained in the water during the difficult process of getting Captain Cone aboard the motor launch.

4. At Captain Cone's request I am very glad to express the appreciation of the United States Navy for the courageous and prompt efforts of this man in assisting the rescue.

The memo was rubber stamped:

> N.C. Twining.
> Captain U.S. Navy,
> Chief of Staff,
> Signed for Vice-Admiral
> In His Absence.

Vice-Admiral Sims sent the following message to Chief Special Mechanic James B. Mason.

21 October 1918

From: Force Commander
To: James B. Mason, Chief Special Mechanic, U.S.N.
Via: Senior Officer Present, Base Six.
Subject: Commendation for gallantry.

(1) I desire to express my sincere appreciation to you of the work performed by you upon the sinking of the S.S. Leinster.

(2) Your apparent disregard of yourself on this occasion, your untiring efforts and cool conduct, were of the very highest order and reflect great credit on you personally and upon the Naval Service.

(3) Cool conduct and self sacrifice in emergencies in the saving of human life, whoever or whatever he may be are always duties worthy of the highest praise.

(4) In this particular case, in addition to my appreciation for your gallant work I can add my most heart-felt thanks for saving Captain Hutch I. Cone, who is not only a dear and personal friend of mine, but is an officer not only of great value to the U.S. Naval Service but to the entire 'Allied Cause.'

(5) I have transmitted copy of the report in your case to the Secretary of the Navy, Bureau of Navigation, and have taken pleasure in recommending you for a Gold Life-Saving Medal.

The Royal Navy

There were 25 members of the Royal Navy on board the *Leinster*.[156] Many appear to have been Irish men and women returning from leave. George Richard Colin Campbell was the second highest-ranking member of the Royal Navy on the ship. Known as Colin, the thirty-four year old Lieutenant-Commander was born at Ballyeglish, Moneymore, Co. Derry, the son of a clergyman. A career naval officer, he had been promoted to Lieutenant-Commander in 1916. He joined the Admiralty Compass Department, rising to become superintendent of the Magnetic Compass Branch. With Dr. G.T. Bennett he invented the Campbell-Bennett Aperiodic Compass.[157] Travelling with Campbell on the *Leinster* was his wife Eileen and 4½ year old daughter, also named Eileen. All three Campbells were lost in the sinking. Eileen Campbell's body was recovered from the sea with her baby still tightly clutched in her arms. They were brought to the mortuary of St. Michael's Hospital, Kingstown, where Colin's father, the Reverend Edward Campbell, identified them. Colin's body was recovered later. All three are buried in Grangegorman Military Cemetery, Dublin. Their grave has a beautiful headstone with a sculpted ship's anchor. There appears to be a dual symbolism in this. Firstly, Colin Campbell was a naval officer. Secondly, a slip of paper was recovered from one of his pockets, on which was written *"Cast all our cares to God, by his anchor hold."*

Leading Seaman William O'Sullivan and Able Seaman David White (41) travelled together by train from Cork. O'Sullivan was returning to *H.M.S. Carysford* and White to *H.M.S. Pembroke*.[158] When they got to Dublin they met a female cousin of White's, who was returning to work in England. The three of them took the train to Kingstown, where they boarded the *Leinster*. David White and his cousin were lost in the sinking. William O'Sullivan survived. Four years previously he had survived the sinking of *H.M.S. Aboukir*. (On 20 September 1914 the cruisers *H.M.S. Aboukir*, *H.M.S. Cressy* and *H.M.S. Hogue* were all sunk within a few minutes by the U-9 with the loss of 1459 lives.) White's wife Mary was pregnant at the time her husband was lost. She named their son George Paul Leinster. Growing up he was known as Leinster. This was later abbreviated to Lennie.

Following employment as an Invoice Clerk, Arthur Eade enlisted in the Royal Navy in 1912.[159] He started out as a Probationary Sick Berth Attendant on *H.M.S. Vivid*, a Base Ship at Devonport. Then, after medical training at Plymouth Hospital, he served on *H.M.S. Vivid*, *H.M.S. Gibraltar* and *H.M.S. Adventure*. Afterwards he was posted to Haulbowline Hospital, Queenstown and subsequently to the depot ship *H.M.S. Colleen.*, also at Queenstown. On

10 October 1918 Eade (25) was lost on the *Leinster* with his *H.M.S. Colleen* shipmates Signalman John Christy and Yeoman of Signals Chief Petty Officer Herbert Pilgrim.

Commander W. Baggott, based at Kingstown., was the highest-ranking member of the Royal Navy on board the *Leinster*.[160] He survived the sinking. He was the man who asked Bill Sweeney if he were in charge of the lifeboat *Big Bertha*.

Leinster's Gunners

For hundreds of years British merchant ships had carried guns to protect them from attack. In wartime the merchant ships were a valuable resource for the British navy.[161] During World War 1, as submarine attacks against British merchant shipping grew, an aft gun was mounted on merchant ships as a defensive measure. Members of the Royal Navy were put on board the ships to man the guns. According to Patrick O'Sullivan in *Lusitania: Unravelling the mysteries* the vast majority of merchant ships did not have an aft gun in place before 1917.[162] CDSPCo crew agreement lists for 1918 show that the company had 12 gunners on their ships on the Kingstown to Holyhead route. As they had three ships in use in 1918 this would have averaged four gunners per ship. Presumably some of them would have been off duty at any given time. Managing Director Edward Watson's figures show that there were three gunners on the *Leinster* on 10 October 1918.

Ordinary Seaman Fred Hough RNVR (21) was from Manchester. His mother, Mary, was a widow. On 10 October 1918 she lost her son Fred. Seaman A.B. Hartnett was injured in the sinking. He was treated at King George V Hospital, Dublin. A partial list of survivors and casualties records the word *Leinster* after his name, as it does for other surviving crewmen. Yet he is not mentioned on any of the crew lists in the newspapers and does not appear on the CDSPCo 1918 Crew Agreement List. Therefore it seems reasonable to assume that he was one of the ship's gunners. Leading Seaman George Leatherbarrow RNVR was killed in the sinking. From Liverpool, he was 34 years old. Commonwealth War graves Commission records show that he was serving on the *R.M.S. Leinster* at the time of his death.

Rear-Admiral William Sims in his book *The Victory at Sea* says that: *"Those who advocated arming the merchant ships as an effective method of counteracting submarine campaigns had simply failed to grasp the fundamental elements of submarine warfare. They apparently did not understand the all-important fact that the quality which makes the submarine so difficult to deal with is its invisibility. In six weeks, in the spring and early summer of 1917, thirty armed merchantmen were torpedoed and sunk off Queenstown and in no case was a periscope or a conning-tower seen. The English never trusted their battleships at sea without destroyer escort, and certainly if a battleship with its powerful armament could not protect itself from submarines, it was too much to expect that an ordinary armed merchantman would be able to do so."*

The Wrens[163]

On 26 November 1917 Sir Eric Geddes, First Lord of the Admiralty, wrote to King George V. *"Sir Eric Geddes, with his humble duty, begs to inform Your Majesty that the Board of Admiralty have under consideration the possibility of substituting women for men on certain work on shore directly connected with the Royal Navy, and as a result of full enquiry, it is recommended that a separate women's service should be instituted for this purpose."*

"It is submitted for Your Majesty's approval that the service should be called THE WOMEN'S ROYAL NAVAL SERVICE, and that the members of the service should wear a distinctive uniform, details of which will be submitted to your majesty for approval in due course….." The letter was rubber stamped in red *"The King has signified his approval"* and dated 28 November 1917. Recruiting of officers and other ranks began soon afterwards. The latter were recruited through local employment exchanges. This proved a deterrent to many middle-class potential recruits. The members of the new service were soon being referred to as *Wrens*. They worked as typists, bookkeepers, telegraphists, telephonists, wireless operators, drivers, laundresses, cooks and waitresses.

There were three *Wrens* on board the *Leinster*. They were Maureen Waters, Josephine Carr and Miss Barry (first name unknown). Twenty-year-old Maureen Waters, from Ballintemple, Cork was the daughter of wine merchant John J. Waters. A letter she wrote to her family after the sinking was published in the *Cork Examiner* on 14 November 1918. The *Cork Examiner* report said that Maureen Waters last saw Josephine Carr in the reading room as the ship left Kingstown and did not know what had happened to her. The report continues by quoting Maureen Waters's letter to her family. *"We were on the starboard side sitting up near the bow, when the ship was hit on the other side. I never thought we were torpedoed. I thought it was a gun firing on our own boat. Then we saw water rushing over the deck. I put on a lifebelt. I waited for a man to put on his and then asked him to put mine right. Miss Barry and I were quite calm. We could not have properly realised it. Then I met with Cora.* (Cora Daly, wife of Major Louis Daly of the Leinster Regiment. They had been married in Cork two days previously.) *We kissed each other goodbye. She had no lifebelt nor was Louis to be seen. I told her a man further up had lifebelts. We got onto the top deck and went around to try and find where we were to go. We saw lifeboats already launched in the water empty and nearly died when we thought we would have to jump down into them. I caught a sailor and asked him where we were to go. He said the other side. I then saw Cora get into a lifeboat and screamed at Miss Barry. We got in and were swung down.*

On our way we saw Louis on the bridge waving and smiling at us. I cried then but stopped to console poor Cora.

(Later comments in the letter about Captain Birch show that they were on Bill Sweeney's lifeboat, 'Big Bertha'.) *We reached the water. No one let the ropes go, so we were tied to the sinking ship and our oars were tied to the seats with ropes. It was awful. A man yelled for penknives. I remembered mine was in my coat pocket. Miss Barry also had hers. So I tell you we were not long in passing them to the men and they cut the oars loose, also the ropes which tied us to the ship. Just then the second torpedo came on our side. How we were not swamped there and then God alone knows. I saw half the 'Leinster' go up in the air, and volumes of water, and thought we would get it all down over us but we didn't. I then looked behind and the ship was standing straight upright almost, propeller in the air, and we were hardly three yards away. I just prayed as I never did before and buried my head in Cora's lap, never even hoping to be saved. Needless to say, our boat was crammed and we had only three oars left. All the others broke. To see the crowds of unfortunate people struggling in that awful sea was terrible. We had a very clearheaded man who took command of our boat. He was splendid.* (She is obviously referring to Bill Sweeney.)

We got clear of the wreckage and hauled Captain Birch into our boat, but his eye was out and one leg broken. We were about an hour and a half in that boat in the most appalling sea as I ever saw, with three oars and bailing for dear life with caps etc. when we saw three or four destroyers come into sight. They picked up people floating on rafts first. Then one (H.M.S. Lively) *came around to us. Oh, the relief! The getting on board was the worst of all. She came close to us and there was a desperate rush to grab ropes or a sailor's hand. Cora said 'Oh, my God, we're swamped!' She looked around quickly. The destroyer washed over onto us. It was terrible. I know I went right under and thought I was never coming up again. But I did and was between the destroyer and our boat, hanging on with one hand and my legs just inside the gunwale of our boat. Three times I had a sailor's hand, but not securely enough, and three times I went down. After the second time I went under I saw Cora being hauled up. Then a man saw me going down between boats and gave me a tug onboard our lifeboat. A wave came and I made a desperate grab at the same sailor's hand, and with the other grabbed the rope around the deck part of the destroyer and there I hung. I nearly lost consciousness and I faintly heard ' One, two, three, - -haul' and I was pulled on board. Three sailors cut the lifebelt off and worked my arms and made me drink rum. I know I was conscious all the time."*

The letter goes on to detail the kindness she received on board the destroyer. It continues: *"Poor Miss Barry was washed out of the lifeboat and screamed 'For God's sake save me.' A sailor jumped off the destroyer and saved her. They were both hauled on board by ropes. She was all right after a few minutes. We also had a sweet child of about three years with us. Her mother was drowned."* Waters added that she was dressed in naval officer's clothes when landed at Kingstown. Mentioning the relief it was to her friends to find her safe, she concludes: *"Louis (Daly) was found later at the Castle Hospital suffering very much from his legs, which were gashed by the fall he got in the second concussion.* (i.e. when the second torpedo struck.) *The agony he suffered was immense. But thank God he is saved."*

Josephine Carr (19) died on the *Leinster.* A shorthand typist in the Woman's Royal Naval Service, she had joined the service less than a month before, on 17 September 1918. She was probably on her way to take up her first position. She was the first ever *Wren* to be killed on active service. Born in Cork, she was the daughter of Samuel and Kathleen Carr, 4 Bethesda Row, Blackrock.[164] As Josephine Carr was of woman or rating rank, presumably her two friends were of similar rank. The uniform worn by ratings was a long shapeless dress, tied in the middle. It had a smaller version of the male naval rating's collar. Ratings wore a pudding basin hat, black stockings and heavy footwear. Travel regulations said: *"Officers of the WRNS will travel first class, and women third class."* Members of the WRNS could buy a standard meal at railway eating rooms for 1/- (one shilling). WRNS were employed only on shore-based duties. Their humorous motto was *"Never at Sea."* Josephine Carr, the first ever *"Wren"* to die on active service, died at sea.

The Royal Air Force

On 1 April 1918 the Royal Flying Corps (RFC) and the Royal Naval Air Service (RNAS) merged to form the Royal Air Force. There were at least 14 members of the RAF on the *Leinster*.[165] Most of them were lost. Among the officers who died was Lieutenant Christopher Domegan, who had worked with the Irish Land Commission before joining up. He initially served with the Royal Irish Fusiliers. Judging by their ranks, the majority of the RAF appear to have been ground crew. Among those lost were Corporal Dennis Creedon (31), Banteer, Co. Cork, Private Second Class Cardiff (first name unknown), James's Street, Dublin, Private Second Class John Corrigan, Birr, Co. Offaly and Private Second Class Edward Kelly, Granard, Co. Longford. While the Irishmen were probably returning from leave, Englishman Corporal Harry Alderidge and Scotsman Air Mechanic Second Class William Crichton were probably going on leave. They were stationed at the 19th Training Squadron at the Curragh, Co. Kildare. Both were lost. Private Second Class Thomas Woodgate, Callan, Co. Kilkenny, was returning to duty with 23rd Training Squadron R.A.F. when he was lost on the *Leinster*. He had joined the RFC seven months previously.[166] Of the Irish who joined the British armed services in 1918, fifty-six per cent went to the RAF.[167] Among other things, they were probably attracted by the technical opportunities on offer.

The man who sank the *Leinster:*

The life and career of Robert Ramm

Robert Heinrich Ramm was born on 3 December 1890 in the village of Klein-Daberkow, Mecklenburg, in the northeast of Germany.[168] Mecklenburg adjoins the Baltic Sea, has a mild climate and is a farming region. It is mostly flat, with some low hills and is dotted with many small lakes.[169] Ramm was the son of a large tenant farmer on land owned by the Grand-Duke of Mecklenburg. He was educated at the Schiller-Realgymnasium (secondary school) in Stettin,[170] about 70 Kilometres (43.5miles) east of his village. He left school in Easter 1910 after obtaining his *Abitur* (final examination certificate) and having applied to become an officer cadet in the German navy. The navy was a comparatively recent development of the German state. The army was the senior service and its officer corps was dominated by the nobility and the sons of higher civil servants. The navy recruited its officers from among the middle class, who were eager to have their sons wear the Emperor's uniform.

Ramm's education qualified him for entry as a naval officer cadet. But the final decision as to whether he would be accepted rested with the *Sea Cadet Entrance Commission*. This body met in private, did not keep minutes and were not required to reveal the reasons for their decisions. Their judgements were made on the basis of the social and financial status of an applicant's family. The Commission received information from schools, police, magistrates and district military commanders. Income was an important factor in the decision. In 1910 the average yearly industrial wage was approximately 1,300 Marks. The parents of naval cadets were required to pay 1,505 Marks for their first year's training and 1,000 Marks per year for the following three years. For the succeeding four years they were expected to pay 600 Marks per year in order to allow their son, at junior lieutenant rank, to maintain the lifestyle of an officer.[171]

The Ramm family obviously met the social and financial requirements. On 1 April 1910 Robert Ramm was one of 207 young men who reported to Kiel as Sea Cadets. The German Navy has a tradition of referring to cadet intakes by the year in which they join. Thus Ramm was a member of *Crew 1910.* Almost half of the cadets of *Crew 1910* were the sons of senior academics, 26 were from the lower nobility, 37 had a merchant or industrial background and 32 came from other middle-class backgrounds. Among the intake of *Crew 1910* were Karl Dönitz, commander of Germany's U-boat service during World War Two and Hans Joachim Emsmann.[172] Ramm became particularly friendly with Emsmann, who was the son of an admiral.

After six weeks of physical training and infantry drill Ramm was assigned to the training ship *S.M.S. Hansa*. Here on a long sea voyage he learned basic sailing skills, together with grounding in gunnery, navigation and engine-room practice. The engine room training included three weeks stoking the boilers. Sea Cadets had to learn in just over ten months what Royal Naval officers, who entered the service at thirteen, were trained over a period of five years. The end of *Hansa's* voyage was followed by a period of leave and promotion to the rank of *Fähnrich zur See* (midshipman). This was followed by a year at the naval school at Flensburg-Mürwik, near the Danish border. The training was mostly theoretical, covering navigation and seamanship, naval regulations, maths, engineering, hydraulics, shipbuilding, ship recognition, gunnery, and mining. There was an hour per week of English and French. The men were also taught fencing, horse riding and dancing. Drinking, smoking and playing of music were prohibited within the grounds of the school. Outside the grounds drinking was only permitted at inns used by the officer corps. At concerts and the theatre the midshipmen had particular seats reserved for them. In the early summer of 1912 the men were sent on specialized courses in gunnery, torpedoes and infantry exercises.

For the final year of their training midshipmen served aboard sea-going ships of the fleet. Ramm was posted to the battleship *S.M.S. Hessen*. On 1 October 1913 he completed the required three and a half years as a cadet. He now faced his final test. The German navy had a custom whereby the officers of their ship elected cadets to officer status. Election had to be unanimous and there was no appeal. The custom *"was designed as the final bar to any dilution of the social and spiritual homogeneity of the officer corps."* Following his election to officer status Ramm would have sworn the following oath on the Imperial flag or on an officers drawn sword: *"I, Robert Ramm, swear a personal oath to God the Almighty and All-knowing that I will loyally and honourably serve His Majesty the German Kaiser, Wilhelm 11, my supreme war lord, in all and any circumstances on land and sea, in peace and in war and will act in a correct and suitable manner for a righteous, brave, honourable and duty-loving soldier."*

Ramm was appointed to the post of radio officer on the *S.M.S. Hessen*, with the rank of Leutnant zur See (sub-lieutenant).[173] On 28 June 1914 heir to the Austrian throne Archduke Franz Ferdinand, and his wife Sophie were assassinated during a visit to the Bosnian capital Sarajevo. The event triggered off a series of reactions by the major European powers that led to the outbreak of World War 1. Ramm's post as radio officer would have given him access to some of the naval signals transmitted during the mounting crisis. He was serving on the *Hessen* on the outbreak of war. He had fallen in love with Gerda, the sister of his friend Hans Joachim Emsmann. Like all officers intending to marry, he had to apply for permission to the Kaiser's personal office. Royal consent was given. The official records say *"He was one of the first of the crew* (i.e. Crew 1910) *to start a family by marrying the sister of his friend Emsmann."* Robert Ramm and Gerda Emsmann were married on 10 November 1915.[174]

Ramm's classmate Karl Dönitz married a general's daughter. Ramm married an admiral's daughter. While the upper ranks of the army were dominated by the nobility and had a higher social status than the navy, it might be worthwhile looking at the living arrangements of the Dönitz family to get some general idea of the conditions in which the Ramm family may lived. Peter Padfield, Dönitz's biographer, said that the family had *"a moderately large house near the harbour at Kiel, it had a master bedroom, two children's and a maid's rooms, a dining and a drawing room."* Padfield goes on to say that *"Ingeborg's marriage settlement must have helped: probably it formed a substantial part of their joint capital whose interest allowed them to live in a style befitting a general's daughter."* Presumably the Ramms were living in the slightly lesser style befitting an admiral's daughter.

Apart from a few forays by a small number of ships, the German navy had been confined to port by the stronger Royal Navy since the outbreak of war. The focus of the German navy had concentrated on developing its U-boat arm. Suitable officers were required for the U-boats. Some of them volunteered. Others, like Karl Dönitz, appear to have been assigned to the U-boat service. Whether Robert Ramm volunteered or was assigned, he started at U-boat school in February 1916. The official report of his career to date says *"Ramm was good at both theory and practice. He had a great interest in all types of sport. He socialised very well. While serving as Fähnrich on S.M.S. Hessen, he was commended for the high level of training achieved by the crew of the light guns he commanded. He found it easy to inspire enthusiasm in his men."*[175] In April 1916 he was appointed watch officer on U-76, a mine-laying submarine. U-76 was put into commission on 11 May 1916, with Kapitänleutnant Waldemar Bender as commander and Leutnant zur See Robert Ramm as one of the boat's senior officers.[176] The submarine had a total crew of 32. On 30 July it laid a minefield off Longstone on the east coast of England.

In an attempt to block the shipment of war materials to Russia, the mine laying submarines U-75 and U-76 were sent to operate off the Kola peninsula, on the north-west coast of Russia.[177] Robert Ramm was aboard U-76 off the Kola Peninsula on 1 October 1916, when his wife Gerda gave birth to their first child, Robert junior. Over the next two days U-76 laid minefields off the entrance to the White Sea.[178] Between them, U-75 and U-76 laid a total of 72 mines. The mines resulted in the sinking of four ships, including the neutral Norwegian steamer *Botnia*. At the end of the mission, presumably, Ramm was able to meet his newly born son, whom the official records say was nicknamed *'Seemann'* (i.e. Sailor).

*

Heligoland is a 2.1 sq km (one square mile) island in the North Sea, 70 kilometres (43.5 miles) off the coast of Germany. It was a German naval base during the First World War.[179] On 9 January 1917 U-76 left Heligoland, to again lay mines on the northwest Russian coast. The boat arrived at its destination on 21 January. Kapitänleutnant Bender planned to enter Alexandrowsk harbour, sink the freighters there and lay mines in the vicinity. During the night of 21-22 January a ship travelling without lights accidentally rammed U-76. According to Kapitänleutnant Bender, due to falling snow, the submarine's crew did not see the approaching steamer until she was close to them. U-76 started to dive but was struck just behind the conning tower. Water started to flood the engine room. The submarine surfaced. The steamer sailed on, apparently unaware that she had rammed a U-boat. Unable to dive, U-76 set out on the long trip home.

Six days later, in stormy weather, U-76 was near Söröy Island, off the north coast of Norway. The boat had developed engine problems that the crew were unable to repair and the boat's batteries were almost flat. U-76 was in danger of being swept onto the rocks at Söröy Island. It was decided to find a sheltered cove, land the crew and scuttle the submarine. The crew spotted the Norwegian fishing vessel *Alia* and fired a distress flare. They also hoisted the international signal for vessel in distress. The *Alia* took off Leutnant zur See Robert Ramm and most of the crew. Kapitänleutnant Waldamar Bender, Chief Engineer Fritz Herman and a mechanic stayed on board the submarine to scuttle her. The three men jumped overboard when U-76 started to sink. Chief Engineer Fritz Herman was lost in the stormy sea. The *Alia* took U-76's crew to Hammerfest, Norway.[180] There they were confined in a local hall. Bender sent a telegram to the German ambassador asking that he arrange for their release as shipwrecked sailors. As Norway was neutral, Robert Ramm and his crewmates should have been interned.[181] However, Bender gave the captain of the *Alia* a thousand Kroner and five hundred Kroner to each of his crew for the rescue and to keep quiet about the circumstances under which it had taken place. In return, the captain of the *Alia* said that the submarine had not been scuttled, but had sunk because of damage. He also said the U-boat crew had been outside Norwegian territorial waters when they were rescued. The Norwegians therefore released them as shipwrecked sailors.[182] They were returned to Germany by way of Sweden on 27 January 1917.[183] Robert Ramm's first combat mission on a U-boat had certainly been eventful.

Official records show that Ramm was assigned to No. 1 U-boat Flotilla in February 1917. It is not clear what his duties were upon his return, as he wasn't assigned to a particular U-boat. Perhaps he was marking time until a place became available in another U-boat. In April he was sent on an officers torpedo course. These courses lasted four to eight weeks and were held at the naval school in Flensburg-Mürwik.[184] In June he was assigned as a watch officer to U-49. The submarine was commanded by Kapitänleutnant Richard Hartmann[185] and had a total crew of 36.

On 27 June 1917 U-49 left the port of Emden,[186] bound for an operational area 350 miles west of Ireland. On 1 July, southeast of the Shetlands, the submarine met a convoy of five or six steamers. U-49 torpedoed the Norwegian steamer *Stalheim* (1,469 tons). The ship did not sink and was later towed to harbour. Two days later the submarine sank four ships west of the Shetlands. The ships were the Danish sailing ship *Cimbria* (234 tons), the Danish fishing vessel *Mary Boyes* (100 tons) and the Dutch fishing vessels *Proefneming 1* (112 tons) and *Thor* (105 tons). On 8 July, west of Ireland, the submarine torpedoed the British merchant ship *Obuasi* (4,416 tons). The ship did not sink. U-49 surfaced and sailors went on board with explosives. The *Obuasi's* captain and one of the ship's gun crew were taken prisoner.

On 10 July U-49 torpedoed the British merchant ship *King David* (3680 tons). As with the *Obuasi*, the ship did not sink. The submarine surfaced and, after the crew had taken to the lifeboats, the ship was sunk with U-49's deck gun. The *King David* had been sailing from Brest, France to Archangel, Russia with a cargo of munitions and aeroplanes.[187] The following day the submarine fired a torpedo at the British merchant ship *Muirfield* (3,086 tons). The torpedo missed. U-49 surfaced and opened fire with her deck gun. The ship fired back with her gun. The duel continued for two hours, when U-49 had to break off due to high waves. The submarine followed the ship and torpedoed her shortly after midnight. The crew took to the lifeboats and the ship sank. The ship's first officer and radio operator were taken prisoner. On 15 July U-49 surfaced and sank the British sailing ship *Dunhope* (2,086 tons) with its deck gun. The following day the submarine fired a torpedo at the British merchant ship *Saturnia* (8,611 tons). The torpedo missed. U-49 surfaced and opened fire with her deck gun. The arrival of a British destroyer forced the submarine to dive. Later that day U-49 met up with U-58. The two submarines made a surface attack on the Italian merchant ship *Lamia L.* (2,220 tons). The ship surrendered and the crew took to the lifeboats. U-49 then sank the ship with her deck gun. On 23 July 1917, having returned north of the Shetlands, U-49 docked at Wilhelmshaven.

In August 1917 Robert Ramm was assigned as Watch Officer to U-43, under the command of his old captain from U-76, Kapitänleutnant Waldemar Bender. On 8 September 1917 U-43 left Heligoland. She sailed by way of the Shetlands and west of Ireland. (On 11 September U-49, Ramm's previous boat, still captained by Kapitänleutnant Richard Hartmann, was rammed and sunk by the SS *British Transport* west of the Bay of Biscay. All on board were lost).[188] On 18 September, southwest of Ireland U-43 sank the

Q-ship *Winona* with two torpedoes. After twelve days without encountering further targets the submarine set out on her return journey. Having sailed north of Denmark, into the Baltic, and through the Kiel Canal,[189] she docked at Wilhelmshaven on 7 October 1917. She probably took this route to avoid minefields regularly laid by the British on the north German coast. When the boat docked, Robert Ramm was six days overdue for his son's first birthday.

On 11 December 1917, after almost two months in port, U-43 left Heligoland again under the command of Kapitänleutnant Waldemar Bender and with Robert Ramm as one of the boat's senior officers. Again sailing north of the Shetlands she set out for an operational area northwest of Spain. Christmas 1917 was spent at sea. On 28 December, 180 nautical miles west of Cape Finisterre,[190] U-43 torpedoed and sank the French merchant ship *Magella* (6,265 tons). On 16 January 1918 the submarine docked at Wilhelmshaven, having again returned by way of the Baltic and the Kiel Canal. The boat spent from mid-January to mid-April in dock undergoing repairs. A new captain, Kapitänleutnant Johannes Kirchner, took over command. But by then Robert Ramm had been given his own command. It was UB-123, the submarine that would sink the *R.M.S. Leinster*.

The crew of UB-123

German rank	Royal Navy equivalent	Crewman's name
Oberleutnant zur see	Lieutenant	Robert Ramm
Leutnant	Sub-Lieutenant	Helmut Bahr
Leutnant	Sub-Lieutenant	Ferdinand Lohmeyer
Steuermann	Helmsman (Navigator)	Johann Wyschka
Bootsmannsmaat	Petty Officer	Richard Bernstein
Bootsmannsmaat	Petty Officer	Jac. Friedrich
Bootsmannsmaat	Petty Officer ofder Reserve	the Reserve
Bootsmannsmaat	Petty Officer	Friedrich Hatting
Obermatrose	Able Seaman	Wilhelm Mohring
Obermatrose	Able Seaman	Alfons Schwebke
Matrose	Ordinary Seaman	Willy Frick
Matrose	Ordinary Seaman	Jacob Jeus
Matrose	Ordinary Seaman	Emil Krackow
Matrose	Ordinary Seaman	Otto Oeser
Matrose	Ordinary Seaman	W. Osterkamp
Matrose	Ordinary Seaman	A. Schermer
Matrose	Ordinary Seaman	Willi Scheel
Funkmaat	Petty Officer Radio	Karl Kraatz
Funngast	Ordinary Seaman Radio	Johann Abenthun
Marineingenieur	Marine Engineer	Hermann Meier
Maschinist	Chief Petty Officer Engines	Alfons Elies
Obermaschinistenmaat	Petty Officer Engines	O. Fuhrmann
Maschinistenmaat	Petty Officer Engines	Fritz Drobbe
Maschinistenmaat	Petty Officer Engines	Huettenrauch
Maschinistenmaat	Petty Officer Engines	P. Reinhardt
Maschinistenmaat	Petty Officer Engines	August Repp
Maschinistenmaat	Petty Officer Engines	Walter Siegling
Obermaschinistenwarter	Able Seaman Engines	Richard Hoesterey
Maschinestenanwarter	Ordinary Seaman Engines	Franz Boehle
Maschinistenanwarter	Ordinary Seaman Engines	Hermann Donat
Maschinistenanwarter	Ordinary Seaman Engines	Erich Funke
Maschinistenanwarter	Ordinary Seaman Engines	J. Gernandt
Heizer	Ordinary Seaman Engines (Stoker)	J. Bernhofer
Heizer	Ordinary Seaman Engines (Stoker)	F. Engelmann
Heizer	Ordinary Seaman Engines (Stoker)	Emil Huels
Heizer	Ordinary Seaman Engines (Stoker)	Adolf Leveren
Heizer	Ordinary Seaman Engines (Stoker)	Wilhelm Pluecker

Source: U-boat archives, Cuxhaven, Germany.

Notes

1   *R.M.S. Munster's* Daily Journal, CDSPCo Crew Agreement Lists for 1918. The latter give Penston's age as 47, making him the youngest of the captains of the three mail boats operating in 1918. (At 61, Captain Birch was the oldest).

2   Daily Journal of the *R.M.S. Ulster* and the 1918 Crew Agreement Lists.

3   Sam Williams.

4   *The Clean Sweep* by Arthur Webb. Thanks to Billy McGrath for bringing the book to my attention.

5   Article on Michael Joyce by Brian Donnelly, in *The Limerick Compendium* (1997). Thanks to Jim O'Dea for bringing the article to my attention.

6   While Irish historians invariably cite the former reason, the latter is rarely mentioned.

7   Local Historian Brian Smith.

8   From the Society's records.

9   Parker's post World War 1 career: Undated catalogue of Spink & Son Ltd, London for an exhibition of Life-Saving Awards (W.H. Fevyer Collection) in the records of the Royal Humane Society. The catalogue listed Parker's eight awards. These were the Royal Humane Society Silver Medal, the Order of the British Empire, 1914/15 Star, British War Medal, Victory Medal, 1939-45 Star, Africa Star, and War Medal.

10 Contemporary newspapers.

11 Royal Humane Society records.

12 Contemporary newspapers.

13 Author's conversation with Liam Donovan and sight of Maher's watch.

14 *Sunbeam House: Bray* by Francis Loughrey. Sunbeam House is the successor of *The Cripples Home* and holds the records of the home.

15 Website on John Mc Cormack, Paul W. Worth, 1997. pwworth@jump.net A book on John McCormack (I neglected to record the name) gave the child's name as Rory.

16 Thanks to Sally Copeland Keogh, daughter of Will Copeland, for a copy of the letter.

17 *The Cure of Souls: A History of St. Bridget's Church of Ireland, Stillorgan* by John A. Ingram.

18 National Archives and Records Administration (Washington).

19 After lengthy service she was sold to Pakistan on 10 January 1982. She was decommissioned from the Pakistani navy on 12 April 1998.

20 Ships Daily Journals.

21 Hazel P. Smyth.

22 Hazel P. Smyth.

23 Gerard Crangle.

24 Sources: Dr David Murphy, Dictionary of Irish Biography and Liam Dodd.

25 Frank Coffey.

26 Hugh's son Leslie Owen. His mother told him how his father had saved the young woman.

27 Rupert Jeffares, General Manager of Howth Yacht Club.

28 Dr Margaret Elmes.

29 Tamsin Bunnay.

[30] Mervyn Wall: *Hermitage* and the article *Some memories of the Borough* in Dún Laoghaire Borough Historical Society Journal No. 1. (1990).

[31] Contemporary newspapers.

[32] Declan Whelan's taped interviews with Bill Sweeney and author's conversations with Declan Whelan.

[33] My thanks to Local Historian Brian Smith for copies of the *Dublin Post* articles.

[34] Information on Tom Connolly's service with the Canadian Pacific Line and the story of the model of the *Leinster* from the *Dublin Post* 30 September 1960. My thanks to Local Historian Brian Smith for the article.

[35] Ollie Gray and contemporary newspapers.

[36] Records of the Irish Labour History Museum, Dublin.

[37] Roy Stokes.

[38] Author's conversations with Des Brannigan and Noel Brien, contemporary newspapers and commemorative leaflet.

[39] Sources: *The Chronicle* (Holyhead) 18 October 1918, taped interview with Bill Sweeney and *The Lady of the House* (Christmas 1919 edition).

[40] Captain T.B. Williams. *Airship Pilot No. 28.*

[41] *Dublin Evening Mail* 13 June 1919. My thanks to Liam Dodd, who discovered the article during his own research.

[42] The previous article was by Irish Volunteer leader Bulmer Hobson.

[43] Information on the Crangle family from Gerard Crangle.

[44] Her father James was a boat builder. *Porters 1911 Commercial Directory for Kingstown* shows the Clancy family living at 4 Crofton Avenue, Kingstown.

[45] Porter's 1911 Commercial Directory of Kingstown shows Dr Patrick Merrin at 79 Upper George's Street, Kingstown.

[46] The *Leinster* exhibition in the Maritime Museum, Dún Laoghaire has an *"Application for Registration as a Merchant Seaman."* The undated application is from William Sweeney, Assistant Purser, born 27 April 1897. His height was 5 ft 8 ins. His hair was dark brown and eyes were brown. His next of kin was given as Mrs A. Delaney., 9 Aberdeen Street, Dublin, Ireland. So presumably his mother had died by the time he made the application.

[47] Thanks to John Cave of Holyhead Maritime Museum who gave me a copy of the account. It is not known why Chief Steward Lewis prepared the account in January 1919.

[48] Connolly's name is not on the crew agreement list drawn up in early 1918. On 8 June 1918 Cabin Boy Llewellyn Williams (18), from Holyhead, left the company, when he was *"called to the colours."* Presumably Tom Connolly was recruited to replace him. This would have meant that at the time of the sinking he would have been employed by the company for a maximum of four months. Source: 1918 Crew Agreement List.

[49] *The Evening Press* (Dublin) 11 October 1968.

[50] Eric Anthony and *The Chronicle* (Holyhead) 18 October 1918.

[51] Frank Coffey.

[52] *Irish Press* 11 October 1968

[53] William Byrne.

[54] Interview published in *Southside* newspaper 7 February 1996.

[55] Details on John Flood from Ninian Faulkiner and John Lush.

56 In CDSPCO Crew Agreement Lists for 1918 Ryan's first name is given as William, age as 47 and place of birth as Tipperary. Perhaps he was known as Paddy or perhaps Bill Sweeney got Ryan's first name wrong 61 years after the event.

57 *Memorial Inscriptions of Deansgrange Cemetery, Blackrock, Co. Dublin Vol 1* by Dún Laoghaire Genealogical Society.

58 Seán M. Redmond.

59 *The Chronicle* (Holyhead) 18 October 1918.

60 Haulwen McClean, Robert H. Williams and *The Chronicle* (Holyhead) 18 October 1918.

61 Peter Scott Roberts.

62 Brian Ellis and *The Chronicle* 18 October 1918.

63 Frank Coffey.

64 On 4 September 1915 the liner *Hesperian* was sailing from Liverpool to Montreal. On board was the body of American Mrs Frances Washington Stephens who was lost from the *Lusitania* and recovered from the sea. The *Hesperian* was sunk by U-20, the same submarine that sunk the *Lusitania*. Some people have been torpedoed twice and lived to tell the tale. The unlucky American woman didn't survive either sinking by U-20. Her life was lost in the first sinking. Her body was lost in the second. Source: *Lusitania: An Irish Tragedy* by Senan Molony and *The Lusitania: Unravelling the Mysteries* by Patrick O'Sullivan.

65 Mairwen Carr.

66 Bill Sweeney. Career details from the Highlanders Regimental Museum.

67 The battalion had been stationed in Ireland since November 1917. Initially, it was at Birr, Co. Offaly. In March 1918 it was sent to Ballyvonare (near Buttervant), Co. Cork. In April it was posted to Limerick and later was sent back to Ballyvonare. Source: *British Regiments, 1914-18* by Brigadier E.A. James.

68 Daily Journals of the *Provinces*. The ships, however, were not being used as troop transports in the same way that *R.M.S. Connaught* had been. Military personnel going on leave or returning from leave travelled on the ships as passengers.

69 ADM 137/1817:129719, Public Records Office, Kew Gardens Surrey.

70 Declan Byrne in *Wicklow Roots* No 5 (2000).

71 Contemporary newspapers and *The Irish Guards in the Great War* by Rudyard Kipling (reprint) (Kent 1997).

72 Joy O'Gorman.

73 *A Doctor on the* Leinster by Fr Ignatius Fennessy OFM Journal of the Genealogical Society of Ireland Vol. 5 No. 2 Summer 2004.

74 Contemporary newspapers, copy of his will from National Archives, Dublin and document T 1/12540 Public Records Office, Kew, Surrey.

75 Local Historian Brian White, contemporary newspapers, Rudyard Kipling *The Irish Guards in the Great War*.

76 Interviewee Martin Murphy in the book *Tralee's Old Stock Reminisce: An Oral History of Tralee and Its Surroundings* by Mick O'Neill. My thanks to Kate Healy Coburn for bringing the book to my attention

77 Contemporary newspapers, Document T 1/12540 Public Records Office, Kew, Surrey. Chief Engineer William Mathias (married to Elizabeth, sister of William John Lewis) also lost. William and Elizabeth Mathias lived Newry Street, Holyhead, same street as William John Lewis.

78 Theresa Moriarty *Industrial Controls and Irish Trade Unionism* in *Ireland and the Great War: A War to unite us All?* (Manchester, 2002).

79 Kate Healy Coburn and Author Mick O'Neill in *Tralee's Old Stock Reminisce: An Oral History of Tralee and its Surroundings*.

80 Francis Loughrey in *Sunbeam House, Bray*.

81 Contemporary newspapers, Aideen Byrne and Annette Proffitt.

82 Dr David Murphy, Dictionary of Irish Biography.

83 James McGuinn *Sligo Men In the Great War*.

84 Jim Herlihy, author of *The Royal Irish Constabulary*.

85 Dr Margaret Elmes.

86 Michael Joyce's daughter Maureen O'Brien, his granddaughter Anne O'Brion, an article on Michael Joyce by Brian Donnelly, in *The Limerick Compendium* (1997). My thanks to Jim O'Dea for bringing the article to my attention.

87 Information on the King and Harmsworth families and the letters quoted: Ruth Dudley Edwards *Newspapermen: Hugh Cudlipp, Cecil Harmsworth King and the Glory Days of Fleet Street*.

88 Lieutenant Lucas Henry St. Aubyn King, 4th Battalion King's Royal Rifle Corps was killed on 8 May 1915. Between 8 May and 10 May the battalion suffered 493 casualties during heavy shelling. Luke was 20 years old. His body was never found and he is commemorated on the Menin Gate Memorial (Panels 51 and 53). Sources: Commonwealth War Graves Commission and Ray Westlake *British Battalions on the Western Front January to June 1915*.

89 S.J. Taylor *The Great Outsiders: Northcliffe, Rothermere and the Daily Mail*.

90 Lieutenant The Honourable Vere Sidney Tudor Harmsworth, R.N.V.R., Hawke Battalion, Royal Naval Division was killed on 13 November 1916 during an attack on Beaucourt. The battalion's leading waves were cut down by machine-gun fire. Aged 21 years, Vere is buried in Ancre British Cemetery: V.E. 19, Beaumont Hamel, France. Sources: Sources: Commonwealth War Graves Commission and Ray Westlake *British Battalions on the Somme*. Captain The Honourable Harold Alfred Vyvyan Harmsworth M.C., 2nd Irish Guards was killed on 12 February 1918. Aged 23 years, he is buried in Hampstead Cemetery: W.B. 620, France.

91 Ruth Dudley Edwards *Newspapermen: Hugh Cudlipp, Cecil Harmsworth King and the Glory Days of Fleet Street*.

92 *The Life-Boat 1 November 1918*. *The Life Boat* is the magazine of the Royal National Lifeboat Institution. Thanks to Jane Smythson, Publications Manager for permission to reproduce the article. Also my thanks to her for giving me A.W. Lewis's first names and the name of the firm for which he worked.

93 Lewis's account has the first torpedo striking much earlier that the accounts of others on board.

94 Details on Charles Blackburne's life and army career: Tonbridge School, Royal Dragoon Guards Regimental Museum, *Who was Who 1916-1928* and *The Chronicle* 18 October 1918.

95 *Dundalk Democrat* 12 and 19 October 1918. My thanks to Donal Hall for copies of same. *Tyneside Irish: 24th, 25th, 26th and 27th (Service) Battalions of the Northumberland Fusiliers* by John Sheen. This gives Samuel McKenna's address as 16 Turnstall Street, Sunderland.

96 Imperial War Museum Information Sheet No 30 *The Royal Defence Corps*, and B.B.C website: Beyond the Broadcast: Making History: *Royal Defence Corps*.

97   Mary Jacques.
98   James Ramsay McDonald (1866-1937). Elected Labour M.P. for Leicester 1906. Became leader of the party in the House of Commons 1911. His pacifist stance during the First World War cost him the leadership of the party in 1914 and his parliamentary seat in the 1918 election. In 1922 he was again elected M.P. and became leader of the parliamentary Labour party. In 1924 he headed the first Labour government. (*The Macmillan Dictionary of Biography* by Barry Jones & M.V. Dixon, London 1981)
99   Mary Jacques.
100 Roger Imes.
101 Royal Irish Constabulary researcher Jim Herlihy.
102 Dr Arnold Burrows, Liz Jones, John Phillpott.
103 The nickname came from a comment made by the Kaiser about the British army. Often misquoted as *"contemptible little army,"* the phrase is more properly translated as *"contemptibly small army."* The British troops immediately adopted the phrase as a badge of honour. *"The Old Contemptibles"* refers to the British soldiers who went in action at the start of the war.
104 *de Ruvigny: The Roll of Honour.* Thanks to Jimmy Taylor for access to this.
105 Information on the Territorials: Ronald Clifton, Historical Information Officer of the Western Front Association and *British Territorial Units 1914-18* by Ray Westlake and Mike Chappell.
106 Information on the Yorkshire Hussars: *British Regiments 1914-1918* by Brigadier E.A. James and Yorkshire Hussars researcher John L. Liffiton.
107 *The Yorkshire Hussars Magazine* Vol. 111, No 11, January 1950. Yorkshire Hussars Researcher John L. Liffiton kindly gave me access to it.
108 *Journal of the Medal Society of Ireland*, No. 49, September 1999.
109 Peter Trigueiro.
110 Nora Hedworth.
111 A partial list of *Leinster* casualties and survivors has a listing for a J. Monc, MSC. Ronald Clifton, Historical Information Officer of the Western Front Association, suggested that this may be an error and should perhaps read MPSC, for Military Provost Staff Corps *"which provided warders for military prisons."* So perhaps Monc was also escorting the prisoner.
112 Joe Devereaux and Hal Giblin.
113 1911 census for Kingstown, *Porters Directory for Kingstown*, 1911.
114 The first ever V.C. awarded was given to a member of the Royal Navy, Charles Davis Lucas, from Co. Armagh, Ireland. Sources: portrait Major Stephen B. Hunt. V. C. Dr David Murphy *Ireland and the Crimean War.*
115 Sigfried Sassoon: *Diaries 1915-1918.*
116 Information on the men of the Royal Welch Fusiliers from *The Chronicle* (Holyhead) 18 October 1918.
117 Thanks to Chris Murphy and Liam Dodd for a copy of the item.
118 Contemporary newspapers, de Ruvigny: The Roll of Honour.
119 John A. Ingram *The Cure of Souls: A History of St. Bridget's Church of Ireland, Stillorgan.*
120 Tom Gallagher.
121 Details on R.A.M.C. officers: Newspapers, Mountjoy School Magazine-Special Issue 1919, Commonwealth War Graves Commission.

[122] It is interesting, however, that Captain Ernest Lee's father received a letter from a doctor telling him that his son had saved a man with a *"metal splint"* on his arm by helping him with his lifebelt.

[123] Details on the Lee family: Michael Lee.

[124] Edward Lee and the 1913 Dublin lockout: *Lockout: Dublin 1913* by Padraig Yeates.

[125] Details on Private James Ratcliffe: Des McCloskey and Marie Lawlor.

[126] Author's article *Sophia Violet Barrett* in Dún Laoghaire Borough Historical Society Journal. No. 5 (1996).

[127] Wynne Gordon.

[128] Marion McNally and contemporary newspapers.

[129] Fr. Ignatius Fennessy OFM *"A Doctor on the Leinster"* Journal of the Genealogical Society of Ireland. Vol. 5 Number 2, Summer 2004.

[130] New Zealand in World War 1: *The World War One Source Book* by Philip J. Haythornthwaite.

[131] Details on New Zealand soldiers: An unsigned and undated partial list of casualties and survivors, Records of the Commonwealth War Graves Commission.

[132] Commonwealth War Graves Commission.

[133] *The World War Source Book* by Philip J. Haythornthwaite and *The Canadian Army At War* by Mike Chappell.

[134] Battlefields of the First World War: A Traveller's Guide by Tonie and Valmai Holt.

[135] An unsigned and undated partial list of casualties and survivors, Commonwealth War Graves Commission.

[136] Information on Edward Milne from Violet Milne McIntyre.

[137] Ann O'Carroll, Commonwealth War Graves Commission, Author's visit to grave and the records of First World War Researcher Jim Strawbridge. The latter give her address as 218 St. George Street, London, Ontario. This is the same address as her sister Mrs Susan K. Bowen. She also had a brother Walter J.

[138] Will Lockhart.

[139] My thanks to Australian researcher Jeff Kildea for details of File AWM18 9953/1/1 at the Australian War Memorial, Canberra. (The file has information on the Australian soldiers who were on the *Leinster*). Other sources: The *World War One Source Book* by Philip J. Haythornthwaite, *Australia during the War*, by Ernest Scott in Volume XI of the Official History and *The Australian Army at War 1899-1975* by John Laffin and Mike Chappell.

[140] A sixth infantry division, formed in early 1917, was disbanded soon after, as casualties necessitated consolidation of the existing divisions.

[141] These fought dismounted at Gallipoli and with horses during the desert campaign in the Middle East.

[142] The former colonies were now called states.

[143] A partial list of survivors and casualties in the National Archives, Dublin contains the name Captain Gale, Australian Army. This name, with a pencil annotation *"NFLD,"* also appears on a note dated 15 October 1918 from *"The Railway Transport Officer, Kingstown."* The note is in file AWM18 9953/1/1 held at the Australian War Memorial, Canberra. However, the very extensive WW1 service records at the Australian War Memorial contain no mention of a Captain Gale. This and the fact that the two sources mentioned have exactly the same errors in the surnames of some of the surviving Australians, --suggesting that they are one source copying another -- leads Australian researcher Jeff Kildea to believe it possible that Captain

Gale's name being on the unsigned and undated partial list of survivors and casualties is an error.

144 Margaret Cross and Kathryn Rundle.

145 Chris Knuckey.

146 The Australian War Memorial Roll of Honour Database.

147 Thanks to Jimmy Taylor for consulting *De Ruigneys Roll of Honour*.

148 History of U.S. Naval Air Service: Naval Historical Centre website www.history.naval.mil Air stations: *A History of the Royal Air Force and United States Naval Air Service In Ireland. 1913-1923* (Irish Air Letter).

149 Details on Captain Cone: Information supplied by United States National Archives and Records Administration (henceforth U.S. National Archives), *Victory at Sea* by Rear-Admiral Sims. (London 1920.) (Henceforth Rear-Admiral Sims).

150 Details from Rear-Admiral Sims, An unsigned and undated partial list of casualties and survivors and the *Cork Constitution* 12 October 1918.

151 Records of American naval casualties from the American Battle Monuments Commission.

152 American records show some of the men as having died on the <u>H.M.S.</u> *Leinster* or, in one case, the *U.S.S. Leinster*. Neither the Royal Navy nor the United States Navy had a ship named *Leinster*. Source: *Conway's All the World's Fighting Ships 1860-1905, Conway's All the World's Fighting Ships 1906-1921*.

153 A copy of the report is held by the Maritime Museum, Dún Laoghaire.

154 *Dublin Evening Mail* 11 October 1918, an unsigned and undated partial list of casualties and survivors, *Cork Constitution* 12 October 1918, *Wexford People* (millennium edition, year 2000) and U.S. National Archives.

155 All U.S. telegrams/messages from U.S. National Archives.

156 Commonwealth War Graves Commission, An unsigned and undated partial list of casualties and survivors and contemporary newspapers.

157 A.E. Fanning *Steady as She goes: A history of the Compass Department of the Admiralty.*

158 Cross referencing of information on David White (supplied by Mary Horgan) and information on William O'Sullivan (supplied by Christine O'Sullivan). Mary Horgan understood that White and O'Sullivan were on deck when the first torpedo struck. She said that he told O'Sullivan that he had to look for his cousin below deck and would see him later. However, O'Sullivan told a newspaper reporter that he was asleep in a lower cabin when the first torpedo struck.

159 George Callaghan's article *Arthur Eade* in the *Journal of the Medal Society of Ireland*. No 57, June 2002.

160 An unsigned and undated partial list of casualties and survivors.

161 Of the English fleet that engaged the Spanish armada on 21 July 1588 sixty-five out of the one hundred ships were privately owned. In later wars British merchant ships were used as auxiliary warships, troop transports, munitions ships and hospital ships. During the Crimean War, the Cunard company put eight of their ships at the disposal of the British government. The practice has continued to present times. During the Falklands War liners like the *Queen Elizabeth 2* and *Canberra* were requisitioned as troop transports. Source on the use of British merchant ships in wartime: *Lusitania: Unravelling the mysteries* by Patrick O''Sullivan. *"Sixty-five out of the one hundred of the English fleet were privately owned"*: The Channel 4 television programme *Secret History: The Spanish Armada* (transmitted on 23 December 2001)

162 This statement is supported by the fact that His Majesty's Stationary Office publication (1919) on British ships sunk during the First World War shows that the *R.M.S. Connaught* did not have defensive armament when she was sunk on 3 March 1917.

163 Information on the Wrens: Lesley Thomas, Curator of the *Wrens* museum, and *The Wrens 1917-1977: A history of the Women's Royal Naval Service* by Ursula Stuart Mason.

164 Commonwealth War Graves Commission and Researcher Jim Strawbridge. The fact that she was the first ever Wren to be killed on active service: Lesley Thomas, Curator of the *Wrens* museum and *The Chronicle* (Holyhead) 18 October 1918. When she signed up, she gave her age as 27.

165 Commonwealth War Graves Commission and an unsigned, undated partial list of casualties and survivors.

166 Patrick Woodgate.

167 Keith Jeffrey *Ireland and the Great War* (Cambridge 2000).

168 My thanks to Dr. Stefan Graf (Germany) and Jörn Jensen (Denmark) for information on Robert Ramm's background and career.

169 www.freepages.genealogy.rootsweb.com *Mecklenburg, The Land, Map and History* by Daniel Schlyter.

170 Stettin, is northeast of Berlin. 55 Kms (34 miles) from the North Sea, it was the main port for Berlin between 1720 and 1945. Now named Szczecin, it is part of Poland. Source: *Reader's Digest Guide to Places of the World.*

171 The status of the navy in German life, cadet entry requirements, composition of *Crew 1910,* details of training and quotations. Peter Padfield's *Dönitz: The Last Fürher.*

172 Karl Dönitz (1891-1980) was a U-boat commander in World War One. During World War 2 he commanded Germany's U-boat fleet. He subsequently became head of the German navy. Upon the death of Adolf Hitler, he took over, for ten days, as Germany's head of state. Hans Joachim Emsmann was born on 20 June 1892, the son of an admiral. He joined the navy in April 1910. He served on *S.M.S. Thüringen* and *S.M.S. Würtemberg.* In May 1916 he was assigned to XV Torpedo boat half-flotilla. In June 1916 he was appointed commander of the recently launched minesweeper M32. He went to U-boat school in September 1917. During 1918 he commanded UB-5, UB-10, UB40 and UB-116. On ten patrols he sank 27 ships, totalling 9,221 tons. Sources: uboat.net

173 *Crew 1910* member Karl Dönitz was also a radio officer. His appointment to the rank of Leutnant zur See was gazetted (i.e. officially came into effect) on 27 September 1913. It seems likely that Robert Ramm's appointment was also gazetted from that date.

174 Research by Dr Stefan Graf (Germany).

175 Research by Dr Stefan Graf (Germany).

176 Information on U-76's voyages: provided by Jörn Jensen from records compiled by German Admiral Arno Spindler and from *Ehrenrangliste der Kaiselichlich Deutschen Marine 1914-18* compiled by Kontreadmiral a.D. Stoelzel (Berlin, 1930).

177 Details on the mine laying: the internet site uboat.net

178 An almost enclosed inlet of the Barents Sea, on the north coast of Russia. The sea covers 95,000 square kilometres (36,670 square miles). It largely freezes over in

winter, although icebreakers keep its main ports open. Source: *Reader's Digest Guide to Places of the World.*

179 Originally part of Denmark, Heligoland (called Helgoland by the Germans) was held by the British from 1814 until 1890, when it was handed over to Germany in exchange for the island of Zanizibar off the east African coast. It was also used as a German naval base during the Second World War. Source: *Reader's Digest Guide to Places of the World.*

180 Fishing port and one of the most northerly towns in the world. On Kvaloy Island, 59 miles (95 km) southwest of North Cape, it lies 285 miles (460 kms) north of the Article Circle. In 1891 it became the first European town to have electric street and domestic lighting. Sources: *Reader's Digest Guide to Places of the World* (London, 1995) and the *Insight Guide: Norway* (Apa Publications (HK) Ltd, 1991).

181 Norway was neutral during the First World War. The country benefited from its neutrality, particularly during the first two years of the war. Germany was willing to buy all the fish Norway could supply. Britain responded by signing a secret agreement with Norway, backed up by the threat to cut off supplies of British oil and coal. Under the agreement Britain would buy most of the Norwegian fish surplus. In turn Norway agreed not to export vital copper pyrites to Germany. But in all other respects Norway was free to trade with both sides. Norway suffered from the German submarine campaign. Most of the Norwegian merchant fleet was under charter to Britain. Half of it was sunk in the war, resulting in the death of 2,000 Norwegian merchant seamen. Source: Rowlinson Carter in *Insight Guide: Norway* (Apa Publications (HK) Ltd, 1991).

182 Source on U-76's sinking and aftermath: *Verschollen: World War1 U-Boat Losses* by Dwight R. Messimer.

183 The wreck of U-76 was raised in July 1971, but plans to preserve her fell through due to structural decay. Source Researcher Brian Viglietti of uboat.net

184 The *Frequently Asked Questions* feature of the World War 1 section of the internet site uboat.net

185 Richard Hartmann born 19 August 1883. Joined navy April 1903. Subsequently Director of Naval Intelligence at Borkum-West station. September 1915 became commander of U-2 at the U-boat training school. Ramm may have met him there when he did his U-boat training in February 1916. In April 1916 Kapitänleutnant Hartmann was appointed commander of U-49. Source on Hartmann and U-49: Researcher Jörn Jensen (Denmark).

186 Port in northwest Germany facing Dutch territory across the estuary of the Ems River. Source: *Reader's Digest Guide to Places of the World.*

187 Source: *British Merchant Ships sunk by U-Boats in the 1914-1918 War* by A.J. Tennant.

188 Sources: *Verschollen: World War 1 U-Boat Losses* by Dwight R. Messimer. and the internet site www.ku.edu/~kansite/ww_one/naval/sm1000ihtm *German Submarine losses from all causes during World War One.* Compiled by J. David Perkins from V.E. Tarrant's *The U-Boat Offensive 1914-1918* and R.M. Grant's *U-Boats Destroyed.*

189 The Kiel Canal connects the Baltic Sea at Kiel with the river Elbe at Brunsbuettel. The canal, formerly known as *Kaiser Wilhelm Canal*, was completed in 1895. Source: Internet site: www.navis.gr/canals/kiel.htm

190 A rocky headland in the northwest of Spain. The western most point of the Spanish mainland. Source: *Reader's Digest Guide to Places of the World.*

Appendix 1

Why was the Irish Sea's greatest loss of life forgotten?

There are at least three reasons for the widespread amnesia that was required to forget such a momentous event.

- Within a year of the sinking, armed conflict broke out between Irish Nationalists and British forces. The conflict resulted in the establishment of an Irish state. Because of this, it later suited each side to deliberately forget the part played by Irish men and women in the First World War (Irish officialdom wanted to construct a myth of perpetual Irish resistance to British rule down through the centuries. As the involvement of Irish men and women in the British forces directly challenged the myth, this awkward fact was written out of Irish history. British officialdom, possibly still smarting from the fact of Irish independence, did nothing to highlight the contribution made by the Irish during the First World War.) The sinking of the *Leinster* became part of the general memory loss.

- Historians have hugely understated the scale of the *Leinster* tragedy. Authors as varied as R.H. Gibson and Maurice Prendergast in *The German Submarine war 1914-1918* (London 1931), Ray Sloan in *Early Aviation in North Wales* (North Wales, 1989), A.J. Tennant in *British Merchant Ships sunk by U-Boats in the 1914-1918 War* (Kent 1990) and Martin Gilbert in *First World War.* (London 1994) all say that 176 people died in the sinking. The Commonwealth War Graves Commission also quote the figure of 176 in their records. Alan Palmer in *Victory 1918* (New York 1998) seems to approach the true extent of the disaster when he says that: *"More than 500 passengers and crew were reported to have drowned in the Irish Sea that day, including Americans crossing from Dublin."* But he goes on to say that: *"Thankfully the final figure was far less."* The error by all of these authorities is probably due to their consulting His Majesty's Stationary Office publication *British Vessels and Merchant Ships lost at sea 1914-1918* (London 1919). This official publication records 176 deaths for the *Leinster*. At the beginning of the book, however, is a note that casualty numbers do not include any troops onboard ships

278

at the time of their sinking. As most of those who died on the *Leinster* were military personnel, they are not included in the figure published by H.M.S.O. This, I believe, is probably the cause of the mistake by the authors and the Commonwealth War Graves Commission. The huge under statement of casualties, published by eminent authorities, has helped to hide the scale of the *Leinster* tragedy in official history.

- The *Leinster* disaster has also been largely forgotten due to lack of information about the people who died. The sinking is remembered to some extent in Dún Laoghaire and Holyhead, the towns from where most of the ship's crew came. Local historians refer to *"Those who died on the Leinster."* Unfortunately, it is difficult to remember nameless people. True remembrance could not take place until the names and stories of those who were on the ship were known.

Appendix 2

Why wasn't the *Leinster* escorted?[1]

CDSPCo ships were given occasional escorts from the end of 1917. The *Leinster* was attacked on 27 December 1917 (see *War and the City of Dublin Steam Packet Company* Appendix 5). Her Daily Journal for 28 December recorded a delay of 8 hours at Holyhead awaiting Admiralty orders to sail. She finally sailed with a convoy escorted by two U.S. destroyers. Also on 28 December, on the trip from Kingstown, she was protected by American destroyer No. 48 (*U.S.S. Parker*).

On 3 January 1918 a U.S. destroyer and a seaplane escorted the *Leinster* from Holyhead. On the return journey from Kingstown *"a destroyer"* protected her. On 4 January a U.S. destroyer accompanied her on the trip from Kingstown. On 6 January she was escorted by *"Destroyer C.C.9"* on the voyage to Kingstown, and by U.S. destroyer *Wadsworth* from Kingstown the same day. On 7 January the *Wadsworth* brought her from Holyhead. Several times in the Daily Journal in January 1918 Captain Birch recorded the comment *"No escort."* This suggests that perhaps he had come to expect an escort as being the norm and the lack of an escort as being worthy of comment. But he must have soon realised that the provision of an escort was the exception rather than the rule and the comments stopped.

On 9 February the *Leinster* was escorted in both directions by U.S. destroyers 26 and 47 (*U.S.S. Patterson* and *U.S.S. Aylwin*). On 10 and 11 February the U.S. destroyer 36 escorted her from Kingstown to Holyhead. On 7 April she was accompanied by *"destroyers"* from Holyhead to Kingstown. On 22 April American destroyer 92 guarded the *Leinster* from Holyhead to Kingstown. The only other times that destroyer escorts were provided were on 15 and 16 August. On the first date the ship was travelling from Holyhead and was escorted by the destroyers D-01 and D-77. On the second occasion, also while travelling from Holyhead, she was protected by destroyers 75 and 98.

December 1917 and January and February 1918 were the only times that the *Leinster's* Daily Journal recorded being escorted by U.S. destroyers. The story told by the editor of *Lady of the House*, in the section on Captain Birch, mentioned that the *Leinster* arrived in Holyhead escorted by a U.S. destroyer and left for Kingstown without an escort. Therefore the events described would have had to have happened in late December 1917 or January/early February 1918.

*

The *Leinster* was also occasionally escorted by airships. Airships were cigar-shaped balloons filled with lighter than air gas. They used engines to manoeuvre through the air. The crew travelled in control cars hanging beneath the balloons. The earlier type of control cars were aeroplane fuselages. Cables running from the control cars were used to operate elevators and rudders in the tail of the balloons to steer the airships.[2] Airships were used for anti-submarine patrols. They were stationed at Pembroke and Anglesey in Wales and Luce Bay in Scotland. A number of sub-stations for the airships were set up in Ireland. These were used for mooring airships overnight before their return to base. The sub-stations were at Ballyliffin, Co. Donegal, Larne, Co. Antrim (both were sub-stations for Luce Bay in Scotland), Malahide Castle, Co. Dublin (sub-station for Anglesey) and Johnstown Castle, Co. Wexford (sub-station for Pembroke). A sub-station at Ballyquirke (also known as Killeagh), Co. Cork, was still under construction at the end of the war. It was to have been a sub-station of Pembroke.[3]

The *Leinster* received airship escort between May and August 1918. Her Daily Journal during this period often recorded airship protection for part of the journey. This usually happened on voyages from Kingstown, when the ship was met in the Irish Sea by an airship from Anglesey. On other occasions the Daily Journal noted that the ship had an airship escort, presumably for the entire journey. The *Leinster* first had airship protection on 7 May 1918. She was accompanied on the voyage from Kingstown by SSZ51 and from Holyhead by SSZ 34 and 35. During the rest of the month she was escorted from Kingstown on 8 May (SSZ 51), 9 May (SSZ 50), 10 May (SSZ 51), 17 May (SSZ 34 and 35), 18 May (SSZ51), 19 May (SSZ 34), May 25 (SSZ 51) and May 27 (SSZ 50). She was escorted from Holyhead on 9 May (SSZ 50) and 29 May (SSZ 50).

The *Leinster* was taken out of service for overhaul following a voyage from Kingstown on 30 May. Two days later Captain Birch was taken on a flight in an airship. Captain T.B. Williams mentions the event in his book *Airship Pilot 28*. *"Captain Birch and I had become friends as we were on and over the Irish Sea so often together. I took him for a flight in SSZ 35 on the 1ˢᵗ June, and he arranged with the Triplex Company, of which he was a shareholder, to send me some flying goggles which I still have.* (Williams's book was published in 1974) *When I was flying with the Italians later in the year I was sent an account of his death, which I found very distressing. He had been blown off the bridge of the Irish Mail Steamer by a German torpedo."*

The *Leinster* returned to duty on 29 June, when she made a night sailing, leaving Holyhead at 2.45 a.m. From 5.30 a.m., until her arrival at Kingstown, she was accompanied by SSZ 51. The following month she was escorted three times on the Kingstown to Holyhead voyage. On 4 July, 29 July and 30 July she was escorted by SSZ50. She was escorted by the same airship on the Holyhead to Kingstown trip on 29 July.

August 1918 was the final month during which the *Leinster* received airship protection. She was escorted on the Kingstown to Holyhead voyage on 3 August (SSZ 34), 13 August (SSZ 51) and 16 August (SSZ 33 and 35). Protection was provided on the trip from Holyhead on 3 August (SSZ 33), 9 August (SSZ 31), 15 August (SSZ 33 and 35).

The *Leinster* was sunk almost two months after she last received airship escort. On the evening of 9 October 1918 an airship was damaged in the trees at Malahide Castle airship station, Co. Dublin.[4] This fact has been cited in a number of articles about the *Leinster* sinking. It has been suggested that, but for the damage to the airship, the *Leinster* would have been escorted the following day. No evidence has been produced to support this theory. Contrary evidence is suggested by the fact that the *Leinster* hadn't been escorted by airship for almost two months prior to her sinking.

Appendix 3

How often did the *Leinster* carry troops?

1917 Kingstown-Holyhead:

29 December, 31 December. Total 2.

1918 Kingstown-Holyhead:

5 January, 10 January, 4 July, 11 July, 17 July, 25 July, 26 July, 3 August, 6 August, 9 August, 10 August, 13 August, 20 September, 22 September, 23 September, 27 September, 1 October and 10 October. Total 18.

1918 Holyhead-Kingstown:

8 January, 22 July, 26 July, 6 August, 8 September, 11 September, 13 September, 14 September, 15 September, 17 September, 22 September, 23 September, 29 September, 30 September, 7 October. Total 15.

On 10 October 1918 the *Leinster* was carrying military from Kingstown to Holyhead when she was sunk by UB-123.

The *Leinster's* Daily Journal for 28 December 1917 recorded the carriage of *"Military equipment."* On 24 April 1918 *"Naval Luggage"* was carried. On 12 July the *Leinster* brought *"U.S. Navy stores"* and on 23 July *"U.S. Navy luggage."* On 17 and 26 September *"U.S. Navy luggage"* were again carried. All of the luggage was carried from Kingstown to Holyhead.

The *Leinster* carried troops twice during 1917 and 33 times in 1918. She carried military baggage twice in 1917 and 5 times in 1918. By far the greatest amount of carriage of military personnel and luggage occurred between July and 10 October 1918. As there was little military carriage before that time, this would appear that Second Lieutenant Hugh Parker's appointment as the *Leinster's* Military Adjutant on 28 June 1918 was in anticipation of, rather than a response to, military carriage. Up to that time troops traveling to and from Dublin used the ships docking at Dublin port. The appointment of Parker would appear to suggest that the numbers using the port had caused risen to such an extent that it was planned that any "overflows" would be channeled through Kingstown.

However, while sometimes carrying troops, the *Leinster* was never used as a troopship in the sense that the *R.M.S. Connaught* was used in the English Channel. Even in the July to 10 October period she carried troops or military luggage a total of 34 times. Given that she crossed the Irish Sea twice a day, every day, during this period (with one partial crossing on 10 October) this means that she had military carriage less than 17% of the time. Did the Germans specifically target the *Leinster*? Or the CDSPCo mail ships in general? Naval Historian Dwight R. Messimer has spent years studying German First World War naval records. He told me that he has never found a record of U-boats ever having specifically targeting any specific ship or group of ships. Did the Germans know that for under 17% of the time during the final months of her life the *Leinster* was carrying troops? The answer to that would surely have to be no. Their intelligence could not have been that precise. She had carried troops from Kingstown to Holyhead four times in September 1918 and – before 10 October – had last carried them on 1 October. From Robert Ramm's point of view he was very lucky to sink the *Leinster* on an October morning when she happened to have been carrying troops.

Source: The *Leinster's* Daily Journal.

Appendix 4

An administrative problem:
Troops who embarked on the *Leinster* without having their names recorded

Mention has already been made of the fact that Australian researcher Jeff Kildea consulted File AWM18 9953/1/1 at the Australian War Memorial, Canberra. The file has details of Australian soldiers who traveled on the *Leinster*. The file contains a letter dated 1 November 1918 from the Commandant of the Administrative Headquarters, AIF London to the Secretary of the Department of Defence, Melbourne. Part of the letter reads: *"It appears — according to a confidential report issued by the G.O.C., troops Ireland — that 18 other ranks embarked at Kingstown without their names being taken at the gangways. No embarkation cards were received for these men. This oversight was due to the late arrival of the 3rd mail train and the consequent rush to complete the embarkation by the scheduled time of sailing.*

No doubt complete lists were in the possession of the office i/c of embarkation. Unfortunately this officer was among the casualties and no records were found on his body. (According to Bill Sweeney the officer in charge of embarkation was Captain Harold Locke, Royal Irish Regiment).

It is the desire of the authorities that the fact that record of 18 military personnel embarking by the "Leinster" is not held, be kept secret. This for obvious reasons. Possession of this knowledge by absentees in Ireland might lead to unfortunate complications."[5]

According to a typed note the source of the information was a *"Phone report from War Office 12.10.18."* As the documentation does not state the nationality of the *"18 other ranks"* it would appear that they were of different nationalities.

*

Another document in File AWM18 9953/1/1 at the Australian War Memorial, Canberra is a report by Warrant Officer S. E. Yeomans who was sent to Ireland by AIF Headquarters to investigate the loss of AIF personnel in the sinking. This contains the statement: *"I interviewed some members of the Embarkation Staff from whom I obtained a list of names, amongst that being one who subsequently proved to be a Captain in the Nova Scotia army."*[6]

My thanks to Jeff Kildea for the information in this appendix.

Appendix 5

War and the City of Dublin
Steam Packet Company[7]

During the First World War the Admiralty could requisition British and Irish merchant ships. Initially, however, the war brought no change to the CDSPCo. The company continued to operate the four *Provinces* on the Kingstown to Holyhead route. It also continued to operate its service from the North Wall, Dublin to Liverpool.

1915

On 31 January 1915 the *Leinster* left Holyhead at 2.13 p.m. As there was a moderate northwest gale blowing, passengers were below deck. Twenty-five miles east of the Kish Light Ship a surfaced submarine was seen, about a mile north of the ship. Two men were seen in the conning tower of the submarine. Captain Birch altered the *Leinster's* course southward. The submarine gave chase. She followed the *Leinster* for about quarter of an hour before giving up. The *Leinster* docked at the Carlisle Pier, in Kingstown, twenty-eight minutes later. Speaking of the chase by the submarine, Captain Birch told a reporter for *The Freeman's Journal* "*as soon as we saw her we showed her a clean pair of heels.*" He said that he believed that the submarine was the same one that had sunk a number of ships the previous day. A notice on Carlisle Pier warned passengers "*a submarine was seen in the Channel today.*" Three people who had intended travelling to Holyhead on the *Ulster* changed their minds when they read the notice. The *Ulster* sailed at 8.20 p.m., under the command of Captain Robert Newton. There were a large number of passengers on board, including a theatrical company. The ship's lifeboats were ready for an immediate launch.[8]

As the war continued, the Admiralty began to requisition more ships. In 1915 the *R.M.S. Connaught* was requisitioned. On 5 May 1915 she left Holyhead for Southampton. For almost two years she was used to transport troops from Southampton to France. Some of the CDSPCo ships on the Dublin to Liverpool route were also requisitioned. Under Admiralty orders the *Louth* sailed between Aberdeen, Scotland and Bergen, Norway until

August 1918. The *Carrickfergus* and the *Wicklow* were used to transport troops.

1916

On Monday 24 April 1916 the Irish Volunteers and the Irish Citizen Army proclaimed a republic and took over the centre of Dublin. The British army rushed troops to Dublin from the rest of Ireland. They also moved troops from Britain. On 25 April the *R.M.S. Ulster* was at Holyhead. Captain Robert Newton received orders to sail to Liverpool to pick up troops. Thirty-eight officers and 1,239 men were carried to Kingstown. On 26 April the ship sailed for Liverpool and returned with 29 officers and 778 men. She also carried a cargo of artillery shells, a large quantity of small arms ammunition and 834 hand grenades, *"about ninety tons in all."* On 27 April the *Ulster* brought 24 officers and 845 men to Kingstown. During May 1916 the *Leinster, Munster* and *Ulster* were delayed leaving Kingstown on a number of occasions, due to military checks on passengers and baggage. These security provisions were probably to prevent the escape of any of those involved in the fighting in Dublin.

The *Ulster's* journal of 22 May 1916 records that, under Admiralty orders, she zigzagged on her voyage from Kingstown. This tactic, designed to hinder attacking submarines, was recorded in the journals of the *Provinces* on most days from then until the end of the war.

1917

On 3 March 1917 the *R.M.S. Connaught* was sunk by U-48 in the English Channel. She was returning to Southampton, from where she had transported troops to Le Harve, France the previous evening. Three crewmen were lost in the sinking. Captain Thompson reported the sinking to CDSPCo Managing Director Edward Watson three days later. All the ships papers, including her log, went down with the ship. Several of the crew who survived the sinking of the *Connaught* were lost on the *Leinster*.

On 13 October 1917 the *Ulster* was sailing from Kingstown to Holyhead. Her journal records: *"10.50 a.m. Sighted ship's boat capsized, with four men on it. Circled around until patrol boat came to pick up. 11.04 a.m. Proceeded at full speed."* The men were probably from the crew of the Guinness ship *W.M. Barkley* (569 tons), which was sunk by UC-75 the previous day. Four of her crew were lost including the captain.[9]

Towards the end of 1917 the *Provinces* began to regularly carry troops across the Irish Sea. This started with two of the ships departing from their regular route. On 10 November the *Ulster* carried 679 officers and men from Holyhead to Dublin. The following day she carried 25 officers and 691 men on the same route. Between 15 and 30 December the *Munster* brought troops in both directions between Holyhead and Dublin. She carried 29 officers and 2,834 men to Dublin. She brought 73 officers and 10,300 men from Dublin. On 28 December, in addition to troops, the *Munster* carried 23 munitions workers from Dublin. An unspecified number of munitions workers were also carried from Dublin on 30 December. Their total is included among 470 *"soldiers and munitions workers."*

Meanwhile, the *Ulster* and *Leinster* were also carrying troops. During December the *Ulster* carried military and civilian passengers on four occasions, twice from Kingstown to Holyhead and twice in the opposite direction. The *Leinster* carried military and civilian passengers on two occasions from Kingstown.

On the morning of 27 December 1917 the *Leinster* left Kingstown. Her journal records: *"10.55 a.m. Twelve miles east of Kish torpedo fired at ship from submarine which had previously been seen. Torpedo missed ship by some twenty yards. Sent out wireless to all in range. 12.05 p.m. Passed British destroyer steering west."* The *Leinster* had been attacked by U-100, commanded by Kapitänleutnant Freiherr Von Loe. Debris in its other torpedo tubes prevented the submarine from firing more torpedoes. U-100 surfaced and the blockages were cleared. Later that day it sank the *S.S. Adela* off the coast of Anglesey., Wales.[10] The Tedcastle and McCormick ship had been sailing from Dublin to Liverpool. Twenty-four crewmen were lost.[11]

The following day the *Leinster* spent eight hours at Holyhead waiting for Admiralty order to sail. She then sailed in a convoy escorted by two U.S. destroyers. On the return voyage to Holyhead she was escorted by a single U.S. destroyer. The *Ulster* was escorted by a U.S. destroyer on the return voyage on 28, 29 and 30 December.

1918

The first week of 1918 saw the *Munster* continue to bring troops from Dublin to Holyhead. On 2 January she carried two officers, 919 men and nine munitions workers. On 4 January she brought one officer, 895 men and 71 munitions workers. Her journal records that she travelled in convoy with the *Leinster* and that they were escorted by a U.S. destroyer. (Strangely, the *Leinster's* journal did not record these facts.) On 26 January the CDSPCo ship *Cork*, (1232 tons) was sailing from North Wall, Dublin to Liverpool. She was sunk by U-103 off Lynas Point, Anglesey. Twelve lives were lost.[12]

On 6 February the *Leinster* was sailing to Holyhead. Her journal records: *"10.44 a.m. Stopped to pick up shipwrecked crew. 11.02 a.m. Proceeded."* The survivors were nine of the crew from the *Mexico City* (5078 tons). The ship had been torpedoed by U-101 at 7.45 p.m. the previous day. Twenty-nine men including the captain had died.[13] On 15 March the *Leinster* was sailing to Kingstown. The officer of the watch saw a submarine that did not attack. The incident was recorded in her journal. *"At 4.41 a.m. ' Stand by.' At 4.45 a.m. Emergency telegraph on full speed to avoid submarine close alongside."* The *Leinster* was sailing from Holyhead to Kingstown on 17 March, St. Patrick's Day, when she collided with a steamer and had to return to port for inspection. The following day while sailing from Holyhead she again had to turn back due to a fault in the starboard engine.

H.M. Stationary Office publication *British Vessels Lost at Sea 1914-18* says that on 22 March a torpedo was fired at the *Ulster*. The torpedo missed the ship. The *Ulster's* Daily Journal does not mention the incident. On 6 April the *Ulster* left Kingstown at 8.50 a.m. From 9.30 a.m. she was escorted by two Royal Navy destroyers. The escorts didn't deter a German submarine from firing a torpedo that passed 80 to 100 yards astern. The two destroyers turned in the direction of the submarine and dropped three depth charges. At 3.50 p.m. on 13 April the *Munster* was attacked by a submarine off the coast of Wales. A torpedo passed about a ship's length astern. H.M. Stationary Office publication *British Vessels Lost at Sea 1914-18* (which also records unsuccessful attacks on British ships) says that on 13 April a torpedo was fired at the *Munster*. The torpedo missed. The *Munster's* Daily Log does not mention the incident.

The *Leinster* sailed from Holyhead on 21 April. Her journal records: *"4.31 a.m. Stopped and reversed to avoid collision with vessel ahead without lights which turned out to be a submarine. 4.33 a.m. Emergency telegraph put on full speed ahead."* On 23 April there was labour trouble at Kingstown. The *Leinster's* mail had to be unloaded by the military. There was no train on the pier. That evening the mails arrived from Dublin by road. The *Leinster's* journal of 14 August recorded the following during a voyage to Holyhead. *"10.30 a.m. Sighted submarine distance three miles. Increased speed and steered south from her. Sent wireless signal which was answered."*

After docking in Holyhead on 7 September the *Ulster* was taken out of service until 5 October. The route was now covered by the *Leinster* and the *Munster*. The *Leinster's* Journal began to record the fact that a number of passengers had to be left behind. On 14 September 1918 her journal recorded: *"Number of passengers shut out at Kingstown last night one hundred military. Number of passengers shut out at Holyhead this morning one hundred civilians, two hundred military."* Similar remarks were recorded on 11 other voyages over the next few weeks. The *Munster* only recorded such comments on two occasions during the same period. On 5 October the *Munster* was taken out of service at Holyhead. She didn't return to duty until 26 October, by which time the *Leinster* had been sunk.

On 10 October 1918 the *Ulster* left Holyhead at 7.00 a.m. She reached the Kish Light Vessel at 9.42 a.m. Soon afterwards she passed north of the outbound *Leinster*. The latter was sunk soon afterwards. That afternoon *Ulster's* Daily Journal recorded a delay while *"waiting Admiralty instructions to sail."* She left Kingstown at 3.11 p.m. and docked at Holyhead at 6.21 p.m.

The *Munster* returned to service on 26 October 1918. A number of articles on the *Leinster* sinking say that towards the middle or end of October 1918 the *Ulster* was struck by a torpedo that failed to explode. This is not mentioned by either the ship's Daily Log or H.M. Stationary Office publication *British Vessels Lost at Sea 1914-18*.

On 11 November 1918 the *Munster*, under the command of Captain James Penston, docked at Kingstown at 10.30 a.m. Half an hour later the armistice came into force. The war was over. The *Ulster*, commanded by Captain Robert Newton, docked at Holyhead at 11.50 a.m.

Appendix 6

U-48 and the sinking of the *R.M.S. Connaught*

On the outbreak of war the Admiralty were legally entitled to take over any British or Irish merchant ships they required. Initially, no demands were made on the CDSPCo mail ships. Eventually, the Admiralty requisitioned *R.M.S. Connaught*. On 5 May 1915 she left Holyhead for Southampton. For almost two years she was used to transport troops from Southampton to France.

Kapitänleutnant Berndt Buss was born on 12 September 1892. He joined the navy in April 1901, eventually becoming commander of torpedo boat G194. In June 1915 he went to U-boat school and on 22 April 1916 was appointed to command U-48. Among other exploits, on 6 July 1916 the submarine captured the British steamer *Pendennis*. On 14 October 1916 she captured the Russian steamer *Suchan* (3,781 tons). When the steamer was brought back to Germany she was found to have a cargo of four automobiles and a large quantity of ammunition. On 28 February 1917 U-48 left the naval base at Heliogoland, under the command of twenty-four year old Berndt Buss. The submarine made her way into the English Channel.

*

Le Harve, northern France, 3 March 1917

The *R.M.S. Connaught* left the harbour bound for Southampton at about 10 a.m. She had arrived from Southampton the previous evening, carrying troops. She had been escorted and had travelled without lights. This morning she did not have an escort. Captain Thompson had a crew of 76 under his command. There were no passengers on board. Visibility was good and there was a moderate sea breeze. At 1.45 p.m. U-48's periscope was sighted a hundred yards off the starboard. Almost simultaneously the submarine fired a torpedo, which exploded aft on the starboard side. The explosion destroyed the wireless aerial, so an S.O.S. could not be sent. A quarter of an hour later a second torpedo struck amidships on the port side. Some of the crew were in the dining room at the time of the attack. An Irishman, a Welshman and a Channel Islander who were cleaning the second-class cabins were killed.[14]

The remaining 74 crew-members took to the lifeboats. The *Connaught* sank within four minutes of the second torpedo striking. Her position was 50.08 North, 00.45 West. Shortly afterwards submarine U-48 approached the lifeboats. The Germans asked for the ship's captain. As had been agreed beforehand, Captain Thompson hid in the locker of the chief officer's boat. The crew told the Germans that they supposed he had been killed. U-48 left. The hospital ship *Grantully Castle* picked up the *R.M.S. Connaught* survivors around 9 p.m. Among them were several who would be on the *Leinster* during her final voyage.

U-48 sank a number of other ships over the next few days. On 9 March, off Eddystone, she torpedoed the British steamer *East Point* (5234 tons). Buss then took the submarine to sixty feet, preparing to attack another steamer he had spotted. Unknown to him, the *East Point* was still under way. When U-48 came up to periscope depth the *East Point* rammed her in the conning tower. The conning tower hatch flew open and the sea began to pour in. The torpedo officer and a seaman dropped down into the control room. But Kapitänleutnant Berndt Buss and Navigator Stuermann Adolf Bergmann had been knocked unconscious. The crew, having no option, closed a lower hatch and the submarine dived, with Buss and Bergmann still in the flooded conning tower. Because of the amount of water on board, the submarine sank quickly and hit the bottom at a depth of 70 meters. The crew managed to regain control and took the boat to 40-50 meters and left the area. In the evening U-48 surfaced. Buss and Bergmann were by this time long dead. The sea was clear of shipping. After an inspection of the damage, the crew held a funeral service for their captain and navigator at 49.48 north, 4.11 west. After an improvised repair of the damaged conning tower, a test dive was made. After 10 minutes at 25 meters depth the conning tower was full of water. The submarine surfaced and – travelling on the surface – set out for home. The following day, 10 March 1917, U-48's log recorded that the boat was under the command of Oberleutnant zur See der Reserve Hinrich Hashagen, the older of the watch officers on board. On 12 March, northwest of Ireland, the boat sank the French ship *Guerveur* (2596 tons) after a brief exchange of gunfire. U-48 arrived at Wilhelmshaven on 16 March, having travelled north of the Shetlands.

The submarine's next commanding officer was Kapitänleutnant Edeling. On 24 November 1917 U-48, commanded by Edeling , ran aground on Goodwin Sands. She came under fire from the destroyer *HMS Gypsy* and several drifters. U-48's gun crew returned fire, but they were outgunned. Edeling ordered that the submarine be destroyed with explosive charges. The crew abandoned the boat, which then blew up. Edeling and 18 of his crew were killed by continuing enemy fire. Seventeen of the crew were captured.

Sources:

U-boat researcher Jörn Jensen of uboat.net.
Find and Destroy: Antisubmarine Warfare in World War 1 by Dwight R. Messimer.
Verschollen: World War 1 U-boat Losses by Dwight R. Messimer.
Holyhead in the Great War by R.E. Roberts.
British Merchant Ships sunk by U-boat in the 1914-1918 War by A.J. Tennant.
Records of the Commonwealth War Graves Commission.
Guides to the Microfilmed Records of the German Navy 1850-1945: No. 1 U-Boats and T-Boats 1914-1918. National Archives and Records Service, U.S. General Services Administration. Washington (1984).
Daily Journal of R.M.S. Connaught. MSS 2920-2946, 27 volumes of the Journals of the Connaught 6/10/1860-16/4/15, National Library, Dublin.

Appendix 7

The men who died on the *R.M.S. Connaught*

Abbreviations: S. = son of.   B. = born.

Able Seaman Henry Charles Jasper (39).   B. St. Helier, Jersey, Channel Islands. S. William John. & the late Ann Elizabeth Jasper. Husband of Mabel Bessie Jasper (née Bravis), 37 Threefield Lane, Southampton.

Able Seaman John Moran (33). B. Kingstown., Co. Dublin, Ireland. S. Denis & Mary Moran. Husband of Kathleen Moran (née Kelly), 7 Crofton Avenue, Kingstown, Co. Dublin.

Able Seaman William Charles Parkhurst (46).   B. Swansea, Wales. S. late John & Mary Parkhurst. Husband of Harriett Ruth Parkhurst (née Upward), High Street, Totton, Hampshire.

None of their bodies were recovered.   All three are commemorated with many of their *Leinster* colleagues on the Tower Hill Memorial, London.

❖   My thanks to the Commonwealth War Graves Commission for information on the *R.M.S. Connaught* casualties.

Appendix 8

Crewmen lost on the tanker *Eupion* 3 October 1918

Abbreviations: S. = son of. B. = born. Tower Hill = Commemorated on Tower Hill Memorial. Kilrush = Buried North-East Corner of Kilrush Church of Ireland, Co. Clare.

Walter Clarke Anderson (35), Chief Steward. S. Walter James Clarke Anderson & Teresa Anderson. Husband of Annie Anderson (nee Fallowfield), 56 Duncan St., Barrow-in-Furness. B. Barrow-in-Furness. Tower Hill.

Christopher Clark (29), Third Mate. S. Christopher Granger Clark & Hannah Hodson Clark, *Hazelwood*, Langholm Rd., East Holdon, Sunderland. B. Robin Hood's Bay, Yorkshire. Kilrush.

John Charles Doherty (23), Seaman. S. Mary & the late Patrick Doherty. Husband of Catherine Doherty (nee Maguire), 67 Regent St., Liverpool. B. Galway. Tower Hill.

George Halter (18), Wireless Operator. S. George & Charlotte B. Halter, 21 Lewes Rd., Welling, Kent. Buried Woolwich (Plumbstead) Cemetery, London. Commonwealth War Graves Commission Records show him as *"Died of sickness 3rd October 1918."* This appears to suggest that he was picked up after the sinking, but died as a result of injuries.

Luciano Lago (31), Sailor. Husband of Matilda Rivas de Lago, Chapela, Pontevedra, Spain. B. Spain. Tower Hill.

David Mann, Royal Naval Reserve. Commemorated on panel 31 of the Portsmouth Naval Memorial, Hampshire.

Jose Olivares (34), Seaman. B. Mexico. Tower Hill.

W. Van De Put (28), Fireman. B. Holland. Tower Hill.

Arie Van der Neut (24), Fireman. S. Pieter Van der Neut, 18 Tyloostraat, Sassenheim. B. Holland. Tower Hill.

Charles Walker (25), Assistant Steward. S. Charles & Sarah Elizabeth Walker, 20 Edward St., Brantford, Ontario. B. Brantford, Canada. Kilrush.

Sidney Frederick Walters (28), Second Mate. S. John & Eleanor Walters, Myddrin House, Lloyd's Terrace, Newcastle Emlyn, Carmarthenshire. B. Newcastle Emlyn. Kilrush.

Source: Records of the Commonwealth War Graves Commission.

Notes

1   The source for this section is the *Leinster's Daily Journal*.
2   *Airship Pilot No. 28* by T.B. Williams.
3   *A History of the Royal Air Force and United States Naval Air Service in Ireland. 1913-1923* by Karl E. Hayes.
4   A History of the Royal Air Force and United States Naval Air Service in Ireland 1913-1923 by Karl E. Hayes.
5   Jeff Kildea is researching the connection between Australian troops and Ireland during the First World War. His research indicates that in 1918 Australian military authorities were concerned that significant numbers of Australian deserters and absentees were making their way to Ireland to evade capture or to avoid returning to their units.
6   Jeff Kildea believes that this might refer to the Captain Gale mistakenly listed as an Australian survivor. (See footnote 14 in The Colonials). The pencil note *"NFLD"* mentioned in that footnote might refer to Newfoundland (commonly abbreviated as Nfld), with WO Yeomans confusing this with Nova Scotia.
7   The information in this section is from *The B&I Line* by Hazel P. Smyth, the Daily Journals of the CDSPCo mail boats and *Holyhead in the Great War* by R.E. Roberts.
8   The events of 31 January 1915 were reported in *The Freemans Journal* (Dublin) the following day. The U-boat was almost certainly U-21, which had sunk the first-ever merchant ships to be sunk in the Irish Sea.
9   *British Merchant Ships sunk by U-Boats in the 1914-1918 War* by A.J. Tennant.
10 *Death in the Irish Sea* by Roy Stokes, *British Merchant Ships sunk by U-Boats in the 1914-1918 War* by A.J. Tennant and *Guides to the Microfilmed Records of the German Navy 1850-1945: No 1: U-Boats and T-Boats 1914-1918* (National Archives and Records Service, Washington 1984.)
11 *British Merchant Ships sunk by U-Boats in the 1914-1918 War* by A.J. Tennant.
12 *British Merchant Ships sunk by U-Boats in the 1914-1918 War* by A.J. Tennant.
13 *British Merchant Ships sunk by U-Boats in the 1914-1918 War* by A.J. Tennant.
14 As the second-class cabins were at the rear of the ship it seems likely that the first torpedo killed the three crewmen.

Friends of the Leinster
October 2003 commemorations

Holyhead

John Cave (Chairperson)
Eric Anthony (Liaison with *Leinster* relatives)
Richard Burnell
Jeff Evans
John D. Hodgkinson
Major Stephen B. Hunt (Retd.)
Alan J. Prince

Dún Laoghaire

Philip Lecane (Chairperson and liaison with *Leinster* relatives)
William Byrne (Secretary)
Tom Franks
Commandant Pat Holahan
Garda Cian Long
Garda Inspector Tom Lundon
Jim Lyons
John Moore
Very Rev. Patrick J. Mangan P.P., V.F.
Breasal Ó'Collaí
Sister Margaret Mary Ryder
Anna Scudds
Colin Scudds
Dr Philip Smyly
Commandant Gerry Tracy
Noel Vaughan
Peadar Ward

BIBLIOGRAPHY

Books

- Barry, Dr J.M. *Old Glory at Queenstown*. Cork 1999.
- Bence-Jones, Mark *Twilight of the Ascendancy*. London 1987.
- *British Vessels Lost at Sea 1914-18*. A reprint of the original HMSO publication of 1919. Cambridge 1977.
- Bourke, Edward J. *Shipwrecks of the Irish Coast 1105-1993*. Dublin 1994.
- *Burkes Landed Gentry 1912*.
- Campbell, Vice-Admiral Gordon *My Mystery Ships*. London 1937.
- Coakley, Davis *Baggot Street: A Short History Of the Royal City of Dublin Hospital*. Dublin 1995.
- Chappell, Mike *The Canadian Army at War*. Osprey Men-At-Arms Series No. 164. London 1996.
- Coggins, Jack *Prepare to Dive: The Story of Man Undersea*. Folkestone 1973.
- *Conway's All The World's Fighting Ships 1860-1905*. New York 1979.
- *Conway's All The World's Fighting Ships 1906-1921*. London 1997.
- Dallas, Gregor *1918: War and Peace*. London 2000.
- Dictionary of Irish Biography, Royal Irish Academy.
- De Courcy Ireland, John *History of Dun Laoghaire Harbour*. Blackrock, Co. Dublin 2001.
- De Ruvigny, Marquis, *The Roll of Honour: A Biographical Record of members of his Majesty's Naval & Military Forces who fell in the Great War: Volumes 1 to 5*. Reprinted, London 2000
- Dudley Edwards, Ruth *Newspapermen: Hugh Cudlipp, Cecil Harmsworth King and the Glory Days of Fleet Street*. London 2004.
- Dún Laoghaire Borough Historical Society *Historical Street Directory of Kingstown-Dún Laoghaire*. Dún Laoghaire 2000.
- Eames, Aled *Ships and Seamen of Anglesey*. Llangefni 1981.
- Fanning, A.E. *Steady as She goes: A history of the Compass Department of the Admiralty*. London 1986.
- Gallery, Rear-Admiral Daniel V. *We Captured a U-Boat*. London 1958.
- Gilbert, Martin *First World War*. London 1994.
- Gilligan, H. A. *A History of the Port of Dublin*. Dublin 1988.
- Haythornthwaite, Philip J. *The World War One Source Book*. London 1994.
- Hayes, Karl E. *A History of the Royal Air Force and United States Naval Air Service in Ireland 1913-1923*. Dublin 1988.

- Henderson, D.V. *Heroic Endeavour: A Complete Register of the Albert, Edward And Empire Gallantry Medals and How They Were Won.* Wiltshire 1988.
- Hirschfeld, Wolfgang *Hirschfeld: The Secret Diary of a U-Boat,* as told to Geoffrey Brooks. London 2000.
- Hitches, Mike *The Irish Mail.* Gloucestershire 2000.
- Holding, Norman *More sources of World War 1 Army Ancestry.* Federation of Family History Societies Birmingham 1991.
- Holt, Tonie and Valmai *Battlefields of the First World War: A Traveller's Guide.* London 1999.
- Hopkins, A.E. *A History of Wreck Covers.* (Undated).
- Hughes, D. Lloyd and Williams, Dorothy M. *Holyhead: The Story of a Port.* Holyhead 1967.
- Ingram, John A. *The Cure of Souls: A History of St. Bridget's Church of Ireland, Stillorgan.*
- James, Brig. E.A. *British Regiments 1914-1918.* London 1993.
- Jeffrey, Keith *Ireland and the Great War.* Cambridge 2000.
- Kipling, Rudyard *The Irish Guards in the Great War.* (reprint) Kent 1997.
- Loughrey, Francis *Sunbeam House Bray.* Ireland 1997.
- Loughrey, Francis *Old Bray and its neighbourhood.* Ireland 1998.
- Laffin, John and Chappell, Mike *The Australian Army at War 1899-1975.* Osprey Men-At-Arms Series No. 123. London 1998.
- Mac Ginty, Tom *The Irish Navy: A Story of Courage and Tenacity.* Kerry 1995.
- Mason, Ursula Stuart *The Wrens 1917-77: a history of the Women's Royal Naval Service.* Reading 1977.
- McNeill, D.B. *Irish Passenger Steamship Services Volume 2: South of Ireland.* Devon 1971.
- Messimer, Dwight R. *Find and Destroy: Antisubmarine Warfare in World War 1.* Maryland 2001.
- Messimer, Dwight R. *Verschollen: World War 1 U-Boat Losses.* Maryland 2002.
- Murphy, David *Ireland and the Crimean War* Dublin 2002.
- Nixon, W. M. *Howth, a Centenary of sailing.* Howth Yacht Club, 1995.
- O'Neill, Mick *Tralee's Old Stock Reminisce: An Oral History of Tralee and Its Surroundings.* Tralee, Co. Kerry, 2001.
- O'Sullivan, Patrick *The Lusitania: Unravelling the Mysteries.* Cork, 1998.
- Padfield, Peter *Dönitz: The Last Führer.* London, 2001.
- Padfield, Peter *War Beneath The Sea: Submarine Conflict 1939-1945.* London, 1995.
- Pearson, Peter *Dún Laoghaire Kingstown.* Dublin 1981.

- Pope, Stephen & Wheal, Elizabeth-Anne *The Macmillan Dictionary of The First World War.* London 1997.
- *Porters Post Office Guide and Directory of Kingstown, Blackrock, Dalkey and Killiney.* 1911.
- Ranson C.C., Fr. Joe *Songs of the Wexford Coast.* Wexford, 1948. Republished by James Hammel (Junr.) Wexford, 1975.
- *Readers Digest Guide to Places of the World.* London 1995.
- Roberts, R. E. *Holyhead and the Great War.* Holyhead 1920.
- Rössler, Eberhard *The U-Boat: The evolution and technical history of German submarines.* London 2001.
- Sassoon, Siegfried *Diaries 1915-1918.* London 1983.
- Sheen, John *Tyneside Irish: 24th, 25th, 26th and 27th (Service) Battalions of the Northumberland Fusiliers* South Yorkshire 1998.
- Simms, Rear Admiral William Sowden in collaboration with Hendick, Burton J. *The Victory at Sea.* London 1920.
- Smyth, Hazel P. *The B & I Line.* Dublin 1984.
- Stenton, Michael and Lees, Stephen (editors) *Who's Who of Members of Parliament Vol 2 1886-1918.* Sussex 1978.
- Stokes, Roy *Death in the Irish Sea: The sinking of the R.M.S. Leinster.* Cork 1998.
- Stern, Robert C. *Battle Beneath the Waves: U-boats at War.* London 1999.
- Tennant, A. J. *British Merchant Ships sunk by U-Boats in the 1914-1918 War.* Gwent 1990.
- Terraine, John *Business in Great Waters.* Hertfordshire 1999.
- *The Irish Air Corps 1922-1997. An Official Souvenir.* Dublin 1997.
- *The Naval Who's Who 1917.* London 1981 reprint.
- The Parish of Holy Trinity, Killiney *Holy Trinity Church Killiney 1858-1996.* Dublin 1996.
- Wall, Mervyn, *Hermitage.* Dublin 1982.
- Webb, Arthur *The Clean Sweep* London 1968.
- Wenborn, Neil, *The Pictorial History of the U.S.A.* London 1991.
- Werner, Herbert A. *Iron Coffins: A U-Boat Commander's War 1939-1945.* London 1969.
- Westlake, Ray *British Battalions on the Western Front January to June 1915.* South Yorkshire 2001
- Westlake, Ray and Chappell, Mike *British Territorial Units 1914-18.* Oxford 1991.
- *Who Was Who 1961-1970 Vol 6.*
- Whitton, Lieutenant-Colonel Frederick Ernest, C.M.G. *The Prince of Wales's Leinster Regiment Royal Canadians Vol 2 1914-1922.* Republished Cork 1998.
- Williams, Captain T. B. *Airship Pilot No. 28.* London 1974.

- Williamson, Gordon *U-boats of the Kaiser's Navy.* Oxford 2002.
- Yeates, Padraig *Lockout Dublin 1913.* Dublin 2000.

Articles

- Byrne, Declan Review of the book *A Life of the Hymn-writer, Mrs Alexander 1818-1895* by Valerie Wallace (Dublin 1995) in Wicklow Roots No 5 (2000).
- Callaghan, George *Arthur Eade* in the Journal of The Medal Society Of Ireland. No 57, June 2002.
- Carr, Mary *The Seán Dunne papers in the ILHS Museum and Archives* Saothar 20, Journal of the Irish Labour History Society (1995).
- Daly, Louis Dominic Account of the Sinking of the R.M.S. Leinster in The Britannia, Journal of the Norfolk Regiment, Vol. 1, Number 1, March 1927.
- De Courcy Ireland, John *Maritime History & Tradition* in *The Book of Dún Laoghaire* Dublin 1987.
- Elmes, Margaret *Maud's Story* Journal of the Genealogical Society of Ireland. Vol. 3 No. 2 Summer 2002.
- Fennessy OFM, Fr. Ignatius *A Doctor on the Leinster* Journal of the Genealogical Society of Ireland. Vol. 5 No.2 Summer 2004.
- Sorter John Higgins's account of the sinking in the *Postal Worker* and Contemporary newspapers accounts of his testimony.
- Isherwood, J. H. *Irish Mail 'Provinces'.* Sea Breezes, Vol. 20, No 115. July 1955.
- Lecane, Philip *Sophia Violet Barrett.* Dún Laoghaire Borough Historical Society Journal No 5 (1996).
- Lecane, Philip *The sinking of the S.S. Adela* Dún Laoghaire Genealogical Society Journal Vol. 8 No. 2 Summer 1999.
- Liffiton, John L. *The last passenger ship sunk in the Great War* Journal of the Medal Society of Ireland. No. 49 (September 1999).
- Loughrey, Frank *Bray and the First World War* Journal of the Old Bray Society Vol. 1, No. 8. (2001).
- McDonnell, Annette *Adam Smyth (1875-1918) Post Office Sorter on Royal Mail Steamer Leinster* Journal of the Genealogical Society of Ireland. Vol. 5. No 1, Spring 2004.
- McGill, Captain H. N, R.D., R.N.R. (Retd) as told to Captain Barry O'Brien *The Sinking of The Leinster* in the magazine *Great War Adventures* Seventh Series (Each issue was described as a series) Late 1933 or early 1934.
- Petree, J. Foster *Charles Wye Williams (1779-1866).* The Transactions of The Newcomen Society Volume XXXIX 1966-67.

- Quinn, Tony *Great War Memorial, St. Patrick's Church, Dalkey* Dún Laoghaire Borough Historical Society Journal No 13 (2004).
- Richards, O.M. *Salved from S.S. Leinster.* Photocopy of an article from a philately journal. I have not been able to establish the source.
- Sides, Ann B. *When submarine UB-123 attacked the ferry Leinster, it torpedoed Germany's last hope for a 'soft peace' in 1918.* Military History, Herndon, October 1998. Vol 15, Issue 4.
- Smyth, Hazel *Some Notes on Charles Wye Williams, His Family, Their Life and Times.* Dublin Historical Record Vol. XLIX No. 1 (Spring 1996).
- Tutty, M. J. *The City of Dublin Steam Packet Company* in Dublin Historical Record Vol. XVIII No.3 June 1963
- Wall, Mervyn *Some memories of the Borough* Dun Laoghaire Borough Historical Society Journal No. 1 (1990)
- West, Margery *Some Corner of an Off-Shore Island* Bulletin of The Western Front Association No. 42 (June 1995)
- Yeates, A.C. *70 Years of the Irish Mail* in Sea Breezes July 1961.
- *The Yorkshire Hussars Magazine Vol. 2, No. 10, October 1919* and Vol. 3, No. 11, January 1950.

Newspapers

- Irish Times 9 October and 10 October 1902
- Cork Examiner, Evening Herald (Dublin), Irish Independent, Irish Times, Weekly Irish Times and The Times. Various dates October and November 1918
- The Chronicle (Holyhead) 18 October 1918.
- The Irish Independent. 31 March 1951.
- The Sunday Express December 1963, article by Seán Dunne T.D. in association with Raymond Foxall.
- Evening Press 11 October 1968.

Public Records

- Daily Journals of *R.M.S. Connaught, R.M.S. Leinster, R.M.S. Munster and R.M.S. Ulster* for the years 1914-1918. Manuscript Room of the National Library of Ireland, Dublin.
- Daily Particulars of the working of the Irish Mail Service Euston-Dún Laoghaire, May 1861-October 1920. Manuscript Room of the National Library of Ireland, Dublin.
- Typed partial list of some of the survivors and casualties. Obtained from the Public Records Office, Kew Gardens, Surrey by Author Roy Stokes.

- Tapes of interviews conducted by Declan Whelan with Bill Sweeney in 1979 National Maritime Museum, Dún Laoghaire, Co. Dublin.
- Records of the Commonwealth War Graves Commission.
- Crew Agreement Records at the Maritime History Archives of the Memorial University of Newfoundland. Obtained by William Byrne.
- James Mason's account of the sinking. National Maritime Museum, Dún Laoghaire.
- H. L. Parker's account of the sinking. Obtained from the Public Records Office, Kew Gardens Surrey by Author Roy Stokes.

The Internet

- Website on Count John Mc Cormack, Paul W. Worth, 1997. *pwworth@jump.net*
- Uboat.net
- The Australian War Memorial Database

Letters and email

Letter to Seán Dunne T.D. from Daniel Nolan, The Kerryman newspaper, 9 December 1964.
Letters and emails from and to *Leinster* relatives and researchers.

Telephone

Circumstances of Acting Captain Hugh Love Parker's O.B.E. Telephone conversation with staff member, Chancery Office, St James's Palace, London 9 February 2001.

Ship's Plans

No. 4 Design, submitted to Edward Watson on 29 July 1895. Obtained by Author Roy Stokes.

INDEX